OXFORD STUDIES IN ME1

OXFORD STUDIES IN METAPHYSICS

Editorial Advisory Board
David Chalmers (University of Arizona)
Tamar Gendler (Cornell University)
Sally Haslanger (Massachusetts Institute of Technology)
John Hawthorne (Rutgers University)
E. J. Lowe (University of Durham)
Brian McLaughlin (Rutgers University)
Kevin Mulligan (Université de Genève)
Theodore Sider (Rutgers University)
Timothy Williamson (Oxford University)

Managing Editor
David Manley (Rutgers University)

OXFORD STUDIES IN METAPHYSICS

Volume 1

Edited by
Dean W. Zimmerman

CLARENDON PRESS · OXFORD

OXFORD
UNIVERSITY PRESS

Great Clarendon Street, Oxford OX2 6DP
Oxford University Press is a department of the University of Oxford.
It furthers the University's objective of excellence in research, scholarship,
and education by publishing worldwide in
Oxford   New York
Auckland Cape Town Dar es Salaam Hong Kong Karachi Kuala Lumpur
Madrid Melbourne Mexico City Nairobi New Delhi Taipei Toronto
Shanghai
With offices in
Argentina Austria Brazil Chile Czech Republic France Greece
Guatemala Hungary Italy Japan South Korea Poland Portugal
Singapore Switzerland Thailand Turkey Ukraine Vietnam

Oxford is a registered trade mark of Oxford University Press
in the UK and in certain other countries

Published in the United States
by Oxford University Press Inc., New York

© the several contributors 2004

The moral rights of the authors have been asserted

Database right Oxford University Press (maker)

First published 2004

All rights reserved. No part of this publication may be reproduced,
stored in a retrieval system, or transmitted, in any form or by any means,
without the prior permission in writing of Oxford University Press,
or as expressly permitted by law, or under terms agreed with the appropriate
reprographics rights organizations. Enquiries concerning reproduction
outside the scope of the above should be sent to the Rights Department,
Oxford University Press, at the address above.

You must not circulate this book in any other binding or cover
and you must impose this same condition on any acquirer

British Library Cataloguing in Publication Data
Data available

Library of Congress Cataloging in Publication Data
Data available

ISBN 0-19-926772-3
ISBN 0-19-926773-1 (pbk.)

3 5 7 9 10 8 6 4

Typeset by Kolam Information Services Pvt. Ltd, Pondicherry, India
Printed in Great Britain by
Biddles Ltd., King's Lynn, Norfolk

For David Lewis,
in memoriam

PREFACE

Oxford Studies in Metaphysics is dedicated to the timely publication of new work in metaphysics, broadly construed. The subject is taken to include not only perennially central topics (e.g. modality, ontology, and mereology; metaphysical theories of causation, laws of nature, persistence through time, and time itself; and realism and anti-realism in the many senses of these terms); but also the rich clusters of metaphysical questions that emerge within other subfields, such as philosophy of mind (e.g. questions about supervenience and materialism, the nature of qualia, mental causation), philosophy of science (e.g. the metaphysical implications of relativity and quantum physics, the ontology of biological species), and philosophy of religion (e.g. theories of universals, causation, or modality that incorporate theological assumptions; examination of the metaphysics of theism, such as the doctrine of divine simplicity or the Molinist's "counterfactuals of freedom"). In addition to independent essays, volumes will often contain critical discussion of a recent book, or a symposium in which participants respond to one another's criticisms and questions. Future volumes will include essays by winners of the *Oxford Studies in Metaphysics* Younger Scholar Prize, described within.

DWZ

New Brunswick, NJ

CONTENTS

Prologue: Metaphysics after the Twentieth Century   ix

Oxford Studies in Metaphysics:
  Younger Scholar Prize Announcement   xxiii

I. PRESENTISM

1. Tensed Quantifiers   3
   David Lewis

2. Symposium: Defining Presentism
   —On Presentism and Triviality   15
     Thomas M. Crisp
   —Presentism, Triviality, and the Varieties of Tensism   21
     Peter Ludlow
   —Reply to Ludlow   37
     Thomas M. Crisp

3. A Defense of Presentism   47
   Ned Markosian

4. Presentism and Truthmaking   83
   Simon Keller

II. UNIVERSALS

5. A Theory of Properties   107
   Peter van Inwagen

6. How Do Particulars Stand to Universals?   139
   D. M. Armstrong

7. Non-symmetric Relations   155
   Cian Dorr

III. FREEDOM, CAUSAL POWERS, AND CAUSATION

8. The Mental Problems of the Many   195
   Peter Unger

9. Properties and Powers   223
   John Heil

10. The Intrinsic Character of Causation   255
    Ned Hall

11. Recombination, Causal Constraints, and Humean Supervenience: An Argument for Temporal Parts?   301
    Ryan Wasserman, John Hawthorne, and Mark Scala

Index   319

PROLOGUE: Metaphysics after the Twentieth Century
Dean W. Zimmerman

THE LATEST "BATTLE OF THE BOOKS"

Metaphysics, as currently practiced in the English-speaking world, is a heterogeneous discipline, comprising a wide variety of philosophical questions and methods for answering them. *Oxford Studies in Metaphysics* is intended to favor no particular set of questions or philosophical school, and to feature the best work on any metaphysical topic from every philosophical tradition.

"Yes, yes, of course that's the sort of thing everyone *says*. But there's obviously a big difference between analytic philosophy and other kinds. In metaphysics the contrast is particularly stark, and people on either side of the analytic/non-analytic divide don't have much to do with those on the other. So where does *Oxford Studies in Metaphysics* fall? Is it to be a venue for analytic metaphysics, or for the kinds of metaphysics that are practiced outside analytic circles?"

Given the frequency with which lines are drawn in the sand using the label "analytic", and the ferocity with which battle is often joined, I suspect that many philosophers with an interest in metaphysics will find this question to be a natural one. (The question is, in effect, "Which side are you on, boy?") But the term "analytic" means different things to different people; an attempt to answer the question in a simple and straightforward way would invite serious misunderstanding. It should either be rejected as too ambiguous to be answered, or answered with a thousand qualifications. Lacking both the good sense to do the former, and time and space to do the latter, I attempt an unsatisfactory compromise. With a couple of crude distinctions, I convey my impressionistic sense of the differences that are typically being indicated when philosophers call some metaphysicians, but not others, "analytic". Then, with a few paragraphs of "potted history", I describe the origins of the deepest divide between groups of contemporary metaphysicians and show how unfortunate and unnatural it is.

Readers who already have a sense of the divisions within metaphysics, and a passing familiarity with the history of the subject (or no interest in either), should now please skip ahead to the more intrinsically worthwhile contents of the volume. Only those who have found themselves bewildered (and perhaps occasionally blind-sided) by the bitter struggles and strange alliances one sometimes encounters in contemporary metaphysics have any reason to read on—and then only if they want to hear my version (idiosyncratic, no doubt) of the story of how we got here.

I begin by recording some ways I have noticed present-day metaphysicians in the English-speaking academy lining up on one side or another of a supposed "analytic/non-analytic" divide. Two ways of drawing the distinction—a very common one, and then a much more specialized one—provide the means to distinguish three metaphysical "camps".

1. Many contemporary metaphysicians belong to movements that broke away during the first half of the last century from what passed, at that time, for "analytic philosophy". For many in these movements, "analytic" became a dirty word, and "analytic metaphysics" practically a contradiction in terms. Call philosophers in these circles *"non-analytic metaphysicians"*. Paradigmatic non-analytic metaphysical movements include process philosophers (the heirs of A. N. Whitehead: Charles Hartshorne, Robert Neville, David Weismann, and many others[1]), neo-Thomists (Norris Clarke, Ralph McInerny), personalists (Borden Parker Bowne, Peter Bertocci, Austin Farrer, Josef Seifert, Erazim Kohak, Karol Wojtyla), some phenomenologists (J. N. Mohanty, Dallas Willard), neo-Platonists (J. N. Findlay), some types of idealist[2] (the non-Berkelian types: W. E. Hocking, G. R. G. Mure, Brand Blanshard), and a few Hegel-inspired but non-idealist system-builders (Paul Weiss, William Desmond). Non-analytic metaphysicians of all varieties usually characterize "analytic philosophy" as fundamentally hostile to the deeper questions of metaphysics.

But the pool of metaphysicians who would be called "analytic philosophers" by these non-analytic metaphysicians is itself far from

---

[1] Nicholas Rescher is one friend of process thought who is perfectly at home among analytic metaphysicians.

[2] Present-day idealists in the tradition of Berkeley, such as John Foster and Howard Robinson, tend to be analytic metaphysicians; fans of 19th-century idealism, on the other hand, are mainly non-analytic metaphysicians.

homogeneous; and there are divisions within it that have sometimes *also* been seen as a difference between metaphysicians who are or are not "analytic" in some (hard-to-specify) narrower sense.

2. Many professional philosophers who publish in metaphysics have no qualms about describing themselves as "analytic philosophers". They take up the traditional problems of metaphysics without apology, and offer philosophical theories meant to resolve them. Call them *"analytic metaphysicians"*, and think of Roderick Chisholm, Saul Kripke, and David Lewis as paradigmatic. In fact, I have the impression that this category includes the vast majority of philosophers active in metaphysics today—at least, the majority of those publishing books with academic presses or articles in scholarly journals.

3. My final group of metaphysicians is neither very cohesive nor very large; but its members do have some important things in common. (*a*) They resemble non-analytic metaphysicians in thinking that metaphysics as practiced by Chisholm, Kripke, Lewis, *et al.* is a dead end; (*b*) they tend to call this (putatively) misguided style of metaphysics, but not their own, "analytic"; but (*c*) they nevertheless would generally be thought of as "analytic philosophers" by the non-analytic metaphysicians (and also by many other non-analytic philosophers—e.g., followers of "continental" figures such as Foucault and Derrida).[3] For lack of a better term, I will call these philosophers *"new wave metaphysicians"*; and I am thinking of the more recent work of Hilary Putnam and John McDowell as paradigmatic—if paradigms are possible for this category. New wave metaphysicians are analytic metaphysicians from the point of view of the non-analytic metaphysicians, yet *not* analytic metaphysicians by their own, apparently stricter, standard.

(Of course plenty of philosophers within the ambit of analytic philosophy, broadly construed, regard metaphysics *in toto* as moonshine; new wave metaphysicians, by contrast, are philosophers who still ask, and offer some sort of answer to, many traditional metaphysical questions.)

Analytic metaphysicians generally take as little interest in what goes by the name "metaphysics" in non-analytic circles as they do in the "metaphysics" found in New Age bookstores. Non-analytic

---

[3] As a general rule, philosophers who use the word "analytic" to pick out the sort of philosophy they *don't* like tend to apply the term very broadly, while those called by that name tend to be more discriminating—an understandable situation.

metaphysicians repay the compliment, since they tend to think of analytic philosophy—construed broadly so as to include the work of both analytic and new wave metaphysicians—as inherently antimetaphysical (as, indeed, it was for a time—but more on that later). More generally, there is a great gulf fixed between analytic philosophers (broadly construed) and other philosophers, including non-analytic metaphysicians. Precious little news travels across it, and a journal or book series initiated on one side will be largely invisible to those on the other. And there is little prospect of the disappearance of this division in the near future, since there have been casualties on both sides—and much more than hurt feelings caused by snide remarks. Departments have split down the middle, tenure has been denied, papers and books have been rejected, and the source of the injury has been "the other side".

Analytic and new wave metaphysicians, on the other hand, remain in considerable dialogue (justifying the non-analytic metaphysicians' perception that they belong to a common tradition), although new wave metaphysicians tend not to engage the positive views of their counterparts in much detail, since they regard their methods as fundamentally misguided.

WHAT IS "ANALYTIC PHILOSOPHY" ANYWAY?

F. H. Bradley was famous for saying that to make distinctions is to falsify one's subject matter. Well, he was right—at least with respect to *these* distinctions and *this* subject matter. There are, of course, no sharp lines to be found where I have tried to draw them. Philosophers can be found who occupy intermediate positions. Some use the word "analytic" in slightly different ways, and some refuse to use the term at all—not a bad policy, given how multivalent and emotionally charged it has become. I feel certain, nevertheless, that there are fairly deep divisions running between groups of metaphysicians *more or less* along the fault lines I've tried to sketch. And the slippery term "analytic" is often used—by different philosophers in different ways—to mark them.

But are philosophically interesting territories being distinguished by these means? Are there "analytic" and "non-analytic" approaches to metaphysics that differ from one another in principled ways? What does "analytic" mean, in the expression "analytic philosophy"?

The word "analytic" is associated, in some people's minds, with the doctrine that most traditional philosophical problems, including all the metaphysical ones, are pseudo-problems arising from misunderstandings about how words work; that philosophical problems can all be solved (or dissolved) by some sort of purely linguistic investigation. After all, isn't "analysis" a matter of *a priori* reflection upon the meanings of words, and "analytic philosophy" the kind that prefers to talk about words rather than about the world? Isn't the origin of "analytic philosophy" some kind of "linguistic turn"?

I don't want to deny that the term "analytic" may have been used by some philosophers, fifty or sixty years ago, to mean something along these lines. But it should not be forgotten that, when it was first used to describe the philosophical movement that begins with Frege, Russell, Moore, and Wittgenstein, the expression "analytic philosophy" did not carry these connotations. And its extension today includes *mainly* philosophers who reject general deflationary attitudes toward metaphysics. It would be odd to identify the meaning of the term "analytic philosophy" with a set of doctrines peculiar to a generation of philosophers falling in the *middle* of the history of analytic philosophy.

How *did* the word "analytic" come into the tradition? The answer is pretty clear. Bradley railed against "analysis" in the late 1800s. When you try to break some fact down into components, he claimed, the result is not the fact you started with, nor even a set of things that were parts of the original fact. We not only murder to dissect, but we murder all the organs, and all the cells, etc., until there's *nothing* left that was in the living animal. When Russell became a realist, he attacked this element of Bradley's idealism, defending the thesis that the components of facts *can* be identified by analysis—even though the original fact would admittedly not appear on a mere list of its components. It was on Russell's lips that "analysis" became, first, a rallying cry in the revolt against idealism; and then the name of the whole movement spawned by the revolt. But in the mouths of both Russell and Bradley, "analysis" was the name of a non-linguistic activity; it was the prying apart (in thought) of the very contents of the world, a procedure with serious ontological implications. Analysis was definitely *not* a mere search for the definitions of words, nor a mere elucidation of concepts—at least, not if concepts are taken to be mental entities of some kind.[4]

---

[4] According to the early Russell, "concepts" are just properties—mind-independent universals—that someone or other happens to be thinking about.

Today, once again, the label "analytic" has no anti-metaphysical implications—or, at least, it shouldn't, given its actual extension. Most contemporary philosophers in the analytic camp reject blanket dismissals of traditional metaphysical problems, and recognize that "philosophical analysis" inevitably involves much more than simply unpacking the meanings of ordinary words and idioms. I suspect that, by now, the majority of all those, living or dead, who have been called "analytic philosophers" would reject any sort of radical "linguistic turn". There was a period when many analytic philosophers—perhaps even the majority—believed that the problems of metaphysics were either demonstrably meaningless, or resolvable by the clarification of terms or the recitation of platitudes "in a plonking tone of voice". But it was a relatively short phase in the history of a longer philosophical tradition—a phase I describe in more detail below.

So being an analytic philosopher does not mean that one tries to turn all philosophical problems into problems about language. Some analytic philosophers have tried to do so, but most have not. What, then, *are* the distinctive features of analytic philosophy—in the broad sense in which both analytic and new wave metaphysicians count as "analytic philosophers"? I'm tempted to answer: there are none. Philosophers who fly the "analytic" flag—or who find the flag often pinned to their chests by others, like it or not—are united by no single substantive doctrine or methodology.

Yes, analytic philosophers have great respect for advances in formal logic, and for rigorous argument. But Whitehead managed to put himself outside the analytic fold without renouncing his role in *Principia Mathematica*. In fact, only the most radical non-analytic philosophers explicitly impugn logic and rational argument.

Yes, some analytic philosophers behave as though philosophy began with Frege. But that can hardly be a distinctive trait, since very many of them also take history seriously; and, in any case, many non-analytic philosophers are just as guilty of writing as though philosophy began with Hegel, or Husserl, or Heidegger, or . . . whomever the next big "H" will prove to be.

The only definitions of "analytic philosophy" that come close to tracking actual application of the term (in its broadest use) are ones that appeal to *historical connections* and *self-identification*. Consider A. P. Martinich's counterfactual criterion, which comes as close to accuracy as any proposal I have seen: analytic philosophers are those who "would have done philosophy the way Moore, Russell, and Wittgenstein did it if they had been doing philosophy when Moore, Russell, and Wittgenstein were".[5] Interpreting this counterfactual is tricky, and some qualifications must be made. On a first reading, the criterion will seem too permissive. Everyone who attempts to characterize the distinctive marks of analytic philosophy (including Martinich) seems to agree that the movement springs from the work of Frege, Moore, Russell, and Wittgenstein. Clearly, Martinich intended that philosophers who came before them should be excluded—despite the fact that some of those earlier philosophers would surely have been on the side of Russell, Moore, and company had they been born later or lived longer. On the other hand, some finesse is required to interpret the counterfactual in such a way that *later* philosophers are not ruled out for the wrong reasons. Some of today's philosophers, though analytic by everyone's lights, are notorious cultural and philosophical conservatives. It's likely that, had they been alive in 1910, they would have defended the idealists against Russell and Moore, simply out of respect for their elders!

Perhaps the best way to understand Martinich's suggestion is this: the distinctive thing about analytic philosophers is that they see themselves as the rightful heirs of Russell and Moore, or of philosophers who saw themselves as the rightful heirs of Russell and Moore, or.... "Analytic", so understood, is an adjective grounded, rather loosely, in the way philosophers think about their debts to their predecessors active at the beginning of the twentieth century. To be an analytic philosopher is to accept a version of the history of philosophy according to which the heroes at the beginning of the last century were Frege, Russell, and Moore—not Bradley, Bosanquet, and Bergson. It is to admire the philosophical impact of the analytic revolutionaries, and to hope to be a similar "force for good" in one's own time.[6]

---

[5] "Introduction", *The Blackwell Companion to Analytic Philosophy*, ed. by A. P. Martinich and David Sosa (Malden, Mass.: Blackwell, 2001), p. 5.

[6] When forced at gunpoint to pick "the greatest philosopher of the 20th century", I often answer, "Russell". A few of my friends have been scandalized by this response: "Only a morally virtuous and deeply self-aware person can be a truly 'great' philosopher," they say, "and Russell was neither." Perhaps they are right about Russell's character. And I suppose they are right about what it takes to be a great philosopher, if "philosophy" essentially involves showing others how to live. But that's not what I mean by "philosophy"; someone who does metaphysics, or epistemology, or logic is doing philosophy, and perhaps doing it *extremely well*, even if she is clueless about all sorts of ethical and practical matters. There are intellectual skills that can make someone a philosophical

Is there a sensible reason to use the word "analytic" in a narrower way, so that it does not apply to new wave metaphysicians, who tend to dislike the label? The question is hard to answer, since members of the little group of philosophers I'm calling "new wave" differ among themselves in the reasons they give for dissatisfaction with the practice of "analytic-metaphysics-as-usual". My suspicion is that it is not very sensible for new wave metaphysicians to characterize the "bad" sort of metaphysics, but not their own, as "analytic". But it also seems to me not worth arguing about. *Oxford Studies in Metaphysics* is certainly intended to be a forum broad enough to include (among other things) both old school analytic and new wave metaphysics. But there was never much danger of someone suspecting that one of the two might be excluded. From now on, I shall ignore narrower uses of the term "analytic". This means that the category will include some philosophers who prefer not to call themselves "analytic philosophers". Nevertheless, construing the term this broadly fits with widespread usage. Many socialists prefer not to call themselves "socialists". One can understand their reservations, and recognize the importance of subtler distinctions they want to make, while continuing to use the word in such a way that it applies to them.

THE FALL AND RISE OF METAPHYSICS IN THE TWENTIETH CENTURY

So why do many people—particularly non-analytic philosophers and scholars in other disciplines—still regard "analytic philosophy" as hostile, in principle, to the traditional problems of metaphysics? Those who think that anti-metaphysical doctrines are among the defining features

giant, but that are quite compatible with massive moral failure and deep character flaws. Of course the same is true of the skills required to be a great mathematician or composer.

Does this prove that I have an "impoverished conception of philosophy" (as I have sometimes been told)? Perhaps; but it's an impoverished conception that has been the accepted meaning of the term for hundreds of years—we're all paupers now. The activities that go on under this impoverished heading need not be valueless just because they are not some *other* activity—such as demonstrating, by precept and in practice, the nature of the good life for human beings. It is true that, in some eras, all philosophers were quasi-religious figures who taught their disciples how to live. But it is also true that, in some eras, all philosophers were scientists who developed theories of motion and chemical change. Contemporary philosophers need not be worthless just because we no longer attempt to do either one—or so I tell myself.

of analytic philosophy are mistaking the movement as a whole for the forms it took during the middle third of the last century—a period during which many philosophers in the United States and nearly all of the most influential philosophers in England were under an antimetaphysical spell of one sort or another.

The story of the fall and rise of metaphysics in the twentieth century is well known, in broad outline, because it is the flip side of an even more famous story: the story of the rise and fall of three of the most important philosophical "schools" of the century—logical empiricism or positivism, the "therapeutic" view of philosophy advocated by the later Wittgenstein, and the sort of ordinary language philosophy inspired by J. L. Austin. These movements offered a succession of reasons for thinking that metaphysical claims are about as meaningful as whistling; or, more pessimistically, that they are "as blank as a fart" (to borrow Jacques Renault's colorful phrase).

The beginning of this dark age (dark for metaphysics, anyway) might well be set at 1935—the year of Carnap's *Philosophy and Logical Syntax*, an English distillation of *Logische Syntax der Sprache*—or 1936—the year of Ayer's *Language, Truth, and Logic*. For the next twenty-five years, philosophy was dominated by movements opposed to the very idea of metaphysics: first by positivism, then by Wittgensteinian "quietism" and the ordinary language philosophy championed by Austin. Metaphysics languished during the years of occupation.

But the anti-metaphysical biases of this period in the history of analytic philosophy appear, in retrospect, as an aberration. They were not present during the first phase of the analytic movement: the revolt against British idealism effected by Russell and Moore. (Frege's monumental achievements came a bit earlier; but his influence upon English-speaking philosophers was at first mainly indirect, mediated by Russell.) Russell and Moore, however, were neither dismissive of the traditional problems of metaphysics, nor anti-theoretical in the solutions they proposed. In Moore's early papers and classic lectures of 1910–11 (which helped to set the agenda for much of Russell's work[7]), and in Russell's classic essays and books from the same period (e.g. *The Problems of Philosophy*, *Mysticism and Logic*, *Our Knowledge of*

---

[7] Moore's lectures were published much later as *Some Main Problems of Philosophy* (London: Allen & Unwin, 1953). Russell adverts to these "unpublished writings" in *The Problems of Philosophy* (Oxford University Press, 1912), p. 6.

the External World), nearly all the traditional problems of metaphysics are discussed, and positive solutions are defended. It is no surprise that Russell's later philosophical books, such as the ambitious *Inquiry into Meaning and Truth* (1940), were unpopular and largely ignored; he explicitly rejects the verificationism of the positivists and the "quietism" of Wittgenstein and his followers, defending instead the possibility of discovering metaphysical truths. Despite his unrivalled initial influence, by mid-century Russell could hardly have been more out of step with the philosophical trends.

Of course there were plenty of other first-rate philosophers doing metaphysics in the usual way right through the 1930s and 1940s. G. F. Stout, C. D. Broad, C. A. Campbell, H. H. Price, D. C. Williams, C. J. Ducasse, G. Dawes Hicks, William Kneale, A. C. Ewing, and a handful of others produced impressive work that is continuous with that of Brentano and Meinong on the one side, and today's analytic metaphysicians on the other. At the time, the eyes of the philosophical world were elsewhere, however; and so, when metaphysics re-emerged a decade or two later, these philosophers were relatively obscure figures. None, save Russell, had widespread immediate impact upon the new generation of metaphysicians.[8]

(The seriousness with which Moore took metaphysics was largely lost upon the next generation or two. Some of Wittgenstein's most able students saw Moore as a sort of John the Baptist, making the way straight for their teacher's appearance on the philosophical scene.[9]

---

[8] Here and there, I detect a metaphysical heritage passed on from this "lost generation" to the next. Chisholm has emphasized the inspiration of Russell and Moore, but also that of his undergraduate teacher and then colleague, Ducasse. A quick reading of Ducasse's *Nature, Mind, and Death* (LaSalle, Ill.: Open Court, 1951) is enough to show that Chisholm's metaphysical agenda owes at least as much to Ducasse as to Moore and Russell. Richard Swinburne—whose significant contributions to metaphysics are overshadowed somewhat by the scope and impact of his work in philosophy of religion—was a doctoral student of H. H. Price. Swinburne could be seen as carrying Price's dualistic metaphysics into the next generation.

[9] Cf. the contributions of John Wisdom, Norman Malcolm, and Alice Ambrose to *The Philosophy of G. E. Moore*, ed. by P. A. Schilpp (La Salle, Ill.: Open Court, 1942). Chisholm, on the other hand, saw Moore primarily as a traditional metaphysician and epistemologist. He took Moore's appeals to the propriety of ordinary language to be echoes of Thomas Reid's commonsense philosophy, not harbingers of Wittgensteinianism. (While a student at Harvard, Chisholm met Moore and had the job of showing him around Cambridge; he later said that Moore was the "one person [who] impressed me even more than Russell did": Chisholm, **"Self-Profile"**, in *Roderick M. Chisholm*, ed. by Radu Bogdan (Dordrecht: D. Reidel, 1986), p. 4.)

I suspect that their reading of Moore screened him off, to some extent, from many of the younger philosophers in the post-Quinean metaphysical renaissance.)

Recent years have seen a revival of interest in Broad and Williams; but thousands of pages of well crafted metaphysics sank without a ripple. Call me old-fashioned, but I quite enjoy the authors of this "lost generation"; I find it easier to adopt their perspectives than to get into the heads of the more naturalistically inclined among my contemporaries. And I expect that metaphysics would have been better off today had this generation been allowed to make its mark.

The anti-metaphysical movements that eclipsed these philosophers dominated the discipline for two or three decades. But by the time of Quine's attack on empiricism and defense of ontology, the darkest days were over. These two aspects of Quine's philosophy were rightly perceived as friendly toward traditional metaphysics; their impact was felt well before 1953, when the collection *From a Logical Point of View* was published. Since then, metaphysics' star has been on the rise. Throughout the 1960s and 1970s, the case files of most traditional metaphysical problems were reopened, one after another—in many instances, over Quine's strenuous objections. Advances in modal logic paved the way for the revival of essentialist metaphysics, preeminently in Kripke's *Naming and Necessity*. By the end of the 1970s the familiar metaphysical questions about universals, events, causation, numbers, and so on were nearly as central to analytic philosophy as they had been in the days of Russell and Moore. The revival of metaphysics even brought back such venerable chestnuts as "libertarian" (i.e. incompatibilist) theories of free action, substance dualism, and the ontological and cosmological arguments for the existence of God.

Although plenty of contemporary analytic philosophers still *dislike* metaphysics, hardly any would now pretend to have a principled reason for dismissing the entire budget of traditional metaphysical questions as pseudo-problems. And many of our best minds venture into deep metaphysical waters with no sign of fear. A list of the one hundred most prominent analytic philosophers of the last fifty years would include a sizable number who are famous, in large part, for their contributions to metaphysics—e.g. Quine, Nelson Goodman, P. F. Strawson, Wilfrid Sellars, Roderick Chisholm, D. M. Armstrong, Hilary Putnam, David Wiggins, Derek Parfit, Donald Davidson, Saul Kripke, Alvin Plantinga, Sydney Shoemaker, and David Lewis.

MEET THE NEW METAPHYSICS, SAME AS THE OLD METAPHYSICS

What is distinctive about the approach most analytic philosophers take to the ancient problems of metaphysics? I'm tempted, once again, to answer: nothing. Russell and Moore broke decisively with the dominant metaphysics of their day, idealism. But they also saw themselves as champions of a patently metaphysical doctrine of their own: a version of realism more robust than most contemporary philosophers would believe. And they did not imagine themselves to be the first to hold their metaphysical positions. They recognized aspects of their own views in those of immediate predecessors such as Meinong and Brentano, whose work they discussed in detail. Russell frankly acknowledged the similarity between Leibniz's monadology (which he examined in its own right very early on, in *The Philosophy of Leibniz*) and the realist metaphysics he developed in *Our Knowledge of the External World*. Russell and Moore may have derided the obscurity and lack of rigor they detected in the work of the most influential metaphysicians of their day. (The three "B"s—Bradley, Bosanquet, and Bergson—were singled out for particularly harsh treatment.) But in their own more positive work, the only truly unprecedented developments were due to the fact that advances in formal logic shed some genuinely new light upon several familiar philosophical problems.

Russell and Moore certainly saw themselves as part of a "revolution in philosophy"; but the revolutionary aspect of analytic philosophy was, to begin with, primarily the overthrow of idealism in favor of realism, and advocacy of the "new logic". It was a revolution intended not to banish traditional metaphysical problems altogether, but to solve them in more commonsensical—or at least more *comprehensible*—ways. The ambitiously anti-metaphysical revolutionary myths were promulgated during a period fifteen to twenty-five years later: all metaphysical statements have been shown to be nonsense according to self-evident criteria of meaningfulness; or metaphysical problems are due entirely to insensitivity to the way language is actually used, and one after another is being exorcised by a sufficiently subtle recitation of truisms. As these myths took hold, Russell's metaphysically loaded brand of realism quickly became almost as unfashionable as the idealism of Bradley and Bosanquet.

TOWARD REUNION IN METAPHYSICS

If my version of history is at all close to the truth, the non-analytic metaphysicians' conviction that analytic philosophy is *inherently* anti-metaphysical is quite erroneous, however understandable. The first generation of analytic philosophers were interested in most of the traditional problems of metaphysics; the anti-metaphysical period in analytic philosophy was comparatively short (albeit exceptionally virulent); and there was no lasting revolution in methodology that distinguishes metaphysics in analytic circles from what one finds in earlier periods and other traditions. Today's analytic metaphysicians have the tools of modern logic at their disposal; but, otherwise, it's pretty much business-as-usual. For good or ill, the problems they tackle are not significantly different from those that faced the philosophers of earlier eras; and they defend positions readily identifiable as variously Platonist, Aristotelian, Thomistic, rationalist, Humean, and so on.

The impression that there is a deep, principled difference between analytic philosophy and other traditions has proven pernicious for the health of metaphysics (and other subfields, too, no doubt), separating natural allies and preventing healthy criticism from being heard across various analytic/non-analytic divides. It is to be hoped that metaphysicians who think of analytic philosophy as fundamentally hostile to metaphysics will discover that the classic, substantive questions of their subject are high on the analytic agenda once again—indeed, that they have been quite high on the agenda for well over half of analytic philosophy's history, including its earliest chapters. And it is also to be hoped that metaphysicians in analytic circles will be open to the best contemporary work originating within metaphysical traditions too long alienated from analytic philosophy—e.g., neo-Thomism, neo-Platonism, process philosophy, personalism, idealism.

Eventually, perhaps even before *Oxford Studies in Metaphysics* has gone the way of all publishing ventures, the label "analytic" will have ceased to seem useful to any of us—whether as badge of honor or term of abuse. Of course the disappearance of the already fuzzy boundary between analytic philosophy and other traditions should not be expected to usher in an idyllic era of philosophical agreement! But it might well mark the beginning of a period when the genuine differences and affinities among philosophical movements are easier to see than they are at present.[10]

---

[10] I am grateful to Tamar Gendler and Alvin Plantinga for many helpful comments and suggestions.

THE *OXFORD STUDIES IN METAPHYSICS* YOUNGER SCHOLAR PRIZE

Sponsored by the A. M. Monius Institute and administered by the editorial board of *Oxford Studies in Metaphysics*, the essay competition is open to scholars who are within ten years of receiving a Ph.D. and students who are currently enrolled in a graduate program. (Independent scholars should inquire of the Editor to determine eligibility.) The award is $2,500. Winning essays shall appear in *Oxford Studies in Metaphysics*.

Essays should generally be no longer than 10,000 words; longer essays may be considered, but authors must seek prior approval by providing the Editor with an abstract and word count by November 1, 2004. Submissions must be postmarked by November 30, 2004, to be assured of consideration for this year's prize. Refereeing will be blind; authors should omit remarks and references that might disclose their identities. The winner will be determined by a committee of members of the editorial board of *Oxford Studies in Metaphysics*, and announced in February 2005.

Inquiries and submissions should be addressed to:
Dean Zimmerman, Editor
Oxford Studies in Metaphysics
Philosophy Department
Rutgers University
Davison Hall, Douglass Campus
New Brunswick, NJ 08903

The A. M. Monius Institute is a non-profit organization dedicated to the revival of traditional metaphysics. Information about other activities of the A. M. Monius Institute may be found at www.ammonius.org.

Part I

PRESENTISM

1. Tensed Quantifiers

David Lewis

Some of our idioms of quantification embed verbs, e.g 'there is', 'there exists'. When they do, those verbs can be tensed, forming what I shall call *tensed quantifiers*. There are past-tensed quantifiers, e.g. 'there was', 'there has been', 'there existed'. There are future-tensed quantifiers, e.g. 'there will be', 'there is going to exist'. There are tensed quantifiers with compound tenses, 'there had existed', or 'there will have been'. And sometimes, at least, the unmarked quantifier phrase 'there is' or 'there exists' acts as a present-tensed quantifier.

Some of us are *four-dimensionalists*. We think that things are spread out through time just as they are through space. Our most inclusive domain of quantification—disregarding, for now, 'abstract' entities and unactualized possibilia—consists of past, present, and future things. We four-dimensionalists have a ready-made way to understand tensed quantifiers: the tenses mark restrictions of the quantifiers to sub-domains of that most inclusive domain. They impose a restriction, perhaps, to past things; or to future things; or to present things; or to things that are past from some contextually definite point in the past. Or they may impose a restriction to things that will at some future time be past—which is no restriction at all.[1]

(All four-dimensionalists agree that the unmarked idioms of quantification sometimes are present-tensed, and carry a restriction to present things. Some four-dimensionalists think, rightly in my view, that sometimes instead the unmarked idioms carry no restriction. They may be used to quantify over the entire domain of past, present, and future things. But other four-dimensionalists may insist that the unmarked quantifiers invariably carry a restriction to present things, so

© Estate of David K. Lewis, 2002

I thank John Bigelow, M. J. Cresswell, Allen Hazen, Mark Johnston, Lloyd Humberstone, Gideon Rosen, Ted Sider, Michael Smith, Dean Zimmerman, and the audience at the Australasian Association of Logic conference, 1999, for valuable comments.

[1] Except in certain structures of two-way branching time.

that if we want to quantify unrestrictedly over all things throughout time, we must resort to circumlocution. Either we can express an unrestricted quantification disjunctively; 'there are, were, or will be'; or else we can express it by means of a compound tense; 'there will have been'.[2] But this disagreement among four-dimensionalists is no kind of disagreement about metaphysics or logic—only a disagreement about English usage.)

Others are not four-dimensionalists but *presentists*. Presentists think that our most inclusive domain of quantification (still disregarding abstracta and possibilia) is just the domain of present things. Past and future things are unreal.[3] There is therefore no question of restricting the most inclusive domain so as to quantify over past or future things. There is likewise no question of shifting the domain of quantification from the domain of present things to a different domain of past things, or a domain of future things. There are no such domains to shift to. For the presentist, the unmarked quantifier is a present-tensed quantifier, just because the unmarked quantifier is an unrestricted quantifier, and quantification over present things is as unrestricted as you can ever get.

The presentist is likely to think that a past- or future-tensed quantifier is an unmarked quantifier within the scope of a tense operator. 'There has been...' means 'it has been that (there is...)'. 'There will be...' means 'It will be that (there is...)'. A tense operator, in turn, is a sentential modifier that works not by restricting domains of quantification (and not truth-functionally) but in some different way.

Modal irrealists will say that there is ample precedent for non-restricting sentential modifiers. For instance: 'possibly' and 'necessarily'; or 'if it were that so-and-so'; or 'according to such-and-such story'. It is harder for a modal realist to find a precedent for a non-restricting sentential modifier. But here's a precedent that even I can accept: the initial modifier in the sentence 'According to Graham Priest, some sets are and are not self-members.' So I agree with the presentists that there can be such a thing as a non-restricting (and non-truth-functional) sentential modifier.

---

[2] 'There were going to be' would do instead, provided we could avoid taking it as an allusion to perhaps-unfulfilled plans.

[3] For a forthright presentist manifesto, see A. N. Prior, 'The Notion of the Present', *Studium Generale*, 23 (1970): 245–8.

Set aside the deadlocked dispute over the plausibility of presentism, and ask simply how well it works on its own terms. So long as our tensed quantifiers are singular, it works fairly smoothly.[4] The presentist does as well as the four-dimensionalist in explaining the truth of 'There has been a king[5] named John', and in explaining the possible truth of 'There will be a king named Wilbur.'

But what if our tensed quantifiers are plural? Start with the simplest case: numerical quantification with a specified finite number. 'There have been two kings named Charles' or 'There will have been three kings named Charles.' (Let's insert a tacit 'at least'. If we can handle 'at least n' for all n, we can of course define 'at most n' and 'exactly n'.) The straightforward presentist translation of the tensed quantifier isn't right. There have been two kings named Charles, but not both at the same time. So 'It has been that (there are two kings named Charles)' is false.

What's to do? In general, we can build a numerical quantifier out of two or more singular quantifiers: 'There are two books here' means 'There is a book here, and there is another book here.' So we might try to build our tensed numerical quantifier out of two singular tensed quantifiers: 'There has been a king named Charles, and there has been another king named Charles.' Or, in long-winded regimentation to make explicit that each tensed singular quantifier is a quantifier within the scope of a tense operator: 'It has been that (there is a king named Charles); and it has been that (there is another king named Charles).'

That translation is all very well by four-dimensionalist lights, but I don't think a presentist has any right to it. The word 'another' seems to mean that a king Charles in the domain of quantification introduced by the first 'there has been' is different from a king Charles in the domain introduced by the second. But the presentist insists that the tense operators neither restrict nor shift domains of quantification. These kings, whether the same or whether different, are by presentist lights unreal. So what sense can it make to speak of whether they are the same or different?

However, a presentist can allow tense operators to modify not only sentences but verb phrases, giving us the modified-having by real,

---

[4] Not perfectly. Allen Hazen points out that a sentence like 'Never have all the kings of England been alive simultaneously' poses difficulties similar to those raised by tensed plural quantifiers.

[5] Of England. Let this be understood henceforth.

present things of properties they don't really (that is, presently) have, but that they have had or that they will have. (Analogously, using our precedent for a non-restricting modifier, we might say that the real person Russell had-according-to-Graham-Priest the property of failing to follow where argument led.) Allowing tense operators to function adverbially licenses us to quantify into the scope of tense operators, though not to quantify from the scope of one tense operator into the scope of another. If so, it is well formed (though not yet true) to say 'There is a king named Charles, and it has been that (there is another king named Charles).' But what we can say, we can say within the scope of a tense operator. So we have this nested translation, which I believe conforms to presentist strictures: 'There have been two kings named Charles' means 'It has been that (there is a king named Charles and it has been that [there is another king named Charles]).'

A similar translation is available for 'There have been three kings named Charles' in which the tense operators are nested three deep: 'It has been that (there is a king named Charles and [it has been that (there is another king named Charles and [it has been that (there is yet another king named Charles, different from both of these)])]).' And so on for larger finite numbers. To translate 'There will have been three kings named Charles' we could simply prefix 'It will be that...' to the translation above; or else we could nest the compound tense operator 'It will be that (it has been that...)' three deep.

It's a bit of good luck that kings persist through time, and that there are never two simultaneous ones. Else to say that there have been two kings named Charles, we'd require an extra disjunct to cover the case where there have been two, and they were instantaneous and simultaneous. A general translation of 'There have been two so-and-sos' should be: 'It has been that (there is a so-and-so, and either [there is another so-and-so or it has been that (there is another so-and-so)]).' Exercise: write out the translation of 'there have been seventeen so-and-sos', presupposing nothing about which if any of the seventeen are instantaneous and which if any of them are simultaneous.

Not all numbers are finite. If the hypothesis of two-way eternal recurrence is true, there have been infinitely many kings named John, and there will be infinitely many more of them. The four-dimensionalist says that, restricting his domain to past things, or restricting it instead to future things, there are infinitely many kings named John in the restricted domain. The presentist, if he sticks to the brute-force method we've been considering so far, requires a construction with tense operators nested *ad infinitum*.[6]

Further, some plural quantifiers do not specify a number, and some specify a number only vaguely. There have been some kings named George, and indeed there have been several of them; though never has it been the case that there are several kings named George. Once the presentist can translate tensed numerical quantifiers, he can give us a disjunction of these translations: 'There have been one or there have been two or... or there have been infinitely many.'[7] And in the case of the vague 'several', perhaps he can somehow leave it undecided just which disjuncts are and which are not included in his translation.

The presentist is accustomed to boast that his metaphysics of time is the view of the common man, uncorrupted by philosophy. The unsuspected complexities that we've just been exploring should therefore come as very bad news. I think the presentist might do better to abandon this brute-force method of translation, and seek some other way to handle tensed numerical or plural quantifiers. I have two alternative suggestions to offer him.

He might take to heart the lesson that nonexistent objects can cast existent shadows. Terence Parsons used this strategy to good effect in investigating Meinongian quantification: the nonexistent golden mountain has as its shadow the existent property-bundle of goldenness and mountainhood. Even the round square casts a shadow: the bundle of roundness and squareness, uninstantiable but nevertheless existent. Parsons imagines a bogus Meinong who quantifies over property-bundles, but expresses himself in such a way that he seems to be quantifying over nonexistent objects. Bogus Meinong parallels real Meinong closely enough that if real Meinong somehow fell into contradiction, bogus Meinong would too. Yet bogus Meinong offers us

---

[6] In the infinite case, it matters whether we translate 'There will have been infinitely many...' by prefixing 'It will be that' to a translation of 'There have been infinitely many...', or whether instead we give an infinite nesting of 'it will be that (it has been that...)' operators. If there is a first sunrise, and every sunrise forevermore is followed by another (and time isn't circular), will there have been infinitely many sunrises? Some of those I have asked, but not all, say yes. The second translation endorses their opinion, the first does not.

[7] I'd like to insist that he should cover the case where for all we know there may be proper-class many; see Daniel Nolan, 'Recombination Unbound', *Philosophical Studies*, 84 (1996): 239–62. Then I ask just how long it is possible for an infinitary construction to get. But I shall be merciful and not press the point.

nothing more peculiar than a presumably-consistent theory of property-bundles.[8]

Likewise a presentist might hold that nonexistent past and future things have existent surrogates, and that we are free to quantify, with or without restrictions, over the domain of these surrogates. There have been two kings named Charles because there are two surrogates for past kings named Charles. Under the hypothesis of eternal recurrence there would have been infinitely many kings named John because there would be infinitely many surrogates for past kings named John. There have been several kings named George because there are several surrogates for past kings named George. This presentist account, call it *surrogate four-dimensionalism*, closely imitates genuine four-dimensionalism. It works just as smoothly. Except for the need to keep inserting the words 'surrogates for', it can be just as simple. One way to keep it simple is to suppose that present, existing things have surrogates too. That way, we can speak uniformly of surrogates, even when we happen to be quantifying over present things that need no surrogates. If we didn't pursue uniformity in this way, 'There will be a king named Charles' would have to be disjunctive: 'Either there is a surrogate for a future king named Charles, or else some real, presently existing thing will be a king named Charles.'

Bogus Meinong's surrogates for nonexistent objects were property-bundles: set-theoretical constructions out of actually existing properties. Whether or not that is a safe policy for bogus Meinong—myself, I doubt that it is—it is not a safe policy for the surrogate four-dimensionalist. The only properties available as building materials for surrogates are properties that presently exist. Either our surrogate four-dimensionalist must commit himself to a dubious platonism which says that properties exist regardless of whether they are instantiated; or else he must assume that presently instantiated properties will suffice to construct all the requisite surrogates for past and future entities. It may be that long ago, when the cosmos was young and its symmetries were still unbroken, fundamental properties were instantiated that have never occurred since. These archaic properties are needed as constituents of the bundles that serve as surrogates for long-ago things, yet they are

---

[8] Terence Parsons, 'A Prolegomenon to Meinongian Semantics', *Journal of Philosophy*, 71 (1974): 561–80; *Nonexistent Objects* (Yale University Press, 1980). The metaphor of non-existent objects casting existent shadows is illustrated on the cover of *Nonexistent Objects*.

not to be had.⁹ Nor do I see what might replace them as constituents of surrogates. So I think the surrogate four-dimensionalist would do best not to offer any set-theoretical recipe for the construction of surrogates. He would then resemble not so much bogus Meinong as Alvin Plantinga, an actualist who invokes uninstantiated 'essences' as surrogates for possibilia.¹⁰

Now the surrogate four-dimensionalist owes us an account of how his surrogates differ from the things that genuine four-dimensionalists believe in and he does not. He will very likely say that whereas the genuine four-dimensionalist thinks that past and future kings are 'concrete', he believes rather that the surrogates for past and future (and present) kings are 'abstract'. (Remember, we granted that a presentist's most inclusive domain of quantification might contain abstract entities as well as present things.) What, I wonder, could he mean by 'abstract'?

When Quine calls something 'abstract', he means that it is some sort of set-theoretical construction. Well and good;¹¹ but we have just seen why a surrogate four-dimensionalist would be ill-advised to offer set-theoretical recipes for surrogates.

When Locke said that some of our ideas were 'abstract', and when Berkeley denied it, they were talking about a lack of specificity: the idea of a triangle which is not specifically equilateral, nor right isosceles, nor.... Well and good; but I don't think that is what our surrogate four-dimensionalist could mean. How is the surrogate for Elizabeth I any less specific than Elizabeth II is?

When Donald C. Williams called (most) tropes 'abstract', he meant that they were less than the whole of what was to be found at their space–time locations. Likewise when Nelson Goodman distinguished between concrete and abstract individuals, concreta were sums of qualia that were maximal with respect to togetherness, whereas abstract individuals were sums that had no concreta as parts. And when D. M. Armstrong says that 'thin' particulars and universals are

---

⁹ This problem of archaic properties resembles the problem of alien properties I raised against linguistic ersatzism in *On the Plurality of Worlds* (Oxford: Blackwell, 1986), pp. 159–65.

¹⁰ *The Nature of Necessity* (Oxford University Press, 1974), pp. 70–7.

¹¹ Provided that, as is often thought, sets are a distinctive kind of thing. But not if sethood is a structural status, akin to coming seventeenth. Seventeenth terms are not a distinctive kind of thing; everything is a seventeenth term of some sequences and not of others. For a structuralist view of sethood, see my 'Mathematics is Megethology' in *Papers in Philosophical Logic* (Cambridge University Press, 1998).

abstracted from 'thick' particulars, he too means that they are only part of what's there. (More or less. They are 'unmereological parts', whatever that means.) Well and good; but I don't think this is what our surrogate four-dimensionalist can mean, since the surrogate for Elizabeth I no more coexists with other things at the same location than Elizabeth II herself does.[12]

He well might mean that the surrogate has no space–time location at all. But is that really so? Surely there is *some* salient relationship between the surrogate for Elizabeth I and sixteenth-century England. Not so, says the presentist, because there is no such thing as sixteenth-century England. But at least he must grant that there is some salient relationship between the surrogate for Elizabeth I and the surrogate for sixteenth-century England. Why does that relationship not give us a perfectly good sense in which the surrogate for Elizabeth I is located? We might well be able to say why not, if we already understood how things and their surrogates, and likewise locations and their surrogates, are thought to differ. But that difference is exactly what we're trying to understand, so far without success.

Finally, our surrogate four-dimensionalist might say of surrogates, as Plantinga says of essences, that they are properties. Some of us sometimes conceive of a property as the class of all its actual and possible instances. Well and good; but this conception is unavailable to a presentist, since he denies the reality of the past and future instances. We might instead conceive of a property as a proper part of the total content of a space–time location. Well and good; but we've already seen that this conception does not apply to surrogates. Or we might think of a property as something repeatable, capable of appearing in its entirety many times over. Well and good; but surrogates are not repeatables. Under the hypothesis of eternal recurrence, there have been infinitely many kings named John. If the relevant surrogates are supposed to be things that there are infinitely many of, we need different surrogates for all the different king Johns of all the different epochs. A repeatable surrogate won't do.

Nor is it helpful to say that a surrogate is a property because it is the kind of thing that can be instantiated. What we know best about being

---

[12] D. C. Williams, 'On the Elements of Being', *Review of Metaphysics*, 7 (1953): 3–18 and 171–92, especially 6–7; Nelson Goodman, *The Structure of Appearance* (Harvard University Press, 1951), sec. VII.8; D. M. Armstrong, *A World of States of Affairs* (Cambridge University Press, 1997).

instantiated is that it's what properties do; the notions of property and of instantiation come as a package deal. If you told me that Kevin Sheedy, though in most respects nothing like a property, can nevertheless be instantiated (and indeed has been), I would have no idea what you might mean. Likewise if you tell me that surrogates can be instantiated, that makes sense only if you have already shown me how to think of them as properties.

Now I've run out of ideas for what it might mean to call a surrogate 'abstract', or to call it a 'property'. Absent other suggestions, the difference between our presentist's surrogate kings and the four-dimensionalist's genuine past and future kings has become ineffable. All we have is a claim that somehow, we know not how, the surrogate four-dimensionalist is entitled to have it both ways. He says in one voice that there is a domain of things spread out through time, and in another voice that there is not.

I think the presentist would do better to look elsewhere for a solution to the problem of tensed plural quantifiers. A safe refuge, I think, is to claim that he just has a primitive understanding of them. Nobody can deny that tensed plural quantifiers are part of the language that we all speak, and that we all understand. If they cannot be analysed as unmarked quantifiers within the scope of tense operators, and if they cannot be understood as quantifiers over a domain of surrogates, so be it. Analysis—who needs it?

The primitivist story could be told in two superficially different versions. I think they are just terminological variants.

Version I. To be a quantifier is to function semantically like a quantifier. There must be a domain of entities, there must be a way for members of that domain to satisfy predicate phrases, and a quantifier phrase indicates whether some, or all, or none, or two, or infinitely many, or several, or... things in the indicated domain satisfy a predicate. Since there are no domains of past or future things, 'tensed quantifiers' are not really quantifiers.

Version II. To be a quantifier is to function inferentially like a quantifier. Tensed quantifiers are indeed quantifiers, because they obey (appropriately tensed forms of) the usual rules of quantificational logic. However, the usual semantic story about domains and satisfaction does not apply to them.

Primitivism is unambitious; the primitivist will reply that the ambition to analyse tensed quantifiers was misguided.

Primitivism is unambitious in a second way, and I think the primitivist should find that rather more worrying. Recall our complex translations of tensed plural quantifiers in terms of nested tense operators and unmarked singular quantifiers. The primitivist does not wish to offer these translations as analyses of sentences with tensed plural quantifiers. But he must still acknowledge that they are *a priori* equivalent to sentences with tensed plural quantifiers. It would be nice if he could explain how these equivalences are known to us. But once he denies that the equivalences are analytic, I don't know what other explanation he can offer.

It may be suggested that the presentist ought to help himself not to primitive tensed quantifiers, but rather to primitive 'span' operators: tense operators of a different kind than we have so far considered. I do not know how to characterize span operators in terms acceptable to a presentist. But to a four-dimensionalist (or to a presentist who understands four-dimensionalism although he does not believe it) I can say that instead of meaning 'at some past (or future) moment', a span operator means 'at some past (or future) interval'. Things can be true not only of moments but also of intervals, so why should we not have operators that allow us to say so?

Let us translate 'There have been two kings named Charles' as 'It HAS been that (there are two kings named Charles)', where 'it HAS been' is the past-tensed span operator. By four-dimensionalist lights, this will mean that it is true of some interval in the past that there are two kings named Charles. The presentist cannot accept that explanation, but he might nevertheless accept the translation with the span operator taken as primitive. Likewise we could translate 'There will be four kings named Wilbur' as 'It WILL be that (there are four kings named Wilbur)', using a future-tensed span operator. Likewise we could translate 'There will have been three kings named Charles' as 'It will be that (it HAS been that [there are three kings named Charles])'. (The outer future tense operator need not be a span operator.)

I object that span operators are so badly behaved that nobody should claim to have a primitive understanding of them. For one thing, they create ambiguities even when prefixed to a sentence that is not itself ambiguous. 'It HAS been that (it is raining and the sun is shining)' might mean that there is some past interval throughout which rain fell from a sunny sky—a 'sun-shower'. Or instead it could mean that there is some past interval with at least one rainy sub-interval and it least one sunny sub-interval. Likewise 'It HAS been that (there are two popes)' could mean that there is some past interval throughout which there are two popes, in which case it is true in virtue of the great schism during which there were rival popes in Avignon and Rome. Or instead it could mean that there is some past interval with two different popes in two non-overlapping subintervals, in which case it would have been true even if there had never been a schism.

For another thing, span operators can be prefixed to contradictions to make truths. 'It HAS been that (it rains and it doesn't rain)' is true, at least under one of its disambiguations—the two-subintervals disambiguation. But span operators will make different truths when prefixed to different contradictions, and sometimes will not make truths at all. Sometimes they will even make new contradictions, as in the case of 'It HAS been that (it rains nonstop and it doesn't rain nonstop)' which cannot reasonably be given a two-subintervals disambiguation. Therefore they are hyperintensional operators: the intension of a sentence formed using a span operator is not a function of the intension of the embedded sentence.

The motivating idea that we should be able to say that something is true not of a moment but of an interval suggests that we should discard the two-subintervals disambiguations. That would avoid both the ambiguity and the making of truths from contradictions. But it would also wreck the plan to use span operators to translate tensed quantifiers. If 'It HAS been that (there are two kings named Charles)' had to mean that there is a past interval throughout which there are two kings named Charles, it would be false, whereas we wanted it to be the translation of something true. If, on the other hand, we discarded the throughout-an-interval disambiguations, we would still have the problem with embedded contradictions, and we would also lose touch with our original motivating idea.

A four-dimensionalist can safely use span operators (though I don't know why he would find them worth the bother), because he has another language available to remove ambiguities and to explain why sentences with embedded contradictions may nevertheless be true. He can do as I have done, and quantify explicitly over past and future intervals and their subintervals. But a presentist who takes span operators as primitive has no such resources available to him. I conclude that primitivism about span operators is not a satisfactory presentist solution to the problem of tensed quantifiers. Primitivism about the tensed quantifiers themselves is a better bet.

To conclude. I have offered three solutions to the problem of tensed plural quantifiers: brute-force translation, surrogate four-dimensionalism, and primitivism. I have not given decisive refutations of any one of the three. But I've argued that each one bears a burden either of implausible complexity or else of unfinished business.

Late, of Princeton University

2. Symposium: Defining Presentism

On Presentism and Triviality
Thomas M. Crisp

One sometimes hears the following argument put against presentism. Presentists say: "Only present things exist." But consider the verb "exist" in the quoted sentence. Is it tensed or untensed? Suppose tensed: then the presentist's thesis amounts to the claim that only present things exist now—a trivial truism. Suppose untensed: then her thesis is equivalent to the claim that only present things existed, exist, or will exist—a manifest falsehood: plenty of things (e.g. the Roman Empire) existed or will exist which aren't present. The upshot: presentism is a trivial truism or an obvious falsehood. Either way, it's not a very interesting piece of metaphysics.[1]

Let us call this the "triviality argument" against presentism. I shall argue for two claims in this paper. First, the triviality argument is unsound. And second, its conclusion is false: presentism is neither banal nor manifestly false. I begin by spelling out the triviality argument more carefully.

1. THE TRIVIALITY ARGUMENT EXPLAINED

Presentists say that only present things exist.[2] But the sentence

(Pr) Only present things exist

---

[1] Lawrence Lombard raises a version of this objection (Lombard 1999, pp. 254–5), as does Craig Callender (2000, S588–S589). For discussion, see Sider (1999, pp. 325–7); Zimmerman (1998, pp. 209–10); Merricks (1995, p. 523; 1999, pp. 421–2); Hinchliff (2000, pp. S576–S577); and Rea (2003).

[2] This way of putting the thesis, or something close to it, is fairly common in the literature. Bigelow characterizes presentism as the thesis that "nothing exists which is not present" (1996, p. 35). Markosian thinks of it as the view that "necessarily, it is always true that only present objects exist" (Ch. 3 below, fn. 1). Merricks suggests that presentism is

is ambiguous. Its verb "exist" plausibly admits of a tenseless and two tensed readings. Each reading of the verb yields a slightly different thesis. Presentism, let us assume, is one of these three theses.

We begin with the tensed readings of (Pr). There are two plausible options. We could take its verb as present tensed, yielding

(Pr$_a$) Only present things exist now (i.e. at present).

But this, presumably, is not what the presentist has in mind since (Pr$_a$) is a trivial truism; for what is a "present thing" but a thing that exists at present?

Perhaps the presentist means (Pr)'s "exist" is to be read *disjunctively*, yielding

(Pr$_b$) Only present things existed, exist, or will exist.

But (Pr$_b$) is manifestly false: the Roman Empire existed but isn't a present thing; my great grandchildren will exist but aren't present things. So it's false that only present things existed, exist, or will exist.

If "exist" isn't plausibly regarded as tensed, maybe it's a tenseless verb, one that indicates nothing about pastness, presentness, or futurity. Some who "take tense seriously" will object that there *are* no tenseless verbs.[3] But let us suppose they're wrong and that presentism is the claim that

(Pr$_c$) Only present things (tenselessly) exist.

A brief comment about (Pr$_c$). Some think that numbers, properties, and the like exist *timelessly* or *atemporally*. (Pr$_c$) should not be read as the claim that only present things exist in this way. To be a present thing is to be a temporal thing, a thing that exists *in time*. The presentist may be benighted, but he doesn't mean to claim that only present things exist timelessly or atemporally.

How then are we to understand (Pr$_c$)? The idea here is that we can speak of a thing as "existing" without thereby saying anything about whether it exists now, in the past, or in the future. To say of x that it exists in this sense is to claim merely that our most inclusive quantifiers range over x. x may be past, present, or future; we say nothing about

the thesis that "all that exists, exists at the present time" (1995, p. 523). Zimmerman characterizes it as the thesis that "the only things that exist are those that exist at present" (1998, p. 209).

[3] See e.g. Smith (1993, ch. 6); Tichy (1980, pp. 177–9).

which when we say of x that our widest quantifiers "pick it up". So, to say that only present things (tenselessly) exist is to say something like: for every x (using our most unrestricted quantifier), x is a present thing.

Could the presentist have this reading of (Pr) in mind? Once again, presumably not, since it's a simple matter of logic that if, for every x, x is a present thing, then for every x, x existed, exists, or will exist only if x is a present thing. But notice: to claim that, for every x, x is a G only if x is an F is just to claim that only Fs are Gs. So to say that, for every x, x existed, exists, or will exist only if x is a present thing is to say that only present things existed, exist, or will exist. And the latter claim, recall, is just (Pr$_b$), a trivial falsehood. (Pr$_c$) implies a trivial falsehood. Since it's obvious that this is so, it's obvious that (Pr$_c$) is false.

We can now put the triviality argument precisely. First, we suppose that presentism is one of the theses yielded by disambiguation of (Pr). There are three plausible disambiguations, (Pr$_a$), (Pr$_b$), and (Pr$_c$); so

(P1) Presentism is either (Pr$_a$), (Pr$_b$), or (Pr$_c$).

But

(P2) (Pr$_a$) is trivially true, and
(P3) (Pr$_b$) and (Pr$_c$) are trivially false.

Accordingly,

(C) Presentism is either a trivial truism or a manifest falsehood.

Fortunately for the presentist, the foregoing argument is unsound.

2. THE TRIVIALITY ARGUMENT EXAMINED

(P3) says that it is manifestly false that only present things existed, exist, or will exist. Says the objector: this is manifestly false because there were and will be things that aren't now present—e.g. the Roman Empire, my great-grandchildren. Since it's manifestly true that there were and will be things that aren't now present, it's manifestly false that only present things existed, exist, or will exist.

But here there is confusion. Again, to say that only Fs are Gs is to say that, for every x, if x is a G, then x is an F. Thus, to say that only present things existed, exist, or will exist is to say that

(Pr$_b'$) For every x, if x existed, exists, or will exist, then x is a present thing.

(Pr$_b'$) invokes an *unrestricted* quantifier, one that ranges over *everything*. The presentist who construes her thesis thus proposes of each thing x in our most inclusive domain of quantification that, if x existed, exists, or will exist, then x is a present thing. We can state the same thing differently by shifting to a restricted quantifier, one whose domain is restricted to the class of all things in time, the class of all things that existed, exist now, or will exist. (Of course, for those of us who think *all* things are temporal things, this amounts to no restriction at all.) Then we get:

(Pr$_b''$) For every x, x is a present thing

where here we quantify restrictedly over the domain of all things in time—henceforth, D$_t$.

The triviality objector proposes that (Pr$_b''$) is trivially false and points to the Roman Empire as an obvious counter-example. The idea, presumably, is that D$_t$ includes something—viz. the Roman Empire—that existed but is not present. But is it an obvious truth that D$_t$ includes something identical with the Roman Empire which existed and is no longer present? Clearly not. Here we need to distinguish between the *de dicto* assertion that

(RE$_1$) *WAS*(for some x, x is the Roman Empire and x will not exist in t$_\alpha$)

where "t$_\alpha$" names the present moment, and the *de re* assertion that

(RE$_2$) For some x, x was the Roman Empire and x is no longer present.

RE$_1$ is a *de dicto* claim predicating past truth of the proposition [For some x, x is the Roman Empire and x will not exist in t$_\alpha$]. Most everyone—presentist or no—will grant that RE$_1$ is an obvious truth.[4] RE$_2$ is a *de re* claim to the effect that the open sentence "x was the Roman Empire and x is no longer present" is satisfied by some *res* in D$_t$. This claim isn't nearly as obvious. It's certainly no Moorean fact[5] that the domain of temporal

---

[4] Let us set aside those of us in the grip of philosophy who doubt that there are such things as empires.

[5] To borrow from Armstrong, "one of the many facts which even philosophers should not deny" (1978, pp. 440–1).

things is still populated with something non-present and identical with the Roman Empire. Were it a Moorean fact that *eternalism*—the view that our most inclusive domain of quantification includes past, present, and future entities—is true, I suppose it would be a Moorean fact that D_t includes the Roman Empire. But it's not just *obvious* that eternalism is true: it's not just obvious that our widest domain of quantification still includes wholly past objects like the Roman Empire. If eternalism is true, we need serious argument to see that it is.

If there is an obvious truth in the neighborhood, then, it's the truth expressed by RE_1. But this truth is consistent with the claim that, quantifying over all things in time, for every x, x is present. It thus provides no counter-example to (Pr_b''). Similar comments apply to the suggestion that (Pr_b'') is false because there will be things—e.g. my great-grandchildren—that aren't yet.

The triviality objector's argument for the claim that (Pr_b'') is trivially false is less than impressive. Moreover, (Pr_b'') is *not* trivially false. No doubt some philosophers take themselves to have good reason for thinking eternalism true and (Pr_b'') false. Perhaps they do have good reason. Again, though, it's not just *obvious* that the domain of temporal things includes non-present objects. Eternalism might *be* true, but seeing this requires substantive metaphysical argument.

I conclude that my opponent is mistaken in thinking that (Pr_b'') is manifestly false. Thus, I reject premise (P3) of her argument. The triviality argument is unsound.

3. NEITHER TRIVIALLY FALSE NOR TRIVIALLY TRUE

Not only is the triviality argument unsound, its conclusion is false. Let us think of presentism as the thesis expressed by (Pr_b'').[6] According to (C), this thesis is either a trivial truism or a manifest falsehood. I've already argued that it's not manifestly false. It's obvious, I think, that it's also not trivially true. Suppose that eternalism is true. Then our most inclusive domain of quantification includes wholly past and wholly

---

[6] This way of putting presentism isn't quite right. To put the thesis most accurately, we need the "ALWAYS" operator: presentism is the claim that it's *always* the case that, for every x, x existed, exists, or will exist only if x is a present thing. Else, for a brief moment, presentism is true in a Broad/Tooley style growing block universe with a first moment (see Broad 1923, pp. 53–84; Tooley 1997). Some think that a further emendation is needed, the addition of a "□". I won't take a stand on that here.

future objects, where these are objects that occupy past times or future times, but not the present time. If so, then it's false that for every x—quantifying over all temporal entities—x is a present thing. The Roman Empire existed, for instance, and it isn't a present thing. Since, according to the eternalist, the domain of temporal things includes the Roman Empire, if eternalism is true, (Pr_b'') isn't. But eternalism isn't manifestly false: I, at any rate, can't just *see* that the domain of temporal things includes no wholly past or future entities. Since eternalism isn't manifestly false, (Pr_b'') isn't trivially true.

I conclude that the triviality argument against presentism fails. Its failure is two-fold: it is unsound, and its conclusion is false.

Florida State University

REFERENCES

Armstrong, D. M. (1978) *Universals and Scientific Realism*, Cambridge University Press.
Bigelow, J. (1996) "Presentism and Properties," *Philosophical Perspectives*, 10: 35–52.
Broad, C. D. (1923) *Scientific Thought*, London: Kegan Paul.
Callender, C. (2000) "Shedding Light on Time", *Philosophy of Science*, 67 (Proceedings): S587–S599.
Hinchliff, M. (2000) "A Defense of Presentism in a Relativistic Setting", *Philosophy of Science*, 67 (Proceedings): S575–S586.
Lombard, L. (1999) "On the Alleged Incompatibility of Presentism and Temporal Parts", *Philosophia*, 27: 253–60.
Merricks, T. (1995) "On the Incompatibility of Enduring and Perduring Entities", *Mind*, 104: 523–31.
Merricks, T. (1999) "Persistence, Parts, and Presentism", *Noûs*, 33: 421–38.
Rea, M. (2003) "Four-Dimensionalism" in *The Oxford Handbook of Metaphysics*, ed. M. Loux and D. Zimmerman, Oxford University Press.
Sider, T. (1999) "Presentism and Ontological Commitment", *Journal of Philosophy*, 96: 325–47.
Smith, Q. (1993) *Language and Time*, Oxford University Press.
Tichy, P. (1980) "The Transiency of Truth", *Theoria*, 46: 165–82.
Tooley, M. (1997) *Time, Tense & Causation*, Oxford University Press.
Zimmerman, D. (1998) "Temporary Intrinsics and Presentism", in *Metaphysics: The Big Questions*, ed. P. van Inwagen and D. Zimmerman, Malden, MA: Blackwell.

Presentism, Triviality, and the Varieties of Tensism
Peter Ludlow

INTRODUCTION

Following Thomas Crisp, let's consider the following stock argument against presentism. Presentists want to say that only present things exist. Question: is the predicate 'exists' tensed or not? If 'exists' is tensed, then this comes to the claim that only present things *presently* exist (and who would argue with *that*?). Alternatively, the presentist might reformulate the claim as "everything that did exist, exists, or will exist presently exists". But prima facie this seems absurd, since, for example, the Roman Empire existed but does not presently exist.

Crisp claims that he can defuse this argument by showing that it is unsound. Unfortunately, as we will see, the solution offered by Crisp does not work for those who subscribe to a view that I will call *Very Serious Tensism*, and I will argue that a number of his additional claims unravel once we give up the tenets of Very Serious Tensism. Ultimately, however, I think that a workable solution to the problem may be available if one gives up Very Serious Tensism and exercises proper caution.

Going into a little more detail, Crisp formalizes the anti-presentism argument as follows.

First, there are three possible versions of presentism:

(Pr_a) Only present things exist now (i.e. presently exist)
(Pr_b) Only present things existed, exist, or will exist
(Pr_c) Only present things (tenselessly) exist

I am indebted to Thomas Crisp for discussion, and to Ted Sider and Dean Zimmerman for heroic efforts at making sense of earlier incarnations of this paper and for providing a number of helpful suggestions and comments. Thanks also are due to Jason Stanley, who read Ted and Dean's e-mail missives over my shoulder and offered lots of advice, some of which I paid attention to, understood, and incorporated.

(Pr_c) collapses into (Pr_b),[1] but (Pr_b) is manifestly false and (Pr_a) is trivially true. Accordingly, the formalized argument goes as follows.

(P1) Presentism is either (Pr_a), (Pr_b), or (Pr_c)
(P2) (Pr_a) is trivially true
(P3) (Pr_b) and (Prc) are trivially false (or rather, (Pr_c) collapses into (Pr_b) and (Pr_b) is trivially false)
(C) Presentism is either a trivial truism or a manifest falsehood

That's the argument. What is the presentist to do?

Crisp claims that the solution to this problem is to stand our ground on (Pr_b) and argue that it is not trivially false. The strategy involves seeing that (Pr_b) can be formulated either as (Pr_b') or (Pr_b''), where we take the domain of quantification to be restricted to items in time (that is, setting aside timeless objects if there be any).

(Pr_b') For every x, if x existed, exists, or will exist, then x is a present thing
(Pr_b'') For every x, x is a present thing

How does this help with the case of the Roman Empire (which, recall, existed but is not present)? Well, for the presentist the domain of quantification does not include the Roman Empire, so, for example, (Pr_b'') makes no claim about the Roman Empire presently existing. On the other hand, we can still make sense of the past tense claim that the Roman Empire existed if we leave 'The Roman Empire' safely embedded within the scope of the past tense operator, as follows.

(RE1) WAS(for some x, x is The Roman Empire)

The idea is that (Pr_b'') and (RE1) can be happily conjoined, allowing us to say both that the Roman Empire existed and that everything exists presently. This has been a standard move for presentists since Prior (1967, 1968), and there are a number of familiar complications that are put on the back burner by Crisp here.[2] In the discussion to follow, I'll

---

[1] If you think this step looks suspicious, you're right; I'll come back to it later.
[2] One problem with this is that (running into the teeth of Kripke 1980) we apparently need a descriptive theory of names for this to work. If names are referring expressions, then of course no embedding is going to help keep their referents out of the domain of discourse. So for example Prior (1967, 1968) argued that, since Queen Anne was deceased, a description would have to go in for her name in a sentence like 'Queen Anne existed'. Presumably one will want to say that 'the Roman Empire' is (or stands proxy for) a description of some form—likewise for 'the Holy Roman Empire'.

also set aside these matters to take up the more narrow issue of whether the strategy is workable for all presentists, and I'll explore some of the complications that arise in formulating the definition of presentism.

WHY CRISP'S SOLUTION IS NO HELP TO THE VERY SERIOUS TENSER

Consider the following doctrine.

> **(Very Serious Tensism)** Every natural language predication is inherently tensed. There are no untensed predications—in particular, no time-indexed verbs/predications—in natural language, hence none can be employed in the meta-language of the semantics for natural language.[3]

Another stock worry has to do with cross-temporal relations. For example, suppose I wanted to utter something like the following:

(i) I resemble Fitz Hugh Ludlow

Since Fitz Hugh (author of *The Hashish Eater*) is long departed from this planet (in several senses, but here I merely mean that he is dead), we have a difficulty with the resemblance relation. We need the name 'Fitz Hugh Ludlow' to remain within the scope of a past tense operator. The problem is that we have a present tense resemblance relation, which means that its argument positions are not in the scope of past tense.

Finally, what do we say about sentences that require span operators (consider David Lewis's example—'There have been many queens named Anne'—as well as considerations raised in Zimmerman 1998)), or, for that matter, objects that can go in and out of existence (like committees and nations)?

(ii) Something existed, does not exist now, but will exist again

This seems to be blocked on Crisp's story, since it involves quantification into the scope of the past and future tense operators. In effect,

(iii) $(\exists x)$ PAST(exists(x)) & ~exists(x) & FUT(exists(x))

These are of course just standard problems for the presentist, and they are widely known. I'm also not saying that Crisp should have solved these problems. I myself wrote an entire book (Ludlow 1999) defending presentism without directly addressing these problems (although in my defense, I did develop a theory of E-type temporal anaphora and I did introduce some presentist-friendly span operators that were intended to be employed in dealing with these issues). These problems will have to be addressed eventually, however.

---

[3] There are a number of details I'm skipping over here. For example, a Very Serious Tenser would presumably hold that a verb with past tense morphology, like 'walked', is going to include a past tense morpheme ('-ed') and an inherently present tensed verb ('walk'). Both morpheme and stem would carry tense. Another possibility, employing an event-style analysis, would have 'John walked' come to something like this: 'there is an e, e is a walking and John is the agent of e' was true. This sort of analysis, which was discussed

By saying that there are no time-indexed verbs or predicates, I mean that no natural language predicates are of the form 'Pred(x,t)', which would mean something like x is (timelessly) Pred-at-t.

The problem is that Crisp's solution to the triviality objection offers little comfort for the Very Serious Tenser. To help the Very Serious Tenser, Crisp needs to find a form of quantification that doesn't involve predication. Why? Because if we say something like 'for every x, such that x is...', we have that auxiliary 'is' involved, and according to Very Serious Tensism that 'is' must be tensed. Crisp thinks that he can meet this challenge—easily, in fact—by giving the account of presentism in (Pr_b'') above, or in its alternative formulation (Pr_b'). In Crisp's words, "(Pr_b') involves an *unrestricted* quantifier, one that ranges over *everything*. The presentist who construes her thesis thus proposes of each thing x in our most inclusive domain of quantification that if x existed, exists now, or will exist then x is a present thing." (Pr_b'') is supposed to have similar virtues.

The problem for Crisp is now this: what are we to make of the predicates 'thing' and 'in our most inclusive domain of quantification'? They are surely predicates, and by Very Serious Tensism they are therefore tensed.[4] Accordingly, his claim comes to "each present thing presently in our domain of quantification is a present thing". The triviality objection is reborn.

I don't think that talk of the "domain of quantification" is going to be at all helpful to Crisp here, for the simple reason that he's going to have to say something about what makes it into the domain of quantification; and no matter how general one makes the characterization of membership it is still going to involve a tensed predicate. Indeed, even if one dispenses with any meaningful characterization of the domain and tries to give a trivial account like 'x is in the domain iff it is in the domain', there is still the relational predicate 'is in', which is tensed.

One might object that one *can* say tensed things about what goes into the domain that wouldn't render presentism trivial. For example, one could make the following speech:

in Ludlow (1999, sect. 8.2), might then take the gerundive tense (as in 'walking') as being a basic inherent tense. Notice also that there are a lot of *is*'s in this analysis, and the Very Serious Tenser is presumably going to take all of them as being tensed as well.

[4] If you think it sounds strange to talk about nominal predicates like 'thing' as being tensed, hang on. Below I'll show that, even if they aren't strictly speaking tensed, this problem will re-emerge when we attempt to give a semantics for these constructions.

"Absolutely *everything* goes in the domain. Even among present things, there are to be no restrictions: big things, small things, short things, tall things—all of them go in. And future objects go in too, if they exist. For example, anything that *will be big*, anything that *will be small*, anything that *will be short*, and anything that *will be tall* goes into the domain. Likewise, anything that *was* a dinosaur goes in."

Can't the present thus say some significant things about the domain using tensed language without making it trivial that only presently existing things are in the domain?[5]

Unfortunately, this strategy doesn't help. Crisp's idea is that you can avoid worries about 'every thing' if you appeal to an independent notion of widest possible domain of quantification that is somehow more basic than the quantified expression with its restriction. The suggestion of saying "*everything* goes in the domain" inverts matters by relying on a more primitive notion of quantification to explain what goes in the domain. That's fine, but then it renders the talk of the domain superfluous. In effect, it amounts to the next strategy I will take up—taking the quantifier 'everything' to be primitive.

So, *could* Crisp avoid these difficulties by just introducing unrestricted quantification directly and taking it to be primitive—i.e. not defined in terms of domains of quantification? This strategy is more promising, but ultimately I think that it also fails. The problem is this: if unrestricted quantification is primitive, then one must give unrestricted quantifiers a disquotational semantics. The reasoning here is that a semantical primitive just is a term or expression that is given "as is" in the meta-language without any further reduction.

Problem: there are no unrestricted quantifiers in natural language, so you can't give unrestricted quantifiers a disquotational semantics. Now you might say, "who cares about the semantics of natural language, I'll provide a regimented meta-language that departs from natural language in that it *has* unrestricted quantification." That's a possible reply, but this meta-language is going to stand in need of interpretation, and this interpretation must (ultimately) take place in a language that we understand—i.e. a natural language.

That probably went by pretty fast, so let me try to spell it out a bit more carefully. I'll begin with the following doctrines:

---

[5] This hypothetical objection is in fact not hypothetical at all, and has been put to me by Ted Sider in more or less precisely those words.

(SAS) Seriousness about Semantics: Inherent semantic properties of natural languages cannot be regimented away by introducing meta-languages that lack those properties. (Ultimately, those introduced meta-languages will need to be interpreted in a natural language meta-language.)

(PUP) Phonologically Unrealized Predicates are ubiquitous.

(SAQ) Seriousness about Quantification: Inherent properties of natural language quantifiers cannot be regimented away in the meta-language. (For example, if all natural language quantification is restricted—possibly by a phonologically unrealized predicate—natural language quantification cannot be regimented into unrestricted quantification.)

(NLQR) Natural Language Quantification is Restricted.

If one is serious about semantics, one has to recognize that there are a number of predicates in natural language that are phonologically unrealized—i.e. not visible on the printed page and not pronounced. So, for example, there is no visible difference between present tense 'hit' and past tense 'hit', but by hypothesis there is a phonologically unrealized past tense morpheme attached to the latter verb. (PUP) is the thesis that such phonologically unrealized predicates are ubiquitous in natural language—and they had better be if one is a Very Serious Tenser, given that many natural languages don't have overt morphological tense. Accordingly, if you endorse Very Serious Tensism you appear to be committed to (PUP).

Now if you are committed to Seriousness about Semantics, then you must also endorse Seriousness about Quantification (which is actually something of a corollary of Seriousness about Semantics). This means that there are no properties of natural language quantification that you can regiment away. Unfortunately, all natural language quantification is restricted (NLQR), so the introduction of unrestricted quantification into the meta-language would require regimenting the meta-language. So you're stuck.

Here is a rough formalization of the argument.

(P1) Seriousness about Semantics is true

(P2) Seriousness about Semantics entails Seriousness about Quantification

(P3) Seriousness about Quantification entails that if all natural language quantification is restricted, then all meta-linguistic quantification is (ultimately) restricted

(P4) All natural language quantification is restricted (possibly by phonologically unrealized predicates)

(P5) If unrestricted quantification is a primitive, then some meta-linguistic quantification must (ultimately) be unrestricted

(C) Unrestricted quantification can't be a primitive

If this is right, then there's not much hope for the primitive-quantifier strategy, but of course everything turns on premise (P4).[6] Is it really the case that there is no unrestricted quantification in natural language? First, let's get clear on what we mean by restricted quantification. (Crisp uses the terminology differently,[7] so we have to be careful here.) By a restricted quantifier, I mean a quantifier expression that comes with a (possibly phonologically unrealized) predicate restriction. So for example in 'All men are mortal', 'men' is the restriction on the quantifier (or *determiner*) 'all'. Now it is standard practice in formal logic to dispense with these restrictions (or at least to *appear* to dispense with these restrictions) in cases like '$(\exists x)F(x)$' and '$(\forall x)G(x)$'. Natural language is not so accommodating, as examples (1) and (2) show:

(1) ⁎Every is mortal
(2) ⁎No exists

Even where we seem to get by without an explicit restriction, as in 'all is lost', it is pretty clear that we understand an implicit predicate as in (3):

(3) All [hope] is lost

Now one might object that we do give the semantics for '$(\exists x)F(x)$' and '$(\forall x)G(x)$', and that when we do so we use unrestricted quantification in the meta-language. But do we? Notice that our informal gloss on these is something like "there is an x, such that x is F" and "for all x, x is G". I'm not going to raise a fuss about the verb 'is' in 'there is an x'—we can avoid that by employing a locution like 'for some x'. The real problem is that the philosopher's syntax is fractured if taken at face value. The first occurrence of 'x' is standing in for a predicate and the second is standing in for a grammatical object (grammatical argument). To see this,

---

[6] I don't mean that the other premises cannot be challenged. They do seem to be premises that most philosophers of language, having reflected a bit, would find uncontroversial. (P4) is the premise that might spark controversy since it is an empirical claim.

[7] When Crisp speaks of 'restricted quantification' he means that the domain of quantification is restricted. It's clear enough what he means, but the usage is non-standard so I'm not going to follow it here.

consider (Pr_b″) with linguistic category labels substituted for the variable positions. We get something like (4), where 'N' stands for *Noun* (a predicate) and 'NP' stands for *Noun Phrase* (an argument), the index 'i' indicates the relevant binding relationship, and the asterisk (∗) indicates that the linguistic structure is somehow ill-formed.[8]

(4) ∗For [every N_i], NP_i is a present thing

Strictly speaking, (4) is ungrammatical, similar in form to (5):

(5) ∗For [every boy_i], he_i is a present thing

Both represent examples of catastrophic type-mismatch—identifying predicate positions with argument positions.

Now of course we can understand utterances of (5), but presumably only by instituting some tacit repairs. The thought is that if we are confronted by utterances of (5) we recognize that they are ill-formed and make some minimal modification to their structure in order to process them. In this case, we might try something along the lines of (5r), where the repair is effected by shifting the index from the noun to the NP:

(5r) [$_{NP}$ every boy]$_i$ [$_s$ he_i is present]

In this case we can give a standard generalized quantifier semantics for 'every boy' (more on this in a bit). We can repair (4) as well, this time by introducing a phonologically unrealized predicate N to serve as the restriction on the quantifier, which in turn allows us to shift the index to the NP 'every N' (the 'e' is what linguists call a trace (of movement of the NP) and it is interpreted as a bound variable):

(4r) [$_{NP}$ every N]$_i$ [$_s$ e_i is present]

The problem is that any repair that is going to make (4) well formed is going to involve the introduction of a phonologically unrealized predicate. Since, by Very Serious Tensism, any such predicate must be tensed

---

[8] We can think of a noun phrase (NP) like 'every boy' as being composed of a noun (N)—in this case 'boy'—and a determiner—in this case 'every'. The noun by itself is ordinarily taken to be a predicate. The noun phrase is not a predicate but is an argument that is capable of saturating some predicate (as in 'every boy is mortal') or perhaps a quantificational element that binds into an argument position. (That is, it might bind a pronoun as in 'every boy is such that he is mortal'.) Some noun phrases will evince more complexity (e.g. 'every tall boy with red hair') and others will—on the surface at least—appear to have less complexity (e.g. the pronoun 'he' or the demonstrative 'that').

(whatever the abstract noun N is—'exists', 'is self-identical'—it must be tensed), the triviality argument rears its head once again.

One might object here that, just because N is tensed, it doesn't follow that it must be *present* tensed, and hence the mere introduction of a tensed predicate N will not be enough to make the triviality argument go. One might insist that N could be past tensed and that this would allow us to dodge the triviality objection.[9] For example, one might hold that it is not at all trivial to say "every former dinosaur is present"—a non-presentist would reject that; 'former dinosaur' is past tensed, so tensed.[10] Applying this argument to (4r), the idea would be that an utterance of (4r) comes to the claim that every former-N, present-N, and future-N is present and that this is hardly something that is trivially true—any non-presentist would reject it.

Matters are a little complicated here. In the first place, it seems doubtful that 'former dinosaur' is past tensed. It is arguable that 'former dinosaur' is a present tensed predicate that is true of absolutely nothing. Being a former dinosaur, like being a former Beatle or a former Syracuse professor, is in fact a property that one has in the present. 'Former dinosaur/Beatle/Syracuse professor' is *presently* true of those individuals that were dinosaurs or Beatles or Syracuse professors but are no longer. The English word 'former' just isn't a tense; 'former N' is a present tense predicate, whatever the N. Indeed, even if we had past tense morphology (i.e. elements like '-ed') on our nouns, it is not clear that PAST-Syracuse-prof wouldn't just mean that you are *currently* a former Syracuse professor.

In languages that *have* overt temporal morphology on their nouns, matters play out differently, but not in a way that is very useful for defusing the triviality objection. According to Burton (1997), with a fair bit of cross-linguistic consistency (e.g. in the Coast Salish languages Squamish and Halkomelem and the Ojibwe language), these morphemes tend not to work like the verbal tenses—rather, they are

---

[9] This suggestion needs to be dressed up a little bit. One idea would be that there is not only a phonologically unrealized noun, but also a phonologically unrealized tense (TNS), so that we have the following:

(4r') [$_{NP}$ every TNS-N]$_i$ [$_s$ e$_i$ is present]

One would do it this way to preserve some symmetry with the verbal tense system—in particular, the idea that the basic predicate is inherently present tensed and the morphemes add past and future tense.

[10] This potential objection is due to Ted Sider.

understood as devices marking death, destruction, and loss. For example, 'my pencil-PAST' means my currently broken (or lost) pencil, 'the dog-PAST' means the dead (or lost) dog.[11]

If it is really the case that nouns cannot have future or past tense, then one might be tempted to say that they aren't tensed at all. That is, one might try to hold that the restricting noun in (4r) is untensed. In effect, this strategy gives up Very Serious Tensism but hangs on to a nearby doctrine which we could call *Very Serious Tensism—VO* (VO because it applies to verbs only).

> (**Very Serious Tensism—VO**) Every natural language *verb* is inherently tensed. There are no untensed verbs—in particular, no time-indexed verbs—in natural language, hence none can be employed in the meta-language of the semantics for natural language. There may, however, be predicates (nouns, for example) that are untensed.

The verb/noun distinction may be unstable in some languages, and there is also the issue of what to say about cases where nominals wear overt temporal morphology (do we make an exception for them?), but let's set these complications aside for the time being and see if this relaxation of Very Serious Tensism buys us anything.

Unfortunately, this gambit won't buy us much—not if we want a compositional semantics (i.e. a theory of meaning) to be possible. To see this, we need to consider a simple semantic theory for (4r) employing generalized quantifier (GQ) theory. The basic idea behind GQ theory is that determiners like 'every' and 'some' denote relations between sets of objects. So, for example, consider the sentence (5r) again. In this case 'boy' denotes the set of all boys and 'is present' denotes the set of all things that are present. (For the sake of simplicity, I'm just considering an extensional fragment of English, and am overlooking issues about co-extensive predicates.) Using "[[ϕ]]" to speak of the meaning or denotation of an expression ϕ, we have the following:

(6) [['boy']] = {x: x is a boy}
(7) [['is present']] = {x: x is present}

---

[11] On the other hand, 'my father-PAST' would mean something like my late (i.e. deceased) father, presumably because being a father is a property that one keeps one's whole life. It still seems to be a present tense property, however, and any true claim involving the expression would require a past tensed verb.

The determiner 'every' denotes a relation holding between sets of objects; in this case,

(8) [['every']] = {<X,Y>: |X-Y| = 0}

Skipping some details, our little semantics tells us that 'every boy is present' is true just in case the following holds:

(9) |{x: x is a boy} - {x: x is a present}| = 0

That is, take the set of all boys, and remove all of those that are also in the set of everything that is present. If the result is a set with cardinality 0 (i.e. if the result is the empty set), then what you said is true.

This is a very simple semantics, but we can already see that the move to Very Serious Tensism—VO has bought us nothing. The first problem comes in with the axiom for 'boy', where the set membership is identified via the meta-linguistic locution 'is a boy'—notice that the pesky verb 'is' has returned. Even if we try to finesse this away somehow, there is the 'is' of identity (disguised as '=') in the same rule (6), and an 'is' of predication (cardinality of X–Y *is* zero) in the rule for 'every' (8). Finally, there is the meta-linguistic expression '*is* the denotation of' which is used in the interpretation of (6)–(8). The point is that the semantics is larded with explicit and implicit occurrences of the auxiliary 'is', and, even by Very Serious Tensism—VO, these are supposed to be tensed.

Any compositional semantic theory is going to run into this eventually. For example, in giving a Davidsonian semantics for (5r), the semantics for the restricting noun 'thing' is going to require an axiom like "x is a semantic value of the noun 'thing' iff x *is* a thing" or perhaps "'thing' *is* true of x". Notice again that pesky 'is'. In addition, the sentence-level theorem will be something of the form '*is* true iff there *is* an x, such that x *is* a semantic value of 'boy' and x *is* a semantic value of "is present". Want to introduce properties? Then you get "x *is* the semantic value of the noun 'thing' iff x *is* the property of being a thing." A sentence-level theorem will be something like "is true iff there *is* an x that *has* the property denoted by 'boy' and *has* the property denoted by 'present'". Even if you try and avoid the auxiliary 'is' (and 'has') and do some Heideggerian language mangling, saying that "x things", you have converted 'thing' into a verb, which is supposed to be tensed according to Very Serious Tensism—VO.

In sum, Crisp's proposal is just no help to either variety of Very Serious Tensism. At this point it looks like the only move available is to

32 | *Peter Ludlow*

give up on the idea of Very Serious Tensism under either formulation, and allow at least limited use of a tenseless predicate 'be'. Now matters begin to get subtle.

CRISP'S ARGUMENT AND THE LESS SERIOUS TENSER

Let's set aside Very Serious Tensism and suppose that we can allow both tenseless verbs and tensed verbs, and suppose further that the tensed verbs are not reducible to the detensed verbs and vice versa. So, for example, "x will exist" is not reducible to "x tenselessly exists at t, where t is later than the time of utterance" and vice versa; and "x tenselessly exists" does not reduce to "x existed, exists or will exist" and vice versa. Let's give a name to this doctrine:

> (**Less Serious Tensism**) There are genuine tensed predicates and genuine tenseless predicates in natural language, and they are not interreducible.

If for some reason the tensed predicates were reducible to the detensed predicates (or vice versa) then we would either have Very Serious Tensism or serious detensism (i.e. a completely detensed metalanguage), and then all is lost for the presentist.[12]

Does Crisp provide solace for the Less Serious Tenser? Not really. In fact, this is the point at which some of his claims begin to fall apart. The first problem is that if we adopt Less Serious Tensism then the various versions of Pr_b offered above are no longer equivalent. Let's review those formulations.

> (Pr_b') For every x, if x existed, exists or will exist, then x is a present thing
> (Pr_b'') For every x, x is a present thing

If one were a detenser or a Very Serious Tenser then these formulations are arguably equivalent, but that doesn't seem to be the case if Less Serious Tensism is true. This is so for it is *logically* possible that there be things that exist (tenselessly), but of which no tensed existence

---

[12] All is lost, because if the tensed predicates are reducible to detensed predicates presentism doesn't get off the ground, and if the detensed predicates collapse into the tensed predicates, then we are back to Very Serious Tensism, which cannot escape the triviality objection.

predicates are true. It follows that these formulations of (Pr$_b$) are not equivalent.

If this is not obvious, perhaps some additional clarification is in order. If Less Serious Tensism is true, then we need to introduce two sets of tenses—genuine tenses (PAST$_t$, PRES$_t$, and FUT$_t$), and regimented (or detensed) "tenses" (PAST$_d$, PRES$_d$, and FUT$_d$) which are not genuine tenses at all but state relative B-theory positions—for example stating that some event is PAST$_d$ if it (tenselessly) holds earlier than the time of utterance. We would then want to provide two different versions of (Pr$_b$′) to avoid conflating these predicates:

(Pr$_b$′-t)   For every x, if x existed$_t$, exists$_t$, or will exist$_t$, then x is a present$_t$ thing

(Pr$_b$″-t)   For every x, x is a present$_t$ thing

(Pr$_b$′-d)   For every x, if x existed$_d$, exists$_d$, or will exist$_d$, then x is a present$_d$ thing

(Pr$_b$″-d)   For every x, x is a present$_d$ thing

Whether we are using the tensed (-t) formulations or the detensed (-d) formulations, it is logically possible that there are things that are (for example) PAST$_t$ but not PAST$_d$ and vice versa. In such cases, the universal quantifiers in (Pr$_b$″-t) and (Pr$_b$″-d) will range over *both* kinds of objects, and this is why they will diverge in truth value from (Pr$_b$′-t) and (Pr$_b$′-d) respectively. To illustrate, suppose that everything that existed$_t$, exists$_t$, or will exist$_t$ is indeed a present$_t$ thing, but suppose also that there is an object (or proposition) that did$_t$ not exist$_t$, does$_t$ not exist$_t$, and will$_t$ not exist$_t$ but which does$_d$ exist$_d$. In such a case (Pr$_b$′-t) is true but (Pr$_b$″-t) is false.[13]

Similarly, Crisp's claims about the relationship between (Pr$_c$) and (Pr$_b$) come unhinged once we adopt Less Serious Tensism. Recall those propositions:

---

[13] Such cases are logically possible, but are they also metaphysically possible? Arguably yes. Imagine a world in which tensers and detensers are both partly right: the tensed predicates are not true of every object; in certain regions of the world 4-dimensionalism is true, but in other regions of the world there is a kind of dynamic time and reality is fundamentally tensed. Now, imagine an object x that inhabits the detensed region of the world. Given our inertial frame it is past$_d$ but it is still not past$_t$ because no fundamentally tensed properties are true of x. All of x's temporal properties are reducible to its space–time location. This would not be true of objects in other parts of such a world. We could even imagine that these worlds overlap a bit, so that there are regions in which some objects have only tensed properties and other objects have only detensed properties.

(Pr$_b$) Only present things existed, exist or will exist
(Pr$_c$) Only present things (tenselessly) exist

Why suppose that (Pr$_c$) collapses into (Pr$_b$)? Crisp seems to think that this is just a matter of logic, but if we adopt Less Serious Tensism matters are actually very subtle. We need to consider what happens when we have both genuinely tensed and genuinely detensed predicates. In such a case it is difficult to see why (Pr$_c$) should collapse into (Pr$_b$) any more than (F$_c$) collapses into (F$_b$).

(F$_b$) Only present things walked, walk, or will walk
(F$_c$) Only present things run

It may seem intuitive to us that everyone who runs must also walk, but of course it is certainly logically possible that there be things that run but do not walk and vice versa. Likewise we may feel some intuitive pull to say that everything that existed$_t$, exists$_t$, or will exist$_t$ must exist$_d$, but this is false.

On the other hand, if we adopt an auxiliary hypothesis about the syntax of natural language—one that I'm inclined to hold in any case—then we *can* uncover a logical relation between these formulations of presentism—although certainly not the relation that Crisp discerns. Even if we reject Very Serious Tensism, we presumably are committed to our doctrine being well-formed in natural language—call this doctrine *Seriousness about Syntax*—but (Pr$_b''$) (as well as (Pr$_b'$)) is still formulated in unrestricted quantifier notation, which on the face of it violates Seriousness about Syntax (for reasons discussed in the previous section). What that means is that if (Pr$_b''$) is coherent there is more structure to it than meets the eye. If we want to make that implicit structure apparent, then we need to make its nominal restriction explicit, yielding (Pr$_b''$-NL), where we have a universal substitutional quantification (Π) into the restriction position. (We employ a *universal* quantifier because we want to say that whatever the restriction, the individual quantified over is present.)[14]

(Pr$_b''$-NL) (ΠN)[every N] is a present$_t$ thing

---

[14] Do we have to worry about the unrestricted substitutional quantifier here? I don't think so; we could easily add a restriction like 'term' or 'noun'. This leads to the more interesting question of whether natural language admits of substitutional quantification at all (whether restricted or not). Suffice it to say for now that I think it does. See Kripke (1976) for some discussion of this issue.

In this case, since we are not Very Serious Tensers, some of the substitution instances for N can be our tenseless predicates. Making this explicit, we have (Pr_b''-NL'):[15]

(Pr_b''-NL') (IIN)Only present$_t$ things are (possibly tenselessly) N

Interestingly, (Pr_c) is just the universal instantiation of this—the case where the abstract predicate N is 'tenselessly exists'. For bookkeeping purposes, we can reintroduce (Pr_c) with the tensed and detensed predicates made explicit[16] (I am also substituting 'are existent' for 'exists' to keep the linguistic categories consistent[17]):

(Pr_c') Only present$_t$ things are existent$_d$

There is a logical relation holding between (Pr_c') and (Pr_b''-NL') after all, but it is hardly logical equivalence, and it would be a mistake to think that the former reduces to the latter. This would be like thinking that 'Socrates is a philosopher' reduces to 'Everyone is a philosopher' because the former is a special case of the latter. Indeed, if one is interested in defending one of the two doctrines, it is a good bet that the less general doctrine will be easier to defend. To illustrate just one case in point, adopting (Pr_c) allows us to skirt some difficulties about the possibility of non-existent objects that are, for example, tenselessly red while failing to tenselessly exist. I don't think we want to be in the position of saying that if there are such objects they must be present (in the tensed sense)—something that seems to be entailed by (Pr_b''-NL').

So let's consider (Pr_c) on its own merits. This is a claim that any B-theorist or four-dimensionalist is going to be happy to reject, but it is not manifestly false—or at least, no more obviously false than is presentism in general. Arguably, then, Crisp has dismissed the most promising formulation of presentism.

---

[15] It is an open question as to whether this position can be developed without the use of substitutional quantifiers. However, if this linguistic proposal is correct, then substitutional quantification of this nature would be widespread in natural language, completely independently of concerns about presentism.

[16] I'm not entirely clear on whether it is also possible to have a version of (Pr_c) in which the predicate 'present' is detensed, so I'll set aside that possibility for now.

[17] A smoother way to handle this would be to have the substitutional quantification into all predicate positions rather than noun positions. For present purposes, this won't make any difference.

In sum, I think that a plausible definition of presentism can be offered, but only if one is careful to distinguish tensed from untensed predicates. As shown above, however, once we allow both types of predicate (and take both types to be primitive), matters become complicated in a hurry. I would suggest that, given the complexity of these issues, any claims made in this context must be made with more than a little caution.

University of Michigan

REFERENCES

Burton, S. C. (1997) "Past Tense on Nouns as Death, Destruction, and Loss", in K. Kusimoto (ed.), *Proceedings of NELS 27*, Amherst, MA: Graduate Linguistics Student Association, University of Massachusetts, pp. 65–77.

Kripke, S. (1976) "Is There a Problem about Substitutional Quantification?" in G. Evans and J. McDowell (eds.), *Truth and Meaning*, Oxford University Press, pp. 325–419.

Kripke, S. (1980) *Naming and Necessity*, Harvard University Press.

Ludlow, P. (1999) *Semantics, Tense, and Time: An Essay in the Metaphysics of Natural Language*, Cambridge, MA: MIT Press.

Prior, A. N. (1967) *Past, Present and Future*, Oxford University Press.

Prior, A. N. (1968) *Time and Tense*, Oxford University Press.

Zimmeman, D. (1998) "Temporary Intrinsics and Presentism", in P. van Inwagen and D. Zimmerman (eds.), *Metaphysics: The Big Questions*, Oxford: Basil Blackwell, pp. 206–19.

Reply to Ludlow
Thomas M. Crisp

Professor Ludlow proposes that my solution to the triviality problem for presentism is of no help to proponents of

(**Very Serious Tensism**) Every natural language predication is inherently tensed. There are no untensed predications—in particular no time-indexed verbs/predications—in natural language, hence none can be employed in the meta-language of the semantics for natural language.

My solution, again, is this. Presentism, I say, should be formulated as the claim that

(Pr_b') For every x, if x existed, exists, or will exist, then x is a present thing

and (Pr_b')'s quantifier should be interpreted as an unrestricted quantifier, one that ranges over *everything*. So interpreted, (Pr_b') says of each thing in our most inclusive domain of quantification that it existed, exists, or will exist only if it is a present thing. And to say this is to say something that is neither trivially true nor manifestly false.

But Ludlow thinks that Very Serious Tensism (VST) gives trouble. Given VST, the predicates "thing" and "in our most inclusive domain of quantification" are tensed. And if these predicates are tensed, says Ludlow, the interpretation I give of (Pr_b') in the previous paragraph comes to this:

(Triv) Each *present* thing *presently* in our most inclusive domain of quantification existed, exists, or will exist only if it is a present thing.

But (Triv) is trivial. If (Triv) is what (Pr_b') comes to, then *it* is trivial and my attempt to rescue presentism from banality has failed.

Thanks to Peter Ludlow and Ted Sider for helpful correspondence.

By way of reply: I have no idea whether VST is true. I suspect not, but suppose I'm wrong. Does it follow that (Pr_b') is a trivial truth? Not obviously. If (Triv) were the right interpretation of (Pr_b'), it would be trivial all right. But the presentistic Very Serious Tenser will deny that (Pr_b') says the same thing as (Triv). She'll say, rather, that (Pr_b') comes to

(Pr_b' + VST) For every *past, present, or future* thing, if it *existed, exists,* or *will exist,* then it *is* a present thing

and that (Pr_b' + VST) expresses an unrestricted quantification over every (past, present, or future) thing whatsoever.[1] (Pr_b' + VST) accords with the strictures of VST—all of its predicates and verbs are tensed— and is neither trivially true nor manifestly false. (That it's not trivially true is obvious. Some will object that it's manifestly false by invoking the Roman Empire as a counter-instance. *It* existed and it isn't present! But for reasons given in my initial piece, this way lies confusion.)

Objection: (Pr_b' + VST), I say, expresses an unrestricted quantification. But if Ludlow and VST are right, there *is* no unrestricted quantification. This is because VST implies that all quantifier expressions in natural language come with (possibly phonologically unrealized) tensed predicate restrictions. (To illustrate: when we say "all men are mortal", "men" is a predicate restriction on our quantifier expression "all". Given VST, "men" is implicitly tensed, so that what we really say is something like "all present men are mortal" or maybe "all past, present, and future men are mortal".) Since all natural language quantifier expressions are so restricted, all natural language quantification is restricted quantification.

Reply: Fine, let all quantification in ordinary language be restricted. It doesn't follow that all quantification in "the philosophy room" is restricted. Perhaps we don't use unrestricted quantifiers in everyday life, but we know perfectly well what they come to in the philosophy room.

Says Ludlow: Not so. Quantifiers introduced in the philosophy room need to be interpreted, and interpretation must ultimately take place in a language we understand—i.e. natural language. If we don't have

---

[1] I presuppose that, for the very serious tenser, quantification over the domain of past, present, and future things is as unrestricted as quantification gets. To think otherwise is to think that some things are neither past, present, nor future. But I'm not sure that this position can be coherently stated in language that accords with the strictures of VST.

unrestricted quantification in ordinary language, then neither do we have it in the philosophy room.

In sum, VST implies that all quantifier expressions—whether used in or out of the philosophy room—come with (possibly phonologically unrealized) tensed predicate restrictions, and that, therefore, all quantification is restricted. Wherefore, my attempt at giving a non-trivial, VST-friendly interpretation of (Pr$_b$') by reading it as (Pr$_b$' + VST) fails. The latter, I say, is an unrestricted quantification. But, given VST, there *are* no unrestricted quantifications.

Thus far the objection. But here we need a distinction. Ludlow uses "restricted quantifier" to mean "a quantifier expression that comes with a (possibly phonologically unrealized) predicate restriction". (So on his usage, "all objects are self-identical" invokes a restricted quantifier: the quantifier "all" is restricted by the predicate "objects".) I use "restricted quantifier" differently. I say that a quantifier is restricted if it ranges over some limited portion rather than the whole of reality. This is to be contrasted with an unrestricted quantifier, one that ranges over the whole of reality, one whose domain is reality *in its entirety*.

If Ludlow and VST are right, there is no unrestricted quantification in his sense: all quantifiers come with tensed predicate restrictions. But this is of interest to my project only if VST also implies that there is no unrestricted quantification in my sense. When I said that (Pr$_b$' + VST)'s quantifier is to be taken as unrestricted, I meant unrestricted in *my* sense, not Ludlow's.

Does VST imply that there is no unrestricted quantification in my sense? I can't see any reason for thinking so. At any rate, Ludlow has given us absolutely no reason for thinking so. I say that a quantifier is unrestricted if it ranges over reality in its entirety rather than a limited portion thereof. Were I a very serious tenser, I'd put it thus: a quantifier is unrestricted (in my sense) if it ranges over all past, present, and future things, leaving out none. (Again, I presuppose that, for the very serious tenser, quantification over the domain of past, present, and future things is as unrestricted as it gets.)

So when I say "every past, present or future thing is (was or will be) self-identical", what I say is naturally interpreted as expressing quantification over every past, present, or future thing, leaving out none (especially if I say it in the philosophy room). Given VST, then, what I say is naturally interpreted as an unrestricted quantification in my sense. Since my quantifier phrase—"every past, present or future thing"—meets the requirements of VST (its determiner "every" is restricted by the tensed predicate "past, present, or future thing"), it looks to me as if VST is perfectly consistent with the existence of quantifiers that are unrestricted in my sense.

If so, if VST is consistent with unrestricted quantification in my sense, then stating a VST-friendly, non-trivial thesis of presentism is simplicity itself. Read "every past, present or future thing" as an unrestricted quantifier in my sense and let presentism be the thesis that

> (Pr_b' + VST) For every past, present or future thing, if it existed, exists, or will exist, then it is a present thing

or, more simply,

> (Pr_b''+ VST) Every past, present, or future thing is a present thing

Both formulations accord with VST; both are non-trivial. (David Lewis, for instance, would have thought that the predicate "past, present, or future thing" applied to a non-present Roman Empire. A. N. Prior would have disagreed. Who's right? Prior, I think, but that he's right is hardly trivial.)

But Ludlow has a reply. Consider the claim that "every former dinosaur is present". Since its quantifier "every" is restricted by the past tensed predicate "former dinosaur", it accords with the strictures of VST. More, it looks to be non-trivial: The non-presentist will think that "former dinosaur" applies to non-present dinosaurs; the presentist will disagree.

Ludlow objects that "every former dinosaur is present" *is* trivial—trivially true. This is because "former dinosaur" isn't past tensed at all, but *present* tensed:

> It is arguable that 'former dinosaur' is a present tensed predicate that is true of absolutely nothing. Being a former dinosaur, like being a former Beatle or a former Syracuse professor, is in fact a property that one has in the present. 'Former dinosaur/Beatle/Syracuse professor' is *presently* true of those individuals that were dinosaurs or Beatles or Syracuse professors but are no longer. The English word 'former' just isn't a tense; 'former N' is a present tense predicate, whatever the N. Indeed, even if we had past tense morphology (i.e. elements like '-ed') on our nouns, it is not clear that PAST-Syracuse-prof wouldn't just mean that you are *currently* a former Syracuse professor. (p. 29 above)

So "former dinosaur", if Ludlow is right, is a present tensed predicate that applies (if it applies) only to present things that *were* dinosaurs. Since obviously there are no such things, "every former dinosaur is present" is trivially true in the way that "every flying pig is present" is trivially true.

Ludlow will say the same thing about "past, present, or future thing" in (Pr_b' + VST) and (Pr_b'' + VST). "Past, present, or future thing", he'll say, is a present tensed predicate that means something like "present thing that was, is, or will be a thing".[2] So read, (Pr_b'' + VST) comes to "every present thing that was, is, or will be a thing is present", and is trivially true.

Is Ludlow right? Does "past, present, or future thing" mean "present thing that was, is, or will be a thing"? This is very hard to believe. When I say "past football games were televised", does "past football games" mean "present things that were football games"? I should think not. It could be true now that past games were televised, even if no present thing *was* a football game. Maybe Ludlow is right that "past football games" is in some sense a present tensed predicate. But if it is, it's a present tensed predicate that applies to non-present football games located in the past (if there are such things).

Likewise, I say, with "past thing". Maybe there is a sense in which it's a present tensed predicate. Fine. But as I use it, it means "thing that *was*", or "thing to which I bear the *later than* relation". So interpreted, it applies to things that *were*, things located in the past (provided there are such things, of course), whether or not they're also located in the present. So for example, if eternalism is true, it applies to the Roman Empire. Likewise with "past, present, or future thing". Even if there's a sense in which it is a present tensed predicate, it's a present-tensed predicate that applies to non-present things like the Roman Empire (if there are such things). Wherefore, it's not true that "every past, present, or future thing is present" means "every present thing that was, is, or will be a thing is present". Wherefore it's not true that "every past, present, or future thing is present" is trivial.

So far, then, VST implies nothing very interesting about my solution to presentism's triviality problem. I say that the problem is solved by

---

[2] This suggestion, or something very close to it, was made by Ludlow in correspondence.

formulating presentism as the claim that, quantifying unrestrictedly (in my sense),

> (Pr_b') For every x, if x existed, exists, or will exist, then x is a present thing

If VST is right, there are phonologically unrealized tensed predicate restrictions on (Pr_b')'s quantifier. Suppose so. Then (Pr_b') needs disambiguation. I propose the following:

> (Pr_b' + VST) For every past, present, or future thing x, if x existed, exists, or will exist, then x is a present thing

or, more simply,

> (Prb'' + VST) Every past, present, or future thing is a present thing

Both accord with the strictures of VST; both are non-trivial. Accordingly, I conclude that Ludlow is mistaken. VST makes no trouble at all for my proposed solution to the triviality problem.

Ludlow thinks that I've got further trouble if we set aside VST and suppose that there are both irreducibly tenseless and irreducibly tensed predicates and verbs. To suppose this is to adopt Less Serious Tensism:

> (**Less Serious Tensism**) There are genuine tensed verbs/predicates and genuine tenseless verbs/predicates in natural language, and they are not interreducible

According to Ludlow, Less Serious Tensism (LST) makes trouble for my claim that

> (Pr_b') For every x, if x existed, exists, or will exist, then x is a present thing

is equivalent to

> (Pr_b'') For every x, x is a present thing

This is because, if LST is true, we need two sets of tenses: genuine tenses and detensed tenses that state relative B-theory positions. So we can say of Fred that he existed$_t$, where here we apply an irreducibly tensed existence predicate to him. But we can also say of him that he existed$_d$, where here we apply a detensed existence predicate of him (a predicate true of him iff his existence is earlier than the time of this utterance).

Given LST, what we say of Fred in the one case is not reducible to what we say of him in the other.

If there are these two sets of tenses, then as they stand (Pr_b') and (Pr_b'') are ambiguous. We may restate them as:

(Pr_b'-t) For every x, if x existed, exists$_t$, or will exist$_t$, then x is a present$_t$ thing

(Pr_b''-t) For every x, x is a present$_t$ thing

or as

(Pr_b'-d) For every x, if x existed$_d$, or will exist$_d$, then x is a present$_d$ thing

(Pr_b''-d) For every x, x is a present$_d$ thing

Either way, says Ludlow, there is reason to doubt that the first and second claim in each pair are equivalent. This is because he thinks that it's possible that there be objects that existed$_d$, exist$_d$, or will exist$_d$ but did not exist$_t$, do not exist$_t$, and will not exist$_t$, and that there be objects that existed$_t$, exist$_t$, or will exist$_t$ but did not exist$_d$, do not exist$_d$, and will not exist$_d$. (I doubt that this *is* possible, but set this aside.) If so, then it could be that everything that existed$_t$, exists$_t$, or will exist$_t$ is a present$_t$ thing, but that some things (things that existed$_d$, exist$_d$, or will exist$_d$ but did not exist$_t$, do not exist$_t$, and will not exist$_t$) are not present$_t$. If so, then it could be that (Pr_b'-t) is true and that (Pr_b''-t) is false; likewise with (Pr_b'-d) and (Pr_b''-d). Wherefore my claim that (Pr_b') and (Pr_b'') are equivalent stands refuted.

But I stand by my claim. I wrote:

to say that only present things existed, exist or will exist is to say that

(Pr_b') For every x, if x existed, exists or will exist, then x is a present thing

(Pr_b') invokes an *unrestricted* quantifier, one that ranges over *everything*.... We can state the same thing differently by shifting to a restricted quantifier, one whose domain is restricted to the class of all things in time, the class of all things which existed, exist now, or will exist.... Then we get

(Pr_b'') For every x, x is a present thing

where here we quantify restrictedly over the domain of all things in time. (p. 18 above)

What I claimed, then, was this:

(∗) The sentence "for every x, if x <u>existed, exists, or will exist</u>, then x is a <u>present</u> thing" is equivalent to the sentence "for every x, x is a <u>present</u> thing" if we interpret the first sentence's quantifier as unrestricted (in my sense) and the second sentence's quantifier as restricted to the domain of things that <u>existed, exist or will exist</u>.

Now, if LST is right and there are Ludlow's two tenses. The underlined occurrences in (∗) of "existed, exists, or will exist" and "present" are ambiguous. Occurrences of the former can be interpreted as "existed$_t$, exists$_t$, or will exist$_t$" or as "existed$_d$, exists$_d$, or will exist$_d$". Occurrences of the latter can be interpreted as "present$_t$" or as "present$_d$". Since I meant to use "existed, exists, or will exist" univocally, a reasonable disambiguation of (∗) will interpret both occurrences of "existed, exists, or will exist" in the same way; likewise with "present". There are four ways of disambiguating. First way: interpret each occurrence of "existed, exists, or will exist" as "existed$_t$, exists$_t$, or will exist$_t$" and each occurrence of "present" as "present$_t$". Then (∗) is true: (Pr$_b'$-t) and (Pr$_b''$-t) are manifestly equivalent if the former's quantifier ranges over *all* entities—including those that existed$_d$, exist$_d$, will exist$_d$, existed$_t$, exist$_t$, or will exist$_t$—and the latter's quantifier ranges over just those things that existed$_t$, exists$_t$ or will exist$_t$. Second way: interpret "existed, exists, or will exist" in (∗) as "existed$_d$, exists$_d$, or will exist$_d$". Then, again, (∗) is manifestly true. Likewise with the next two ways. Given a reasonable disambiguation of what I said, then, what I said was true.

Ludlow also thinks that LST gives trouble for my claim that

(Pr$_c$) only present things (tenselessly) exist

implies

(Pr$_b$) Only present things existed, exist or will exist.

I reasoned as follows. To say of something that it *tenselessly* exists is just to say that our most inclusive quantifiers range over it. It may be past, present, or future; we say nothing about *which* when we say of it that our widest quantifiers "pick it up". So, I said, to say that only present things (tenselessly) exist is to say something like: for every x (using our most unrestricted quantifier), x is a present thing.

Now, if (Pr$_c$) amounts to the claim that, quantifying unrestrictedly over our most inclusive domain of quantification, everything is a present thing, then (Pr_c) trivially implies that, quantifying unrestrictedly over that same domain, everything that existed, exists, or will exist is a present thing. But to say that everything that existed, exists, or will exist is a present thing is just to say that, for every x, if x existed, exists, or will exist, then x is a present thing, which is just to say that only present things existed, exist, or will exist. In short, (Pr_c) implies (Pr_b).

Not so, says Ludlow—not if LST is true. His argument here is a bit compressed; perhaps it's meant to go as follows. Given LST, we have Ludlow's two tenses and (Pr_b) and (Pr_c) need disambiguation. Take (Pr_c). If we interpret it as Ludlow's

(Pr_c') only present$_t$ things are existent$_d$

where "existent$_d$" applies to a thing x iff x has some B-position or other, and we interpret (Pr_b) as

(Pr_b-t) only present$_t$ things existed$_t$, exist$_t$, or will exist$_t$

then there's reason to doubt that (Pr_c) implies (Pr_b). This is because, says Ludlow, it's *possible* that there be things that existed$_t$, exist$_t$, or will exist$_t$ but fail to exist$_d$. If so, then it might be true that only present$_t$ things are existent$_d$, but false that only present$_t$ things existed$_t$, exist$_t$, or will exist$_t$.

In reply, I find it very hard to conceive of the possibility envisaged by Ludlow. For it to be true that only present$_t$ things are existent$_d$, but false that only present$_t$ things existed$_t$, exist$_t$, or will exist$_t$, there would need to be non-present things that existed$_t$, exist$_t$, or will exist$_t$ but nevertheless are not earlier than, later than, or simultaneous with anything. I doubt that this is possible.

But suppose I'm wrong. Then I still say that (Pr_c) implies (Pr_b) (read as (Pr_b-t)). For I did not intend (Pr_c) to be read as (Pr_c'). I said that (Pr_c) amounts to the claim that, quantifying unrestrictedly (in my sense), everything is present. To quantify unrestrictedly in my sense is to quantify over *all* things—including things that existed$_d$, exist$_d$, will exist$_d$, existed$_t$, exist$_t$, or will exist$_t$. Obviously enough, if all such things are present$_t$, then all things that existed$_t$, exist$_t$, or will exist$_t$ are present$_t$. But to say that all things that existed$_t$, exist$_t$, or will exist$_t$ are present$_t$ is just to say that only present$_t$ things existed$_t$, exist$_t$, or will exist$_t$. I stand by my claim, then, that (Pr_c) implies (Pr_b).

Finally, Ludlow complains that I dismiss the most promising formulation of presentism, (Pr_c). But this isn't entirely accurate. I do put an argument in the mouth of my opponent that (Pr_c) is trivially false, but I don't endorse her argument. (Quite the contrary. Her argument is that (Pr_c) is trivially false because it implies (Pr_b), a trivial falsehood. But I spend the bulk of the paper arguing that (Pr_b) is not a trivial falsehood.)

So I don't exactly dismiss (Pr_c). That said, I don't think of it as the most felicitous formulation of presentism. This is because, as I construe it, it says that—quantifier wide open—everything is present. But suppose you believe that all things in time are present but that some "atemporal" things—e.g. sets, properties, and God—are not present. Then you reject (Pr_c). Still, I'm happy enough to call you a presentist. You're a presentist, I say, because you accept (Pr_b).

Florida State University

3. A Defense of Presentism
Ned Markosian

1. INTRODUCTION

Presentism is the view that only present objects exist.[1] According to Presentism, if we were to make an accurate list of all the things that exist—i.e. a list of all the things that our most unrestricted quantifiers range over—there would be not a single non-present object on the list.

Apologies to Mark Hinchliff for stealing the title of his dissertation (see Hinchliff, *A Defense of Presentism*). As it turns out, however, the version of Presentism defended here is different from the version defended by Hinchliff: see Section 3.1 below. I'm grateful to West Virginia University for a research grant that helped support the writing of an earlier draft of this paper. And although they didn't give me any money, I'm even more grateful to Stuart Brock, Matthew Davidson, Greg Fitch, Geoffrey Goddu, Mark Heller, Hud Hudson, Aleksandar Jokic, Trenton Merricks, Bradley Monton, Joshua Parsons, Laurie Paul, Sharon Ryan, Steven Savitt, Ted Sider, Quentin Smith, and Dean Zimmerman for helpful comments on earlier versions of the paper, and to Greg Fitch, Tom Ryckman, and Ted Sider for many helpful discussions of these topics.

[1] More precisely, it is the view that, necessarily, it is always true that only present objects exist. At least, that is how I am using the name 'Presentism'. Quentin Smith has used the name to refer to a different view; see his *Language and Time*. Note that, unless otherwise indicated, what I mean by 'present' is *temporally present*, as opposed to *spatially present*.

For discussions of Presentism and Non-presentism, see R. M. Adams, "Time and Thisness"; Augustine, *Confessions*; Bigelow, "Presentism and Properties"; Brogaard, "Presentist Four-Dimensionalism"; Chisholm, *On Metaphysics*; Chisholm, "Referring to Things that No Longer Exist"; Christensen, *Space-Like Time*; Fine, "Prior on the Construction of Possible Worlds and Instants"; Fitch, "Does Socrates Exist?"; Fitch, "Singular Propositions in Time"; Hinchliff, *A Defense of Presentism*; Hinchliff, "The Puzzle of Change"; Keller and Nelson, "Presentists Should Believe in Time Travel"; Long and Sedley, *The Hellenistic Philosophers*, Vol. 1, *Translations of the Principal Sources with Philosophical Commentary* (especially the writings of Sextus Empiricus); Lucretius, *On the Nature of the Universe*; Markosian, "The 3D/4D Controversy and Non-present Objects"; McCall, *A Model of the Universe*; Merricks, "On the Incompatibility of Enduring and Perduring Entities"; Monton, "Presentism and Spacetime Physics"; Prior, "Changes in Events and Changes in Things"; Prior, "The Notion of the Present"; Prior, *Papers on Time and tense*; Prior, *Past, Present and Future*; Prior, "Some Free Thinking About Time"; Prior, "A Statement of Temporal Realism"; Prior, *Time and Modality*;

Thus, you and I and the Taj Mahal would be on the list, but neither Socrates nor any future grandchildren of mine would be included.[2] And it's not just Socrates and my future grandchildren—the same goes for any other putative object that lacks the property of being present. All such objects are unreal, according to Presentism. According to Non-presentism, on the other hand, non-present objects like Socrates and my future grandchildren exist right now, even though they are not currently present.[3] We may not be able to see them at the moment, on this view, and they may not be in the same space–time vicinity that we find ourselves in right now, but they should nevertheless be on the list of all existing things.

I endorse Presentism, which, it seems to me, is the "common sense" view, i.e. the one that the average person on the street would accept. But there are some serious problems facing Presentism. In particular, there are certain embarrassingly obvious objections to the view that are not easily gotten around. The aims of this paper are (i) to spell out the most obvious objections that can be raised against Presentism, and (ii) to show that these objections are not fatal to the view. In section 2 I will spell out the embarrassing problems facing Presentism that I will be concerned with, and in Section 3 I will consider various possible solutions to those problems, rejecting some but endorsing others.

Prior and Fine, *Worlds, Times and Selves*; Sextus Empiricus, *Against the Physicists*; Sider, "Presentism and Ontological Commitment"; Sider, *Four-Dimensionalism*; Smith, *Language and Time*; Smith, "Reference to the Past and Future"; Tooley, *Time, Tense, and Causation*; Wolterstorff, "Can Ontology Do without Events?"; and Zimmerman, "Persistence and Presentism".

[2] I am assuming that each person is identical to his or her body, and that Socrates's body ceased to be present—thereby going out of existence, according to Presentism—shortly after he died. Those philosophers who reject the first of these assumptions should simply replace the examples in this paper involving allegedly non-present people with appropriate examples involving the non-present bodies of those people.

[3] Let us distinguish between two senses of 'x exists now'. In one sense, which we can call the *temporal location* sense, this expression is synonymous with 'x is present'. The Non-presentist will admit that, in the temporal location sense of 'x exists now', it is true that no non-present objects exist right now. But in the other sense of 'x exists now', which we can call the *ontological* sense, to say that x exists now is just to say that x is now in the domain of our most unrestricted quantifiers, whether it happens to be present, like you and me, or non-present, like Socrates. When I attribute to Non-presentists the claim that non-present objects like Socrates exist right now, I mean to commit the Non-presentist only to the claim that these non-present objects exist now in the ontological sense (the one involving the most unrestricted quantifiers).

2. PROBLEMS FOR PRESENTISM

2.1 Singular Propositions and Non-present Objects

One of the most obvious problems facing Presentism concerns singular propositions about non-present objects.[4] A singular proposition depends for its existence on the individual object(s) it is about. Thus, Presentism entails that there are no singular propositions about non-present objects.[5]

This is a very counterintuitive consequence. Most of us would have thought that there are many propositions about specific non-present objects (like Socrates, for example). And it seems clear that a proposition that is specifically about a non-present object would count as a singular proposition about that object. Thus, it is natural to think that sentence (1), for example, expresses a singular proposition about Socrates:

(1) Socrates was a philosopher.

Similarly, most of us would have thought that we often believe singular propositions about non-present objects, like the proposition that is apparently expressed by (1).

But according to Presentism, there are never any singular propositions about non-present objects, and hence no sentence ever expresses any such proposition, and no person ever believes any such proposition. This is surely a strange consequence of Presentism.[6]

Here is a variation on the same problem. Consider the time when Socrates ceased to be present. According to Presentism, Socrates went out of existence at that time. Thus, according to Presentism, all singular propositions about Socrates also went out of existence at that time. Now consider someone—Glaucon, say—who knew Socrates, and believed various singular propositions about him in the period right before Socrates ceased to be present, but who was unaware of Socrates's

---

[4] In what follows I'll adopt Robert Adams's definition of 'singular proposition', according to which "a singular proposition about an individual x is a proposition that involves or refers to x directly, perhaps by having x or the thisness of x as a constituent, and not merely by way of x's qualitative properties or relations to other individuals" (Adams, "Time and Thisness", p. 315). By the "thisness" of x, Adams means "the property of being x, or the property of being identical with x". I will refer to such a property below as x's *haecceity*.

[5] Adams would disagree; he maintains that there are singular propositions about past objects even though those past objects no longer exist. See Section 3.4 below.

[6] Greg W. Fitch is an example of someone who rejects Presentism for this reason. See Fitch, "Singular Propositions in Time".

unfortunate demise. When Socrates ceased to be present and thereby popped out of existence, according to Presentism, all of those singular propositions about him also popped out of existence. But there was poor Glaucon, who we can suppose did not change in any important intrinsic way when Socrates ceased to be present. According to Presentism, although Glaucon did not change in any significant intrinsic way when Socrates ceased to be present, he nevertheless did undergo a very important change right at that moment: Glaucon all of a sudden went from believing all of those singular propositions about Socrates to not believing any of them—through no fault of his own, and without any knowledge that his beliefs were changing in such a dramatic way! Isn't that a strange and absurd consequence of the view?

2.2 Relations between Present and Non-present Objects

There is more. If there are no non-present objects, then no one can now stand in any relation to any non-present object. Thus, for example, you cannot now stand in the *admires* relation to Socrates; I cannot now stand in the *grandson* relation to my paternal grandfather; and no event today can stand in any causal relation to George Washington's crossing the Delaware. These are all fairly counterintuitive consequences of Presentism, and it must be acknowledged that they pose serious problems for the view.[7]

2.3 Presentism and Special Relativity

A third challenge for Presentism comes from an empirical theory in physics, namely, the Special Theory of Relativity. It is apparently a

---

[7] W. V. Quine is an example of a philosopher who rejects Presentism because of the problem of relations between present and non-present objects; see his *Quiddities*, pp. 197–8.

For discussions of the special version this problem that has to do with causation, see Bigelow, "Presentism and Properties"; Tooley, *Time, Tense, and Causation*; and Zimmerman, "Chisholm and the Essences of Events". Tooley rejects Presentism because of the causal version of the problem, while Bigelow and Zimmerman propose solutions to the causal version of the problem that are inspired by the writings of Lucretius and the Stoics (see Lucretius, *On the Nature of the Universe*; Sextus Empiricus, *Against the Physicists*; and Long and Sedley, *The Hellenistic Philosophers*, vol. 1, *Translations of the Principal Sources with Philosophical Commentary*, especially the writings of Sextus Empiricus). (It should be noted, however, that Bigelow's proposed solution to the causal version of the problem seems to require the existence of singular propositions about non-present objects.)

consequence of that theory that there is no such thing as absolute simultaneity, and this suggests that which things are *present* is a relativistic matter that can vary from one reference frame to another. This in turn suggests that the Presentist is committed to the claim that what *exists* is a relativistic matter, so that it may well be the case that Socrates exists relative to your frame of reference but does not exist relative to my frame of reference. This would surely be an untenable consequence of the view.

2.4 Past and Future Times

Here is the fourth embarrassing problem for Presentism that I will discuss in this paper. It is very natural to talk about times. We often speak as if times are genuine entities, and we often appear to express propositions about times. But Presentism seems to entail that there is no time except the present time. Thus, Presentism also seems to entail that there are no propositions about any non-present times, and that we never say anything about any such times. These would be very odd consequences of Presentism, to say the least. If they are indeed consequences of the view, then some account of why they are not completely unacceptable is needed. And if they are not consequences of the view, then some explanation of this fact is required.

3. PRESENTIST SOLUTIONS TO THESE PROBLEMS

3.1 Non-existent Objects that Have Properties and Stand in Relations

Let me begin my discussion of responses to these problems by mentioning some possible solutions that I do not endorse. One response available to the Presentist for dealing with both the problem of singular propositions about non-present objects and the problem of relations between present and non-present objects (and perhaps the problem of past and future times as well) involves a view that has been advocated by Mark Hinchliff.[8] Hinchliff distinguishes between *Serious Presentism* and *Unrestricted Presentism*. Serious Presentism is the conjunction of Presentism with the claim that an object can have properties, and stand

---

[8] See Hinchliff, *A Defense of Presentism*, ch. 2 and 3, and "The Puzzle of Change", pp. 124–6.

in relations, only when it exists, while Unrestricted Presentism is the conjunction of Presentism with the claim that an object can have properties, and stand in relations, even at times when it does not exist.

Thus, according to Unrestricted Presentism, Socrates can now have properties like *having been a philosopher*, and can stand in the *admired by* relation to me, even though he no longer exists. Moreover, according to Unrestricted Presentism, we can now express singular propositions about Socrates (such as the proposition expressed by (1)), even though Socrates does not exist.

There is a great deal to be said for this response to our problems. But the response comes with a price—namely, accepting the claim that an object can have properties, and can stand in relations, at a time when it does not exist—that I personally am not willing to pay. That is, my pre-philosophical intuitions commit me not only to Presentism but also to Serious Presentism. This is of course not meant to be an argument against Unrestricted Presentism. But it does mean that the response to these two problems that is available to the Unrestricted Presentist is not available to me.

3.2 No Singular Propositions

Another solution available to the Presentist for dealing with the problem of singular propositions about non-present objects would be simply to deny that there are any singular propositions about concrete objects in the first place. I don't know of any Presentist who adopts this position specifically for the purpose of defending Presentism, but the view that there are no singular propositions about concrete objects has been discussed by Chisholm (who was in fact a Presentist) and various others.[9] One who says that there are no singular propositions about concrete objects at all will have to give an account of sentences that seem to express singular propositions about such objects, like the following.

(2) Peter van Inwagen is a philosopher.

For example, such a person could say that (2) expresses the same general proposition as

(2a) (∃x)(x is the referent of 'Peter van Inwagen' and x is a philosopher).

---

[9] See e.g. Chisholm, *The First Person*.

Instead of involving van Inwagen himself, or referring directly to him, this proposition involves the property of being the referent of 'Peter van Inwagen' (as well as the property of being a philosopher and the relation of coinstantiation).

If the Presentist insists that there are no singular propositions about concrete objects at all, not even singular propositions about present concrete objects, then he or she can say that there is nothing peculiar about maintaining that sentences that appear to express singular propositions about past or future concrete objects really express general propositions about the way things were or will be. For on this view, even when Socrates was present the sentence

(3) Socrates is a philosopher

did not express any singular proposition about Socrates. Instead, it expressed some general proposition, such as the one expressed by the following sentence.

(3a) (∃x)(x is the referent of 'Socrates' and x is a philosopher).

Thus, there is nothing odd about saying that (1) does not now express a singular proposition about Socrates. Instead, the Presentist might say, what (1) really expresses is the past-tensed version of the proposition expressed by (3a), which proposition can be more perspicuously expressed by the following sentence (in which 'P' is the past-tense sentential operator, short for 'it has been the case that').

(1a) P(∃x)(x is the referent of 'Socrates' and x is a philosopher).

Similarly, a Presentist who does not believe in singular propositions about concrete objects in the first place will say that there was no immediate change in Glaucon's beliefs brought about by Socrates's ceasing to be present, since all of Glaucon's beliefs "about" Socrates involved purely general propositions all along.

Unfortunately, however, this no-singular-propositions-about-concrete-objects strategy is not appealing to me, for one main reason: it presupposes a controversial thesis—that there are no singular propositions about concrete objects—that I am not willing to endorse. It seems pretty clear to me that there are in fact singular propositions about existing concrete objects (such as the singular proposition that Peter van Inwagen is a philosopher), that many sentences express such propositions, and that many of us often believe such propositions.

3.3 Singular Propositions with Blanks

Another response to the problem of singular propositions about non-present objects would involve appealing to a view about empty names that has been developed by Kaplan, Adams and Stecker, Braun, Salmon, and Oppy.[10] I cannot do justice to the view in question in the limited space I have here, but the basic idea is that a sentence with an empty name in it, like 'Harry Potter wears glasses', expresses just the kind of singular proposition that a similar sentence with a normal name (such as 'Woody Allen wears glasses') expresses, except that the singular proposition expressed by the sentence with the empty name contains a blank where the other singular proposition contains an individual.[11] A Presentist who took this line could say that sentences like (1) do indeed express singular propositions, albeit singular propositions with blanks in them rather than ordinary singular propositions.

Although I think that there is a lot to be said for the singular-propositions-with-blanks view as a theory about empty names, I do not think that the view is of much use to the Presentist when it comes to our current problem. The reason is that combining Presentism with the singular-propositions-with-blanks view yields the result that the sentences 'Socrates was a philosopher' and 'Beethoven was a philosopher' express the same singular proposition (namely, the singular proposition that ____ was a philosopher). And if the goal of the Presentist is to give some account of sentences like (1) that has plausible consequences regarding the meanings and truth values of those sentences, this result will clearly not do.

3.4 Haecceities to the Rescue?

A fourth strategy for dealing with the problem of singular propositions about non-present objects would be to appeal to unexemplified *haecceities*. Haecceities are supposed to be properties like the property of being identical to Socrates, each of which can be exemplified only by one unique object. Those who believe in haecceities typically believe that a

---

[10] See Kaplan, "Demonstratives"; Adams and Stecker, "Vacuous Singular Terms"; Braun, "Empty Names"; Salmon, "Nonexistence"; and Oppy, "The Philosophical Insignificance of Gödel's Slingshot".

[11] For the sake of simplicity, I am now talking as if singular propositions literally contained the individuals they are about, as opposed to merely referring to them directly in some way.

haecceity comes into existence with its object, and continues to exist as long as it is exemplified by that object. That much is relatively uncontroversial. But some Presentists also believe that a haecceity continues to exist even after its object ceases to exist. On this view, which has been defended by Robert Adams, there is a property—Socrates's haecceity, which we might call "Socraticity"—that came into existence with Socrates and was uniquely exemplified by Socrates, and that continues to exist today, even though it is no longer exemplified.[12] Thus, according to Adams, sentences like (1) *do* express singular propositions about the relevant concrete objects after all, even though those concrete objects no longer exist. The idea is that a sentence like (1) now expresses the proposition that there was a unique x who exemplified Socraticity and who was a philosopher, and that this proposition somehow involves or directly refers to Socrates, in virtue of having Socraticity as a constituent. (It is worth noting here that Adams believes in unexemplified haecceities of past objects, but not of future objects. Thus, Adams's version of the haecceity approach purports to solve the problem of singular propositions about non-present objects for the case of past objects but not for the case of future objects. On his view, there are no singular propositions about future objects.)

Unfortunately, there are several problems with the haecceity approach. One problem with the approach, at least as it is defended by Adams, is that, although it allows us to say that there are now singular propositions about past objects, like Socrates, it does not allow us to say that there are now any singular propositions about future objects, like my first grandson.[13] Thus, Adams's version of the haecceity approach to the problem of singular propositions about non-present objects involves an important asymmetry between the past and the future. And it seems to me that any adequate Presentist solution to the problem should treat the past and the future as perfectly analogous.[14]

A second, and more serious, problem with the haecceity approach is that it requires an ontological commitment to the haecceities of non-existent objects, and the claim that there are such things is a controversial claim that many Presentists, including myself, are not willing to accept. If we are to understand Socraticity as the property of being identical to Socrates, for example, then it seems that Socrates must be

---

[12] See R. M. Adams, "Time and Thisness".
[13] Since Adams doesn't believe in haecceities of future individuals.
[14] Adams responds to this objection in "Time and Thisness": see pp. 319–20.

a constituent of Socraticity. But in that case, it's hard to see how Socraticity could continue to exist after Socrates goes out of existence.[15]

A third problem facing the haecceity approach is that it is not at all clear that the proposition that there was a unique x that exemplified Socraticity and that was a philosopher is really a singular proposition about Socrates. That is, it's not clear that this proposition involves or refers to Socrates directly. Consider the proposition that there was a unique x that was Plato's best teacher and that was a philosopher. That proposition is not a singular proposition about Socrates. And it seems to me that these two propositions are alike in this respect, so that if the one is not a singular proposition about Socrates then neither is the other. After all, what is the difference between Socraticity and the property of being Plato's best teacher in virtue of which a proposition containing the former property is a singular proposition about Socrates while a proposition containing the latter property is not?

Finally, there is a fourth problem with this approach which combines the second and third problems to generate a dilemma for the haecceity approach. Either the proposition that there was a unique x that exemplified Socraticity and that was a philosopher is really a singular proposition about Socrates, or it is not. If it is not, then the haecceity approach has not given us a singular proposition about Socrates. And if it is, then that must be because there is something special about Socraticity in virtue of which propositions containing it are singular propositions about Socrates, whereas propositions containing the property of being Plato's best teacher are not. But it seems like the only feature that Socraticity could have to give it this distinction is having Socrates himself as a constituent. And in that case, it looks like Socraticity cannot exist without Socrates after all.

3.5 Paraphrasing

Accepting (i) the view that there can be singular propositions about non-existent objects, or (ii) the view that there are no singular propositions

---

[15] Adams suggests that individuals are not constituents of their haecceities (see "Time and Thisness", p. 320.) But I have a hard time understanding how Socrates could fail to be a constituent of Socraticity, although, admittedly, what we say about this matter depends partly on what we say about the tricky subject of the nature of constituency. In any case, whatever we say about the nature of constituency, it seems clear to me that this principle will be true: *The property of being identical with x exists only if x itself exists.* For it seems to me that, for any relation and for any object, the property of standing in that relation to that object will exist only if the object exists.

A Defense of Presentism | 57

at all, or (iii) the singular-propositions-with-blanks view, or (iv) the view that there are unexemplified haecceities that can "stand in" for non-present, concrete objects in singular propositions about those objects would allow the Presentist to solve the problem of singular propositions about non-present objects in a more or less straightforward way.[16] But as I have said, none of these strategies will work for me. A fifth strategy for dealing with the problem of singular propositions about non-present objects involves the technique of paraphrasing sentences that seem to be about non-present objects into purely general past-and future-tensed sentences.[17] We have already encountered this technique above, when we considered paraphrasing

(1) Socrates was a philosopher

as

(1a) P($\exists$x)(x is the referent of 'Socrates' and x is a philosopher).

The idea is that, once Socrates ceases to be present and thereby goes out of existence, according to Presentism, (1) has the same meaning as (1a). That is, once Socrates ceases to be present, (1) ceases to express a singular proposition about Socrates. Instead, according to this line of thought, (1) begins at that point to express the general proposition expressed by (1a).

This paraphrasing approach differs from the no-singular-propositions approach in that, on the paraphrasing approach, it is admitted that there are singular propositions about present objects; the claim on this approach is that, once an object ceases to be present, all singular propositions about it go out of existence, so that sentences about it—like (1) in the case of Socrates—must then be understood in some other way, as suggested by (1a). The paraphrasing approach also differs from the haecceity approach in that it does not entail the existence of any controversial items such as unexemplified haecceities.

But the paraphrasing approach is not without its own problems.[18] Perhaps the main difficulty with this approach is that the relevant

---

[16] I say "in a more or less straightforward way" partly because, as I noted above, Adams's version of the haecceity approach purports to solve the problem of singular propositions about non-present objects for the case of past objects but not for the case of future objects.

[17] Something like this strategy is tentatively suggested by Prior in "Changes in Events and Changes in Things" (see pp. 12–14). The paraphrasing strategy is explicitly endorsed by Wolterstorff in "Can Ontology Do without Events?" (see pp. 190 ff).

[18] For a discussion of further problems for the paraphrasing approach, see Smith, *Language and Time*, pp. 162 ff.

paraphrases just don't seem to have the same meanings as the originals. For example, (1) seems to be about a man, while (1a) seems to be about a name. Also, (1) has the form of a sentence that expresses a singular proposition, while (1a) has the form of a sentence that expresses a general proposition. Moreover, it seems pretty clear that (1) did not have the same meaning as (1a) back when Socrates was still present,[19] and it would be strange to say that the two sentences differed in meaning at one time and then had exactly the same meaning at a later time, even though (we can assume) there were no changes in the interpretation of the relevant language between those two times.[20]

3.6 Indirect Relations Between Present and Non-present Objects

We will return to the problem of singular propositions about non-present objects, and consider a variation on the paraphrasing strategy, below. First, however, let us consider two strategies that I want to endorse for dealing with the problem of relations between present and non-present objects. The first strategy I have in mind involves insisting that there never really are relations between objects that are not contemporaneous, but trying to accommodate our intuition that there are by appealing to various other truths that are "in the ballpark". The strategy will also involve pointing out that the fact that there cannot be direct relations between two objects at a time when one of those objects is not present, and hence does not exist, is an instance of a more general phenomenon. The more general phenomenon occurs whenever we are inclined to say that two things stand in some relation to one another even though they do not both exist.

For example, we are inclined to say that Chelsea Clinton stands in the *sibling* relation to her possible brother, who does not exist.[21] Since there really is no possible brother for Chelsea to be related to, it is not literally

---

[19] Let's pretend, for simplicity's sake, that English existed in its present form back then. For arguments that seem to show that (1) did not have the same meaning as (1a) back when Socrates was present, see Kripke, *Naming and Necessity*.

[20] I'm grateful to Greg Fitch for making this point in correspondence.

[21] For the remainder of this paper I will be assuming that Actualism is true, i.e. that there are no non-actual objects. This is because I am offering a defense of Presentism, and Presentists tend to be Actualists as well. (In fact, I do not know of a single Presentist who is not also an Actualist.) But all of the points I make based on this assumption could be made—although in a much more cumbersome way—without assuming that Actualism is true.

true that she stands in the sibling relation to any such person. But we can capture what is true about this case with a sentence in which the relevant existential quantifier lies within the scope of a modal operator, like the following (where the diamond is the modal operator standing for 'it is possible that'):

(4) ◇(∃x)(x is a brother of Chelsea).

Because the existential quantifier in (4) lies within the scope of a modal operator, (4) does not entail the actual existence of any possible brother of Chelsea. For this reason, (4) is acceptable even to the Actualist, who can say that, although it is not literally true that Chelsea stands in the sibling relation to her possible brother, there is nevertheless a literal truth in the ballpark that we can point to in order to justify our intuition that Chelsea does stand in that relation to some possible brother.

Similarly, the Presentist can maintain, when we are inclined to say that a present object stands in some relation to a non-present object, as in the case of my grandfather and myself, that the thing we are inclined to say is not literally true. But in such a case, the Presentist can maintain, there is nevertheless a general truth in the ballpark that is literally true, and that we can point to in justifying our intuition. In the case of my grandfather, we can express this general truth with a sentence in which the relevant existential quantifier lies within the scope of a tense operator, like the following:

(5) P(∃x)(x is the grandfather of Ned).

A similar technique will work even in a case in which the two objects in question never existed at the same time. For example, when we are inclined to say that I stand in the *great-great-grandson of* relation to my great-great-grandfather, the Presentist can appeal to the following sentence, which is literally true:

(6) P(∃x)[x is the grandfather of Ned and P(∃y)(y is the grandfather of x)].[22]

---

[22] There is a further assumption that is required for this approach to work. It is the assumption that, in every case in which there is some truth to the claim that a certain present object stands in some relation to a putative non-present object, there will be sufficient "linking objects" that will connect the present object to the putative non-present object, the way my grandfather links me to my great-great-grandfather. I am inclined to accept this assumption, although I won't attempt to defend it here.

The matter is more complicated in the case of *causal* relations among entities that are never contemporaneous, but I see no reason not to think that the same basic strategy will work even in such cases. Here is a very brief sketch of one way in which the indirect relations approach could be applied to the case of causal relations among non-contemporaneous events. It is natural to think that events generally take some time to occur, and also that direct causal relations between events always involve events that are contemporaneous for at least some period of time. If we grant these assumptions, then it will turn out that, whenever we want to say that one event, e_1, causes another, much later event, e_{23}, there will be a causal chain of linking events connecting e_1 and e_{23}, such that each adjacent pair of events in the chain will be contemporaneous for at least some period of time.[23]

3.7 Similarities between Time and Modality; Differences between Time and Space

Some may feel that this approach still leaves something to be desired, however, since it remains true, even according to the Presentist who takes this line, that there is still no direct relation between me and my grandfather. Also, it looks as if the type of account exemplified by (6) won't work when we want to say that I stand in the *admires* relation to Socrates. This is where the second strategy that I want to endorse for dealing with the problem of relations between present and non-present objects comes in. The second strategy involves emphasizing fundamental similarities between time and modality while at the same time emphasizing fundamental differences between time and space. The

---

[23] A great deal more space than I have here would be required to do justice to the causal version of the problem of relations between non-contemporaneous entities. For more extended discussions of the problem, see Bigelow, "Presentism and Properties"; Lucretius, *On the Nature of the Universe*; Sextus Empiricus, *Against the Physicists*; Sider, *Four-Dimensionalism*; the writings of the Stoics in Long and Sedley, *The Hellenistic Philosophers*, vol. 1, *Translations of the Principal Sources with Philosophical Commentary*; Tooley, *Time, Tense, and Causation*; and Zimmerman, "Chisholm and the Essences of Events".

It is worth noting that at least some Presentists are reductionists about events, insisting that all talk that appears to be about events is really talk about things (see e.g. Prior, "Changes in Events and Changes in Things"). Such Presentists will perhaps have an easier time than others of dealing with the problem of causal relations between non-contemporaneous events, since for them the problem will turn out more or less straightforwardly to be just a special case of the general problem of relations between present and non-present objects.

claim that putative objects like Socrates, my grandfather, and my future grandchildren do not really exist, and can neither feature in singular propositions nor stand in direct relations to existing objects, is much less counterintuitive on the assumption that time is fundamentally like modality and fundamentally unlike the dimensions of space. But it can be plausibly argued that this is in fact the case. In fact, Prior and others have argued for the first part of this claim (time's fundamental similarity to modality);[24] and Prior, myself, and others have argued for the second part (time's fundamental dissimilarity to the dimensions of space).[25] Thus, according to this line of thought, putative non-present objects like Socrates and the others have more in common with putative non-actual objects like Santa Claus than they have in common with objects that are located elsewhere in space, like Alpha Centauri. It's very plausible to say that, although Alpha Centauri is located far away from us in space, it is no less real because of that. And similarly, it is very plausible to say that Santa Claus *is* less real in virtue of being non-actual. The question, then, is whether putative non-present objects like Socrates are in the same boat as Alpha Centauri in this regard or, instead, in the same boat as Santa Claus. And once it is accepted that time is fundamentally similar to modality, and fundamentally different

---

[24] See Prior, "The Notion of the Present"; Prior, *Time and Modality*; Prior and Fine, *Worlds, Times and Selves*; Fine, "Prior on the Construction of Possible Worlds and Instants"; and Zalta, "On the Structural Similarities between Worlds and Times". One of the main similarities between time and modality has to do with the similarities between modal logic and tense logic, and in particular the way the tense operators function just like modal operators. Another main similarity between time and modality involves similarities between worlds (construed as abstract objects) and times (construed as abstract objects). A third similarity between time and modality, at least according to the Presentist, has to do with ontology, and the fact that the past and the future are as unreal as the merely possible.

[25] See Prior, *Past, Present, and Future*; Prior, "Thank Goodness That's Over"; Prior, *Time and Modality*; Markosian, "On Language and the Passage of Time"; Markosian, "How Fast Does Time Pass?"; Markosian, "The 3D/4D Controversy and Non-present Objects"; and Markosian, "What Are Physical Objects?". Here are some of the main ways in which it is claimed that time is unlike the dimensions of space. (1) Propositions have truth-values at times, and a single proposition can have different truth-values at different times, but the corresponding things are not true about space. (2) The so-called "A-properties" (putative properties like pastness, presentness, and futurity) are genuine, monadic properties that cannot be analyzed purely in terms of "B-relations" (binary, temporal relations such as earlier-than and simultaneous-with), but there are no genuine spatial properties analogous to the A-properties. (3) Time passes—that is, times and events are constantly and inexorably changing from being future to being present and then on to being more and more remotely past—but nothing analogous is true of any dimension of space.

from space, then the natural answer to this question is that Socrates is in the same boat as Santa Claus.

Someone might object at this point by saying something like the following. "You're overlooking an important fact about Socrates: he was once real. For that reason, it is a big mistake to lump him together with Santa Claus, who never was real and never will be real. Socrates ought to be in the same boat as Alpha Centauri, not in the same boat as Santa Claus."

My reply to this objection is that it misses the point about the fundamental similarity between time and modality and the fundamental difference between time and space. Given the fundamental similarity between time and modality, being formerly real is analogous to being possibly real. And given the fundamental difference between time and space, there is no reason to think that being real at a remote temporal location is analogous to being real at a remote spatial location. So, although I admit that it might seem a little counterintuitive, I think it is actually a desirable consequence of Presentism that I cannot now stand in any direct relations to Socrates, or my grandfather, or any other non-present object, just as I cannot stand in any direct relations to Santa Claus, or my possible sister, or any other non-actual object.

What about admiring Socrates, then? The problem, it will be recalled, is that it would be natural to say that I stand in the *admires* relation to Socrates, but according to Presentism I cannot do so, since Socrates does not now exist. What I want to say in response to this problem is that there is an exactly analogous problem with non-actual objects, and that the solution to the modal case will also work for the temporal case.

Consider Sherlock Holmes, for example. I admire him too, almost as much as I admire Socrates. Or anyway, I am inclined, when speaking loosely, to say that I admire Sherlock Holmes. But of course I can't really stand in the *admires* relation to Sherlock Holmes if, as I am assuming, Actualism is true and Sherlock Holmes doesn't really exist.[26] What truth is there, then, in the intuitive idea that I admire Sherlock Holmes? Surely the correct answer will involve an analysis roughly along these lines:

---

[26] This is perhaps an oversimplification. Some people would say that Actualism is true and that Sherlock Holmes *does* really exist. For some people believe that fictional characters are abstract, actual objects (like sets of properties); see e.g. van Inwagen, "Creatures of Fiction"; Howell, "Fictional Objects: How They Are and How They Aren't"; Emt, "On the Nature of Fictional Entities"; Levinson, "Making Believe"; and Salmon, "Nonexistence". For the sake of simplicity, I will ignore this point in what follows.

(7) There are various properties, p_1-p_n, such that (i) I associate p_1-p_n with the name 'Sherlock Holmes', and (ii) thoughts of either p_1-p_n or the name 'Sherlock Holmes' evoke in me the characteristic feeling of admiration.

Note that (7) can be true even though it's also true that, when the characteristic feeling of admiration is evoked in me by the relevant thoughts, the feeling is not directed *at* any particular object. Thus, (7) captures what is true in the claim that I admire Sherlock Holmes, without requiring that there actually *be* such a person as Sherlock Holmes.

Note also that (7) is consistent with the truth of this claim:

(7a) There are various properties, p_1-p_n, such that (i) I associate p_1-p_n with the name 'Sherlock Holmes', (ii) thoughts of either p_1-p_n or the name 'Sherlock Holmes' evoke in me the characteristic feeling of admiration, and (iii) according to the Conan Doyle story, $(\exists x)(x$ has p_1-p_n and x is the referent of 'Sherlock Holmes').

Thus, it can be true that (loosely speaking) I admire Sherlock Holmes, and also true that my admiration is connected with the actual story.

If this is right, then we can say a similar thing about my admiration of Socrates: namely,

(8) There are various properties, p_1-p_n, such that (i) I associate p_1-p_n with the name 'Socrates', and (ii) thoughts of either p_1-p_n or the name 'Socrates' evoke in me the characteristic feeling of admiration.

And (8), like (7), can be true even though it's also true that, when the characteristic feeling of admiration is evoked in me by the relevant thoughts, the feeling is not directed *at* any particular object. Thus, (8) captures what is true in the claim that I admire Socrates, without requiring that there presently *be* such a person as Socrates.

Now, (8) is consistent with the truth of this additional claim:

(8a) There are various properties, p_1-p_n, such that (i) I associate p_1-p_n with the name 'Socrates', (ii) thoughts of either p_1-p_n or the name 'Socrates' evoke in me the characteristic feeling of admiration, and (iii) $P(\exists x)(x$ has p_1-p_n and x is the referent of 'Socrates').

Thus, it can be true that (loosely speaking) I admire Socrates, and also true that my admiration is connected with the actual course of history in such a way that I am indirectly related to Socrates.[27]

Time's alleged similarity with modality and alleged dissimilarity with space are relevant here. For the plausibility of (8) as an analysis of what is correct about the intuitive idea that I am an admirer of Socrates depends on the claim that the case of Socrates is similar to the case of a non-actual object like Sherlock Holmes, and not similar to a case involving someone who is (temporally) present but very far away.

Here is a related point. As a way of developing the objection to Presentism involving Glaucon and the sudden change in his beliefs when Socrates ceased to be present, the Non-presentist might say something like the following:

> Consider the time right before Socrates suddenly ceased to be present and the time right after. And consider the states Glaucon was in at these two times. If you just look at Glaucon, there is virtually no difference between how he is at the first of these times and how he is at the second (since we are assuming that Glaucon did not change in any important intrinsic way when Socrates ceased to be present). How is it possible, then, that there is such a big difference between Glaucon before Socrates ceased to be present and Glaucon after Socrates ceased to be present? How is it possible that the earlier Glaucon believes the singular proposition that Socrates is a philosopher and the later Glaucon does not believe that proposition, when the two Glaucons are so similar?

And here is my reply to this objection. Imagine someone arguing as follows:

> Consider two possible worlds: the actual world, in which George W. Bush really exists, and a merely possible world—call it "w_1"— in which some very powerful being is playing an elaborate trick on all of us by making it seem as if there is a man named "George W. Bush" when in fact there is not. Let the two versions of me in the two worlds have exactly the same intrinsic properties, and let

---

[27] I mentioned (in n. 22) that the indirect relations strategy is based on the assumption that there will in general be sufficient "linking objects" to generate the requisite truths. Notice that, in the case of the truth about my admiring Socrates that is captured by sentence (8a), it is the name and the properties in question that do the linking.

my experiences in the two worlds be exactly alike, so that, whenever I experience a television image of Bush in the actual world, I experience a qualitatively identical television image of (what appears to be) Bush in w_1. Now, if you just look at my intrinsic properties, there is no difference between how I am in the actual world and how I am in w_1. How is it possible, then, that there is such a big difference between me in the actual world and me in w_1? How is it possible that the actual me believes the singular proposition that Bush is president and the me in w_1 does not believe that proposition, when the two versions of me are so similar?

The correct response to someone who argues like this would be that the me in w_1 cannot believe any singular proposition about Bush, for the simple reason that Bush does not exist in that world. No object, no singular proposition; and no singular proposition, no belief in that singular proposition. That's how there can be such a big difference between the two versions of me even though they are so similar. And, I am suggesting, it is the same with poor Glaucon and the time after Socrates has ceased to be present. He cannot believe any singular proposition about Socrates at that time for the simple reason that Socrates does not exist at that time. No object, no singular proposition; and no singular proposition, no belief in that singular proposition. That's how there can be such a big difference between Glaucon before Socrates has passed out of existence and Glaucon after Socrates has passed out of existence.[28]

3.8 A Variation on the Paraphrasing Strategy

Emphasizing the similarities between time and modality can also help the Presentist to deal with the problem of singular propositions about non-present objects by employing a variation on the paraphrasing strategy discussed above. Recall that, on that strategy, the claim was that

---

[28] It is worth mentioning here that the Presentist line I am defending on beliefs about non-present objects commits me to at least one version of "externalism" about beliefs: namely, the thesis that which propositions one believes is not determined solely by one's intrinsic properties, but rather is partly determined by features of the external world, such as whether there is an object for the relevant belief to be about. This is what makes it possible for Glaucon to go from believing various singular propositions about Socrates to not believing any such propositions, even though he doesn't change in any intrinsic way. (I am grateful to Ted Sider for making this point in correspondence.)

(1) Socrates was a philosopher

now has the same meaning as

(1a) P(∃x)(x is the referent of 'Socrates' and x is a philosopher).

This approach was rejected because, upon reflection, it seems pretty clear that (1) and (1a) do not really have the same meaning at all.

But now consider the case of the two worlds discussed in the above example: the actual world, in which George W. Bush exists, and w_1, in which a very powerful being is playing a trick on all of us by making it seem as if there is a guy named "George W. Bush" when there really is no such person. We surely don't want to say that in w_1 the sentence

(9) George W. Bush is president of the US

expresses a singular proposition about Bush, even though (9) does have the *form* of a sentence that expresses a singular proposition about a man named "George W. Bush". And the reason we don't want to say that (9) expresses a singular proposition in w_1 is that there is no such man in that world, so that there can be no such singular proposition there. But this doesn't mean that we have to say that (9) is utterly meaningless in w_1.

The way to say that (9) has some meaning in w_1, even though it doesn't there express a singular proposition about Bush, is to distinguish between two different kinds of meaning that a declarative sentence can have. One type of meaning that a declarative sentence can have is simply the proposition (if any) expressed by that sentence. Let's call this the *propositional content* of the sentence.[29] Sentence (9) has no propositional content in w_1.[30] But another type of meaning that a

---

[29] The propositional content of a sentence is, strictly speaking, a feature of individual tokens of the sentence rather than a feature of the sentence type itself (since it is, strictly speaking, sentence tokens that express propositions, rather than sentence types). But I will for the most part talk loosely here, as if propositional content were somehow a feature of sentence types.

[30] That is, tokens of (9) that occur in w_1 do not express any proposition. This claim is consistent with the claim that tokens of (9) in the actual world do express a (singular) proposition, and also with the claim that tokens in the actual world of the sentence

(9a) In w_1, George W. Bush is president of the US

express a (false, singular) proposition. (Since, after all, George W. Bush does exist in the actual world, and so does the proposition that he is president of the US in w_1.)

declarative sentence can have is the meaning associated with the truth and falsity conditions for the sentence. I'll follow Greg Fitch in calling this the *linguistic meaning* of the sentence.[31]

Acknowledging the distinction between the propositional content and the linguistic meaning of a sentence allows us to say that, although (9) has no propositional content in w_1, it nevertheless has linguistic meaning in that world. For in w_1, just as in the actual world, (9) will have the following truth condition.

(TC9) 'George W. Bush is president of the US' is true iff $(\exists x)(x$ is the referent of 'George W. Bush' and x is president of the US).

(TC9) tells us, in effect, that if the name 'George W. Bush' picks someone out, and if that individual happens to be president of the US, then (9) is true. Otherwise, according to (TC9), the sentence is not true. In w_1, then, where 'George W. Bush' fails to refer to anything, (9) fails to express a proposition, and thus has no propositional content. That's why it is not true there, and that's why (TC9) gets the correct result in this case.[32]

---

[31] See Fitch, "Non Denoting". As I see it, linguistic meaning will be primarily a feature of sentence types (although it also makes sense to ascribe to a sentence token the linguistic meaning associated with its type). Thus, for example, we can say that the following sentence (type),

(2) Peter van Inwagen is a philosopher,

has this truth condition:

(TC2) 'Peter van Inwagen is a philosopher' is true iff $(\exists x)(x$ is the referent of 'Peter van Inwagen' and x is a philosopher).

But if need be, we can make it explicit that (TC2) should be understood as saying that a given token of 'Peter van Inwagen is a philosopher' is true iff $(\exists x)(x$ is the referent of the relevant occurrence of 'Peter van Inwagen' and x is a philosopher).

[32] But notice that (9) is not false in w_1, either. For, as we have noted, (9) has no propositional content in w_1. (TC9) entails that (9) is not true in w_1, but it does not entail that (9) is also not false in that world. In order to guarantee that result, we will need to accept the following falsity condition for (9).

(FC9) 'George W. Bush is president of the US' is false iff $(\exists x)(x$ is the referent of 'George W. Bush' and it's not the case that x is president of the US).

What this shows is that the linguistic meaning of a sentence should be identified not simply with the truth condition for that sentence, but rather with the combination of the truth and falsity conditions for the sentence. (I will sometimes gloss over this point in what follows.)

Notice that all of this is consistent with the denizens of w_1 being utterly convinced that (9) really does express a true proposition (in their world). But since we know something important about their world that they do not know (namely, that there is no referent of 'George W. Bush' in w_1), we are in a position to say, "Poor folks—they think they are expressing a true proposition when they utter (9), when really they are not. All they are doing instead is uttering a sentence with a linguistic meaning but with no propositional content; and on top of that, it's not even a sentence that happens to be true (for according to the correct truth and falsity conditions for (9), it is neither true nor false in w_1)."

Returning to our original sentence,

(1) Socrates was a philosopher,

what I want to say about its situation at the present time is analogous to what I have just said about (9) in w_1. Sentence (1) currently has no propositional content, because it is "trying" to express a singular proposition about the referent of 'Socrates', and there is no such thing. But it doesn't follow that (1) is utterly meaningless. For it has a linguistic meaning. And in fact, as I will argue below, the correct truth condition for (1) is the following:

($TC1_g$) 'Socrates was a philosopher' is true iff $(\exists x)[x$ is the referent of 'Socrates' and P(x is a philosopher)].[33]

At this point the Non-presentist might say, "Fine. If you're willing to outSmart us on the question of whether (1) expresses any proposition, by happily biting the bullet and denying that it does, there's nothing we can do about that. But what about the fact that the majority of English speakers will want to say that (1) happens to be *true*? How do you account for that fact if, as you insist, the sentence does not express any proposition at all?"

Here is my response. I agree that many English speakers will be inclined to say that (1) is true. But I think that there are three main reasons for this, all of which are consistent with the truth of Presentism. The first reason is that some English speakers are at least sometimes inclined toward Non-presentism. Those people are likely to think (sometimes, at least) that (1) expresses something like a true, singular

---

[33] The relevance of the subscript in the name '($TC1_g$)' will be clear shortly.

proposition about Socrates.³⁴ They're making a mistake, but still, this explains why they think (1) is true.³⁵

The second reason why so many English speakers are inclined to say that (1) is true is that even those of us who are confirmed Presentists sometimes prefer not to focus on the Presentism/Non-presentism dispute in our everyday lives. As a purely practical matter, it turns out that you can't be doing serious ontology all the time. But here something like Ted Sider's notion of *quasi-truth* comes in handy.³⁶ The idea is roughly this. Presentists and Non-presentists disagree over a philosophical matter, but we don't necessarily disagree over any non-philosophical matter regarding some empirical fact about the current state of the world. In particular, we Presentists think that the current state of the world is qualitatively indiscernible from the way it would be if Non-presentism and (1) were both true. And that is good enough to make us want to assent to (1), in everyday circumstances, even if we don't really think it is literally true.³⁷

The following technical term can be used to describe the situation:

> S is *quasi-true* = df S is not literally true, but only in virtue of certain non-empirical or philosophical facts.

Now the point can be put this way: Presentists and Non-presentists alike, not to mention people who don't have a view on the Presentism/Non-presentism dispute, all assent to (1), in everyday circumstances, because we all think it is at least quasi-true.

The third reason for the fact that a majority of people will want to say that (1) is true has to do with a very understandable mistake that people tend to make regarding the truth conditions for sentences like (1). The mistake involves blurring a distinction between two kinds of truth

---

³⁴ I say "something like a true, singular proposition about Socrates" because I don't suppose that typical non-philosophers have any view about the existence of singular propositions. But in any case, to the extent that some people have Non-presentist leanings, they will think that (1) is currently true, because they will think that it satisfies the above truth condition.

³⁵ If I became convinced that there were enough of such people, I would have to give up my claim (from Section 1) that Presentism is the view of the average person on the street.

³⁶ See Sider, "Presentism and Ontological Commitment". What I describe in the text is a variation on Sider's actual notion of quasi-truth.

³⁷ Similarly, we think that the current state of the world is qualitatively indiscernible from the way it would be if Non-presentism were true and 'Socrates was a plumber' were false; and that is good enough to make us want to say (when we are not obsessing about philosophical issues) that 'Socrates was a plumber' is false.

condition for sentences that combine names with certain modal operators.[38] The distinction I have in mind can be illustrated by a difference between two different possible truth conditions that we could assign to (1). One truth condition we could assign to (1) is ($TC1_g$), which we have already considered above, and which goes as follows:

($TC1_g$) 'Socrates was a philosopher' is true iff $(\exists x)$[x is the referent of 'Socrates' and P(x is a philosopher)].

The other truth condition we could assign to (1) is the following:

($TC1_s$) 'Socrates was a philosopher' is true iff $P(\exists x)$(x is the referent of 'Socrates' and x is a philosopher).[39]

The difference between ($TC1_g$) and ($TC1_s$) has to do with the scope of the past-tense operator on the right-hand side of the biconditional. In ($TC1_g$) the past-tense operator has narrow scope, while in ($TC1_s$) it has wide scope. ($TC1_g$) tells us, in effect, to grab the thing that is now the referent of 'Socrates', and then to go back to see whether there is some past time at which that thing is a philosopher. ($TC1_s$), on the other hand, tells us, in effect, to go back to past times, and to search for a thing that is the referent of 'Socrates' and that is a philosopher. Thus, the difference between ($TC1_g$) and ($TC1_s$) illustrates a difference between what we might call *grabby truth conditions* and what we might call *searchy truth conditions* for sentences combining names with modal operators.[40]

It should be clear that, if we apply ($TC1_s$) to (1), then, even assuming Presentism, (1) may well turn out to be true. For it may well be the case that there *was* a person who was the referent of 'Socrates' and who was a philosopher.[41] But if we take ($TC1_g$) to be the correct truth condition for (1), on the other hand, then (again assuming Presentism) (1) turns out

---

[38] Following Prior and others, I am counting tense operators as a species of modal operator.

[39] Technical point: in order to accommodate the possibility that Socrates was not named "Socrates" way back when, we may instead want the "searchy" truth condition for (1) (see explanation below) to say something like the following (in which 'F' is the future-tense sentential operator, short for 'it will be the case that').

($TC1_s'$) 'Socrates was a philosopher' is true iff $P(\exists x)$[F(x is the referent of 'Socrates') and x is a philosopher].

[40] I am grateful to Tom Ryckman for suggesting the terms 'searchy' and 'grabby'.

[41] If we take ($TC1_s'$) (see n. 39) to be the correct truth condition for (1), then the point here is that it may well be the case that there *was* a person who *would be* the referent of later occurrences of 'Socrates', and who was a philosopher.

not to be true (which means that it is either false or without a truth value).

So which kind of truth condition should we apply to (1)? I think there is good evidence that, given the way such sentences are understood in English, the answer is that we should apply the grabby truth condition to (1). For consider this sentence

(16) Joe Montana was a quarterback.

The current truth of (16) should depend on how things have been with the guy who is currently the referent of 'Joe Montana'. But if (16) had a searchy truth condition, such as

(TC16$_s$) 'Joe Montana was a quarterback' is true iff $P(\exists x)(x$ is the referent of 'Joe Montana' and x is a quarterback),

then (16) could be true now in virtue of the fact that someone else was formerly both the referent of 'Joe Montana' and a quarterback, even if our current Joe Montana never was a quarterback. And that would be the wrong result. So I think it's clear that (16) now has the following grabby truth condition:

(TC16$_g$) 'Joe Montana was a quarterback' is true iff $(\exists x)[x$ is the referent of 'Joe Montana' and $P(x$ is a quarterback$)]$.

Moreover, I think that, even when (16) loses its propositional content, as a result of Montana's going out of existence, the sentence will not then suddenly come to have a different linguistic meaning; which means that (16) will continue to have the same grabby truth condition it now has even after Montana ceases to exist.

These considerations suggest that the conventions of English are such that two things will normally be true of any standard sentence combining a name and a past-tense operator: (i) like other sentences containing standard uses of names, that sentence will express a singular proposition about the referent of that name, if it expresses any proposition at all; and (ii) that sentence will have a grabby truth condition.[42]

---

[42] Similar remarks apply to sentences containing names and alethic modal operators: they also are meant to express singular propositions about the things named, and they also have grabby rather than searchy truth conditions. For example, the sentence

(17) Joe Montana might have been a plumber

expresses a singular proposition about Joe Montana, and it has the following grabby truth condition:

If I am right about the second part of this claim, then (TC1$_g$) is the correct truth condition for (1). Which means (again, assuming Presentism) that (1) is not true. But still, even if I am right about the correct truth condition for (1), it is quite natural that we sometimes think "True" when we think of (1), for the simple reason that the difference between grabby truth conditions and searchy truth conditions is a fairly subtle difference. I mean, it's really not surprising that the average English speaker would confuse (TC1$_g$) and (TC1$_s$). I can barely tell them apart myself.

If the reader still has doubts about my claim that (TC1$_g$) is the correct truth condition for (1), here is a little empirical test that is easy to do. Go out and corral a typical English speaker on the street. Ask her to consider sentence (1), and to tell you whether it is true. She will most likely say "Yes". Then ask her this question: "Do you think this sentence is true because there *is* a guy called 'Socrates' who was a philosopher, or do you think it is true because there *was* a guy called 'Socrates' who was a philosopher?" I'm willing to bet five dollars that, if you can get her to take this last question seriously, she will opt for the second alternative (the one that corresponds to (TC1$_s$)). And what I think this shows is that, even though the correct truth condition for (1) is (TC1$_g$), the grabby truth condition, the average person on the street is likely to think (mistakenly) that the correct truth condition for (1) is something like (TC1$_s$), the searchy truth condition.

Now, I have argued above that (TC1$_g$) rather than (TC1$_s$) is the correct truth condition for (1). But there is always the possibility that I am wrong about this. If (TC1$_s$) is actually the right truth condition for (1), then the explanation for our inclination to think that (1) is true is even simpler. The explanation is that we think (1) is true because it is (since, presumably, it has been the case that there is a guy called "Socrates" who is a philosopher).[43] But notice that, if we say that

---

(TC17$_g$) 'Joe Montana might have been a plumber' is true iff ($\exists$x)(x is the referent of 'Joe Montana' and $\Diamond$(x is a plumber)).

That is, the correct truth condition for (17) tells us to grab the thing named "Joe Montana" and to check other possible worlds to see whether *that thing* is a plumber in any of them (rather than telling us to go to other possible worlds and search around for a thing that is both named "Joe Montana" and a plumber).

[43] Better yet (again taking into account the possibility that Socrates was not called "Socrates" in his time): If (TC1$_s$') (see n. 39) is the correct truth condition for (1), then the explanation for our inclination to think (1) is true is simply that it is, since, presumably, it has been the case that there is a guy whom we will later call "Socrates" and who is a philosopher.

(TC1$_s$) is the appropriate truth condition for (1), then we must say either (*a*) that (1) is true even though it fails to express a proposition, or else (*b*) that (1) expresses a general proposition, such as the one expressed by this sentence:

(1a) P($\exists$x)(x is the referent of 'Socrates' and x is a philosopher).

And I don't think either of these alternatives is at all tenable.

On the strategy that I am endorsing, then, the claim is not that (1a) has the same meaning (in any sense of 'meaning') as (1). Nor am I claiming that the right-hand side of (TC1$_g$) expresses the same proposition as (1). Rather, the claim is that (1) fails to express any proposition at all, but nevertheless has the linguistic meaning that is captured by (TC1$_g$).[44] In addition, I am admitting that the majority of English speakers would be inclined to say that (1) is true, but I am suggesting that there are three main reasons for this that are all consistent with Presentism: (i) some English speakers are occasional Non-presentists; (ii) Presentists, Non-presentists, and agnostics with respect to the Presentism/Non-presentism dispute are all happy to say that (1) is true, because we all think it is at least quasi-true; and (iii) many English speakers are confused about the correct truth conditions for sentences like (1), mistakenly thinking that they are searchy truth conditions that happen to be satisfied rather than grabby truth conditions that are not satisfied.

3.9 Presentism and Special Relativity

What about the argument from the Special Theory of Relativity (STR) against Presentism? In order to discuss the best Presentist response to it, let's first get clear on exactly how the argument is supposed to go. As I understand it, the argument goes something like this:

The Argument from Relativity

(1) STR is true.
(2) STR entails that there is no such relation as absolute simultaneity.
(3) If there is no such relation as absolute simultaneity, then there is no such property as absolute presentness.

---

[44] Together with the corresponding falsity condition.

(4) Presentism entails that there is such a property as absolute presentness.

(5) Presentism is false.

The rationale for premise (1) is whatever empirical evidence supports STR. The rationale for premise (2) is that STR apparently entails that the relation of simultaneity never holds between two objects or events *absolutely*, but instead only *relative to a particular frame of reference*. The rationale for premise (3) is that, if there were such a property as absolute presentness, then whatever objects or events possessed it would be absolutely simultaneous with one another. And the rationale for premise (4) is that, if Presentism allowed what is present to be a relativistic matter, then Presentism would entail that what exists is a relativistic matter, which would be an unacceptable consequence.[45]

My response to this argument requires a small digression on a general matter concerning philosophical method. It is fashionable nowadays to give arguments from scientific theories to philosophical conclusions. I don't have a problem with this approach in general. But I think it is a seldom-observed fact that, when people give arguments from scientific theories to philosophical conclusions, there is usually a good deal of philosophy built into the relevant scientific theories. I don't have a problem with this, either. Scientists, especially in areas like theoretical physics, cannot be expected to do science without sometimes appealing to philosophical principles.

Still, I think it is important, when evaluating an argument from some scientific theory to a philosophical conclusion, to be aware of the fact that there is likely to be some philosophy built into the relevant scientific theory. Otherwise there is the danger of mistakenly thinking that the argument in question involves a clear-cut case of science versus philosophy. And I think it very rarely happens that we are presented with a genuine case of science versus philosophy.

The reason I raise this methodological point here is that how I want to respond to the Argument from Relativity depends on how philosophically rich we understand STR to be. Does STR have enough philosophical baggage built into it to make it either literally contain or at least entail that there is no such relation as absolute simultaneity?

---

[45] A similar argument from STR can be used against the A Theory of time.

A Defense of Presentism | 75

I don't have a view about the correct answer to this question. But I do know that there are two ways of answering it (Yes and No). So let us consider two different versions of STR, which we can characterize as follows:

$STR^+ = $ A philosophically robust version of STR that has enough philosophical baggage built into it to make it either literally contain or at least entail the proposition that there is no such relation as absolute simultaneity.

$STR^- = $ A philosophically austere version of STR that is empirically equivalent to STR^+ but does not have enough philosophical baggage built into it to make it either literally contain or even entail the proposition that there is no such relation as absolute simultaneity.

Suppose we understand the Argument from Relativity to be concerned with STR^+. Then I think premise (1) of the argument is false, because STR^+ is false. Although I agree that there seems to be a great deal of empirical evidence supporting the theory, I think it is notable that the same empirical evidence supports STR^- equally well. And since I believe there is good *a priori* evidence favoring STR^- over STR^+, I conclude that STR^- is true and that STR^+ is false.

Suppose, on the other hand, that we understand the Argument from Relativity to be concerned with STR^-. Then I reject premise (2) of the argument. STR^- will entail, among other things, that, while it is physically possible to determine whether two objects or events are simultaneous relative to a particular frame of reference, it is not physically possible to determine whether two objects or events are absolutely simultaneous. But this is consistent with there being such a relation as absolute simultaneity. And it is also consistent with there being such a property as absolute presentness.[46]

3.10 Presentism and Past and Future Times

All of this is well and good, but what about the problem of non-present times? Here are two questions that are crucial to this topic:

[46] For more discussions of STR and the A Theory and/or Presentism, see Prior, "The Notion of the Present"; Putnam, "Time and Physical Geometry"; Maxwell, "Are Probabilism and Special Relativity Incompatible?", and Monton, "Presentism and Spacetime Physics".

(Q1) What are times?
(Q2) Are there any non-present times?

And here are the answers to these questions that I want to endorse:

(A1) Times are like worlds.[47]
(A2) In one sense there are many non-present times, while in another sense there are none.

Here's how times are like worlds. Consider the actual world. There are really two of them. There is the abstract actual world, which is a maximal, consistent proposition.[48] There are many things that are similar to the abstract actual world in being maximal, consistent propositions. Each one is a possible world. The abstract actual world is the only one of all of these possible worlds that happens to be true. And then there is the concrete actual world, which is the sum total of all actual facts.[49] The concrete actual world is the only concrete world that exists, and it is what makes the abstract actual world true.

The Presentist can say that it is the same with the present time. There are really two of them. There is the abstract present time, which is a maximal, consistent proposition. There are many things that are similar to the abstract present time in being maximal, consistent propositions that either will be true, are true, or have been true. Each one is a time.[50] The abstract present time is the only one of all of these abstract times that happens to be true right now. And then there is the concrete present time, which is the sum total of all present facts. It is the only concrete time that exists, and it is what makes the abstract present time true. Talk about non-present times can be understood as talk about maximal, consistent propositions that have been or will be true. For example, the time ten years from now can be identified with the maximal, consistent proposition that will be true in ten years.

---

[47] Cf. Prior and Fine, *Worlds, Times and Selves*; Fine, "Prior on the Construction of Possible Worlds and Instants"; and Zalta, "On the structural Similarities Between Worlds and Times".

[48] As before, I am assuming that Actualism is true. There are alternative "ersatzist" accounts that the Actualist can give of possible worlds. See Lewis, *On the Plurality of Worlds*. For our purposes it won't matter what specific account the Actualist gives.

[49] I understand facts to be complex entities, each one consisting of the instantiation of some universal by some thing (in the case of a property) or things (in the case of a relation).

[50] For reasons that have to do with what I will say below about the passage of time, the propositions that I am identifying with abstract times will have to be maximal, consistent, *purely qualitative* propositions.

It might be objected that there is an undesirable consequence of what I have just said, namely that if history were cyclical, repeating itself every 100 years, say, then the time 100 years from now would be identical to the time 200 years from now. In general, it might be objected, the view about times I have endorsed entails that it is impossible for history to be cyclical without time's being closed.[51]

Here is my reply to this objection. On the view I am endorsing, 100 years from now there will be two items that deserve the name "the present time". One will be the concrete present time, i.e. the sum total of all facts then obtaining. The other will be the abstract present time, i.e. the maximal, consistent proposition that will then be true. The latter will be identical to the time 200 years from now, but the former will not.[52] So all that follows from the combination of the view about times I am endorsing with the assumption that history repeats itself every 100 years is that the thing that will be the abstract present time in 100 years is identical to the thing that will be the abstract present time in 200 years.

Here a small digression on the nature of possible worlds may be helpful. It is important to remember when talking about abstract possible worlds that they are not really *worlds*, in the robust sense of the word. They are not composed of stars and planets and flesh-and-blood beings (the way the concrete actual world is). They are not even composed of matter. They are just abstract objects that play a certain role in philosophers' talk about modality. They are ways things could be. That's why there are no two abstract possible worlds that are qualitatively identical. If w_1 is a way things could be, and w_2 is also a way things could be, and w_2 is just like w_1 in every detail, then w_2 is identical to w_1.

Similar remarks can be made about abstract times on the view I am endorsing. It is important to remember when talking about these abstract times that they are just abstract objects that play a certain role in philosophers' talk about temporal matters. They are ways things are, or

---

[51] For a detailed discussion of the possibility of history's being cyclical while time is closed, see Newton-Smith, *The Structure of Time*, pp. 57–78.

[52] Or at least, the view I am endorsing does not entail that, on our assumption about history's being cyclical, the concrete present time in 100 years will be identical to the concrete present time in 200 years. That's because the view does not entail that the objects existing in 100 years will be identical to their counterparts in 200 years, and hence the view also does not entail that the facts containing those objects as constituents will be identical.

have been, or will be. That's why there are no two abstract times that are qualitatively identical. If t_1 is a way things are, or have been, or will be, and t_2 is also a way things are, or have been, or will be, and t_2 is just like t_1 in every detail, then t_2 is identical to t_1.

For that reason, I don't find the relevant consequence of my view about times to be undesirable. In fact, I find it highly desirable. Of course, it *would* be a strike against it if the view entailed that the concrete present time that will obtain in 100 years was identical to the concrete present time that will obtain in 200 years (on the assumption of cyclical history, that is). For in that case, the view would come with an extra commitment—namely, the impossibility of cyclical history without closed time—that some philosophers would find undesirable. But as I have said, this is in fact not a consequence of the view.

Meanwhile, talk about the passage of time—the process by which times become less and less future, and then present, and then more and more past—can also be understood as talk about maximal, consistent propositions. For example, I have said that the time ten years from now can be identified with a certain maximal, consistent proposition. Call that proposition "T". T is false right now, but will be true ten years hence. In other words, the future-tensed proposition *that it will be the case in ten years that T* is true right now. In one year's time the future-tensed proposition *that it will be the case in nine years that T* will be true, and then a year later the future-tensed proposition *that it will be the case in eight years that T* will be true, and so on. To put the point a different way: T will go from instantiating *will-be-true-in-ten-years* to instantiating *will-be-true-in-nine-years* and then *will-be-true-in-eight-years*, and so on. And the process by which T goes from instantiating *will-be-true-in-ten-years* to instantiating *will-be-true-in-nine-years*, and so on, can be identified with the process by which that time—T—becomes less and less future. In a similar way, it will eventually recede further and further into the past. Thus, what appears to be talk about a non-present time's becoming less and less future can be understood as talk about a maximal, consistent proposition's instantiating a succession of properties like *will-be-true-in-ten-years*.

Here, then, is the sense in which there are some non-present times: there are some maximal, consistent propositions that will be true or have been true, but are not presently true. (This is analogous to the sense in which there are some non-actual worlds: there are some maximal, consistent propositions that are not actually true.)

And here is the sense in which there are no non-present times: there is only one concrete time, and it is the present time, i.e. the sum total of all present facts. (This is analogous to the sense in which there are no non-actual worlds: there is only one concrete world, and it is the actual world, i.e. the sum total of all actual facts.)

An Actualist who is also a Presentist (such as myself) can say that the concrete actual world is identical to the concrete present time. It is the sum total of all current facts. Similarly, such a person can say that the abstract actual world is identical to the abstract present time. It is the one maximal, consistent proposition that is actually and presently true.

Western Washington University

REFERENCES

Adams, Fred, and Stecker, Robert, "Vacuous Singular Terms", *Mind and Language*, 9 (1994), pp. 387–401.

Adams, Robert M., "Actualism and Possible Worlds", *Synthese*, 49 (1981), pp. 3–41.

Adams, Robert M., "Time and Thisness", in Peter A., French, Theodore E., Uehling, and Howard Wettstein (eds.), *Midwest Studies in Philosophy*, vol. XI (Minneapolis: University of Minnesota Press, 1986), pp. 315–29.

Augustine, *Confessions* (New York: Modern Library, 1949).

Bigelow, John, "Presentism and Properties", *Philosophical Perspectives*, 10 (1996), pp. 35–52.

Braun, David, "Empty Names", *Noûs*, 27 (1993), pp. 449–69.

Brogaard, Berit, "Presentist Four-Dimensionalism", *The Monist*, 83 (2000), 341–56.

Chisholm, Roderick M., *The First Person* (Minneapolis: University of Minnesota Press, 1981).

Chisholm, Roderick M., *On Metaphysics* (Minneapolis: University of Minnesota Press, 1989).

Chisholm, Roderick M., "Referring to Things that No Longer Exist", *Philosophical Perspectives*, 4 (1990), pp. 546–56.

Christensen, Ferrel M., *Space-Like Time* (Toronto: University of Toronto Press, 1993).

Emt, Jeanette, "On the Nature of Fictional Entities", in Jeanette Emt and Goran Hermerén (eds.), *Understanding the Arts: Contemporary Scandinavian Æsthetics* (Lund: Lund University Press, 1992), pp. 149–76.

Fine Kit, "Prior on the Construction of Possible Worlds and Instants", in Arthur N. Prior and Kit Fine, *Worlds, Times and Selves* (Amherst, MA: University of Massachusetts Press, 1977), pp. 116–61.

Fitch, Greg W., "Does Socrates Exist?", unpublished paper, 2002.

Fitch, Greg W., "Non Denoting", *Philosophical Perspectives*, 7 (1993), pp. 461–86.

Fitch, Greg W., "Singular Propositions in Time", *Philosophical Studies*, 73 (1994), pp. 181–7.

Forbes, Graeme, *The Metaphysics of Modality* (Oxford: Oxford University Press, 1983).

Frege, Gottlob, "On Sense and Meaning", in Peter Geach and Max Black (eds.), *Translations from the Philosophical Writings of Gottlob Frege*, 3rd edn (Totowa, NJ: Rowman & Littlefield, 1980), pp. 56–78.

Hinchliff, Mark, *A Defense of Presentism* (doctoral dissertation, Princeton University, 1988).

Hinchliff, Mark, "The Puzzle of Change", in James Tomberlin (ed.), *Philosophical Perspectives*, vol. 10, *Metaphysics* (Cambridge, MA: Blackwell, 1996), pp. 119–36.

Howell, Robert, "Fictional Objects: How They Are and How They Aren't", *Poetics*, 8 (1979), pp. 129–77.

Kaplan, David, "Demonstratives", in Joseph Almog, John Perry, and Howard Wettstein (eds.), *Themes from Kaplan* (New York: Oxford University Press, 1989), pp. 481–564.

Keller, Simon and Nelson, Michael, "Presentists Should Believe in Time Travel", *Australasian Journal of Philosophy*, 79 (2001), pp. 333–45.

Kripke, Saul, *Naming and Necessity* (Cambridge, MA: Harvard University Press, 1972).

Levinson, Jerrold, "Making Believe", *Dialogue*, 32 (1993), pp. 359–74.

Lewis, David, *On the Plurality of Worlds* (Oxford: Basil Blackwell, 1986).

Long, A. A., and Sedley, D. N., *The Hellenistic Philosophers*, vol. 1, *Translations of the Principal Sources with Philosophical Commentary* (Cambridge: Cambridge University Press, 1987).

Lucretius, *On the Nature of the Universe* (R. Latham, trans.) (Baltimore: Penguin Books, 1951).

Markosian, Ned, "On Language and the Passage of Time", *Philosophical Studies*, 66 (1992), pp. 1–26.

Markosian, Ned, "How Fast Does Time Pass?" *Philosophy and Phenomenological Research*, 53 (1993), pp. 829–44.

Markosian, Ned, "The 3D/4D Controversy and Non-present Objects", *Philosophical Papers*, 23 (1994), pp. 243–9.

Markosian, Ned, "What Are Physical Objects?" *Philosophy and Phenomenological Research*, 61 (2000), pp. 375–95.

Maxwell, Nicholas, "Are Probabilism and Special Relativity Incompatible?" *Philosophy of Science*, **52** (1985), pp. 23–43.

McCall, Storrs, *A Model of the Universe* (Oxford: Clarendon Press, 1994).

Merricks, Trenton, "On the Incompatibility of Enduring and Perduring Entities", *Mind*, **104** (1995), pp. 523–31.

Monton, Bradley, "Presentism and Spacetime Physics", unpublished paper, 2000.

Newton-Smith, W. H., *The Structure of Time* (London: Routledge & Kegan Paul, 1980).

Oppy, Graham, "The Philosophical Insignificance of Gödel's Slingshot", *Mind*, **106** (1997), pp. 121–41.

Plantinga, Alvin, *The Nature of Necessity* (Oxford: Oxford University Press, 1974).

Plantinga, Alvin, "Actualism and Possible Worlds", *Theoria*, **42** (1976); reprinted in Michael J. Loux (ed.), *The Possible and the Actual* (Ithaca, NY: Cornell University Press, 1979), pp. 253–73.

Prior, Arthur N., *Time and Modality* (Oxford: Oxford University Press, 1957).

Prior, Arthur N., *Past, Present and Future* (Oxford: Oxford University Press, 1967).

Prior, Arthur N., *Papers on Time and Tense* (Oxford: Oxford University Press, 1968).

Prior, Arthur N., "Changes in Events and Changes in Things", in Arthur N. Prior, *Papers on Time and Tense* (Oxford: Oxford University Press, 1968), pp. 1–14.

Prior, Arthur N., "The Notion of the Present", *Stadium Generale*, **23** (1970), pp. 245–8.

Prior, Arthur N., "Thank Goodness That's Over", in Arthur N. Prior, *Papers in Logic and Ethics* (London: Duckworth, 1976), pp. 78–84.

Prior, Arthur N., "Some Free Thinking about Time", in Jack Copeland (ed.), *Logic and Reality: Essays on the Legacy of Arthur Prior* (Oxford: Clarendon Press, 1996), pp. 47–51.

Prior, Arthur N., "A Statement of Temporal Realism", in Jack Copeland (ed.), *Logic and Reality: Essays on the Legacy of Arthur Prior* (Oxford: Clarendon Press, 1996), pp. 45–46.

Prior, Arthur N., and Fine, Kit, *Worlds, Times and Selves* (Amherst, MA: University of Massachusetts Press, 1977).

Putnam, Hilary, "Time and Physical Geometry", *Journal of Philosophy*, **64** (1967), pp. 240–7.

Quine, W. V., *Quiddities* (Cambridge, MA: Harvard University Press, 1987).

Salmon, Nathan, "Nonexistence", *Noûs*, **32** (1998), pp. 277–319.

Sextus Empiricus, *Against the Physicists*, vol. 3 (R. G. Bury, trans.) (Cambridge, MA: Harvard University Press, 1960).
Sider, Ted, "Presentism and Ontological Commitment", *Journal of Philosophy*, **96** (1999), pp. 325–47.
Sider, Ted, *Four-Dimensionalism: An Ontology of Persistence and Time* (Oxford: Clarendon Press, 2001).
Smith, Quentin, *Language and Time* (Oxford: Oxford University Press, 1993).
Smith, Quentin, "Reference to the Past and Future", in Q. Smith and A. Jokic (eds.), *Time, Tense and Reference* (Cambridge, MA: MIT Press, 2002).
Tooley, Michael, *Time, Tense, and Causation* (Oxford: Oxford University Press, 1997).
Van Inwagen, Peter, "Creatures of Fiction", *American Philosophical Quarterly*, **24** (1977), pp. 299–308.
Wolterstorff, Nicholas, "Can Ontology Do without Events?" in Ernest Sosa (ed.), *Essays on the Philosophy of Roderick Chisholm* (Amsterdam: Rodopi, 1979).
Zalta, Edward N., "On the Structural Similarities between Worlds and Times", *Philosophical Studies*, **51** (1987), pp. 213–39.
Zimmerman, Dean, "Persistence and Presentism", *Philosophical Papers*, **35** (1996), pp. 115–26.
Zimmerman, Dean, "Chisholm and the Essences of Events", in Lewis E. Hahn (ed.), *The Philosophy of Roderick M. Chisholm* (Chicago: Open-Court, 1997).

4. Presentism and Truthmaking
Simon Keller

1. A PROBLEM FOR PRESENTISM

Saint Augustine's boyhood teachers told him that there are three types of time: past, present, and future. Are we then to say, Augustine asks in his *Confessions*, that the past and future exist? At first, he thinks that they do. It seems, he says, that "when the present emerges from the future, time comes out of some secret store, and then recedes into some secret place when the past comes out of the present". If the past and future are in some secret place, then they must *exist* in that secret place. Further, Augustine says, we can remember the past and predict the future, and "to see that which has no existence is impossible".

Augustine soon changes his mind. Supposing, he says, that past and future things exist, they must, wherever they are, be present. For if they were past in some secret place, they would be there no longer, and if they were future in some secret place, they would not be there yet. The notion of a secret place for past and future things, Augustine concludes, is not very helpful. When we remember the past and predict the future, he now says, we are really making observations about the present. When we remember a past event, we are looking on its image in the present, and when we predict a future event, our prediciton is based upon things that are already present and can be seen. The only things that really exist, he concludes, are present things.[1]

Once Augustine has dispensed with the past and the future, it is difficult to see how a memory or a prediction could ever be *right*. What happens when a past event has differing images in the present—when people have different memories of the same event? Is it

---

I owe large debts to David Lewis and John Bigelow, who have greatly influenced my thinking about this material. Thanks also to Karen Bennett, Michael Fara, Josh Greene, John Hawthorne, Bradley Monton, Michael Nelson, Josh Parsons, Ed Zalta and Dean Zimmerman.

[1] Augustine (1991, bk XI, sects. 22–4).

84 | Simon Keller

possible to have a false memory? What is there to make it false? Could there be past events that no one remembers? Augustine seems to think that past- and future-tensed statements can have truth-values that are independent of what is going on in the present; he thinks, for example, that the prophets have a speical ability to make *correct* predictions. I think that Augustine never quite gets rid of the idea that the past and future are, in some sense, real, and I think that this problem can also be found among some of his philosophical descendants.

These days, those who agree with Augustine's conlusions about time call themselves *presentists*. Presentism is the belief that only present things exist. If something doesn't exist now, says the presentist, then it doesn't exist at all.[2] The most popular alternative to presentism says that past, present, and future things all exist; the universe, on this view, is a four-dimensional space–time manifold, containing everything that has happened, everything that is happening, and everything that will happen. This is a view that I will call *four-dimensionalism*.[3] (Note that this label is sometimes applied to a different view in the philosophy of time: namely, the view that objects have temporal parts—that they persist through time by perduring, rather than enduring.[4] This is not the view that I have in mind.) Four-dimensionalists believe that there are places at which past and future things exist, but that those places are not so secret. Past things exist in the past, and future things exist in the future. Saint Augustine exists in fourth-century Italy.[5]

---

[2] For some defenses of presentism, see Prior (1970), Geach (1972), Zimmerman (1998), Hinchliff (1996), and Bigelow (1996).

[3] For good descriptions of the four-dimensional view of time, see Smart (1966) and Williams (1968). I do not mean to suggest that presentism and four-dimensionalism are the only possible, or the only plausible, views about the nature of time. For one well worked-out alternative, see Tooley (1997).

[4] See e.g. Jackson (1998, p. 138). For the reasons why "four-dimensionalism" is a poor label for perdurantism, see J. Parsons (2000, pp. 399–400).

[5] A little more needs to be said about how presentism and four-dimensionalism come into conflict. It is natural to say that, where the four-dimensionalist believes that the world is four-dimensional, the presentist believes that it is three-dimensional. If presentism is just the claim that only present things exist, however, then the presentist need not be a three-dimensionalist. She could say that only present things exist, but some of those things are four-dimensional. All the things that exist exist presently, the claim would go, but some of them are not instantaneous—they extend into the past or future. Most presentists are in fact committed to three-dimensionalism, but it will be enough for my purposes to assume that there are at least some past or future things in the four-dimensionalist's ontology whose existence is denied by the presentist. Anne Boleyn can serve as an example; the four-dimensionalist, but not the presentist, believes that Anne Boleyn exists. (Thanks to Josh Parsons for clearing my thoughts on this question.)

In this paper, I will describe an ancient and powerful problem for presentism, and consider the ways in which the presentist might respond.[6] The problem is to say how there can be past- and future-tensed truths even though the past and future do not exist. I aim to show that the presentist can avoid the problem only if she endorses some very controversial metaphysical views. While the truthmaking problem (as I will call it) does not stand as a refutation of presentism, it does show that presentism comes at a price. Whether or not presentism is plausible depends upon whether or not that price is worth paying.

The truthmaking problem is best presented as a set of three claims. Two of them seem to be true, and the third is presentism. The problem for presentism is that it is difficult to see how the three claims could all be true together. To solve the problem, the presentist must either deny at least one of the first two claims, or explain how their truth does not force us to deny the third.

First claim: *What is true depends upon what exists.* If some true statement were false, or if some false statement were true, then there would have to be a difference in what things exist, or in what the existing things are like. I will call this claim *Truthmaker.*[7]

It is important to distinguish Truthmaker from the stronger thesis that for every truth there exists something that makes it true.[8]

---

[6] A version of the problem, the "argument from relations", is presented in Bigelow (1996, p. 38). Bigelow finds traces of the argument among the Stoics and Epicureans. For other recent discussions that mention some version of the truthmaking problem, see Adams (1989, pp. 32–3), Lewis (1999a, p. 207), and Lewis (this volume).

[7] I take the name "Truthmaker" from the helpful discussion in Bigelow (1988, pp. 121–34). Now Truthmaker, as it stands, may seem to be trivially true. "Propositions exist," we might say, "so of course it is true that if some proposition had a different truth-value then there would be a difference in what some existing thing is like." But Truthmaker is supposed to make a stronger claim than this. The idea is that there are no contingent truths that hang free of reality; the truth of any contingently true proposition is underwritten by certain existing things that are not themselves propositions. A better way of putting Truthmaker is as follows. *Truth is supervenient upon what things exist and which perfectly natural properties and relations they instantiate, where "things" do not include such things as propositions, and "perfectly natural properties and relations" do not include properties and relations that refer to such things as propositions.* (This is a modification of the formulation settled upon in Lewis 1999a, p. 207—see Lewis's discussion for a more extensive explanation of why this is the best way to express the claim.) From now on, when I talk about the ways in which things would have to be different in order for some contingent proposition to have a different truth-value, I am not talking about differences that exist only at the level of propositions themselves. (Thanks to Mike Fara for help with this question.)

[8] The stronger Truthmaker thesis is advocated in Armstrong 1997. For discussion of Truthmaker theses of various strengths see Lewis (1999a, pp. 196–214) and Lewis (1998).

This stronger thesis would serve just as well in an argument against presentism, but it is far more controversial. There may be some truths—negative existential truths, for example—for which it is not the case that there is some existing thing that makes the truth true.[9] But negative existentials do depend upon what exists in the way that the weaker Truthmaker thesis demands. There would have to be a difference in what exists in order for the proposition *Unicorns do not exist* to be false: unicorns would have to exist.

Other truths, however, cause trouble even for the weaker thesis. The obvious examples are truths about fictional entities—how would the existing world have to differ in order for *Sherlock Holmes lives on Baker Street* to be false?—and we could perhaps add mathematical, modal, and moral truths (although the truthmaking problem for necessary truths is not so easy to formulate). Nevertheless, Truthmaker is very plausible. It expresses an attractive philosophical picture according to which reality is made up of all and only the things that exist, and contingent propositions derive their truth or falsity from the relations in which they stand to the existing things.

(The nature of these relations, it must be admitted, is difficult to pin down, and it may be a little misleading to speak of "truth*making*"—as though the world is populated by a team of truthmakers working hard to cause propositions to change their truth-values. Really, the relations in question are explanatory; the truth of a proposition is somehow explained by a story about things that exist. One way to bring this out is to note that discharging the truthmaking burden with regard to some true proposition often involves pointing to an analytic connection between the proposition and some claim about the existing world. The following, for example, is surely analytic: if there is some existing thing that is identical to John and another that is identical to Mary, and if the first is such as to love the second, then the proposition *John loves Mary* is true. It would be nice to think that finding truthmakers for a proposition *always* involves finding such analytic connections, but there are reasons to be cautious here. First, there are negative existentials; *Unicorns do not exist* is not analytically implied by any claim about what *does* exist. Second, it might be wise to leave room for the possibility that the connection between a proposition and its truthmakers is sometimes synthetic, although still a priori. In any case, Truthmaker should be

---

[9] See Lewis (1999a, pp. 204–5).

regarded as a thesis about a certain mode of explanation, a thesis about what is involved in a proposition's being true.)

For many of us, it is hard to imagine that Truthmaker could be incorrect, regardless of how many headaches it causes. Sometimes it is difficult to explain how certain propositions that we normally regard as true could be made true by what we normally take to constitute the entirety of what exists. When metaphysicians notice such difficulties, however, they do not tend to reject Truthmaker. They are more likely to try to explain how the things that we normally take to exist really are enough to explain why the propositions are true, or to suggest that there are more existing things than we would otherwise have thought, or to argue that the apparent truths are not true after all.[10] Still, there are those who reject Truthmaker, and we will ask later whether this is an option that the presentist should take.

Second claim: *There are past- and future-tensed truths.* More precisely, there are past- and future-tensed truths that seem offhand to mention entities whose existence the presentist denies. It is true, for example, that Anne Boleyn was executed.

Third claim: *Only present things exist.*

I said that the first two claims, when taken together, pose a problem for presentism. But they certainly do not *imply* its falsity. After all, an exactly analogous set of claims could be constructed in order to pose a problem for the view that fictional characters do not exist—we just need Truthmaker, plus the truth that Sherlock Homes lives on Baker Street. The way to respond in that case would be to say that *Sherlock Holmes lives on Baker Street* is not strictly speaking a truth about Sherlock Holmes, who doesn't exist. Really, it's a truth about certain existing stories, or about existing thoughts in the mind of Arthur Conan Doyle, or something like that; and it's because of this that we can say that the truth of *Sherlock Holmes lives on Baker Street* supervenes upon what exists. It's not clear how the truthmaking story would go, but most of us feel sure that it can be accomplished without abandoning Truthmaker and without positing an existing Sherlock Holmes.[11]

---

[10] When it comes to talk of possible worlds, the first strategy is taken in Armstrong (1989) and Rosen (1990), and the second strategy is taken in Lewis (1986). With regard to moral talk, the third strategy is taken in Mackie (1977).

[11] As is pointed out in Bigelow (1996, p. 39). Note that many philosophers *are* prepared to posit existing fictional entities—see e.g. Van Inwagen (1977) and Salmon (1998).

Truths about fictional entities seem to depend upon what exists in the non-fictional world, but past- and future-tensed truths do not seem to depend upon existence in the present. It seems as though the present could be just as it is, without the past- and future-tensed truths being just as they are. Most would agree, for example, that there is nothing about the present world, considered in itself, that rules out the possibility that the world sprung into existence five minutes ago, or that someone combed his hair with his left rather than his right hand on a particular morning last century. So the reason why there is a problem for presentism is that it looks at first as though presently existing things and their properties are not enough to ground past- and future-tensed truths.

Three broad responses are available to the presentist. One is to deny that any past- or future-tensed statements are true. With regard to future-tensed statements, the claim in question might not be so crazy; Aristotle suggests that statements about the future are neither true nor false, because the events that would ground their truth or falsity are yet to come into existence.[12] The corresponding claim about past-tensed truths, however, is highly implausible—Anne Boleyn *was* executed[13]— and I cannot see how the presentist could make it attractive.[14]

---

[12] Aristotle, *De Interpretatione*, ch. 9. See also Tooley (1997).
[13] See e.g. Hibbert (1992, p. 18).
[14] Well, there might be a more principled way of defending the claim that there are fewer past-tensed truths than we might previously have thought. In Prior (1960) and Adams (1989), it is argued that not-yet-existing individuals are not available to be the constituents of propositions, which is to say that there are no true singular propositions about not-yet-existing individuals—it was not true in 1066 that Anne Boleyn would be executed in 1536. Perhaps, then, we could treat no-longer-existing individuals in just the same way, saying that, because Anne Boleyn does not exist now, there are no singular propositions about her (and hence none that is true). This view, however, has the fatal feature of implying that it is not true that Anne Boleyn was executed. (Adams makes this point himself on p. 29, saying that what can plausibly be said about the future cannot plausibly be said about the past.) Now, it might be thought that this feature is not really so fatal, because we can get almost all that we want in the way of past-tensed truth from tensed propositions that involve definite descriptions, rather than from past individuals themselves. While there are no singular propositions about Anne, we could say, it is true that someone who was married to the king, gave birth to a daughter, was called "Anne", ..., was executed. Supposing, however, that there are properties that were once instantiated but are instantiated no more, and that there are no uninstantiated properties, the presentist will run into difficulties in constructing the required definite descriptions— some of the properties that she needs do not, on her view, exist. For further discussion of this general line of thought, see Section 3 below.

A second option is to deny Truthmaker, either by denying that the things upon which past- and future-tensed truth supervenes *exist*, or by denying that past- and future-tensed truth supervenes upon anything. This is an initially tempting strategy, but I will explain why I don't think that either form of Truthmaker-denying presentism (as I shall call it) is acceptable.

Finally, the presentist can be a Truthmaker-preserving presentist, accepting Truthmaker while denying that we need non-present things to ground past- and future-tensed truths. This form of presentism is the most promising, and I will explore two ways in which it might be developed.

2. TRUTHMAKER-DENYING PRESENTISM

2.1 "There are things that don't exist!"

There are, as I say, two ways in which the presentist might try to deny Truthmaker. She can deny Truthmaker either by saying that the things upon which past- and future-tensed truth supervene do not exist, or by saying that past- and future-tensed truth does not supervene upon anything. I'll begin by considering the first of these views, a view that I will call Meinongian presentism.[15] It is an odd view, and it probably represents the less obvious form of Truthmaker-denying presentism, but it is a good place to start.

The Meinongian presentist maintains her presentism by making a very simple move. She accepts that there are non-present things upon which truth supervenes, but denies that they exist. She has no trouble explaining how there can be past- and future-tensed truths; she has all the truthmaking resources of the four-dimensionalist. There are past things, says the Meinongian presentist, but they no longer exist, and there are future things, but they do not exist yet. *Anne Boleyn was executed* is true, says the Meinongian, because Anne Boleyn has the property of having been executed, even though she does not have the property of existing.

---

[15] Named after Alexius Meinong, who is credited with founding the doctrine of non-existent objects. The best recent exposition of the doctrine is in T. Parsons (1980). For a defense of Meinongian *presentism*, see Hinchliff (1988).

There are, however, good reasons to reject a view that relies upon non-existent entities. First, we might find it hard to make sense of the idea of objects that do not exist, but nevertheless *are*.[16] Second, and this is the objection that I'll take up first, we might worry that, once we have admitted non-existent objects into our ontology, existence—and presentism—cease to be very interesting.

What do the Meinongian presentist and the four-dimensionalist disagree about? They agree that Anne Boleyn was executed, and that this is made true by Anne Boleyn, a sword, a swordsman specially brought over from France, and the relations in which those things stand. They agree that Anne stands in a certain relation to the Tower of London, and that this is the same Tower that exists now. Their theories, in fact, are exactly the same, except for the four-dimensionalist's insistence that all those past and future things *exist*.

This general objection can be put another way.[17] If the only difference between what exists and what does not is in a label, then why should we think that *we* are present and existing, while Anne Boleyn is non-present and non-existing? Anne, like us, has all sorts of properties and stands in all sorts of relations to the things around her, and she, like us, thinks that she exists. Who's to say that she is wrong and we are right? And why should we care? If Anne Boleyn were present instead of us, then I would be doing whatever I am doing, and you would be reading this paper. We wouldn't exist, but so what?

At this point, the Meinongian presentist might complain that I am willfully refusing to understand the significance of existence. I say that there is nothing to choose between two theories that agree on what there is while disagreeing about which of those things exist. The Meinongian presentist replies that we all know what existence means, and we all care about what exists and what doesn't, and that's enough to show that the two theories are interestingly different.

Do we have a robust pre-theoretical conception of what it means for something to exist? I think that we do. My own robust conception of existence, however, cannot cope with the notion that there is an X—there *really is* an X—and it has properties—it *really has* properties—but it doesn't exist. Once the presentist commits herself to such

---

[16] If W. V. Quine's views on how to do ontology are correct, then the Meinongian presentist, as someone who quantifies over non-present entities, is not a presentist at all. See Quine (1953, p. 13).

[17] See Williams (1962, p. 752).

things, she loses her right to call upon our unanalyzed conception of existence. That is not to say that philosophers are not allowed to posit non-existent entities, but it is to say that when they do they owe us an explanation of what, apart from a label, sets the existent apart from the non-existent.

There is no real difference between Meinongian presentism and four-dimensionalism. Either we restrict our use of "exists" to present things, adopt an ontology of non-existent objects and call ourselves presentists, or we accept that all these things exist and call ourselves four-dimensionalists. If it's just a battle of linguistic convenience, then the one who posits non-existent objects is going to have a lot of trouble persuading us to adopt her way of speaking. And when it comes to metaphysics, it doesn't really matter.

2.2 "Truth does not supervene upon anything!"

A better way to deny Truthmaker, perhaps, is to say that the truths that are purported to create trouble for presentism are not made true by anything. *Anne Boleyn was executed,* on this view, is just plain true, and we don't need anything, existing or not, to underlie its truth. We might motivate such a move by pointing to all the other truths for which the truthmaking problem arises. If it's so difficult to say what underlies truths about fictional objects and the rest, we might say, then that's a reason to think that the truthmaking impulse should be resisted.[18] This refusal to worry about truthmaking is not unprincipled, but I do not think that it can be sustained. The problem, put briefly, is that it is entirely implausible to say that present-tensed truth does not supervene upon something, and once this is conceded it becomes difficult to produce a respectable reason why past- and future-tensed truth should not supervene upon something as well. That's what the following comments are intended to show.

Start with a present-tense truth: *The Tower of London is on the Thames.* This is a truth about the Tower of London and the Thames, two things that exist and are next to each other. If either the Tower or the Thames did not exist, or if they were not next to each other, then *The Tower is on the Thames* would be false. So there's one proposition

---

[18] I do not know of anyone who has defended this view in print, but it often comes up in conversation.

whose truth depends upon certain things' existing and exhibiting certain characteristics. Now consider a past-tensed truth about those same things: *The Tower of London was on the Thames*. That too is a truth about the existing Tower and the existing Thames, and it's true because those very things *were* next to each other; if either the Tower or the Thames had never existed, or if they had never been next to each other, then *The Tower was on the Thames* would be false.

Next, *Anne Boleyn spent time at the Tower*. Here we have another truth about the existing Tower, and another truth that seems to report a relation that holds between the Tower and something else—not an existing Anne, perhaps, but definitely *something*. And if the Tower had never existed, or if the Anne-like thing was not such as to make it the case that Anne spent time at the Tower, then *Anne Boleyn spent time at the Tower* would not be true. But now we have an Anne-like thing, and surely that is the very thing about which *Anne Boleyn was executed* is a truth. If the Anne-like thing were different in certain respects, then it would not be true that Anne was executed. So the truth of *Anne Boleyn was executed* does, after all, depend upon a certain thing's being a certain way.

Can the presentist depart from this line of thought? There are two points at which it seems vulnerable. The first is in the claim that, if *The Tower is on the Thames* is made true by two existing things and the relation in which they stand, then the same must be the case for *The Tower was on the Thames*. The presentist might say that *The Tower was on the Thames* is true because there *were* two things that stood in a certain relation. It happens that both of those things still exist, but that is not at all to say that we need presently existing things to be a certain way in order for *The Tower was on the Thames* to be true.

This response, however, entails implausible claims about the nature of propositions. *The Tower was on the Thames*, the presentist agrees, is a relational truth, in that it posits a relation that either does or did exist. Normally, we would think that a proposition is a relational proposition because it has constituents that stand, or are claimed by the proposition to stand, in some relation. Our Truthmaker-denying presentist, however, cannot endorse this view. To do so would be to accept that *The Tower was on the Thames* has constituents and that a certain relation holds between those constituents, and that's to say that the proposition's truth does after all depend upon there being things that stand in a certain relation. (It's not enough to say that the proposition's constituents *did* exist and *did* stand in a certain relation, because that would only show that the proposition *did* exist. *The Tower was on the Thames* is true *now*.) And if the presentist rejects the idea that propositions have constituents, then how is she to account for the fact that *The Tower was on the Thames* is a relational truth but *The Tower was a tower* is not?[19]

Another way in which the presentist might resist the argument is to deny the claim that, if *The Tower was on the Thames* reports a relation between two things, then *Anne spent time at the Tower* must do so as well. The presentist, as someone who doesn't believe that Anne exists, perhaps has a reason for saying that any truth that seems to say something about Anne cannot really be saying something about anything, and hence that there is nothing that has to be a certain way in order for propositions that seem to mention Anne to be true. To make this claim, however, is to say that the question of how a sentence should be analyzed sometimes depends upon contingent questions about what exists. Suppose that we are unsure about whether or not the Tower was destroyed in last night's earthquake. If the view in question is correct, then we should also be unsure about whether or not *The Tower was on the Thames* is a relational truth (although we could be sure that the statement is true). Whether *The Tower was on the Thames* reports a relation between two things, on this view, depends upon whether the Tower still exists. And that just seems absurd.

Perhaps the presentist should respond to such arguments by positing presently existing surrogates for non-present entities. *The Tower was on the Thames* can be a proposition that has constituents, runs the thought, without those constituents having to be the Thames and the Tower. And the reason why the proposition is a relational proposition, we could add, is that it posits a relation between two present surrogates for the Tower and the Thames. This strategy is best discussed in the next section, on Truthmaker-preserving presentism.

---

[19] There are probably things that the presentist could say here. Perhaps there is just a brute difference between relational and non-relational past- and future-tensed truths, or perhaps the difference is merely syntactic. We would never make such claims about the difference between relational and non-relational present-tensed truths, however, so these responses appear to be somewhat desperate.

3. TRUTHMAKER-PRESERVING PRESENTISM

3.1 Tensed properties of present things

Truthmaker-preserving presentism accepts Truthmaker while saying that past- and future-tensed truth does not supervene upon non-present being. Earlier, I said that the truthmaking problem is a special problem for presentism because truths about the past and future look at first glance to be underdetermined by truths about the present. The present world could be just as it is, it seems, even if the past- and future-tensed truths were very different. But perhaps the presentist can disagree. Perhaps she can say that the present world does the truthmaking for past- and future-tensed truths.

A version of Truthmaker-preserving presentism is sketched by John Bigelow. The present world, Bigelow says, has many, many past- and future-tensed properties, and these properties are what underlie past- and future-tensed truth. Where four-dimensionalists accept the existence of every past, present, and future individual, Bigelow writes, "presentism trades off this ontological expenditure against a lavish outlay on properties of present individuals".[20] A similar sort of proposal is presented by Roderick M. Chisholm, who speaks not of tensed world properties, but of the past- and future-oriented properties of eternal entities (where an example of an eternal entity is the property of redness).[21]

If the presentist is to claim that tensed properties of present things do the truthmaking for past- and future-tensed truths, then she must see present things as having *fundamental* tensed properties, by which I mean properties that are not to be explained by reference to anything else (like other individuals or other, more fundamental, properties). After all, the four-dimensionalist will agree that the present world has the property of being a world in which Anne Boleyn was executed, but will say that that property is grounded in the properties of the world as it is at another time, namely, the time at which Anne Boleyn is being executed. What is distinctive about the presentist view is the claim that the tensed properties of present things are not to be explained by way of the properties of past or future individuals. Only the presentist says that

---

[20] Bigelow (1996, p. 47).
[21] Chisholm (1990). As far as I can tell, the Bigelow and Chisholm strategies have much the same virtues, and run into much the same problems.

the present world could not be just as it is and yet have a different past or future.[22]

The commitment to past- and future-tensed properties, as Bigelow says, is lavish, and it looks especially lavish when we consider those fundamental properties, if there are any, that have been or will be instantiated but are not instantiated presently.[23] Suppose that there is some property P that is not instantiated by anything now, but will be instantiated by some future individual. Our presentist needs the future-tensed version of P, so she must say either that past- and future-tensed properties can exist even when their present-tensed correlates do not, or that properties like P can exist even when uninstantiated.

Further, the presentist must take care of the fact that non-present instantiations of properties are not just in the past or future, but are at particular moments in the past or future. It's not enough to say that this world is one in which Anne Boleyn was executed: we have to be able to say that it's a world in which Anne was executed at around midday on the 19th of May, 1536. One way for the presentist to deal with such questions is to commit herself to an even greater abundance of properties, properties that encode facts about the times at which relevant events did or will occur; then, the property of having been Q at midday last Thursday is one fundamental property, and the property of having been Q at 1 pm last Thursday is another. Depending on her views about certain other matters, the presentist may have other options available. She might think that she can get the facts about the times at which properties are instantiated just by positing further facts about which properties are instantiated before and after which others.[24] Or she might posit presently existing surrogates for non-present moments, so that a relation can hold between a present individual, a past- or future-tensed property, and a surrogate for a past or future time.

---

[22] Bigelow does not speak of "fundamental" world properties, but they seem to be what he has in mind when he speaks of "the property of being burdened with a certain sort of past, or (as Leibniz put it) being pregnant with a certain sort of future" (Bigelow 1996, p. 47). The relevant burdens and pregnancies are not thought to be grounded in any non-present things.

[23] As Lewis points out, there may be some fundamental properties that were had by individuals early in the history of the universe, but are had by no individuals now; see Lewis (this volume, pp. 8–9).

[24] See Chisholm (1990). Chisholm's proposal is complicated, but the thought, put roughly, is that events, plus the facts about which events are parts of other events, plus the relations in which events stand to eternally existing entities, are enough to make it the case that events occur at particular times.

96 | Simon Keller

In any case, in positing her past- and future-tensed properties, the presentist is taking on commitments that some will find unpalatable. But another important question remains: to which present individuals are these properties attached?

Past- and future-tensed truths, as we saw earlier, have structure, and it is hence not enough for the Truthmaker-preserving presentist simply to posit an abundance of past- and future-tensed world properties. The property of being a world in which Anne was executed, for example, cannot be just a bare property of the world, but must involve the attribution of a property-like thing to an Anne-like thing.[25] I want to consider two stories that the presentist might tell here. I am sure that they are not the only stories that could be told, but their telling will make clear the moral for Truthmaker-preserving presentism.

3.2 Haecceitist presentism

Let me explain how I will use some terms. An individual's *thisness* is its property of being just that individual. Your thisness is a property of you, and of nothing else. The nature of thisnesses is controversial, but one view is that thisnesses are primitive—that they are elements of reality that cannot be reduced to anything more fundamental.[26] Can an individual's thisness exist without the existence of the individual itself? To put it another way, are there uninstantiated thisnesses? If there are, then thisnesses are *haecceities*.[27]

If there are haecceities, then the presentist can suppose that, although there exist no nonpresent individuals, there exist the haecceities of nonpresent individuals. And if thisnesses are primitive—if they are not constructed out of qualitative properties or "suchnesses"—then the presentist can use them to give the right sort of structure to past- and

---

[25] It's not clear what Bigelow and Chisholm would say here. Bigelow speaks of the presentist's investment in the properties of present *individuals* (Bigelow 1996, p. 47), but at another point says that he prefers the language of *world* properties (Bigelow 1996, p. 46).

[26] Another view, associated with Leibniz, is that to have a thisness is to have all the qualitative properties in some large, maximally consistent set, so that to be Anne Boleyn is to marry the king, to give birth to a daughter, to be executed in 1536, to be called "Anne Boleyn", to not have a tail, and so on and on. This Leibnizian view is probably more compatible with what I call atomic presentism—the view that I discuss in section 3.3.

[27] A clear description of the debate about the nature of thisness is given in Adams (1979, pp. 5–10). I am following Adams's terminology. On the conditions for something's being a qualitative property (or a "suchness"), see Adams (1979, pp. 7–9).

future-tensed properties. Here's how a haecceitist presentist might try to account for the truth of *Anne Boleyn was executed in 1536*.

Among the haecceities that presently exist, the presentist can say, are the thisnesses of Anne Boleyn, of the sword with which Anne was executed, and of the swordsman who was specially brought over from France. These properties themselves, says the presentist, instantiate a relation that somehow mirrors the relation that the four-dimensionalist claims to be instantiated by Anne, the sword, and the swordsman. When it comes to making sure that the execution occurred in 1536, rather than at some other time, the presentist might treat times as individuals that themselves have haecceities, and say that the pertinent relation actually holds between the haecceities of Anne, the sword, the swordsman, *and* the property of being a time at around midday on the 19th of May, 1536.[28]

Why do I say that the haecceitist presentist posits a relation between haecceities that "somehow mirrors" the relation that the four-dimensionalist believes to hold between individuals? Because the presentist and the four-dimensionalist cannot be positing exactly the same relation. Where the four-dimensionalist has a relation between individuals, the presentist has a relation between properties—you can execute a person, but you can't execute a property. To take a simpler example, the entities that underlie the truth of *Anne was sophisticated* cannot be just Anne's haecceity and the property of sophisticatedness. Rather, the presentist says that there exists the property of sophisticatedness—a property that can be instantiated by present persons—and there also exists a different property—call it sophisticatedness*—that can be instantiated by thisnesses. Sophisticatedness* is of such a nature that, if it is instantiated by the haecceity of some individual, then it is true that, when that haecceity was or will be itself instantiated, the mentioned individual was or will be sophisticated. Anne's thisness is sophisticated*, and that's enough to make it true that Anne, when she existed, was sophisticated.[29]

---

[28] Or, if she prefers, she could adopt one of the other two strategies suggested a few paragraphs back.

[29] Some further complications. First, the presentist will have to make sure that Anne's hacceity's being sophisticated* has some connection with certain times in the sixteenth century; depending on the time-indexing strategy that she favors, the presentist might want to say that Anne's haecceity is [sophisticated at certain times in the sixteenth century]*. Second, for the sake of consistency, the presentist could add that all instantiations of properties by individuals are mirrored by instantiations of properties by

There are two objections to haecceitist presentism worth mentioning here. The first is obvious: the view posits the existence of strange, unappealing entities that have strange, inelegant properties. I think that the only way for the haecceitist presentist to respond is to try to show that the positing of such entities is a sacrifice worth making—more on this later. The second objection, if successful, strikes more deeply. In committing herself to the existence of haecceities, runs the objection, the presentist is trying to pull much the same trick as was attempted by the Meinongian presentist. Like the Meinongian, the haecceitist is positing one entity for each of the four-dimensionalist's entities, and using them as truthmakers in much the same way. The Meinongian presentist turned out to be a four-dimensionalist with a funny way of speaking. Can the haecceitist presentist really do any better?

I think that she can. First, she can express her presentism in terms that we all can understand; she says not only that no non-present things exist, but that *there are* no non-present things. Second, the haecceitist presentist can say that the entities to which she is committed are of an importantly different type from the corresponding entities that appear in the four-dimensionalist's ontology. When the four-dimensionalist talks about Anne Boleyn, he is talking about a person—a concrete thing—but when the presentist talks about Anne Boleyn, she is talking about a property—an abstract thing.

As David Lewis emphasizes, the presentist still faces the question of what the difference between abstract and concrete entities really comes down to.[30] The correct answer, I think, is that the entities postulated by the presentist count as abstract, rather than concrete, because they are not spatially located; they exist now, but not in any particular place. But how can the presentist say that her entities are not located at non-present times, and are not spatially located at all, when she is committed to the truth of propositions like *Anne Boleyn was executed at the Tower of London in 1536*? Anne was in London in 1536—doesn't this give her location away?

No, the presentist can respond, because what underlies the truth of that statement is not Anne, but her haecceity. Anne's thisness is not

haecceities; if you are presently sophisticated, then your haecceity is sophisticated*. Furthermore, we might add, your haecceity exists*, but Anne Boleyn's doesn't (although it did). Obviously, there are further details to be worked out here.

[30] Lewis (this volume, pp. 9–11).

spatially located and is not in the past. It does, however, stand in relations to certain other thisnesses, and these relations are such as to make it the case that on the 19th of May, 1536, Anne did exist—her thisness was instantiated—and she was to be found at the Tower of London. This sounds very odd, and the objector may reject it as fantastical. Fair enough, but by now the objector is saying not that the presentist is just a four-dimensionalist in disguise, but that it is very difficult to believe that there could be the things that the haecceitist presentist postulates. And that has already been conceded.

3.3 Atomic presentism

I now want to outline a second strategy that the Truthmaker-preserving presentist might employ. Suppose that the world is made up of a number of particles, and that all the contingent truths about the present world supervene upon the way in which those particles are presently arranged and the fundamental properties that they presently instantiate.[31] *The Tower is on the Thames* is true, on this account, because there are certain particles that bear such properties and are arranged in such a way as to constitute the Tower, and there are a number of particles that bear such properties and are arranged in such a way as to constitute the Thames, and these two collections of particles stand in a relation that suffices for the Tower's being next to the Thames.

Next, suppose that each of the particles that make up the world has always existed and always will exist. Finally, suppose that these particles carry their pasts and futures around with them, which is to say that each particle bears fundamental past- and future-tensed properties that give away the facts about where they have come from and where they are

---

[31] It's easiest to imagine such particles as being very, very small, but it might be possible to pursue this strategy by postulating any sorts of eternally enduring particulars which together constitute the entire world. There could, conceivably, be just one such particular—space, perhaps, or God, or the world itself. For reasons that should become clear from my discussion, however, I think that the presentist would have to say not only that the world consists in one eternally enduring particular, but that all the parts of that particular are also eternally enduring—in which case we are back where we started. Note also that there is no need for the atomic presentist to claim that everything in the world just *is* a collection of particles. It's consistent with the view say that a person, for example, cannot be identical with a collection of particles, although a person can exist only if there exists a collection of particles bearing certain properties and arranged in a certain way. Finally, note that there is nothing in the view that claims that all of the particles in the world are *physical* particles.

going. No particle could be just like another, according to the theory, unless it had just the same history and just the same future. It is, on this view, a brute fact about any given particle that it was in a certain place and instantiated certain properties in 1536, and it is a brute fact about the particle that it will be in a certain place and will instantiate certain properties in 2036. These are said to be *brute* facts because they are not to be explained in terms of any more basic facts—facts about what is happening in 1536 or 2036, for example. Terms like "was" and "will be", then, are taken as primitively understood.[32]

How does all of this help the presentist to account for past- and future-tensed truth? Well, there is, according to atomic presentism, no need for non-present things to tell us what the world was like in 1536 or what it will be like in 2036, because the information is all encoded in the past- and future-tensed properties of presently existing atoms. The fundamental past-tensed properties of present particles are enough to make it the case that the particles had certain properties and were arranged in a certain way in 1536, and that is enough to make it the case that Anne Boleyn was executed at the Tower in 1536. Given the properties of the things that make up the present world, says the atomic presentist, there's no other way that things could have been, and that's why the world has the property of being a world in which Anne was executed.

Atomic presentism does not posit haeccaeties, but it does commit its own form of ontological extravagance. If atomic presentism is correct, then the things that we find around us have many more fundamental properties than we would normally suspect. Things that we would normally think to be duplicates of each other turn out not to be, because they do not have the same history and future.

Further, the atomic presentist is committed to the claim that there exist eternal elemental particles that constitute the world at every point in its history. As a claim about the actual world, this is ambitious, but not entirely implausible. Consider, however, the following claim. If X is

---

[32] We had to add extra details to the haecceitist's story in order to account for the fact that events do not just happen, but happen at times, and a similar move is required of the atomic presentist (as I will call her). She might say, for example, that the various past- and future-tensed instantiations of properties by particles stand in (perhaps quasi-) temporal relations, so that it can be true of some particle that it was in place P and of nature X *before* it was in place Q and of nature Y. Then, it can be claimed that the facts about the times at which events happen supervene upon the facts about which events happen before and after which other events, and which events are simultaneous with which others.

presently P, then it will be the case at every future time that X was P. That's true, and seems indeed to be necessarily true; it does not seem possible, for example, that Elizabeth II is Queen now and yet there is a future time at which it will not be the case that Elizabeth II was Queen. But if atomic presentism is correct, then what underlie the truth of *X was P* at future times are the existence and tensed properties of the very same particles that presently underlie the truth of *X is P*. So, if it's necessary that, if X is presently P then it will always be true that X was P, then it's necessary that each of the world's presently existing particles will exist at all future times. The atomic presentist must take it to be a necessary truth that the world is made up of eternally existing particles.

That is not a happy result. Normally, we would think it quite possible that matter could be destroyed, that some fundamental constituent of being could suddenly drop out of existence.[33] And we do not normally think that if a bundle of matter were to be utterly destroyed then a number of past-tensed truths would go along with it. The atomic presentist, however, must either deny the possibility of particles whose lives are not coextensive with the life of the world, or deny that the truths about what is happening now make it necessary that certain past-tensed truths will hold at all future times. If this is not a devastating dilemma, then it is certainly embarrassing.

3.4 Evaluating Truthmaker-preserving presentism

I've tried to show that Truthmaker-preserving presentism is the only viable form of presentism, and I've sketched two ways in which the view might be developed. Each version of the view involves troublesome commitments, but neither is utterly implausible. There are probably other ways in which the presentist might try to describe the present world in such a way as to ground past- and future-tensed truth, but I think that our examination of those two theories has been enough to show that any form of Truthmaker-preserving presentism will come at a high cost. If the Truthmaker-preserving presentist doesn't posit uninstantiated haecceities or fundamental tensed properties, and if she

---

[33] An exactly analogous problem, of course, arises with regard to the possibility that particles could suddenly pop into existence. We'd normally think it to be a necessary truth that, if X is presently P, then it was the case at all past times that X will be P. But if the particles that make for X's being P came into existence only last year, then it was not true until last year that X will be P.

doesn't make surprising claims about what is and isn't possible, then she will surely take upon herself some other undesirable commitments.

The truthmaking problem does not refute presentism, but it does leave the presentist with the twin burdens of choosing an account of what underlies past- and future-tensed truths and of showing that it is worth making the unattractive commitments that such an account will inevitably involve. I will not try to address the question of whether presentism has benefits that outweigh the costs associated with responding to the truthmaking problem, but I do want to close by considering a possible advantage of presentism that arises naturally from the issues addressed in this paper.

I said earlier that the truthmaking problem is a little different when it comes to the question of what underlies necessary truths. The point is that it does not make sense to ask what things would have had to have been like in order for some necessary truth to fail to be true, so if there is to be a truthmaking problem here then we will have to find some other way to formulate Truthmaker. Still, truthmaking concerns do arise for necessary truths in one form or another, as is evidenced by the philosophical debates over what sorts of ontological commitment are required in order to account for moral, mathematical, and modal truths, and it is with regard to the truthmaking problem for modal truths that the presentist may be on stronger ground than her four-dimensionalist rival.

Suppose, as many do, that it is difficult to account for what is possible using only those things that are actual, and suppose, as many do, that realism about possible objects is too high a price to pay to secure the truths of modality. It may be that the only way to navigate between these two suppositions is to posit actually existing surrogates for merely possible objects—perhaps the uninstantiated haecceities of things that never actually exist, or perhaps the irreducibly modal properties of the things that do. If this is right, then the presentist's commitments may no longer seem so unattractive; placed next to the commitments that are required to solve the truthmaking problem for modality, they are relatively benign. Then, the truthmaking problem might not seem like such a problem. Whether the debate about modality ever gets to this point, however, is another question entirely.

Boston University

REFERENCES

Adams, Robert Merrihew (1979) 'Primitive Thisness and Primitive Identity', *Journal of Philosophy* 76:1, 5–26.

Adams, Robert Merrihew (1989) 'Time and Thisness', in Joseph Almog, John Perry, and Howard Wettstein (eds.), *Themes from Kaplan* (Oxford: Oxford University Press), 23–42.

Aristotle, *De Interpretatione*.

Armstrong, D. M. (1989) *A Combinatorial Theory of Possibility* (Cambridge University Press).

Armstrong, D. M. (1997) *A World of States of Affairs* (Cambridge University Press).

Augustine (1991) *Confessions*, trans. Henry Chadwick (Oxford University Press).

Bigelow, John (1988) *The Reality of Numbers* (Oxford University Press).

Bigelow, John (1996) 'Presentism and Properties', in James E. Tomberlin (ed.), *Philosophical Perspectives*, 10 (Cambridge, MA: Blackwell), 35–52.

Chisholm, Roderick M. (1990) 'Events without Times: An Essay on Ontology', *Nous*, 24, 413–28.

Geach, P. T. (1972) 'Some Problems about Time', in P. T. Geach, *Logic Matters* (University of California Press), 302–18.

Hibbert, Christopher (1992) *The Virgin Queen: The Personal History of Elizabeth I* (London: Penguin Books).

Hinchliff, Mark (1988) *A Defense of Presentism*, dissertation, Princeton University (available from University Microfilms).

Hinchliff, Mark (1996) 'The Puzzle of Change', in James E. Tomberlin (ed.), *Philosophical Perspectives*, 10 (Cambridge, MA: Blackwell), 119–36.

Jackson, Frank (1998) 'Metaphysics by Possible Cases', in Frank Jackson, *Mind, Method and Conditionals* (London: Routledge).

Lewis, David (1986) *On the Plurality of Worlds* (New York: Basil Blackwell).

Lewis, David (1998) 'Truthmaking and Difference-making', paper presented at the meeting of the Australasian Association of Philosophy, July.

Lewis, David (1999a) 'Armstrong on Combinatorial Possibility', in David Lewis, *Papers in Metaphysics and Epistemology* (Cambridge University Press), 196–214.

Mackie, J. L. (1977) *Ethics: Inventing Right and Wrong* (London: Penguin Books).

Parsons, Josh (2000) 'Must a Four-Dimensionalist Believe in Temporal Parts?' *The Monist*, 83:3, 399–418.

Parsons, Terence (1980) *Non-existent Objects* (New Haven: Yale University Press).

Prior, A. N. (1960) 'Identifiable Individuals', *Review of Metaphysics*, 13, 684–96.
Prior, A. N. (1970) 'The Notion of the Present', *Studium Generale*, 23, 245–48.
Quine, W. V. (1953) 'On What There Is', in W. V. Quine, *From a Logical Point of View* (Harvard University Press), 1–19.
Rosen, Gideon (1990) 'Modal Fictionalism', *Mind*, 99, 327–54.
Salmon, Nathan (1998) 'Nonexistence', *Nous*, 32, 277–319.
Smart, J. J. C. (1966) 'The River of Time', in A. Flew (ed.), *Essays in Conceptual Analysis* (London: Macmillan), 213–27.
Tooley, Michael (1997) *Time, Tense and Causation* (Oxford: Clarendon Press).
Van Inwagen, Peter (1977) 'Creatures of Fiction', *American Philosophical Quarterly*, 24, 299–308.
Williams, Donald C. (1962) 'Dispensing with Existence', *Journal of Philosophy*, 59, 748–63.
Williams, Donald C. (1968) 'The Myth of Passage', in R. M. Gale (ed.), *The Philosophy of Time* (London: Macmillan), 98–116.
Zimmerman, Dean W. (1998) 'Temporary Intrinsics and Presentism', in Peter Van Inwagen and Dean W. Zimmerman (eds.), *Metaphysics: The Big Questions* (Malden, MA: Blackwell) 206–19.

Part II

UNIVERSALS

5. A Theory of Properties

Peter van Inwagen

1. IT WOULD BE BETTER NOT TO BELIEVE IN ABSTRACT OBJECTS IF WE COULD GET AWAY WITH IT

In their book *A Subject without an Object: Strategies for the Nominalistic Interpretation of Mathematics*[1] (the main topic of the book is well conveyed by its subtitle), John Burgess and Gideon Rosen suggest that—in fact, they argue at some length for the conclusion that—the motivation for undertaking nominalistic reconstructions of mathematics has not been clearly and persuasively formulated.[2] This seems to me to be wrong. At any rate, it seems to me that it is not hard to formulate the motivation (or a sufficient motivation) for this project clearly and persuasively. Suppose one could show this: it would be better not to believe in abstract objects if one could get away with it. Or this, if it is not the same: it would be philosophically desirable to accept only philosophical positions that do not require their adherents to affirm the existence of abstract objects. I will take it that it is evident why someone who accepted this conclusion (or either of them, if they are different) would have a strong motivation for wishing that a nominalistic reconstruction or interpretation of mathematics were available.

In this section I will present an argument for the conclusion that not believing in abstract objects would be a Good Thing—for the conclusion, that is, that one should not believe in abstract objects unless one feels rationally compelled to by some weighty consideration or argument. If we call the thesis that there are abstract objects *platonism*, my conclusion is that a philosopher should wish not to be a platonist if it's rationally possible for the informed philosopher not to be a platonist. And I'll take it for granted that, if one takes this attitude toward platonism, one should take the same attitude toward any theory from

---

[1] John Burgess and Gideon Rosen, *A Subject without an Object*, (Oxford University Press, 1997).
[2] Ibid., Part 1A, "Introduction", *passim*.

which platonism is deducible. Thus, if a theory T entails platonism, that is a good reason not to accept that theory. (This bald statement requires qualification, however. If T is a very attractive theory, the fact that T entails platonism might be a good reason for accepting platonism. Its existence and the fact that it entailed platonism might in fact be just the "weighty reason" for accepting platonism that showed that one should, after all, be a platonist. My point is really a truism: if Theory One entails Theory Two, and is known to do so, then the question whether either of the theories should be accepted or rejected cannot be considered in isolation from the question whether the other should be accepted or rejected.) If, moreover, a theory might, for all anyone knows at present, entail platonism, that is a good reason to try to find out whether it in fact entails platonism—just as, if a theory might, for all anyone knows, entail a contradiction, that is a good reason to try to find out whether it in fact entails a contradiction.

My thesis is no clearer than the term 'abstract object', and, unfortunately, I have nothing very useful to say about what this phrase means. I will note, however, that it is possible to divide the terms and predicates we use in everyday and scientific and philosophical discourse into two exhaustive and exclusive classes by a very simple method. We stipulate that one class shall contain the terms and predicates in the following list: 'table', 'the copy of *War and Peace* on the table', 'Mont Blanc', 'the Eiffel Tower', 'Catherine the Great', 'neutron star', 'intelligent Martian', 'elf', 'ghost', 'angel', 'god', and 'God'. We stipulate that the other shall contain 'number', 'the ratio of 1 to 0', 'proposition', 'sentence' (as in 'the same offensive sentence was scrawled on every blackboard in the building') 'property', 'angle' (as in 'the sum of the opposite angles of a right triangle is equal to a right angle'), 'possibility' (as in 'that possibility is still unrealized'), 'the lion' (as in 'the lion is a large African carnivore of the genus *Felis*'), '*War and Peace*' (as in '*War and Peace* has been translated into thirty-nine languages'), 'the English language', and 'the mixolydian mode'. We then ask philosophers (it had better be philosophers; it's unlikely that anyone else will cooperate) to place each term or predicate of our discourse (let's leave mass terms out of the picture, just to simplify matters) in the class where it will be most at home. (We make it clear that the classification is not to depend on whether the person doing the classifying believes that a term to be classified denotes anything or believes that a predicate to be classified has a non-empty extension. We have, in fact, included such items as 'the ratio of 1 to 0' and 'elf' among our "paradigms", items, that is, that by everyone's reckoning have no semantical correlates, to make our intent on this point clear.) I say that this procedure will yield pretty consistent results. Perhaps not as consistent as the results would have been if the paradigms comprised the names of twenty even numbers and twenty odd numbers and the "new" words our respondents were asked to classify were all names of natural numbers. But pretty consistent. Some of the terms in our list of paradigms may be ambiguous and might be understood by different philosophers in different ways. And some philosophers may have idiosyncratic theories about the items in the extensions of some of these terms. (Most philosophers would put '{Catherine the Great, {the Eiffel Tower}}' in with 'property' and 'the lion'; but the author of *Parts of Classes* might be inclined to think that this term was more at home with 'Catherine the Great' and 'the Eiffel Tower'.) And some terms may just yield inconsistent responses: Amie Thomasson would say that our whole scheme of classification was in at least one respect objectionable, since '*War and Peace*' isn't a clear candidate for membership in either class—for it denotes an object that is non-spatial and has instances (like many of the items in the second list), and is, nevertheless, a contingently existing artifact (like some of the items in the first). Nicholas Wolterstorff would say that our classification scheme was unobjectionable, and that '*War and Peace*' clearly belonged right where we had put it, since it denoted something that was much more like a proposition than it was like a volume on a library shelf. He would add that the idea of a contingently existing, non-spatial object that had instances was incoherent.[3] (I don't think that either of these philosophers could be said to have a theory of the ontology of the novel that was "idiosyncratic" in the way Lewis's theory of classes is idiosyncratic.)

When all the possible qualifications and doubtful cases have been noted, however, there will be, or so I maintain, really substantial agreement as to which class any given term or predicate should be placed in. (There will also be substantial agreement on this point: every term can be placed in one list or the other.) And this implies that, with respect to most terms, most philosophers will be in substantial agreement about the truth-values of the propositions that are substitution-instances of the following schema:

[3] For Amie Thomasson's views, see her book *Fiction and Metaphysics* (Cambridge University Press, 1999); for Nicholas Wolterstorff's, see his *Worlds and Works of Art* (Oxford University Press, 1980).

If X is really, as it appears on the syntactical face of it to be, a term, and if it denotes an object, it denotes an abstract object.

Where did the words 'abstract object' come from? 'Abstract object' as I see it, is just the general term that applies to the objects denoted by the terms in the second class—provided, of course, that those terms have denotations. This is no substantive thesis, not even a substantive thesis about meaning. It is simply a stipulation. By a similar stipulation, we can call the items denoted by the terms in the first class *concrete* objects. (The word 'object', as I use it, is simply the most general count-noun. It is synonymous with 'thing' and 'item' and, no doubt, with 'entity'. That is to say, everything is an object. That is to say, 'For every x, if x is an object, then x is F' is equivalent to 'For every x, x is F' and 'For some x, x is an object and x is F' is equivalent to 'For some x, x is F'.) A similar point applies to the schema 'If X is really, as it appears on the syntactical face of it to be, a predicate, and if it has a non-empty extension, its extension comprises abstract objects.' The qualification 'if X really is a term' is a concession to anyone who thinks (and no doubt this is a very reasonable thing to think in some cases) that some words or phrases that have the syntax of terms do not really "function as denoting phrases".

This is as much as I have to say about the meaning of 'abstract object'. On such understanding of 'abstract object' as what I have said supplies, a "platonist" is someone who thinks that at least some of the linguistic items in the second class really are terms (really are predicates) and really have referents (really have non-empty extensions). If my thesis is wrong—if my lists of paradigms do *not* really partition the terms and predicates we use into two classes, if this is not even an *approximation* to the truth—then my explanation fails, owing simply to the fact that there is no such thing as what I have called 'the second class of terms'.

In my view, as I have said, it is better not to be a platonist—prima facie better, better if we can get away with it. The reason is not profound. I suppose one could classify it as an 'Occam's razor' sort of reason, though I will not make any use of this term.

Think of matters this way. The platonist must think of objects, of what there is, as falling into two exclusive and exhaustive categories, the abstract and the concrete. If x falls into one of these categories and y into the other, then no two things could be more different than x and y. According to orthodox Christian theology, no two concrete things could differ more than God and an inanimate object. But (assuming for the sake of the illustration that all three things exist) the differences between God and this pen pale into insignificance when they are compared with the differences between this pen and the number 4; indeed, the number seems no more like the pen than like God. The difference between *any* abstract object and *any* concrete object would seem to be the maximum difference any two objects could display. The difference between a topological space and the color the Taj Mahal shares with the Washington Monument is no doubt very great, but each is far more like the other than either is like this pen. (Again, of course, we are assuming for the sake of the illustration that all three things exist.)

Now it seems very puzzling that objects should fall into two exclusive and radically different categories. Rather than suppose that this is so, it would be much more appealing to suppose that at least one of these categories is empty—or that the words we have used to describe one or both of the two categories are meaningless. And we cannot suppose that the category that contains the pen, the category of concrete objects, is empty, for that is the category into which *we* fall, and, as Descartes has pointed out, we know *we* exist. (I set aside Quine's amusing reduction of supposedly concrete things to pure sets; we can't discuss everything. I shall mention this reduction again, but only as an example to illustrate a point.) It seems, moreover, that we know a lot more about concrete things than we know about abstract things. We understand them better. Maybe not *well*, but better than we understand abstract things. At least we understand *some* of them better: simple paradigms of concrete things. We do not understand even the simplest, the paradigmatic, abstract objects very well at all. You say there is such a thing as the number 4? All right, tell me what properties it has. Well, it has logical properties like self-identity and having, for no property, both that property and its complement. And it has arithmetical properties like being even and being the successor of three and numbering the Stuart kings of England. But what others? It is, no doubt, non-spatial, and perhaps non-temporal. It is perhaps necessarily existent. At about this point we trail off into uncertainty. Consider, by way of contrast, this pen. It has the same logical properties as the number. It does not have arithmetical properties, but it has functional properties, like being an instrument for making marks on surfaces, and perhaps the functional properties of an artifact are analogous to the arithmetical properties of a number. It has "metaphysical" properties, properties as abstract and general as those we ascribed to the number: it occupies space, it endures through or is extended in time, its existence is contingent. When we have said these things, these things that correspond to what we were able to say about the number, however, we do not trail off into uncertainty. There is *lots* more we can say. We could write a book about the pen, albeit not a very interesting one. We could discuss its color, its mass, its spatial and mereological structure, the chemical composition of its various parts and of the ink it contains, the devices by which ink is drawn from an internal reservoir to the rolling ball that distributes the ink on paper, and so—for practical purposes, at least—*ad infinitum*. If it is not altogether clear what I mean by saying that we have a pretty good understanding of a certain *object* ('object' as opposed to 'concept'), *this* is what I mean: this ability to go on saying true things about the intrinsic features of the object till we drop. And if I say we do not have a very good understanding of the number 4, I mean simply that, if we try to describe its intrinsic features, we soon trail off in puzzlement. We may trail off in puzzlement at some point in our disquisition about the pen: when we try to specify the conditions under which it endures through time or the counterfactual situations in which it would have existed, for example. (If Sartre is right, certain speculations about the pen can lead not only to puzzlement but to nausea.) But we can go on about the pen for an awfully long time before we come to such a point. If this difference in our abilities to describe the pen and the number cannot be ascribed to "a better understanding" of the pen than of the number, what can it be ascribed to? After all, it can hardly be that the number has fewer properties than the pen. If the number and the pen both exist—if the phrases 'the number 4' and 'this pen' both really denote something—then these two objects both have the following feature: each is an object x such that, for every property, x has either that property or its complement. It must therefore be that we know a lot less about the properties of the number than we do about the properties of the pen. And that seems to me to imply that, when we talk about the pen, we have a pretty good idea of the nature of the thing we are talking about, and when we talk about the number, we have at best a radically incomplete idea of the nature of the thing we are talking about.

Platonists, therefore, must say that reality, what there is, is divided into two parts: one part *we* belong to, and everything in this part is more like us than is anything in the other part. The inhabitants of the other part are radically unlike us, much more unlike us than is anything in "our" part, and we can't really say much about what the things in the other part are like. It seems to me to be evident that it would be better not to believe in the other part of reality, the other category of things, if we could manage it. But we can't manage it. In the next section I shall try to explain why we can't get along without *one* kind of abstract object: properties.

2. WE CAN'T GET AWAY WITH IT

What reasons are there for believing in the existence of properties (qualities, attributes, characteristics, features, ...)? I think it is fair to say that there are apparently such things as properties. There is, for example, apparently such a thing as humanity. The members of the class of human beings, as the idiom has it, "have something in common". This appears to be an existential proposition. If it is (the platonist will ask rhetorically), what could this "something" be but the property "humanity"? It could certainly not be anything physical, for—Siamese twins excepted—no two human beings have any physical thing in common. And, of course, what goes for the class of human beings goes for the class of birds, the class of white things, and the class of intermediate vector bosons: the members of each of these classes have something in common with one another—or so it appears—and what the members of a class have in common is a property—or so it appears. But, as often happens in philosophy, many philosophers deny that what is apparently the case is really the case. These philosophers—"nominalists"—contend that the apparent existence of properties is mere appearance, and that, in reality, there are no properties.

How can the dispute between those who affirm and those who deny the existence of properties (platonists and nominalists) be resolved? The ontological method invented, or at least first made explicit, by Quine and Goodman (and illustrated with wonderful ingenuity in David and Stephanie Lewis's "Holes") suggests a way to approach this question.[4]

---

[4] W. V. Quine, "On What There Is", in *From a Logical Point of View* (Harvard University Press, 1961), pp. 1–19 (originally published in the *Review of Metaphysics*, 1948.); W. V. Quine, *Word and Object* (Cambridge, MA: MIT Press, 1960), ch. VII, "Ontic Decision", pp. 233–76; Nelson Goodman and W. V. Quine, "Steps toward a Constructive Nominalism", *Journal of Symbolic Logic*, 12 (1947), pp. 105–22; David and Stephanie Lewis, "Holes", in David Lewis, *Philosophical Papers*, vol. I (Oxford University Press, 1983), pp. 3–9 (originally published in the *Australasian Journal of Philosophy*, 1970).

Nominalists and platonists have different beliefs about what there is. Let us therefore ask this: how should one decide what to believe about what there is? According to Quine, the problem of deciding what to believe about what there is is a very straightforward special case of the problem of deciding what to believe. (The problem of deciding what to believe is, to be sure, no trivial problem, but it is a problem everyone is going to have somehow to come to terms with.) If we want to decide whether to believe that there are properties, Quine tells us, we should examine the beliefs we already have, the theses we have already, for whatever reason, decided to believe, and see whether they "commit us" (as Quine says) to the existence of properties. But what does this mean? Let us consider an example. Suppose we find the following proposition among our beliefs:

> Spiders share some of the anatomical features of insects.

A plausible case can be made for the thesis that this belief commits us to the existence of properties. We may observe, first, that it is very hard to see what an "anatomical feature" (such as "having an exoskeleton") could be if it were not a property: 'property', 'quality', 'characteristic', 'attribute', and 'feature' are all more or less synonyms. The following question is therefore of interest: does our belief that spiders share some of the anatomical features of insects therefore commit us to the existence of "anatomical features"? If we examine the meaning of the sentence 'Spiders share some of the anatomical features of insects', we find that what it says is this:

> There are anatomical features that insects have and spiders also have.

Or, in the "canonical language of quantification",

> It is true of at least one thing that it is such that it is an anatomical feature and insects have it and spiders also have it.

(The canonical language of quantification does not essentially involve the symbols '∀' and '∃'. Natural-language phrases like 'it is true of everything that it is such that' and 'it is true of at least one thing that it is such that' will do as well, for the symbols are merely shorthand ways of writing such phrases. And the canonical language of quantification does not essentially involve variables—'x', 'y' and so on. For variables are nothing more than pronouns: "variables" are simply a stock of typographically distinct third-person-singular pronouns; having such a stock at one's disposal is no more than a device for facilitating cross-reference when one makes complicated statements. In the case of the present simple statement, 'it' works as well as 'x': there is *no* difference in meaning between 'It is true of at least one thing that it is such that it is an anatomical feature and insects have it and spiders also have it' and '$\exists x$ x is an anatomical feature and insects have x and spiders also have x'.)

It is a straightforward logical consequence of this proposition that there are anatomical features: if there are anatomical features that insects have and spiders also have, then there are anatomical features that insects have; if there are anatomical features that insects have, then there are anatomical features—full stop.

Does this little argument show that anyone who believes that spiders share some of the anatomical features of insects is committed to platonism, and, more specifically, to a belief in the existence of properties? How might a nominalist respond to this little argument? Suppose we present the argument to Norma, a convinced nominalist (who believes, as most people do, that spiders share some of the anatomical features of insects). Assuming that Norma is unwilling simply to have inconsistent beliefs, there would seem to be four possible ways for her to respond to it:

(1) She might become a platonist.
(2) She might abandon her allegiance to the thesis that spiders share some of the anatomical features of insects.
(3) She might attempt to show that, despite appearances, it does not follow from this thesis that there are anatomical features.
(4) She might admit that her beliefs (her nominalism and her belief that spiders share some of the anatomical features of insects) are apparently inconsistent, affirm her nominalistic faith that this inconsistency is apparent, not real, and confess that, although she is confident that there is some fault in our alleged demonstration that her belief about spiders and insects commits her to the existence of anatomical features, she is at present unable to discover it.

Possibility (2) is not really very attractive. It is unattractive for at least two reasons. First, it seems to be a simple fact of biology that spiders share some of the anatomical features of insects. Secondly, there are many, many "simple facts" that could have been used as the premise of an essentially identical argument for the conclusion that there are properties. (For example, elements in the same column in the Periodic Table tend to have many of the same chemical properties; some of the most important characteristics of the nineteenth-century novel are rarely present in the twentieth-century novel.) Possibility (4) is always an option, but no philosopher is likely to embrace it except as a last resort. What Norma is likely to do is to try to avail herself of possibility (3). She is likely to try to show that her belief about spiders and insects does not in fact commit her to platonism. If she does, she will attempt to find a *paraphrase* of 'Spiders share some of the anatomical features of insects', a sentence that (i) she could use in place of this sentence, and (ii) does not even *seem* to have 'There are anatomical features' as one of its logical consequences. If she can do this, she will be in a position to contend that the commitment to the existence of anatomical features that is apparently "carried by" her belief about spiders and insects is only apparent. And she will be in a position to contend—no doubt further argument would be required to establish this—that the apparent existence of anatomical features is *mere* appearance (an appearance that is due to certain forms of words we use but needn't use).

Is it possible to find such a paraphrase? (And to find paraphrases of all the other apparently true statements that seem to commit those who make them to the reality of properties?) Well, yes and no. 'Yes' because it is certainly possible to find paraphrases of the spider-insect sentence that involve quantification over some other sort of abstract object than anatomical features—that is, other than properties. One might, for example, eliminate (as the jargon has it) the quantification over properties on display in the spider-insect sentence in favor of quantification over, say, concepts. No doubt any work that could be done by the property "having an exoskeleton" could be done by the concept "thing with an exoskeleton". Neither of the two statements 'At least one thing is such that it is an anatomical feature and insects have it and spiders also have it' and 'At least one thing is such that it is an anatomical concept and insects fall under it and spiders also fall under it' would seem to enjoy any real advantage over the other as a vehicle for expressing what we know about the mutual relations of the members of the phylum *Arthropoda*; or, if one of them does, it will be some relatively minor, technical advantage. It is certain that a nominalist will be no more receptive to an ontology that contains concepts (understood in a platonic or Fregean sense, and not in some psychological sense) than to an ontology that contains properties. When I say it is not possible to get along without asserting the existence of properties, therefore, what I mean is that it is not possible to get along without asserting the existence of properties—*or* something that a nominalist is not going to like any better than properties.

Now the distinction between a "relatively minor, technical advantage" and a really important advantage, an advantage that can be appealed to as relevant in disputes about fundamental ontology, is not as clear as it might be. Here is an example that illustrates this point. Some philosophers, most notably Quine, would agree that we cannot eliminate quantification over abstract objects, but deny that examples like the above, or any other consideration, should convince us that there are *properties*. Quine would insist that the most that any such argument can establish is that we must allow the existence of *sets*. Quine concedes that in affirming the existence of sets he is affirming the existence of abstract objects. The set of all spiders, after all, is not a spider or a sum of spiders or any other sort of concrete object. It is true that if the only use we made of the language of set-theory was exemplified by phrases like 'the set of all spiders' and 'the set of all intermediate vector bosons', we could regard our use of such phrases as being merely a device for referring collectively to all spiders, to all intermediate vector bosons, and so on. But that is not the only use we make of such language; for, if we are going to say the things we want to say, and if we affirm the existence of no abstract objects but sets, we must quantify over sets and we must refer to (and quantify over) sets that have sets as members. (If we wish to express the facts of evolutionary biology, we must say things like 'Any spider and any insect have a common ancestor', and those who believe in no abstract objects but sets cannot say that without quantifying over sets—at least, not unless they are willing to take 'ancestor of' as undefined; if their only undefined term is 'parent of', they must affirm generalizations about individually unspecified sets to express the idea "ancestor of". Or we may wish to make use of the idea of *linear order*—we may, for example, wish to calculate the probability of drawing a face card, an ace, and a heart *in that order*; and those of us who believe in no abstract objects but sets must refer to sets that have sets as members to explain the idea of things-arranged-in-some-linear-order.) Sets, then, are abstract objects; but, Quine says, sets are not properties. And this statement points to a far more important fact than the statement that concepts are not properties. Sets, Quine tells us, are well-behaved in a way in which concepts and properties are not. Or, availing himself of the method of "semantic ascent", he might wish rather to say this: those who contend that general terms like 'concept' and 'property' have non-empty extensions face intractable problems of individuation, problems that do not face those who, in admitting abstract objects into their ontology, content themselves with admitting sets. I mention this position of Quine's (that an ontology that contains sets and no other abstract objects is superior, all other things being equal, to an ontology that contains properties or Fregean concepts) because it is important, but I decline to discuss it because it raises some very difficult questions, questions I cannot attempt to answer within the confines of this paper.[5]

Let us return to the topic of paraphrase. Is it possible to provide sentences like 'Spiders share some of the anatomical features of insects' with *nominalistically acceptable* paraphrases? My position is that it is not. I cannot hope to present an adequate defense of this position, for an

---

[5] I will, however, make one remark, or one connected series of remarks, about Quine's thesis. I doubt whether having an extensional principle of individuation has the fundamental ontological significance that Quine ascribes to it. To begin with, I'm not entirely sure that the idea of a certain sort of entity's having an extensional principle of individuation makes sense. I certainly don't see how to write out a Chisholm-style *definiens* for 'the so-and-sos have an extensional principle of individuation'. And I am far from confident that, if I did understand the concept "sort of thing that has an extensional principle of individuation", I should regard falling under this concept as a mark of ontological good behavior. I don't see why the concept "abstract object of a sort that has an extensional principle of individuation" should be identified with the concept "abstract object of a sort that is well-behaved". In any case, whatever may be the case as regards the individuation of properties, they seem to be perfectly well-behaved (Russell's paradox aside; but sets enjoy no advantage over properties in respect of Russell's paradox). It might be objected—Quine no doubt would object—that properties lack not only an extensional principle of individuation (whatever that is), but lack any principle of individuation of any sort. Properties must therefore (the objection continues) to be ruled *entia non grata* by anyone who accepts the principle "No entity without identity". I reply, first, that it is certainly possible to supply principles of individuation for properties, although any such principle will be controversial. (For example: x is the same property as y just in the case that x and y are coextensive in all possible worlds; x is the same property as y just in the case that x and y are coextensive in all possible worlds *and*, necessarily, whoever considers x considers y and whoever considers y considers x.) Second, the principle "No entity without identity" is ambiguous. It might mean "One should not quantify over entities of a given sort unless one is able explicitly to supply a principle of individuation for those entities." Or it might mean "For every x and for every y, x is identical with y or it is not the case that x is identical with y." I see no reason to accept the first of these principles. The second is certainly unobjectionable (it is a theorem of quantifier logic with identity), but there is no reason to suppose that someone who quantifies over entities of a sort for which he has not endorsed an explicit principle of individuation is committed to its denial.

adequate defense of this position would have to take the form of an examination of all possible candidates for nominalistically acceptable paraphrases of such sentences, and I cannot hope to do that. The question of nominalistically acceptable paraphrase will be answered, if at all, only as the outcome of an extended dialectical process, a process involving many philosophers and many years and many gallons of ink. I can do no more than look at one strand of reasoning in this complicated dialectical tapestry. My statement "We can't get away with it" must be regarded as a promissory note. But here is the ten-dollar co-payment on the debt I have incurred by issuing this note.

Suppose a nominalist were to say this: "It's easy to find a nominalistically acceptable paraphrase of 'Spiders share some of the anatomical features of insects'. For example: 'Spiders are like insects in some anatomically relevant ways' or 'Spiders and insects are in some respects anatomically similar'." A platonist is likely to respond as follows (at least, this is what *I'd* say):

> But these proposed paraphrases seem to be quantifications over "ways a thing can be like a thing" or "respects in which things can be similar". If we translate them into the canonical language of quantification, we have sentences something like these:
>
>> It is true of at least one thing that it is such that it is a way in which a thing can be like a thing and it is anatomical and spiders are like insects in it.
>>
>> It is true of at least one thing that it is a respect in which things can be similar and it is anatomical and spiders and insects are similar in it.
>
> These paraphrases, therefore, can hardly be called nominalistically acceptable. If there are such objects as ways in which a thing can be like a thing or respects in which things can be similar, they must certainly be *abstract* objects.

What might the nominalist say in reply? The most plausible reply open to the nominalist seems to me to be along the following lines.

> My platonist critic is certainly a very literal-minded fellow. I didn't mean the 'some' in the open sentence 'x is like y in some anatomically relevant ways' to be taken as a *quantifier*: I didn't mean this sentence to be read '$\exists z$ (z is a way in which a thing can be like a thing and z is anatomical and x is like y in z)'. That's absurd. One might as well read

'There's more than one way to skin a cat' as '$\exists x \, \exists y$ (x is a way of skinning a cat and y is a way of skinning a cat and $x \neq y$)'. I meant this open sentence to have no internal logical structure, or none beyond that implied by the statement that two variables are free in it. It's just a form of words we learn to use by comparing various pairs of objects in the ordinary business of life.

And here is the rejoinder to this reply:

If you take that line you confront problems it would be better not to have to confront. Consider the sentence 'x is like y in some *physiologically* relevant ways'. Surely there is some logical or structural or syntactical relation between this sentence and 'x is like y in some anatomically relevant ways'? One way to explain the relation between these two sentences is to read the former as '$\exists z$ (z is a way in which a thing can be like a thing and z is physiological and x is like y in z)' and the latter as '$\exists z$ (z is a way in which a thing can be like a thing and z is anatomical and x is like y in z)'. How would *you* explain it? Or how would you explain the relation between the sentences 'x is like y in *some* anatomically relevant ways' (which you say has no logical structure) and 'x is like y in *all* anatomically relevant ways'? If neither of these sentences has a logical structure, how do you account for the obvious validity of the following argument?

Either of two female spiders of the same species is like the other in all anatomically relevant ways.

Hence, an insect that is like a given female spider in some anatomically relevant ways is like any female spider of the same species in some anatomically relevant ways.

If the premise and conclusion of this argument are read as having the logical structure that their syntax suggests, the validity of this argument is easily demonstrable in textbook quantifier logic. If one insists that they have no logical structure, one will find it difficult to account for the validity of this argument. That is one of those problems I alluded to, one of those problems it would be better not to have to confront (one of thousands of such problems).

I suggest that we can learn a lesson from this little exchange between an imaginary nominalist and an imaginary platonist: that one should accept the following condition of adequacy on philosophical paraphrases:

Paraphrases must not be such as to leave us without an account of the logical relations between predicates that are obviously logically related. Essentially the same constraint on paraphrase can be put in these words: a paraphrase must not leave us without an account of the validity of any obviously valid argument.

Accepting this constraint has, I believe, a significant consequence. This consequence requires a rather lengthy statement:

> Apparent quantification over properties pervades our discourse. In the end, one can avoid quantifying over properties only by quantifying over other sorts of abstract object—"ways in which a thing can be like a thing", for example. But most philosophers, if forced to choose between quantifying over properties and quantifying over these other objects, would probably prefer to quantify over properties. The reason for this may be illustrated by the case of "ways in which a thing can be like a thing". If there really are such objects as ways in which a thing can be like a thing, they seem to be at once intimately connected with properties and, so to speak, more *specialized* than properties. What, after all, would a particular "way in which a thing can be like a thing" be but the sharing of a certain property? (To say this is consistent with saying that not just any property is such that sharing it is a way in which a thing can be like a thing; sharing "being green" can plausibly be described as a way in which a thing can be like a thing, but it is much less plausible to describe sharing "being either green or not round"—if there is such a property—as a way in which a thing can be like a thing.) And if this is so, surely, the best course is to accept the existence of properties and to "analyze away" all apparent quantifications over "ways in which a thing can be like a thing" in terms of quantifications over properties.

It is the content of this lengthy statement that I have abbreviated as "We can't get away with it."

This argument I have given above has some obvious points of contact with the so-called Quine–Putnam indispensability argument for mathematical realism.[6] But there are important differences between the two

---

[6] See Hilary Putnam, *Philosophy of Logic* (New York: Harper & Row, 1971). *Philosophy of Logic* is reprinted in its entirety in Stephen Laurence and Cynthia Macdonald (eds.), *Contemporary Readings in the Foundations of Metaphysics* (Oxford: Blackwell, 1998), pp. 404–34.

arguments—I mean besides the obvious fact that my argument is an argument for the existence of properties and not an argument for the existence of specifically mathematical objects. It should be noted that my argument is not that we should believe that properties exist because their existence is an indispensable postulate of science. Nor have I contended that the scientific indispensability of properties is *evidence* for the existence of properties. I have not maintained that, because of the scientific indispensability of properties, any adequate account of the success of science must affirm the existence of properties. For one thing, my argument has nothing in particular to do with science. Science does indeed provide us with plenty of examples of sentences that must in some sense, on some analysis, express truths and also, on the face of it, imply the existence of properties—for example, 'Many of the important properties of water are due to hydrogen bonding.' But our everyday, pre-scientific discourse contains a vast number of such sentences, and these will serve my purposes as well as any sentences provided by the sciences. If our spider-insect sentence is insufficiently non-scientific to support this thesis, there are lots of others. ('The royal armorer has succeeded in producing a kind of steel that has some of but not all the desirable characteristics of Damascus steel'.) My argument could have been presented in, say, the thirteenth century, and the advent of modern science has done nothing to make it more cogent.

More importantly, I have not supposed that the fact (supposing it to be a fact) that quantification over properties is an indispensable component of our discourse is any sort of *evidence* for the existence of properties. That's as may be; I neither affirm that thesis nor deny it. It is simply not a premise of my argument, which is not an epistemological argument. Nor is my argument any sort of "transcendental" argument or any sort of inference to the best explanation; I have not contended that the success of science cannot be accounted for on nominalistic premises. Again, that's as may be. If I have appealed to any general methodological principle, it is only this: if one doesn't believe that things of a certain sort exist, one shouldn't say anything that demonstrably implies that things of that sort do exist. (Or, at any rate, one may say such things only if one is in a position to contend, and plausibly, that saying these things is a mere manner of speaking—that, however convenient it may be, it could, in principle, be dispensed with.) This methodological rule does not, I think, deserve to be controversial. We would all agree, I assume, that, if p demonstrably implies the existence of God, then atheists who propose to remain atheists shouldn't affirm *p*—or not, at any rate, unless they can show us how they could in principle dispense with affirming p in favor of affirming only propositions without theological implications.[7]

I suppose I ought to add—the point needs to be made somewhere—that, if one *could* show how to eliminate quantification over properties in a nominalistically acceptable way, that achievement, by itself, would have no ontological implications. After all, Quine has shown how to eliminate quantification over everything but pure sets (at least, it can be argued that he's shown how to do this), and Church has shown how to eliminate quantification over women.[8] The devices of Quine and Church would be of ontological interest if "containing only pure sets" or "not containing women" were desirable features for an ontology to have. But they're not. If what I said in the first section of this paper is right, however, "containing no abstract objects" is an advantage in an ontology.

I will close this section with a point about philosophical logic—as opposed to metaphysics. My argument fails if there is such a thing as substitutional quantification; and it fails if there is such a thing as

---

[7] For an important objection to this style of reasoning, see Joseph Melia, "On What There's Not", *Analysis*, 55 (1995), pp. 223–9. I intend to discuss Melia's paper elsewhere; to discuss it here would take us too far afield. I wish to thank David Manley for impressing upon me the importance of Melia's paper (and for correspondence about the issues it raises).

[8] In 1958, Alonzo Church delivered a lecture at Harvard, the final seven paragraphs of which have lately been making the e-mail rounds under the title (not Church's), "Ontological Misogyny". In these paragraphs, Church wickedly compares Goodman's attitude toward abstract objects to a misogynist's attitude toward women. ("Now a misogynist is a man who finds women difficult to understand, and who in fact considers them objectionable incongruities in an otherwise matter-of-fact and hard-headed world. Suppose then that in analogy with nominalism the misogynist is led by his dislike and distrust of women to omit them from his ontology.") Church then shows the misogynist how to eliminate women from his ontology. (In case you are curious: We avail ourselves of the fact that every woman has a unique father. Let us say that men who have female offspring have two modes of presence in the world, primary and secondary. Primary presence is what is usually called presence. In cases in which we should normally say that a woman was present at a certain place, the misogynist who avails himself of Church's proposal will say that a certain man—the man who would ordinarily be described as the woman's father—exhibits secondary presence at that place. . . .) "Ontological Misogyny" came to me by the following route: Tyler Burge, Michael Zeleny (Department of Mathematics, UCLA), James Cargile.

Quine's reduction of everything to pure sets (well, of physics to pure sets, but physics is everything for Quine) can be found in his essay "Whither Physical Objects?" which is included in R. S. Cohen, P. K. Feyerabend, and M. W. Wartofsky (eds.), *Essays in Memory of Imre Lakatos* (Dordrecht: D. Reidel, 1976), pp. 497–504. I thank Michael Rea for the reference.

quantification into predicate positions. (Or so I'm willing to concede. If either substitutional quantification or quantification into predicate positions is to be found in the philosopher's tool kit, then defending my thesis—"We can't get away with it"—becomes, at the very least, a much more difficult project.) I say this: substitutional quantification and quantification into non-nominal positions (including predicate positions) are both meaningless. More exactly:

(1) Substitutional quantification is meaningless unless it is a kind of shorthand for objectual quantification over linguistic objects, taken together with some semantic predicates like 'x is true' or 'something satisfies x'. But substitutional quantification, so understood, is of no use to the nominalist; for, so understood, every existential substitutional quantification implies the existence of linguistic items (words and sentences), and those are abstract objects.

(2) Quantification into non-nominal positions is meaningless unless (a) the non-nominal quantifiers are understood substitutionally; this case reduces to the case already dismissed; or (b) it is understood as a kind of shorthand for nominal quantification over properties, taken together with a two-place predicate (corresponding to the 'ε' of set-theory) along the lines of 'x has y' or 'x exemplifies y'. (In saying this, I'm saying something very similar to what Quine says when he says that second-order logic is set theory in sheep's clothing—for the salient feature of the language of second-order logic is quantification into predicate positions. But, since I do not share Quine's conviction that one should admit no abstract objects but sets into one's ontology, I am free to say "Second-order logic is property theory in sheep's clothing".)

I have defended (1) elsewhere.[9] My arguments for (2) would be no more than a reproduction of Quine's animadversions on quantification into non-nominal positions.[10]

---

[9] Peter van Inwagen, "Why I Don't Understand Substitutional Quantification", *Philosophical Studies*, 39 (1981), pp. 281–5. The arguments presented in this paper are similar to the more general arguments of William G. Lycan's fine paper, "Semantic Competence and Funny Functors", *Monist*, 64 (1979). "Why I Don't Understand Substitutional Quantification" is reprinted in my *Ontology, Identity and Modality Ontology, Identity, and Modality: Essays in Metaphysics* (Cambridge University Press, 2001).

[10] See the section of W. V. Quine's *Philosophy of Logic* (Englewood Cliffs, NJ: Prentice-Hall, 1970) entitled "Set Theory in Sheep's Clothing" (pp. 66–8).

3. IF WE AFFIRM THE EXISTENCE OF PROPERTIES, WE OUGHT TO HAVE A THEORY OF PROPERTIES

By a "theory of properties", I mean some sort of specification of, well, the *properties* of properties. If one succeeds in showing that we cannot dispense with quantification over properties, one's achievement does not tell us much about the intrinsic features of these things. When I was presenting what I took to be the prima facie case for nominalism, I said that we didn't know much about the properties of properties. I am now making the point that the sort of argument for the existence of properties I have offered does not tell us much about the nature of properties. The whole of our discourse about things, on the face of it, defines what may be called "the property role", and our argument can be looked on as an attempt to show that something must play this role. (The property role could, in principle, be specified by the Ramsey-style methods that Lewis sets out in "How to Define Theoretical Terms."[11]) But it tells us nothing about the intrinsic properties of the things that play this role that enable them to play this role. In "Holes", Bargle argues that there must be holes, and his argument is in many ways like our argument for the existence of properties; that is, he uses some ordinary discourse about cheese and crackers to define the "hole role", and he attempts to show that one can't avoid the conclusion that something plays this role. Argle, after an initial attempt to evade Bargle's argument, accepts it. He goes on, however, to show how things acceptable to the materialist can play the hole role. In doing this, he spells out the intrinsic properties of the things he calls holes (when they are holes in a piece of cheese, they are connected, singly-perforate bits of cheese that stand in the right sort of contrast to their non-cheesy surroundings), and he, in effect, shows that things with the intrinsic properties he assigns to holes are capable of playing the role that Bargle's argument shows is played by something-we-know-not-what.

We are not in a position to do, with respect to properties, anything like what Argle has done with respect to holes, for, as I have observed, we cannot say anything much about the intrinsic properties of properties. It is of course unlikely that, if we could say anything more than the little we can about the intrinsic properties of properties, we should find

---

[11] David Lewis, "How to Define Theoretical Terms", *Philosophical Papers*, vol. I, Oxford University Press, 1983 pp. 78–95 (originally published in the *Journal of Philosophy*, 1970).

that the things whose properties we had specified were acceptable to the nominalist. It would seem in fact that even the little we can say about the properties of properties is sufficient to make them unacceptable to nominalists. (If this were not so, the whole nominalist–platonist debate would have to be re-thought.) However this may be, the plain fact is: we platonists *can't* describe those somethings-we-know-not-what which we say play the property role in anything like the depth in which Argle describes the things that (*he* says) play the hole role. Argle can describe the things he calls 'holes' as well as he can describe anything; we platonists can describe any concrete object in incomparably greater depth than we can any property.

I wish it weren't so, but it is. Or so *I* say. Some will dissent from my thesis that properties are mysterious. David Lewis is a salient example. If Lewis is right about properties, the property role is played by certain *sets*, and one can describe at least some of these sets as well as one can describe any set.[12] In my view, however, Lewis is not right about properties. In the next section I will explain why I think this. (A qualification: I have said that, according to Lewis, certain sets are suitable to play the property role. In Lewis's view, however, it may be that our discourse defines at least two distinct roles that could equally well be described as "property-roles". It should be said of those sets— the sets that Lewis has pressed into service—that, although they can play *one* of the property roles, they are unsuited for the other—if there are indeed two property roles.[13])

4. LEWIS'S THEORY OF PROPERTIES AS SETS (WITH SOME REMARKS ON MEINONGIAN THEORIES OF PROPERTIES AS SETS)

According to Lewis, the property "being a pig" is the set of all pigs, including those pigs that are inhabitants of other possible worlds than ours. But, in saying this, I involve myself in Lewis's notorious modal

---

[12] See David Lewis, *On the Plurality of Worlds* (Oxford: Blackwell, 1986), sect. 1.5, "Modal Realism at Work: Properties", pp. 50–69.

[13] See David Lewis, "New Work for a Theory of Universals", in *Papers on Metaphysics and Epistemology* (Cambridge University Press, 1999), pp. 8–55 (originally published in the *Australasian Journal of Philosophy*, 1983). See especially the section entitled "Universals and Properties", pp. 10–24 in *Papers on Metaphysics and Epistemology*.

ontology. Let us, for the moment, avoid the questions raised by Lewis's modal ontology and say that Lewis's theory is one member of a species of theory according to all of which the property "being a pig" is the set of all possible pigs. Members of this species differ in their accounts of what a possible pig is. (That is to say, they differ in their accounts of what a *possibile* or *possible object* is, for we are interested not only in the property "being a pig" but in properties generally. According to all theories of this kind, every property is a set of *possibilia* and every set of *possibilia* is a property.) Lewis's theory will be just the member of this species according to which possible objects are what Lewis says possible objects are, and will be like the other members of the species on all points not touching on the nature of possible objects. The other members of the species are Meinongian theories, or at least all of them I can think of are.

What is a possible object? Examination of our use of the adjective "possible" shows that it has no fixed meaning. Its meaning rather depends on the word or phrase it modifies: a possible X is an X that is possibly F, where what F is depends on what X is. A possible proposition is a proposition that is possibly true. A possible state of affairs is a state of affairs that possibly obtains. A possible property is a property that is possibly instantiated. What, then, is a possible pig? A pig can't be true or false, can't obtain or not obtain, isn't instantiated or uninstantiated. A pig just *is*. So—a possible pig is a pig that is possibly *what*? It may be that we sometimes use "possible pig" to mean not something of the form 'pig that is possibly F', but rather 'thing that is possibly a pig'; if so, this is no clue to what 'possible pig', and more generally 'possible object', mean in theories according to which the property "being a pig" is the set of all possible pigs and every set of possible objects is a property. If any such theory is correct, every possible pig must be, without qualification, a pig—and not a merely counterfactual pig or a merely potential pig. And no one, in any context, would ever want to define 'possible object' as 'something that is possibly an object', for, although it is possible not to be a pig (in fact, I've seen it done), it is not possible not to be an object. 'Possible object' must therefore, at least in statements of theories of properties like those we are considering, have a logical structure like that of 'possible proposition' or 'possible property'. A definition of 'possible object' must have the form 'thing that is an object and is also possibly F'. And of course, if the definition is to be of any interest, F must represent a characteristic that does not belong to objects as a necessary and automatic consequence of their being objects. What characteristic could satisfy this condition?

A Meinongian, or, rather, a neo-Meinongian like Terence Parsons or Richard Sylvan, has a simple answer to this question.[14] Just as a possible proposition is a proposition that is possibly *true*, and a possible property is a property that is possibly *instantiated*, a possible object is an object that is possibly *existent*. (We must avoid confusion on the following point. Assuming that there is such a thing as the proposition that $2 + 2 = 5$, it is a possible object and is not a possible proposition. Since all propositions are objects, it might be thought to follow that it was at once a possible object and not a possible object. But to infer that conclusion would be to commit the fallacy of ambiguity. All that follows from its being a possible object and its not being a possible proposition is that it is an object that is possibly *existent* and an object that is not possibly *true*—which is not even an apparent contradiction.) And, the neo-Meinongians maintain, objects are not necessarily and automatically existent. Although any object must *be*, there are objects that could fail to *exist*. In fact, most of the objects that are *do* fail to exist, and many objects that do exist might have been without existing. (Paleo-Meinongians—Meinong, for example—would not agree that any object must be: they contend that many objects, so to speak, don't be.)

What is to be said about neo-Meinongianism? What Lewis says seems to me to be exactly right: the neo-Meinongians have never explained what they mean by 'exist'.[15] We anti-Meinongians and they mean the same thing by 'be'. We anti-Meinongians say that 'exists' and 'be' mean the same thing; the neo-Meinongians say that this is wrong and 'exists' means something else, something other than 'be'. (And, they say, the meanings of the two verbs are so related that—for example—the powers that exist must form a subset of the powers that be.) Unfortunately, they have never said what this "something else" is. I would add the following remark to Lewis's trenchant critique of neo-Meinongianism. The only attempt at an explanation of the meaning of 'exists' that neo-Meinongians have offered proceeds by laying out

---

[14] See Terence Parsons, *Non-Existent Objects* (Yale University Press, 1980); Richard Routley [=Richard Sylvan], *Exploring Meinong's Jungle and Beyond: An Investigation of Noneism and the Theory of Items* (Canberra: Departmental Monograph No. 3, Philosophy Department, Research School of Social Sciences, Australian National University, 1980).

[15] See David Lewis, "Noneism and Allism", in *Papers in Metaphysics and Epistemology* (Cambridge University Press, 1999), pp. 152–63 (originally published in *Mind*, 1990).

supposed examples of things that are but do not exist. But, in my view, the right response to every such example that has ever been offered is either "That does too exist" or "There is no such thing as that." And, of course, if there is no distinction in meaning between 'be' and 'exist', then neo-Meinongianism cannot be stated without contradiction. If 'be' and 'exist' mean the same thing, then the open sentence 'x exists' is equivalent to '$\exists y\ x = y$'. And, if that is so, 'There are objects that do not exist' is logically equivalent to 'Something is not identical with itself'. Since neo-Meinongians obviously do not mean to embrace a contradiction, their theory depends on the premise that 'exist' means something other than 'be'. But, so far as I can see, there is nothing for 'exists' *to* mean but 'be'. In the absence of further explanation, I am therefore inclined to reject their theory as meaningless. It does not, I concede, follow that 'possible object', if it means 'object that possibly exists', is meaningless. If it means that, that's what it means, and that which means something is not meaningless. It does, however, follow, that 'possible object' means the same as 'object'; at least this must be true in the sense in which, say, 'object that does not violate Leibniz's Law' or 'object that is possibly self-identical' or 'object whose being would not entail a contradiction' mean the same as 'object'. And in that case the theory that a property is a set of possible objects cannot be distinguished from the theory that a property is a set of objects *tout court*.

Let us turn to Lewis's version of the properties-as-sets-of-possible-objects theory. According to Lewis, a possible object is indeed simply an object. But some possible objects are, as he says, *actual* and some are *merely* possible. Merely possible objects are not objects that do not exist; that is, they are not objects of which we can correctly say that they do not exist "in the philosophy room". Outside the philosophy room, in the ordinary business of life, we can say, and say truly, that flying pigs do not exist, despite the fact that we say truly in the philosophy room that some possible objects are flying pigs. When we say that there are no flying pigs, our use of the quantifier is like that of someone who looks in the fridge and says sadly, "There's no beer." When I say, in the philosophy room, "There are flying pigs, but they're one and all merely possible objects", I'm saying this: "There are [an absolutely unrestricted quantifier; the philosophy room is just that place in which all contextual restrictions on quantification are abrogated] flying pigs, and they're spatio-temporally unrelated to me."

The problem with Lewis's theory, as I see it, is that there is no reason to think that there is anything spatio-temporal that is spatio-temporally unrelated to me, and, if there *is* anything in this category, I don't see what it has to do with modality.[16] Suppose there *is* a pig that is spatio-temporally unrelated to me—or, less parochially, to us. Why should one call it a "merely possible pig"—or a "non-actual pig"? Why are those good things to call it? This is not the end of the matter, however. Even if a pig spatio-temporally unrelated to us *can't* properly be called a merely possible pig, it doesn't follow immediately that Lewis's theory of properties is wrong. If what Lewis calls the principle of plenitude is true—if, as Lewis maintains, there exists (unrestricted quantifier) a pig having, intuitively speaking, every set of properties consistent with its being a pig—then there might be something to be said for identifying the set of all pigs (including those spatio-temporally unrelated to us) with the property "being a pig". (If there exist pigs having every possible combination of features, there must be pigs that are spatially or temporally unrelated to us: if every pig were spatially and temporally related to us, there wouldn't be room for all the pigs that Lewis says there are.) There might be something to be said for this identification, that is, even if the set of all pigs couldn't properly be called 'the set of all pigs, both actual and merely possible'. But even if there are pigs spatio-temporally unrelated to us, there is, so far as I can see, no good reason to accept the principle of plenitude—even as it applies to pigs, much less in its full generality.

On the face of it, the set of pigs seems to represent far too sparse a selection of the possible combinations of characteristics a pig might have for one to be able plausibly to maintain that this set could play the role "the property of being a pig". According to both the neo-Meinongians and Lewis, the set of pigs has a membership much more diverse than most of us would have expected, a membership whose diversity is restricted only by the requirements of logical consistency (for Lewis) or is not restricted at all (for the neo-Meinongians). If I am right, both Lewis and the Meinongians have failed to provide us with any reason to accept this prima facie very uncompelling thesis.

---

[16] I have gone into this matter in a great deal of detail in "Two Concepts of Possible Worlds", *Midwest Studies in Philosophy*, 11 (1986) pp. 185–213 (reprinted in *Ontology, Identity and Modality*, cited above).

5. A THEORY OF PROPERTIES

There is only one real objection to Lewis's theory of properties: it isn't true. It is a model of what a good theory should be, insofar as theoretical virtue can be divorced from truth. In this section I present a theory of properties that, or so *I* say, does have the virtue of truth. Alas, even if it has that virtue, it has few others. Its principal vice is that it is very nearly vacuous. It can be compared to the theory that taking opium is followed by sleep because opium possesses a dormitive virtue. That theory about the connection of opium and sleep, as Lewis points out somewhere, is not *entirely* vacuous: it is inconsistent with various theses, such as the thesis that taking opium is followed by sleep because a demon casts anyone who takes opium into sleep. The theory of properties I shall present, although it is pretty close to being vacuous, is inconsistent with various theses about properties, and some of these theses have been endorsed by well-known philosophers. (A proper presentation of this theory would treat properties as a special kind of relation.[17] But I will not attempt to discuss relations within the confines of this paper.)

The theory I shall present could be looked on as a way of specifying the property role, a way independent of and a little more informative than specifying this role via the apparent quantifications over properties that are to be found in our discourse. This theory identifies the property role with the role "thing that can be said of something". This role is a special case of the role "thing that can be said". Some things that can be said are things that can be said *period*, things that can be said *full stop*. For example: that Chicago has a population of over two million is something that can be said; another thing that can be said is that no orchid has ever filed an income-tax return. But these things—'propositions' is the usual name for them—are not things that can be said *of* anything, not even of Chicago and orchids. One can, however, say *of* Chicago that it has a population of over two million, and one can also say this very same thing of New York. And, of course, one can say it of Sydney and of South Bend. (It can be said only falsely of South Bend, of course, but lies and honest mistakes are possible.) I will assume that anything that can be said of anything can be said of anything else. Thus,

---

[17] And it would treat propositions as a special kind of relation: it would treat properties as monadic relations and propositions as 0-adic relations.

if there are such things as topological spaces, one can say of any of them that it is a city with a population of over two million, or that it has never filed an income-tax return. I don't know why anyone would, but one could.

Let us call such things, propositions and things that can be said of things, *assertibles*. The assertibles that are not propositions, the things that can be said *of* things, we may call *unsaturated* assertibles. I will assume that the usual logical operations apply to assertibles, so that, for example, if there are such assertibles as "that it has a population of over two million" and "that it once filed an income-tax return", there is also, automatically as it were, the assertible "that it either has a population of over two million or else has never filed an income tax return". (In a moment, I shall qualify this thesis.) It follows that the phrase I used to specify the role I wish to consider—"things that can be said of things"— cannot be taken too literally. For if there are any unsaturated assertibles, and if there are arbitrary conjunctions and disjunctions and negations of such unsaturated assertibles as there are, it will be impossible for a finite being to say most of them of anything. "Things that can be said of things" must therefore be understood in the sense "things that can in principle be said of things", or perhaps "things of a type such that some of the simpler things of that type can be said of things" or "things that can be said of things by a being without limitations". All these ways of qualifying 'said of' could do with some clarification, but I cannot discuss the problems they raise here. (One possible solution to the problem raised by human limitations for our role-specification would be to substitute something like 'can be true of' or 'is true or false of' for 'can be said of' in our specification of the unsaturated-assertible role. This is, in my view, a promising suggestion, but I do think that 'can be said of' has certain advantages in an initial, intuitive presentation of the theory of properties I shall present.)

It seems to me that there are such things as unsaturated assertibles: there are things that can be said of things. It seems to me that there is an x such that x can be said of y and can also be said of z, where z is not identical with y. One of the things you can say about the Taj Mahal is that it is white, and you can say that about the Lincoln Memorial, too. (I take it that 'about' in this sentence is a mere stylistic variant on 'of'.) If, during the last presidential campaign, you had heard someone say, "All the negative things you've said about Gore are perfectly true, but don't you see that they're equally applicable to Bush?" you wouldn't have regarded this sentence as in any way problematical—not logically or syntactically or lexically problematical, anyway. (And if the speaker had said 'perfectly true *of him*' instead of 'perfectly true' your only objection could have been that this phrasing was wordy or pedantic.) I say it seems to me that there are such things. I certainly see almost no reason to *deny* that there are such things, other than the reasons we have (and which I have tried to lay out) for denying that there are abstract objects of any sort. (For assertibles, if they exist, are certainly abstract objects.) I say 'almost no reason' because there are, I concede, powerful "Russellian" objections to admitting assertibles into our ontology. If there are things that can be said, there are things that can be said of things that can be said. We can say of a proposition that it is false or unsupported by the evidence. We can say of "that it is white" that it can be said truly of more than one thing. Now *one* of the things we can say of "that it is white" would seem to be that it isn't white. That's a thing that can be said *truly* about "that it is white"—a thing that can be said of something is obviously not a visible thing, and only a visible thing can have a color—so, *a fortiori*, it's a thing that can be said about "that it is white". It would seem, therefore, that one of the things we can say about "that it is white" is that it can't be said truly of itself. And it would seem that we can say this very same thing about, for example, "that it has a population of over two million". It seems evident therefore that, if there are things that can be said of things, one of them is "that it can't be said truly of itself". What could be more evident than that this is one of the things that can be said (whether truly or falsely) about something? But, of course, for reasons well known to us all, whatever things that can be said of things there may be, it can't be that one of them is "that it can't be said truly of itself". At any rate, there can't be such a thing if—as we are supposing—anything that can be said of something can be said of anything. If, therefore, we accept the conditional 'If there are things that can be said of things, one of them must be "that it can't be said truly of itself"', we can only conclude that there are no things that can be said of things. Well, I choose to deny the conditional. It's true that it seems self-evident. But, then, so does 'If there are sets, there is a set containing just those sets that are not members of themselves.' Everyone who accepts the existence of sets or properties is going to have to think hard about how to deal with Russell's Paradox. There are many workable ways of dealing with the paradox. (Workable in that, first, they generate a universe of abstract objects sufficient to the needs of the working mathematician, and, secondly, none of them is known to lead to a contradiction—and there's no particular reason to think that any of them does.) None of these "workable" ways of dealing with the paradox is, perhaps, entirely satisfying. In the case of first-order set- or property-theories, the workable ways of dealing with the paradox are workable ways of saying that certain open sentences must correspond to sets or properties—and leaving it an open question which, if any, of the others do. The friends of things that can be said of things can easily adapt any of the standard, workable ways of dealing with the paradox to the task of saying which open sentences must correspond to things that can be said about things. These adaptations will, I think, be neither more nor less intellectually satisfying than the "originals".

I propose, therefore, that properties be identified with unsaturated assertibles, with things that can be said of things. It seems unproblematical that unsaturated assertibles can successfully play the property role. And I would ask this: what is the property whiteness but something we, in speaking of things, occasionally predicate of some of them? And what is predicating something of something but *saying* the former *of* the latter? Well, perhaps someone will say that it sounds wrong or queer to say that whiteness is one of the things we can say of the Taj Mahal. I don't think that arguments that proceed from that sort of premise have much force, but I won't press the point. Anyone who thinks that unsaturated assertibles—from now on, I'll say simply 'assertibles'—cannot play the property role but is otherwise friendly to my arguments may draw this conclusion from them: there are, strictly speaking, no properties, but assertibles may be pressed into service to do the work that would fall to properties if it were not for the inconvenient fact that there are no properties to do it. If we suppose that there are assertibles, and if we're unwilling to say that assertibles are properties, what advantage should we gain by supposing that there are, in addition, things that we *are* willing to call properties?

Now if properties are assertibles, a wide range of things philosophers have said using the word 'property' make no sense. For one thing, a property, if it is an assertible, cannot be a part or a constituent of any concrete object. If this pen exists, there are no doubt lots of things that are in some sense its parts or constituents: atoms, small manufactured items... perhaps, indeed, every sub-region of the region of space exactly occupied by the pen at t is at t exactly occupied by a part of the pen. But "that it is a writing instrument", although it can be said truly of the pen—and is thus, in my view, one of the properties of the pen—is not one of the parts of the pen. That it is not is as evident as, say, that the pen is not a cube root of any number. Nor is "that it is a writing instrument" in any sense present in any region of space. It makes no sense, therefore, to say that "that it is a writing instrument" is "wholly present" in the space occupied by the pen. In my view, there is just nothing *there* but the pen and its parts (parts in the "strict and mereological sense"). There are indeed lots of things true of the pen, lots of things that could be said truly about the pen, but those things do not occupy space and cannot be said to be wholly (or partly) present anywhere.

If properties are assertibles, it makes no sense to say, as some philosophers have said, that properties are somehow more basic ontologically than the objects whose properties they are. A chair cannot, for example, be a collection or aggregate of the properties ordinary folk say are the properties of a thing that is not a property, for a chair is not a collection or aggregate of all those things one could truly say of it. Nor could the apparent presence of a chair in a region of space "really" be the co-presence in that region of the members of a set of properties—if only because there is no way in which a property can be present in a region of space. (I hope no one is going to say that if I take this position I must believe in "bare particulars". A bare particular would be a thing of which nothing could be said truly, an obviously incoherent notion.)

Properties, if they are assertibles, are not (as some philosophers have said they are) objects of sensation. If colors are properties and properties are assertibles, then the color white is the thing that one says of something when one says of it that it is white. And this assertible is not something that can be seen—just as extracting a cube root is not something you can do with a forceps. We never see properties, although we see *that* certain things have certain properties. (Looking at the pen, one can see that what one says of a thing when one says it's cylindrical is a thing that can be said *truly* of the pen.) Consider sky-blue—the color of the sky. Let us suppose for the sake of the illustration that nothing—no exotic bird, no flower, no 1958 Cadillac—is sky-blue. (If I say that nothing is sky-blue, it's not to the point to tell me that the sky is sky-blue or that a reflection of the sky in a pool is sky-blue, for there is no such thing as the sky and there are no such things as reflections. And don't tell me that when I look at the sky on a fine day I perceive a sky-blue quale or visual image or sense-datum, for there are no qualia or visual images or sense-data. I may be sensing sky-bluely when I look at the sky on a fine day, but that shows at most that something has the property "sensing sky-bluely"; it does not show that something has the property "being sky-blue".) Now some philosophers have contended that if, as I have asked you to suppose, nothing is sky-blue, it must be possible to *see* the property "being sky-blue". After all (they argue), this property is in some way involved in the visual experience I have when I look at the sky, and this fact can't be explained by saying that when I look at the sky I'm seeing something that has it, for (we are supposing) nothing has it. And what is there left to say but that when I look upwards on a fine day I see the uninstantiated property "being sky-blue"? I would answer as follows: since the property "being sky-blue" is just one of those things that can be said of a bird or a flower or a 1958 Cadillac (or, for that matter, of human blood or the Riemann curvature tensor), we obviously don't *see* it. It's involved in our sensations when we look upwards on a fine day only in this Pickwickian sense: when we do that, we sense in the way in which visitors to the airless moon would sense during the lunar day if the moon were surrounded by a shell of sky-blue glass. And why *shouldn't* we on various occasions sense in the way in which we should sense *if* an X were present when in fact there is no X there?

Some philosophers have said that existence is not a property. Are they right or wrong? They are wrong, I say, if there is such a thing to be said about something as that it exists. And it would seem that there is. Certainly there is this to be said of a thing: that it might not have existed. And it is hard to see how there could be such an assertible as "that it might not have existed" if there were no such assertible as "that it exists".

Some philosophers have said that there are no individual essences or haecceities, no "thisnesses" such as "being *that* object" or "being identical with Alvin Plantinga". Are they right or wrong? They are wrong, I say, if one of the things you can say about something is that it is identical with Alvin Plantinga. Is there? Well, it would seem that if Plantinga hadn't existed, it would still have been true that he might have existed. (It would seem so, but it has been denied.) And it is hard to see how there could be such a thing as the saturated assertible "that

A Theory of Properties | 137

Alvin Plantinga might have existed" if there were no such thing as the unsaturated assertible "that it is Alvin Plantinga".

Some philosophers have said that, although there are obviously such properties as redness and roundness, it is equally obvious that there is no such property as "being either red or not round". They have said, to use a phrase they favor, that the world, or the Platonic heaven, is "sparsely", not "abundantly", populated with properties. Are they right? If properties are assertibles, only one answer to this question seems possible: No. If one of the things you can say about something is that it is red and another thing you can say about something is that it is round, then, surely, one of the things you can say about something is that it is either red or not round. (Mars is either red or not round, and *that*, the very same thing, is also true of the Taj Mahal and the number four—given, of course, that all three objects exist.) It is, of course, our answer to the question 'Is the world sparsely or abundantly supplied with properties?'—"abundantly"—that eventually leads to our troubles with Russell's Paradox. But, again, the alternative doesn't seem possible.

Some philosophers have denied the existence of uninstantiated properties. Is this a plausible thesis? If properties are assertibles, it is a very implausible thesis indeed, for there are obviously things that can be said of things but can't be said *truly* of anything: that it's a—non-metaphorical—fountain of youth, for example. No doubt someone, Ponce de León or some confidence trickster, has said this very thing about some spring or pool. (If there are uninstantiated properties, are there *necessarily* uninstantiated properties? Yes indeed, for one of the things you can say about Griffin's *Elementary Theory of Numbers* is that it contains a correct proof of the existence of a greatest prime. You can say it about *Tess of the D'Urbervilles*, too. It would seem, moreover, that one of the things you can say of something, one of the things that is "there" to be said about a thing, is that it is both round and square.)

Some philosophers have said that properties exist only contingently. This would obviously be true if there could not be uninstantiated properties, but it would be possible to maintain that there are uninstantiated properties and that, nevertheless, some or all properties are contingently existing things. Could this be? Well, it would certainly seem not, at least if the accessibility relation is symmetrical. One of the things you can say about something is that it is white. Are there possible worlds in which there is no such thing to be said of anything? Suppose there is such a world. In that world, unless I'm mistaken, it's not even possibly true that something is white. Imagine, if you don't mind using this intellectual crutch, that God exists in a world in which there's no such thing to be said of a thing—not "said *truly* of a thing": "said of a thing *simpliciter*"—as that it is white. Then God, who is aware of every possibility, is not aware of the possibility that there be something white. (If God could be aware of or consider the possibility that there be something white, he would have to be aware that one of the things that can be said of something is that it is white.) Therefore, there must be no such possibility in that world as the possibility that there be something white. Therefore, with respect to that possible world, the possible world that is in fact actual is not even possible; that is to say, in that world, the world that is in fact the actual world doesn't exist (or exists but is impossible). But then the accessibility relation is not symmetrical. And I should want to say about the proposition that the accessibility relation is symmetrical what Gödel said of the power-set axiom of set theory: it forces itself upon the mind as true. Admittedly, there are steps in this argument that can be questioned and have been questioned—or at least, the corresponding steps in certain very similar arguments have been questioned. (I give one example of an objection, not the most important objection, that could be made to this argument: the argument at best proves that 'that it is white' denotes *an* object in, or with respect to, every possible world; it doesn't follow from this that this phrase denotes the *same* object in every possible world.) But the argument seems convincing to me. At any rate, it is the argument that will have to be got round by anyone who wants to say that properties do not exist necessarily.

There are many other interesting and important theses about properties than those I have considered. But the theses I have considered are, or so it seems to me, all the interesting and important theses to which the theory of properties as assertibles is relevant. The fact that this theory is inconsistent with various interesting and important theses about properties shows that, although it may be very close to being vacuous, it does not manage to be entirely vacuous.[18]

The University of Notre Dame

---

[18] A condensed version of this paper (with the appropriately condensed title "Properties") will appear in a *Festschrift* for Alvin Plantinga.

6. How Do Particulars Stand to Universals?

D. M. Armstrong

The theory advanced in this paper is not mine. It was put forward by Donald Baxter in a remarkable paper read to a departmental meeting at the University of Connecticut in the spring semester of 1999. It is now, I am glad to say, published (Baxter, 2001). Illuminating discussions with Baxter have continued, including his comments on this paper, but I will present what I take to be his central inspiration in my own way. (We diverge on one important point, to be indicated.) His theory seems to me to be very attractive, and well worth further investigation.

The problem of how universals stand to their particulars might seem of little concern to nominalists, where the latter term is taken very broadly to include all metaphysicians who deny the existence of universals, meaning by the term "universals" entities that are strictly identical in their different instantiations. But in fact it should be of considerable interest to these philosophers. For the difficulty of giving a coherent account of the instantiation of universals is regularly used by them as a major reason for denying the existence of these entities. If Baxter's account goes through, then the case for the rejection of universals is significantly, though not of course decisively, weakened.

Suppose that a particular, a as usual, has the non-relational property, good old F, which is a universal. (Baxter's theory should be perfectly hospitable to the idea that the class of universals is, in David Lewis's term, a sparse one, members being perhaps postulated a posteriori on the basis of our best science.) The difficulty is to understand the "fundamental tie" between a and F. The relation cannot be strict identity, because we want to distinguish the particular and its property. But equally, a and F cannot be "distinct existences" because then they cannot be united except by a fully blown relation, call it "I" for "instantiation". Then, as F. H. Bradley and others have pointed out,

John Hawthorne has given me some extremely valuable critical comments on this paper. In some of the footnotes I will reproduce his objections and reply to the points he has made. Thanks also to Dean Zimmerman for his comments.

the problem reappears. How are a, I, and F to be brought together? One can, using Scotist terminology, speak of a "formal" distinction between a and F, a distinction that is more than identity but less than a "real" distinction. But this, alas, seems a label for the problem, not a solution. Baxter's suggestion is that particulars really do participate in their universals (as the young Socrates suggests to Parmenides and Zeno in Plato's *Parmenides*!). Putting it in more contemporary terms, the relation is one of intersection, intersection understood as a case of partial identity.

To grasp the import and strength of Baxter's proposal, it is helpful to recall Plato's notion of the universal as a "one over many". Let us alter this a little, moving it more decisively towards an immanent theory of universals, to give "one running through many". (If the universals are transcendent, how could they intersect with particulars?) But it is also essential to consider the relation between a particular and its properties, in particular its non-relational properties ("intrinsic" properties is the more common term, but it has some misleading associations), where the properties are taken to be universals. Plato seems to have thought that there was no special problem here and discusses it, as far as I know, in only two places (*Sophist* 251 a–d and *Philebus* 14). In each case the discussion is rather brief and dismissive. But, after all, if we are taking the properties to be universals, the problem of how the one particular stands to its many properties ought to be a close relative of the problem of how the one property stands to its many particulars.[1] Perhaps the two problems have the same solution.

Let us be clear how this theory conceives of particulars. It must reject what we might call Universalism, the view that a particular is nothing more than a bundle of universals. This is a view that Russell put forward in his later period, but few other philosophers have been convinced. Instead, we should hold that there is an ineliminable factor of particularity in particulars. There is something that *has* the properties, a subject–attribute view as opposed to a bundle view. (I note in passing that we do not have to make the subject, the "thin particular" as I sometimes call it, something hidden from experience, as Locke notoriously, and I'm sorry to say pusillanimously, hides it. We experience

---

[1] Perhaps Plato really thought of the *immanent* properties of particulars as tropes, as scholars of the *Phaedo* have suggested, leaving the universals, the Forms, in another realm. If so, the symmetry of the situation would have escaped him, and he could not have taken *participation* of particulars in universals as a partial identity.

particulars as *this* and *that* as well as experiencing their properties.) That the properties are all properties of the one particular is a primitive, not further definable, notion. This, I suggest, should be construed as a *oneness*, a genuine one, a *strict* identity, that runs through its many properties.

Baxter's idea then becomes clear. A universal is also a *oneness*, a genuine one, a *strict* identity, that runs through its many particulars. Particulars are ones running through many different universals, universals are ones running through many different particulars. A particular instantiating a universal is an intersection of the two sorts of oneness, a point of partial identity. That, on this theory, is what the formal distinction *is*. The particular and the universal intersect. Consider a cross that has been cut out of a single piece of wood. The intersection of the vertical portion of the cross (which models the particular) and the horizontal portion (which models the universal) gives a rough, but perhaps helpful, model for a's being F.

We have the notion of mere overlap, together with the notion of whole and proper part, in the simple mereological calculus. But the relation between the instantiated particulars and the instantiating universals cannot be mereological. That is why the analogy of the cross is rough only. Metaphysicians generally recognize that a's being F (a "fact" as Russell and Wittgenstein have it, a "state of affairs" in my own terminology) has a non-mereological form of unity. Some, David Lewis in particular, make this a reproach to these alleged entities, on the grounds that there is no other ultimate form of combination in the world except the mereological. If Baxter is correct, however, what we have in a fact or state of affairs is *a non-mereological partial identity*. Particulars and universals participate *in each other*.[2]

It is quite clear that this hypothesized partial identity of particular and universal is not mereological. But if states of affairs (facts) are allowed to exist, as I think they do, then it seems that mereology cannot be the only sort of composition in the world. The state of affairs of a's being F is, it would seem, a complex object, but is not just the mereological sum of a and F. Suppose a is not G, a property instantiated

---

[2] David Lewis pointed out to me that in "classical" (bundle) trope theories, in particular in the case of D. C. Williams (1966), monadic states of affairs are constituted by the *intersections* of two bundles: a compresent bundle of monadic tropes that is the particular, and an equivalence class of exactly resembling tropes that is the universal. An interesting parallel.

elsewhere. Given unrestricted mereological composition, which I uphold, then there exist a mereological sum $a + G$ just as much as $a + F$. But surely a and F are more tied together than a and G? So I say that they form a non-mereological unity. At the same time, a and F do seem to be in some sense *parts* of the state of affairs. So they will have to be non-mereological parts. And if they are partially identical, then this will be non-mereological partial identity.[3]

The great attraction of the theory is that it involves nothing but the particulars and universals. Because the suggested link between the two is partial identity, any need for a fundamental tie, a copula, or what have you, seems to be eliminated. All the trouble that this tie has caused to those of us who accept universals alongside particulars, the tie that so many others use as a major reproach against the postulation of universals, is at a stroke removed. It may be, of course, that Baxter's idea will run into other, equally distressing, difficulties. But in the meanwhile it seems like a theory that we ought to look into closely.

In order to get a grip on the new theory, it may be helpful to begin by applying it to a very simple "world", one not dissimilar to Leibniz's world of monads, but without God. This world is a world of simple particulars and simple universals, where the universals are non-relational properties. It can be represented as a grid (see Figure 1). The ticks have been put in at random to illustrate the points of intersection: the states of affairs. The particulars (lower case) and universals (upper case) are not to be thought of as anything but the columns and rows themselves (in so far as they are filled). Reality, in this simple scheme—or, better because more cautious, first-order and positive real-

	a	b	c	d	e	→
F	√		√			
G	√	√		√		
H			√	√	√	
J	√	√		√		
K		√	√		√	
↓						

Figure 1

---

[3] The notion of non-mereological composition deserves much closer examination, but here this paragraph must suffice. Baxter explains instantiation in terms of what he calls "aspects", but I have found this part of his theory difficult to understand.

ity—*consists* of these criss-crossing identities. It is not a matter of somehow putting together particulars that totally exclude universals, and universals that totally exclude particulars. The tradition has taught us of the apparently insoluble problem that this raises, and we have already adverted to this difficulty. It may help to point out that the totality of the columns and the totality of the rows—the particulars and the universals—each constitutes the *whole* of reality, or, again more cautiously, the whole of positive and first-order reality. Particulars and universals are, on this theory, an inseparable package deal because they each help to *constitute* the other.[4]

A natural corollary is that each atomic particular intersects with at least one universal—a tick in every row—and, still more strongly, that each atomic universal intersects with at least one particular—a tick in every column. The grid-world is thoroughly "Aristotelian" in spirit. Particulars without properties and universals that are uninstantiated

---

[4] I take the liberty of inserting comments by John Hawthorne at this point:

I think it's worth bringing out some of the ways in which partial identity does not fit the format of standard mereology. The closest thing to partial identity in mereology is overlap, but partial identity does not satisfy the standard axioms for overlap: note in this connection: (i) Consider a really simple world with one particular instantiating one universal. Call them P and U. P overlaps U. But there is nothing left over, so to speak, when you "take away" U from P. (We don't have thin particulars anymore.) But standard mereology says, for example, that if P overlaps U and isn't identical to U, then either P overlaps something U doesn't or else U overlaps something that P doesn't. Similarly, standard mereology say that if P overlaps U but isn't a part of U, then there is something that is part of P that is not part of U. And it says that if P overlaps U and is a part of U then either U is identical to P or else there is something that U overlaps that P does not. (ii) Standard mereology says that if x overlaps y and x is part of z then z overlaps y. But partial identity in your sense isn't like overlap in this way. An electron is partially identical to electronhood. But that doesn't mean that anything that the electron is part of is partially identical to electronhood.

I reply that, in the very small world in which Hawthorne asks me to contemplate the relation that holds between P and U, it cannot be compared to mereological *overlap*. A resemblance to such overlap fails for this limiting case. In the actual world, however, the comparison to overlap seems to hold because, in general, universals have multiple instantiations and particulars have multiple properties. And, as I go on to argue in the text, because in the proposed new scheme truths of predication are necessary rather than contingent, merely possible worlds do not have to be taken with great ontological seriousness.

Nor, I think, is it the case that "we don't have thin particulars anymore". The thin particular remains as the particular considered in abstraction from its properties, even though the link to its properties is now a necessary one. But I do accept the point that, even if the electron is partially identical with electronhood (a dubious property!), it does not follow that it is partially identical (in my sense) with anything an electron is part of. That is a difference from mereological parthood.

come out, on this theory, as illegitimate abstractions. A welcome result, I suggest.

It is customary to accept that particulars are contingent existences, and I do not want to contradict this (although I am deeply uncertain about the metaphysical possibility of a world that contains no particulars at all). I have for many years argued that universals, also, are contingent existences, not necessary ones. In our diagram world this modal symmetry can be preserved. However, since the universal is identical in its different instances, to "eliminate" one of the universals in a diminished world is to eliminate each one of its instantiations. It is to eliminate a whole row. Equally, though, the particular is the same particular "in" each of its different properties. To "eliminate" it is to eliminate a whole column.

But what of the points of intersection, the states of affairs? Is it not a central idea in classical logical atomism—in the *Tractatus* in particular—that any state of affairs (fact) might not have existed, *yet everything else remain exactly the same*? The trouble is, though, that in the intersection theory neither the row that is the universal, nor the column that is the particular, would *be* exactly the same. Is the theory forced to say that, given the actual universals and the actual particulars, each intersection, each state of affairs, is then necessary?

We are indeed forced to say this. (Or so I think, although Baxter still upholds the contingency of predication: see Baxter, 2001, pp. 449, 462.) But is it so unacceptable a conclusion? Two respectable developments in contemporary metaphysics go down the same path. First, consider trope theory, the theory that properties exist, but are particulars rather than universals. Many trope theorists, for instance John Heil (2003, sect. 13.3) and Peter Simons[5], hold that particulars are, in C. B. Martin's phrase, *non-transferable*. A property of a particular is essentially a property of that particular. What is this but saying that, though particular and trope may be contingent existences, the fact that this particular has this trope is a necessary truth?

Second, consider David Lewis's counterpart theory. Could a particular have been different in nature from what it actually is? Such a counterpart in another world, Lewis holds, cannot be *strictly* the same as the particular. So it seems to me that his view at least *should* be that

---

[5] Simons, in a personal communication, tells me that, although he upholds this view, he does not explicitly argue for it anywhere in his work.

predications are really necessary.[6] Lewis is, however, prepared to accept a *loose* sense of "identity". There can be counterparts of *a* in other possible worlds, he allows, counterparts that in a loose sense can be said to be "the very same particular".

At any rate, the intersection theory can largely follow Lewis here. Where *a* is in fact F, this is strictly necessary. Nevertheless, there is a sense in which *a* might not have been F. Object *a* and property F might not have existed, but instead there might have been counterpart *a'* and counterpart F' where *a'* is *not* F'. These close counterparts are very like *a* and F respectively, but would lack this particular intersection. Like any counterpart theory, this gives us less than we might have hoped, but perhaps it gives us enough. As a "one worlder", I hope for a counterpart theory that does not invoke possible worlds other than our actual world; and as a naturalist, I hope for a theory that does not postulate actual entities over and above the spatio-temporal system. I believe that these two rather strong demands can be satisfied, but cannot discuss these issues here. The simple world of monads that I have set up for the purposes of discussion is, of course, itself a mere counterpart of the actual world. Indeed, it is a very impoverished counterpart.[7]

---

[6] To those who doubt this, I offer the following argument. Lewis's "pluriverse"—all the possible worlds—is a necessary being. Whatever goes to make up a necessary being must itself be necessary. So a certain particular's having a certain property in a certain world will be necessary. (But we can only know the truth of predications a posteriori because we cannot know exactly which world we are in.)

[7] Hawthorne writes:

Concerning your counterpart theory: The natural way of thinking about how counterpart theory is to work fails. Look at your grid world. Consider a world without *a*. Your idea is that while F would not exist in that world, a counterpart of F would. But if F and *a* don't exist in that world, then none of the particular or universals in the original grid world would exist. The disappearance of *a* and in turn F infects everything else. For if there isn't F there isn't *c*. And if there isn't *c* there isn't H and K and so on. So what would ground the counterpart relation of similarity? We now see that the world without the particular named '*a*' would, strictly speaking, be a world in which none of the universals and particulars in the original grid world would exist. So what would make a property in another world a counterpart of "*a*"? It cannot be similarity between this world and that, construed as some kind of sharing of particulars and universals. So how does one think about the relevant notion of similarity that is to undergird the counterpart relation and in turn the "loose and popular sense" of transworld identity?

Replying to this, I concede that it is true that the need for counterparts will have a great tendency to balloon outwards from the individual case, spreading outward, it may well be, to all the particulars and universals that the world contains. But the problem is much less serious in our actual, very large, world as contrasted with the small world of the diagram. The changes we consider in our actual counterfactuals are normally very small compared

I would hope (without being sure) that the proposed scheme allows two different monads to instantiate exactly the same universals. Such particulars would differ in number only. Similarly, two different universals might be instantiated by exactly the same particulars. What would be the principle of difference for two or more such universals? In the atomist scheme diagrammed in figure 1, these universals are simple. I suggest that such simple co-existent universals also would be no more than numerically different. Just as we need not postulate any haecceity that goes beyond bare numerical identity and difference of simple particulars, so, I suggest, we do not need any quiddity that goes beyond bare numerical identity and difference of simple universals.

I am proposing that instantiation of a universal be construed as an intersection, a partial identity, of the particular and universal involved. Intersection is a symmetrical relation, but instantiation appears to be *asymmetrical*. The universal does not instantiate the particular.[8]

The obvious way to deal with this difficulty is to appeal to the difference between the two *terms* of the relation. One is a particular, the other a universal. Is this not asymmetry enough? The asymmetry, we can then say, supervenes upon this categorial difference between the terms. This answer, however, although I think it is correct, uncovers another difficulty. Can the whole distinction between particular and universal be made out? (Famously, it was attacked by Ramsey, 1925.) In what has preceded in this paper, the two sorts of entities have been brought closer together than most theories bring them. Can they still be distinguished?

I think the distinction can still be made out. There remain important differences between particulars and universals; they have different

with the size of the world as a whole ("small miracles"). As a result, the counterpart particulars and universals that are involved will still have a great resemblance to their counterparts in the actual world.

[8] Hawthorne objects that if higher-order universals are allowed, and I do allow them, then the instantiation of such a universal cannot appeal to a difference between particulars and universals. I think that this is covered by relativization of the notion of a particular, something I argued for back in Armstrong (1978, see p. 133). Suppose that a certain first-order universal, F, itself falls under a universal, K. We can think of F as also being a *second-order* particular falling under the second-order universal K. The asymmetry is then preserved. Incidentally, if one thinks of nomic connection as a higher-order relation holding between first-order universals, and one extends the partial identity idea to this predication, then laws of nature become (strictly) necessary—an unexpected result, but not unwelcome to me.

properties, if that is the right word. Allowing ourselves to move beyond a monadic world, universals have a fixed number of "places" for particulars: they are monadic, dyadic, triadic, etc. It would seem, by the Indiscernibility of Identicals, that the very same universal could not have a different number of places for different instantiations, a principle that I have called Instantial Invariance.[9,10] That is why so-called anadic or multigrade predicates such as "is surrounded by" cannot apply in virtue of a single universal. Particulars, however, are not so limited, and may be found promiscuously instantiating universals of different adicities.

I think the repeatability of universals is a further mark of differentiation. There is no modal limit to their being instantiated at indefinitely many places and times. On some views, particulars may remain strictly identical over time. This is a sort of repeatability, the very same thing at a series of different times, but it is strictly limited by comparison with universals. If these two marks of difference between particulars and universals can be sustained, then these asymmetries between them can be offered as constituting the asymmetry of the "fundamental tie".[11]

Given that the distinction between particulars and universals has first been made out, it is worth noticing that the state of affairs of *a's being F* is itself a particular rather than a universal, because it is not promiscuously repeatable (I think not repeatable at all) in the way that a universal is. (I call this "the victory of particularity".[12]) The world itself is a particular instantiating a hugely complex structural universal (perhaps infinitely complex, if the simplifying assumption of atomism proves unsustainable). This state of affairs is a particular, not a universal. As I have already noted, there is a sense in which, if the intersection thesis is correct, both particulars (the columns) and universals (the rows) exhaust first-order reality, because of the thoroughgoing way that they

[9] Fraser MacBride has pointed out that I require the further premise that the adicity is a non-relational feature of universals (1998, p. 28). Without discussing the matter here, I will just say that I think it is a very plausible premise.

[10] Hawthorne objects that Instantial Invariance applies even to first-order particulars. They have the instantial invariance number 0 in all cases, because they can never be instantiated. This seems to me to be ontologically insensitive. The "0" is a fancy way of saying that they are not the sort of thing that can be instantiated.

[11] Hawthorne objects that this way of differentiating between particulars and universals would rule out the possibility of particulars being bilocated, or, I suppose he would also say, multilocated. But bilocation is a very controversial idea, and in the absence of strong arguments for it I think the intersection theory can simply deny it.

[12] See Armstrong (1997, sect. 8.4).

criss-cross. But, that having been said, the world is a very complex particular, and is not a very complex structural universal. It only *instantiates* (intersects with, on the theory being developed) that very complex universal.

What is the ontological status of the blanks in the diagram? Do we want to fill them with negative states of affairs, as Russell wanted to do in his logical atomism? The answer seems to be that this is quite unnecessary. Speaking strictly, they are not possibilities at all. If *a* is not G, then it is a possibility that *a* should have been G only in the loose sense. For adding a new instance of G is to change what G *is*. So it can only be a counterpart of the true G.

(This leads to a very interesting consequence that quite contradicts previous thinking of mine. If each instantiation of universal F is necessary and no other instantiation of F is possible, then the truthmaker for the truth that this class of particulars is the totality of the Fs seems to be: no more than just these instantiations. In previous work, most recently in Armstrong (1997), I argued, following Russell, that a general fact over and above the sum of the particular instantiations is needed as truthmaker for this truth. But that depended on its being a *contingent* truth. Removing the need for general facts, at least in such contexts, would be a notable ontological economy.)

But what of relations? The scheme as so far adumbrated might perhaps suit a monadologist with universals that are themselves all monadic. But if two particulars are related in a certain way, how can that relation be partially identical with these particulars?

An immediate qualification is in order. I think that we need be concerned here only with *external* as opposed to internal relations. (Though I shall be pointing out shortly that, given the intersection theory, the term "external" is not well chosen.) In the case of internal relations, as I use the term, the relation is wholly determined by its terms—by its "foundations", as it is sometimes put. It is plausible, and I think true, that the relation in these cases is no "addition of being", is not something over and above, the foundations. Or, as we can also put it, the sole truthmakers required for the truth that a certain internal relation holds are the existence of its foundations. Such relations make no troubling demands on the intersection theory. Even our monads in Figure 1, or again "island universes" that are totally cut off from each other because they are different, unconnected, space–times, can have internal relations. The island universes may resemble to different degrees. The monads will at least have the relation of difference. These are real relations, but they are internal ones, and seem to make no ontological demands beyond the existence of the suitable foundations, which are found in their terms.

Even many relations that it is natural to take to be external have an internal component. Consider the marriage relation, for instance. Those who are married must be persons, and, at least in the old understanding of marriage, of different sexes. We are interested here, though, in external relations that have little if any admixture of internality. Causality and the spatio-temporal relations are the generally accepted paradigms.

Working, then, with external relations, let us begin with the cases that, though difficult, present the fewest problems for the intersection thesis. These cases are relations that are, by necessity, symmetrical. This can include relations of any adicity—all that is required is that the relation holds for the terms taken in any order. Spatial and temporal distances are examples of such relations in a Newtonian world, space-time interval in an Einsteinian one.

A plausible thesis naturally presents itself for such relations. They and their converses constitute but one relation. "$a\ R\ b$" and "$b\ R\ a$" are different orderings of the names for the terms of the relation, but they do *not* represent two different, necessarily coexistent, states of affairs. That latter view looks to be quite a serious case of metaphysical double vision. If this is correct, then we can present the putative "intersections" for dyadic cases in what is still a relatively simple spread-sheet (see Figure 2).

Here the universals are supposed to intersect not with individual particulars, but with pairs (or triples, quadruples, and so on). We have seen, I hope, that it is not implausible to interpret the monadic case as a partial identity holding between the particular and the universal. Relations, or at any rate external relations, definitely knit things together,

	{a, b}	{a, c}	{b, c}	→
R	√		√	
S	√	√		
T	√			
↓				

Figure 2

and so to that degree unify them. Consider how two space–times not connected by any external relation seem to be irreducibly *two*. But now in thought supply causal and spatio-temporal relations between the two. They are then much more *one* than they were before the additions! Nominalists would presumably see this as just a fact about us: the conditions under which our minds are led to treat something as a unit. The intersection thesis, however, will be that this unity that external relations introduce is ontological, a matter of partial identity, between the relation, a universal, and the class of the terms that instantiate the universal. Unity, after all, has something to do with identity.

So why should we not interpret this unification as a partial identity, one that holds between the relation and the terms? This seems to be a line that a partial identity theory can plausibly take. We do need to note that it is the pair (say) that provides the locus, as it were, of the identity, rather than the mere mereological sum of the terms. The demarcation of the two terms just *as* these two terms is of the essence. The identity, I therefore suppose, runs through the class of the terms, rather than their mere sum. But this does not seem to pose any particular problem, although no doubt it points to the need for a suitable metaphysics of classes.

We do need to notice, though, that the term "external" is, from the point of view of the intersection hypothesis, not very well chosen. But perhaps it was never well chosen. It has already been pointed out that the external relations unify, and to unify is to make things in some degree or aspect *one*. This point, I think, was appreciated by the Absolute Idealist tradition, but was lost by upholders of analytic empiricism, myself included. (But here I will continue to use the word "external".)

So it seems that we can extend our "spreadsheet model" to include at least some relations. The relations in Figure 2 are external and simple (not further analyzable), and necessarily symmetrical. Instead of a horizontal list of simple particulars, substitute a list of all pairs of these particulars; then, if necessary, have a list of all triples; and so on as far as necessary. (It may be that all fundamental relations are dyadic.) Correlate the list of pairs with the dyadic relations, the triples with triadic relations, and so on. Ticks at intersection points indicate the atomic, but relational, polyadic, states of affairs.

One very interesting thing to notice here, pointed out by Cian Dorr, is that these sorts of relations permit a particularly simple theory of states of affairs (facts) (see Chapter 7 below, particularly n. 42). As a reproach to states of affairs, David Lewis has used the point that different states of affairs may have exactly the same constituents. For instance supposing unrealistically that *loving* is a universal, where *a* loves *b* and *b* loves *a*, he wonders how such different compositions from the very same elements is possible.[13] In the case of monadic atomic states of affairs no such different composition can arise. If your constituents are confined to *a* and F, you can only get one state of affairs. Atomic states of affairs that involve necessarily symmetrical relations also do not violate the principle, provided we agree, as was argued above, that permutations of the terms make no more than a verbal difference. (There will still be a distinction, though, between a state of affairs and the mere mereological sum of the constituents of that state of affairs. $a + F$ is not *a's being F*.)

But what of external relations that are asymmetrical or non-symmetrical? Consider necessarily asymmetrical external relations. Suppose that the external relation R is such that, if *a* has R to *b*, then *b* cannot have R to *a*. What intersection can there be between R and $\{a, b\}$ which would constitute *a*'s having R to *b*? It may seem hard to see. The situation does not seem any better if the relation is merely non-symmetrical. We still have to distinguish between two forms of intersection, where either both forms of intersection exist or just one. What does intersection come to in such a case? Two roads might intersect more than once, and, say, at different angles on the two occasions. But this is the intersection of particulars. Can there be two intersections, two partial identities, intersections of a dyadic universal and its two terms, the first marked for one direction of the relation, the second for the opposite direction?

I originally thought that this difficulty was extremely serious. Baxter, however, has pointed out to me that in fact it can be met without too much difficulty. Let *a* have R to *b*, and let that necessitate that *b* has not got R to *a*. Think of this asymmetric relation as being like a freeway, but with only two lanes (whose different directions can usefully symbolize the two possible directions of the relation). The terms may then be thought of as a highway *intersecting* with one of the lanes—the lane that gets the direction of the relation right—but *flying over* the other

---

[13] Lewis is perhaps basing himself on Nelson Goodman's rejection of what he calls 'Nominalism'. See Goodman, 1958, p. 55: 'a system is nominalistic... if no two entities are generated from exactly the same atoms.'

lane. After all, particulars between which there hold relations that have a direction do, as it were, relate to the different "ends" of the relation differently. That allows for the "two different possibilities" of intersection. It would be necessary to complicate the boxes that represent the intersections in our diagrams. For a necessarily asymmetrical relation there would be two boxes. Ticking one would make it wrong for a tick to appear in the other, although no tick need appear in either. For a genuinely non-symmetrical relation a 2 × 2 matrix would have to be inserted inside such a box, with the four possibilities of the relation holding in both directions, in neither, or in one only. Polyadic external relations of higher adicity, if any such are fundamental, would have as many "lanes"—possibilities of intersection—as possibilities of permuting the terms to give different "directions". One could think of these lanes as "dedicated" lanes, each lane dedicated to a different direction. Such is Baxter's ingenious, yet simple, resolution of the difficulty.

It does seem to work. I do nevertheless hanker for an ontology where the fundamental external relations are symmetrical of necessity (and where that necessity is explained in terms of the identity of the states of affairs involving the relation and the states of affairs where the terms are permuted). In addition to simplifying the theory of states of affairs, an advantage that we have already noticed, such an ontology would permit promiscuous recombination for possibilities (in the loose sense, of course, where possibilities involve mere counterparts). That is to say, none of the blanks in the grids would be determined, positively or negatively, by the ticked squares. An example of negative determination we have just met with concerns those cases where, if a has R to b, b cannot have R to a. A case of positive determination would be a necessarily transitive relation. If a has such a relation T to b, and b has it to c, then ticking the box for a Tc becomes obligatory. It would be nice if reality did not permit such irregularities! (For further argument, see Dorr's already cited paper in Chapter 7 below.)

That this is not an incoherent suggestion (or not obviously incoherent) is shown, for instance, by Randall Dipert (1997), who uses the formalism of graph theory to put forward the idea that the world is constructed with a single symmetric dyadic relation connecting particulars that are bare of non-relational properties. (This bareness is perhaps a dubious feature of his scheme. Should not a particular have at least one non-relational property?) Surface asymmetries can then be seen to emerge from particular arrangements of lines (instantiations of the single relation) connecting dots (the truly bare particulars). We do not of course have to maintain that such an analysis can be effected a priori. It might turn out to be necessary a posteriori.

It may be argued that such schemes are empirically implausible because such relations as *being before* (in time) and *causing* involve fundamental asymmetries. In *A World of States of Affairs* I have argued in detail that these relations, which may be asymmetrical *de facto*, are not necessarily so. (See Chapter 9 for *before* and Chapter 14, Section 4, for *causation*.) Temporal and causal loops, I suggest there, are possibilities. The argument there was developed in the interest of giving the maximum freedom for merely possible recombinations of atoms. In spreadsheet terms, it was concerned with the blanks. But the argument is, if good, available also in the service of a partial identity theory.

A further point. Perhaps we can we take heart from the symmetry that fundamental physics constantly seeks for, and to a considerable degree succeeds in finding, in fundamental laws and conceptions.

If viable, the intersection theory can be extended, perhaps, to properties and relations that attach not to particulars but to universals. For instance, contingent relations between universals, such as the contingent ones that I and others have argued for as constituting the laws of nature, could perhaps be seen as pairwise or n-wise partial, but non-mereological, identities holding between the universals involved. But, given intersection, it seems that the laws would be necessary. And there may be other identities reaching across many—for instance, identity over time—that some might wish to postulate.

University of Sydney

REFERENCES

Armstrong, D. M. (1978) *The Theory of Universals*, Cambridge University Press.

Armstrong, D. M. (1997) *A World of States of Affairs*, Cambridge University Press.

Baxter, Donald L. M. (2001) "Instantiation as Partial Identity", *Australasian Journal of Philosophy*, 79, 449–64.

Dipert, Randall (1997) "The Mathematical Structure of the World: The World as Graph", *Journal of Philosophy*, 94, 329–58.

Heil, John (2003) *From an Ontological Point of View*, Oxford: Clarendon Press.

Goodman, Nelson (1958) "On Relations that Generate", *Philosophical Studies*, 9, 65–6.

MacBride, Fraser (1998) "On How We Know What There Is", *Analysis*, 58, 27–37.

Ramsey, F. P. (1925) "Universals"; most recently published in *Properties*, D. H. Mellor and Alex Oliver (eds.), *Properties*, Oxford University Press, 1997, 57–73.

Williams, D. C. (1966) "The Elements of Being", in his *Principles of Empirical Realism*, Springfield, IL: Charles C. Thomas.

7. Non-symmetric Relations
Cian Dorr

1. PRIMITIVE PREDICATES

Let us say that a relation *r* is *symmetric* iff, whenever *x* bears *r* to *y*, *y* bears *r* to *x*; otherwise, *r* is *non-symmetric*.[1] In this paper I will argue for the thesis that, necessarily, there are no non-symmetric relations.

What is this predicate '...bears...to...' in terms of which 'symmetric' was defined? According to one important theory of relations, this predicate is *primitive*, in the same sense in which the two-place predicate 'instantiates' ('has', 'exemplifies') is primitive according to some theories of properties. When *x* bears *r* to *y*, this is not so *in virtue of* any more basic truths involving *x*, *r*, and *y*; there is no interesting answer to the question '*What is it* for *x* to bear *r* to *y*?' But it is not uncontroversial that 'bears' is primitive in this sense. Various analyses of this predicate have been proposed. For example, a believer in states of affairs might analyse '*x* bears *r* to *y*' as 'there is a state of affairs *s* such that *s* relates *x* to *y*, and *r* is the universal component of *s*.' The predicates '...relates...to...' and '...is a universal component of...' might be taken as primitive, or be analysed still further.

I regard the question of which predicates are primitive in this sense as the most fundamental question of metaphysics. Traditionally, metaphysics aspires not just to answer a long list of questions of the form 'are there Fs?' but to understand the *ultimate structure of reality*. This

---

Thanks to David Armstrong, Kit Fine, Allen Hazen, Jessica Moss, Josh Parsons, Gideon Rosen, Kieran Setiya, Timothy Williamson, and Dean Zimmerman, and to everyone with whom I have discussed this material. I also thank the Research School of Social Sciences at the Australian National University, where the first version of this paper was written. Finally, I would like to express my gratitude to David Lewis for his encouragement and advice.

[1] Russell (1903, p. 25), by contrast, rather misleadingly defines '*not-symmetric*' to mean: not symmetric, and also not *asymmetric*—where an asymmetric relation is one for which there are no *x* and *y* such that *x* bears it to *y* and *y* bears it to *x*.

aspiration should be understood, I think, as equivalent to the quest for a complete list of primitive predicates.[2]

But what do we mean when we ask whether some predicate, like 'bears', is primitive? 'Primitive' means 'unanalysable'; but what does 'unanalysable' mean? Unless we are extremely optimistic about conceptual analysis, we should not take it to mean '*conceptually* unanalysable'. For there are a great many predicates—'is an umbrella', 'is a dog', 'loves', 'is in pain'...—which only an extreme optimist would deny are primitive in *this* sense.[3] The project of listing all these predicates has nothing in common with the traditional metaphysical enterprise of understanding the ultimate structure of reality. Fortunately, we seem to understand a less demanding notion of analysis, better suited to the purposes of foundational metaphysics. We report such "analyses" when we say things like 'to be made of water is to be composed of H_2O molecules', or 'for one thing to be hotter than another is for the former to have a greater mean molecular kinetic energy than the latter'. As these examples make clear, analyses in this sense need not be accessible a priori. They also can be "de re", as when we say 'to be Napoleonic is to resemble a certain person, namely Napoleon', or 'to be an electron is to instantiate a certain universal, namely Electronhood'.[4]

Does this notion of analysis give us the notion of primitiveness we were looking for, or is the list of unanalysable predicates still too long and miscellaneous to be metaphysically significant? I will briefly mention two categories of predicates which might be thought to resist

---

[2] I don't mean to presuppose that it is always a *determinate* question whether a predicate is primitive. Certain views lead naturally to the conclusion that there is a certain amount of indeterminacy in the question. For example, surely there can be no determinate fact of the matter as regards whether it is 'instantiates' or 'is instantiated by' that is primitive: if one of them is primitive, it is indeterminate which it is. I discuss the issue of indeterminacy further in Dorr (2003).

[3] For the optimistic view, see Jackson (1998).

[4] As this last example shows, the question whether a predicate is *primitive* is quite different from the question whether a predicate *corresponds to a universal*. If this analysis is correct, then 'is an electron' corresponds to a universal but is not primitive: the whole point of positing Electronhood is to allow us to give a straightforward analysis of 'is an electron'. And conversely, if 'instantiates' is primitive, there is no corresponding reason to posit a corresponding binary relation of Instantiation. And even if we decide that 'instantiates' is not primitive, surely we should not analyse 'x instantiates y' as 'x bears Instantiation to y'. If we do, we will have taken the first step on Bradley's regress: unless we stop the regress arbitrarily, we will find ourselves analysing 'bears' in turn in terms of a ternary Bearing relation, and so on (Bradley 1897, ch. 3).

analysis without being primitive in the metaphysically interesting sense. First, there are *vague* predicates. The vagueness of 'small', for example, seems to prevent us from stating any interesting truth of the form 'to be small is to ... '. One way to respond to this challenge would be to allow the notion of analysis to have a vagueness correlative to the vagueness of the expressions being analysed. Thus, there might be a range of precise predicates having to do with an object's mass, volume, etc., such that it is determinate that one of them counts as an analysis of 'is small', although there is no specific one of them such that it is determinate that *it* is an analysis of 'is small'.

Second, there is the category of "semantically defective" predicates, comprising various predicates introduced by myths, fictions, and false theories, like 'is a unicorn', 'is a friend of Sherlock Holmes', 'is phlogiston', and perhaps 'is a Form' and 'is a monad'. It is hard to see how any of these predicates could be analysed, but clearly we don't want to count them all as primitive. We could deal with this problem by selecting some arbitrary logical contradiction (like 'is non-self-identical') to be the analysis of all such predicates. Alternatively, we could simply redefine 'primitive' as 'unanalysable, and not semantically defective'.

The notion of analysis I have been describing is naturally associated with a notion of analyticity. Say that a sentence (lacking quotational and intensional contexts) is *metaphysically analytic* iff it can be transformed into a logical truth by

(i) substituting analyses for analysanda;
(ii) substituting co-referential proper names; and
(iii) replacing semantically defective predicates with logically contradictory ones.

Unlike sentences that are analytic in the traditional sense, metaphysically analytic sentences can be a posteriori, like 'everything that is made of water is made of H_2O molecules', 'Hesperus is Phosphorus', and 'there are no unicorns'.[5] Nevertheless, metaphysical analyticity is a stronger notion than metaphysical necessity, at least as the latter notion is generally understood. All metaphysically analytic sentences are metaphysically necessary,[6] but the reverse is not true: 'If Socrates

---

[5] Cf. Kripke (1980, pp. 102–5, 126–7, 156–8).
[6] The only potential counter-examples I can think of are sentences like 'Napoleon exists', which count as logical truths according to standard logic, but are not

exists, Socrates is human' is generally thought to be metaphysically necessary, but it is clearly not metaphysically analytic, since Socrates does not need to be mentioned in the analysis of 'is human'.

2. RELATIONS

I will argue that all relations are necessarily symmetric by arguing that 'all relations are symmetric' is a metaphysically analytic truth. One way to argue for this thesis would be to argue for some analysis of 'bears' on which 'x bears r to y' and 'y bears r to x' turn out to be analytically equivalent. Another way to argue for the thesis would be to argue that the only primitive predicates are those on a certain list, where the predicates on the list are such that the only plausible analyses of 'bears' in terms of them render 'all relations are symmetric' analytic. Consider, for example, what I will call the *simple theory of states of affairs*. According to this theory there are just two primitive predicates: 'is a particular component of' and 'is a universal component of'. Given just these two predicates to work with, it is overwhelmingly natural to analyse 'x bears r to y' as 'there is an s such that x and y are the only particular components of s, and r is the only universal component of s'; and of course, under this analysis, 'all relations are symmetric' is analytic. We *could* give an analysis of 'x bears r to y' on which it is not equivalent to 'y bears r to x'—for example, we could analyse it as 'x is a particular component of r and r is a universal component of y'—but all such analyses are completely implausible.

A third way to argue for the thesis would be to argue that 'bears' is a semantically defective predicate. If it is, then 'there are no x, y, r such that x bears r to y' and hence 'there are no non-symmetric relations' count as metaphysically analytic, for the same reason that 'there are no unicorns' counts as metaphysically analytic. This would be a natural view for a Nominalist—a denier of the existence of universals, including relations—to hold. From a Nominalist point of view, predicates like 'is a universal', 'is a relation', 'instantiates', and 'bears' belong in the same category as 'is phlogiston': the theories that introduce these predicates

---

metaphysically necessary. This difficulty is easily resolved by adopting some version of free logic as our characterization of logical truth.

are so radically unlike the truth that there is no way for the predicates to acquire any non-defective meaning.

In fact, I will not argue for any analysis of 'bears', or for any specific list of primitive predicates, Nominalist or Realist in character. Instead, I will defend the logically weaker claim that whatever the true primitive predicates might be, they do not allow for any credible analysis of 'there are non-symmetric relations' on which this claim is consistent.

Before I proceed with this argument, I should briefly address the most common objection to the thesis. It is obvious that there are non-symmetric *predicates*—alas, we sometimes love those who do not love us. If the claim that there are no non-symmetric relations seems obviously false, that may be because it seems obvious that all (or most) two-place predicates correspond to relations. ('F' corresponds to r iff, for any x and y, x bears r to y iff Fxy.) Obvious though this may seem, I am committed to denying it. In my view, properties and relations are *sparse* as compared with predicates: in fact, it is an open question whether *any* of our current predicates correspond to relations.

This claim deserves a more sustained defence than I can provide in this paper.[7] For what it's worth, I do have a strategy for "explaining away" the appeal of the idea that all predicates correspond to properties or relations. In my view, our ordinary talk about these sorts of entities is governed by a certain fiction, "the fiction of abundant attributes". It is true, according to this fiction, that all predicates correspond to properties or relations; hence, we can *correctly* speak of non-symmetric relations like *loving, being taller than*, and so forth, even though in reality there are no such things. But even those who find this unsatisfactory might be able to make some other sort of sense of the thought that the properties and relations that correspond to most predicates are "derivative" entities rather than "fundamental" ones. If you think you can make sense of this thought, you probably should interpret my thesis—and my quantifiers more generally, at least in formal contexts—as restricted to "fundamental" entities.[8]

---

[7] See Ramsey (1925); Armstrong (1978, ch. 13); Mellor (1991); Dorr (2002, ch. 4–6).

[8] If there are universals, it will sometimes happen that x instantiates y but y does not instantiate x. Hence the predicate 'instantiates' is an example of a non-symmetric predicate. So if my thesis is true, it must be an example of a predicate that corresponds to no relation. This is unproblematic: as we have already seen in n. 4, the analysis of 'x instantiates y' as 'x bears Instantiation to y' seems like a bad idea for independent reasons. I am arguing for the view that there are no non-symmetric *relations*, not for the quite different view that there are no non-symmetric *primitive predicates*.

So far, I have been considering only binary relations; but the discussion extends in a predictable way to relations of higher degree. The only slight difficulty in the way of stating the thesis is the fact that the three-place predicate 'bears' doesn't have any natural counterparts in English that are appropriate for talking about relations of higher degree. We can say 'r holds among x, y, and z' or 'x, y, and z instantiate r'; but these expressions appear grammatically to contain the plural referring term 'x, y, and z'. Hence, just as 'Tom, Dick, and Harry lifted a piano' is logically equivalent to 'Dick, Harry, and Tom lifted a piano', 'r holds among x, y, and z' should, properly speaking, be logically equivalent to 'r holds among y, z, and x'. To get around this difficulty, the best the proponent of non-symmetric relations can do is to say things like 'r holds among x, y, and z, in that order' or 'x, y, and z instantiate r, in that order'; and it isn't very satisfactory to have to use such quasi-quotational devices to express purportedly fundamental metaphysical facts.[9] Since I don't want to rest my case on these facts about English, it seems best to state my thesis using an artificial notation. Let us abbreviate 'x bears r to y' as '$xy\Delta r$'; and let us stipulate that the $(n+1)$-place predicate '$x_1 \ldots x_n \Delta r$' is to be understood as a natural generalization of this predicate, playing the same role for n-ary relations that '$xy\Delta r$' plays for binary relations. Then my claim is that the order of the first n arguments in the formula '$x_1 \ldots x_n \Delta r$' is semantically irrelevant: in other words, when $k_1 \ldots k_n$ is some permutation of the first n integers, '$x_1 \ldots x_n \Delta r$' is metaphysically analytically equivalent to '$x_{k_1} \ldots x_{k_n} \Delta r$'.

The plan for the rest of the paper is as follows. In Sections 3 and 4 I present an argument that 'bears' is not primitive. In Sections 5, 6, and 7 I present and then argue against a range of other systems of primitive predicates which can allow for non-symmetric relations. In Sections 8 and 9 I say more in defence of the thesis that all relations must be symmetric. Finally, in Section 10 I present a new argument for the thesis, in the hope that it will convince some of those who reject the central premise of the main argument.

---

[9] In practice, of course, the qualifier 'in that order' doesn't have to be added every time. Nevertheless, in treating the order of the constituents of a plural referring term like 'x, y, and z' as significant, we are definitely bending the ordinary rules governing such expressions. On the ordinary rules, 'r holds among x, y, and z but does not hold among y, z, and x' should entail 'there are some things such that r holds among them, and some other things such that r does not hold among them, and each of the former things is identical to one of the latter things, and each of the latter things is identical to one of the former things', which is surely inconsistent.

3. CONVERSE RELATIONS AND BRUTE NECESSITIES

Consider the following rather plausible-looking principle:

> CONVERSES. For every r, there is an r^* such that, for any x and y, x bears r^* to y iff y bears r to x.

To put it more succinctly, everything has a converse, where a converse of some entity r is any entity r^* such that, for all x, y, x bears r^* to y iff y bears r to x. (Assuming that 'x bears r to y' entails 'r is a relation', everything that is not a relation is automatically one of its own converses, and so CONVERSES is equivalent to the claim that every *relation* has a converse.)

CONVERSES is not a *logical* truth in the narrow sense—as witness the fact that it becomes false if we replace the non-logical predicate 'bears' with some other predicate, like 'gives'. This fact is not very interesting on its own, but it takes on a new significance if we assume that 'bears' is primitive. For then it follows that CONVERSES is not metaphysically analytic. In no sense is there any *hidden contradiction* in the claim that there counter-examples to CONVERSES. This seems to me to be a very significant fact, as far as the modal and epistemological status of CONVERSES is concerned. I will defend the following two claims: first, if 'bears' is primitive, CONVERSES is not metaphysically necessary; second, if 'bears' is primitive, CONVERSES cannot be known for certain a priori.

The first of these claims follows from the following principle:

> POSSIBILITY. If a sentence S is logically consistent, and the only non-logical vocabulary in S consists of primitive predicates, then ⌈It is metaphysically possible that S⌉ is true.

The thought behind POSSIBILITY is that metaphysical necessity is never "brute": when a logically contingent sentence is metaphysically necessary, there is always some *explanation* for this fact. One sort of explanation involves the notion of metaphysical analyticity. It is metaphysically necessary that everything that is made of water is made of H$_2$O molecules: this is explained by the fact that to be made of water just is to be made of H$_2$O molecules. But this sort of explanation is available only when a sentence contains some *non*-primitive expressions that have such analyses. Another, quite different, sort of explanation involves the notion of essence. It is metaphysically necessary that, if Socrates exists, Socrates is human: this is explained by the fact that Socrates is *essentially* human. But this sort of explanation is available only when a sentence contains some rigid referring terms, or words (like 'Napoleonic' and perhaps 'electron') whose analysis involves such terms. It is not available for what we might call *purely non-referential* sentences, which contain no such expressions; hence it is not available for sentences that contain only primitive predicates and logical vocabulary. Thus, if 'bears' is primitive, the metaphysical necessity of CONVERSES cannot be explained in either of these two standard ways. At the very least, the burden of proof is on someone who wants to maintain the necessity of CONVERSES to come up with some explanation of a different sort.

The second claim—that if 'bears' is primitive, CONVERSES cannot be known for certain a priori—follows from the following principle:

KNOWABILITY. If a sentence S is logically consistent, and the only nonlogical vocabulary in S consists of primitive predicates, then ⌜No-one could know for certain a priori that not-S⌝ is true.

This claim seems to me to follow from the kernel of truth in the traditional empiricist claim that only analytic truths can be known a priori. The traditional empiricist claim needs to be weakened in several ways. First, we should replace 'known' with 'known for certain': if induction is rational, it seems that we must be be able to have a priori knowledge of some general principles like 'the future resembles the past' or 'good explanations are generally true ones', though we cannot justifiably be *certain* of such principles. Second, we should understand 'analytic' not as 'conceptually analytic', but as 'metaphysically analytic': this should be enough to take care of alleged counter-examples like 'nothing is both reddish and greenish all over', or 'any being who feels pain is conscious', or 'anyone who knows that snow is white believes that snow is white'. Third, we should restrict the empiricist thesis to *purely non-referential* sentences, which neither explicitly nor implicitly contain any referring expressions—this will take care of the cases Kripke discussed under the heading of the "contingent a priori", such as 'If m exists, then m is a metre long' (where m is the standard metre). But even when the empiricist doctrine is weakened in all these ways, it still entails KNOWABILITY; for a logically contingent sentence that contains no non-logical vocabulary besides primitive predicates cannot be metaphysically analytic, and must be purely non-referential.

The most important potential counter-examples to POSSIBILITY and KNOWABILITY are the theorems of mathematics, which are often taken to be both metaphysically necessary and a priori. However, many philosophers will be able to find some sense in which they can endorse the claims that numbers and other mathematical entities are "derivative" entities rather than "fundamental" ones, and that this fact is central to a proper understanding of the modal and epistemological status of the truths of mathematics.[10] Hence, if the example of mathematics prompts us to reject certain instances of POSSIBILITY and KNOWABILITY, we can still accept the restrictions of these claims to sentences in which all quantifiers are restricted to fundamental entities. But on its intended interpretation, the quantification in CONVERSES *is* restricted to fundamental entities. So even the restricted versions of POSSIBILITY and KNOWABILITY suffice to entail that, if 'bears' is primitive, CONVERSES is neither metaphysically necessary nor a priori.

Suppose we could somehow show that CONVERSES *is* metaphysically necessary, or a priori; then, by *modus tollens*, we could conclude that 'bears' is not primitive. This argument exemplifies the important role that POSSIBILITY and KNOWABILITY (even in their restricted versions) can play in allowing us to make progress in finding out which predicates are primitive. Using these principles, we can use what we know about metaphysical necessity and knowability a priori to rule out a great many hypotheses about primitive predicates. Since I will be making use of this sort of argument time and again, it will be useful to have a simple formula which encapsulates the conclusions of this section. Let us say that a sentence S is a *brute necessity* iff (i) S is not a logical truth; (ii) the only nonlogical vocabulary in S consists of primitive predicates; (iii) ⌜S is metaphysically necessary⌝ is true, (iv) ⌜One can know for certain a priori that S⌝ is true, and (v) all quantifiers in S are restricted to fundamental entities. Then the principle we need can be stated succinctly as follows: there are no brute necessities.[11]

---

[10] I myself like to make sense of this sort of talk by interpreting 'fundamental' as 'real' and 'derivative' as 'fictional'. But there is no need to insist on this.

[11] This principle is weaker than either POSSIBILITY or KNOWABILITY, since it concerns only sentences that are both necessary and a priori. But it is strong enough for our purposes.

4. SPURIOUS DISTINCTIONS

In this section I will complete the argument that 'bears' is not primitive. I will not actually argue for the claim that CONVERSES is necessary and a priori, but for the weaker claim that *either* CONVERSES is necessary and a priori, *or* 'bears' is not primitive: this weaker premise is still sufficient, given the results of the previous section, to establish the conclusion that 'bears' is not primitive. My aim, in other words, is to argue against the conjunction of the following two claims: first, 'bears' is primitive; second, CONVERSES is not necessary or not a priori. The problem I see with this combination of views is that it forces us to draw *spurious distinctions* between the possibilities (metaphysical or epistemic possibilities—it doesn't matter which) in which CONVERSES fails. We have to distinguish different "possible worlds" where intuitively there should be only one.

Imagine a world containing (among other things) a series of simple particulars, linearly ordered by exactly two independent simple relations, r_1 and r_2. The two relations generate exactly the same order among the objects in the series. (Outside the series, however, the two relations are not linked by any particularly simple laws.) Do they order the series in the same or in opposite directions? In other words, which of the following is the case?

(i) For any distinct x and y in the series, x bears either r_1 or r_2, but not both, to y.

(ii) For any distinct x and y in the series, x either bears both r_1 and r_2 to y, or bears neither r_1 nor r_2 to y.

At any world containing such a series, exactly one of these hypotheses is true. If the actual world satisfied the description, we could ask which of the two possibilities obtained, and, assuming that 'bears' is primitive, there would be a determinately right answer. But I say that there can be no determinately right answer, because the question is not a legitimate one. There is nothing here for us to be ignorant about; no genuine respect in which two possible worlds might be dissimilar.

Let us consider a concrete example of this kind of situation. Suppose we discover that our talk of the charges of particles was actually talk about two different magnitudes: charge varies in discrete steps from -1 to $+1$, and charge* also varies from -1 to $+1$. But in our region of the universe, charge and charge* are always the same (except in the case of a few very rare kinds of particle that exist only inside cyclotrons). If there could be non-symmetric relations, then one way for the theory of charge and charge* to be true would be for there to be two non-symmetric relations such that 'the charge of x is greater than that of y' reports the holding of one of them, and 'the charge* of x is greater than that of y' reports the holding of the other.[12] If CONVERSES were true, there would have to be a total of four non-symmetric relations involved, corresponding to the four predicates 'is of greater charge than,' 'is of less charge than', 'is of greater charge* than', and 'is of less charge* than'. But if CONVERSES is false, there might be only two relations: one for comparisons of charge, and one for comparisons of charge*. If this were so, a question would arise: does the correlation of charge with charge* in our region of the universe consist in the fact that, for any x and y in our region, x bears either both relations or neither to y, or does it rather consist in the fact that, for any x and y in our region, x bears exactly one of the relations to y? Do the relations "point in the same direction", or in opposite directions?

Surely there are not two structurally different possibilities here. If there were a distant region of the universe in which the correlation went the other way, there would be no real question whether it is we, or the inhabitants of that other region, for whom the two relations coincide. Our scientists assign numbers to charges and charges* in such a way that the numbers for particles in our region are the same, and the numbers for particles in their region are of different signs. Their scientists of course do the opposite: they think of their region as the one in which charges and charges* are equal, and of ours as the one in which charges and charges* are opposite. One need hardly be a verificationist to feel that this difference is purely a matter of convention: neither system of notation is in any way "better" than the other, as far as the metaphysics of the situation is concerned. If non-symmetric relations are possible at all, distinct non-symmetric relations order their relata in different ways.

---

[12] This might seem like a rather unlikely way for the theory to be true. It entails that comparisons of charge and charge* are *external*; whereas we might have thought they were internal, true in virtue of the (intrinsic) properties of the particles. In that case there would be a property (unary universal) corresponding to each distinct value for charge and charge*; the fundamental relations underlying the comparisons would hold not between the particles themselves, but between the properties. But the same question about the meaningfulness of comparisons of the "directions" of the two relations will arise whether the relata are properties or particulars.

We might put this point metaphorically by saying that there is no non-arbitrary sense to be made of the way numbers are assigned to the argument places of non-symmetric relations. If we were to assign the number 1 to the "lower charge" and "lower charge*" argument places of the two binary relations in the example, and 2 to the "higher charge" and "higher charge*" argument places, this would be arbitrary. We might as well assign 2 to "lower charge" and "lower charge*", or assign 1 to "lower charge" and 2 to "lower charge*", or 2 to "lower charge" and 1 to "lower charge*". In reality, there are just four different argument places: two belonging to the relation "comparison of charge", and two belonging to the relation "comparison of charge*".[13] That is why it makes no sense to ask whether two particulars are related in the same way or in opposite ways by these two relations, unless the question is intended to be relative to some particular way of making the arbitrary choices.[14]

The hypothesis that 'bears' is primitive must be rejected, since it entails that there is a deep metaphysical fact in these situations, where clearly there is nothing but arbitrariness.[15] Unless 'bears' is semantically defective, it must somehow be analysable.

There are two ways in which a revealing account of what it is for something to bear a relation to something else could help us deal with the present argument. First, the analysis might block the argument for the contingency of CONVERSES by revealing CONVERSES to be metaphysically analytic. However, as far as I can see, the only credible analyses on which CONVERSES is analytic are those on which 'all relations are symmetric' also comes out analytic. The only way I can think of to render CONVERSES analytic without ruling out non-symmetric relations is to build something tantamount to CONVERSES directly into the analysis of 'bears'. Thus, for example, someone might

---

[13] Cf. Williamson (1985, p. 260).

[14] This talk of entities called "argument places" doesn't *have* to be regarded as metaphorical. In Sect. 7 I will consider several theories in which argument places are taken seriously as a fundamental ontological category.

[15] In n. 2 I pointed out that, if either 'instantiates' or 'is instantiated by' is primitive, it should be taken as indeterminate which is the primitive one. Likewise, no one should regard it as a determinate fact that 'x bears r to y' rather than 'y is borne r to by x' is primitive. Thus, it is purely a matter of convention which of these two predicates we should adopt: we could just as well have chosen to mean by 'x bears r to y' what we actually mean by 'y bears r to x'. But this fact doesn't help us to do away with the invidious distinctions that are forced upon us when we take either of these notions as primitive. For, no matter which of the two equally good meanings for 'bears' we adopt, the answer to the question 'Does x (i) bear both or neither of r_1 and r_2 to y, or does it rather (ii) bear exactly one of r_1 and r_2 to y?' will be the same.

propose taking some new predicate 'F' as primitive, analysing 'a bears r to b' as '$Fabr$, and there is an r^* such that for all x, y, $Fxyr$ iff $Fyxr^*$'. But this suggestion is not only incredible but pointless: the spurious structural distinctions between possible worlds are no more palatable when expressed using 'F' than when expressed using 'bears'.

Second, the analysis might allow us to accept the contingency of CONVERSES, and embrace the conclusion that in the imagined scenario either (i) or (ii) is true, while denying that this constitutes a deep structural difference. The idea is that the notion of bearing is relative to a series of arbitrary choices, one for each relation. We might have defined our word 'bears' in such a way as to make (i) true; but someone else could just as well choose a different definition on which (ii) comes out true. And if our use of the word 'bears' doesn't decide the question, it will be *indeterminate* which of these two perfectly good notions is expressed by 'bears', and hence indeterminate which of (i) and (ii) is the true hypothesis and which the false one.[16]

In the next three sections I will consider several systems of primitive predicates which allow 'bears' to be defined only by means of such arbitrary choices.

5. PRIMITIVE LIKE-RELATEDNESS

The first system I will consider is also the most straightforward. We want it to make sense to say 'a is related to b by r in the same way that c is related to d by r'', but not to make sense to say 'a is related to b by r_1 in the same way that c is related to d by r_2'. Well, let's just take the kind of comparison we do want to make sense as our new primitive predicate, rather than defining it in terms of 'bears'. We will symbolize the first sentence as '$ab \uparrow_r cd$'. There is no natural analysis of the second sentence: '$ab \uparrow_{r_1 r_2} cd$' is just ill-formed.

Even if it is the notion of like-relatedness that is primitive, and the notion of bearing that is defined, still there is surely an intimate relation

---

[16] Williamson (1985) holds a view very similar to this, although he allows that *some* sets of relations might have naturally corresponding argument places, so that a single arbitrary choice would suffice to render the notion of bearing determinate for all the members of such a set. Fine (2000) holds essentially the same view regarding what he calls "neutral" relations, although he also believes in less fundamental "biased" relations for which the notion of bearing is unproblematic. Williamson's and Fine's arguments, however, are quite different from mine.

between these two notions, to which we can appeal in informally explaining the intended meaning of '$ab \uparrow_r cd$'. Abbreviating 'x bears r to y' as '$xy\Delta r$', the intended connection is given by the following biconditional:

BICOND $\qquad xy \uparrow_r zw \equiv (xy\Delta r \wedge zw\Delta r) \vee (yx\Delta r \wedge wz\Delta r)$.

If we were taking 'bears' as primitive, it would be natural to take BICOND as a definition of '$\uparrow$'. As it is, given that we are trying to reverse the order of definition, BICOND does not tell us how to go about defining 'Δ' in terms of '$\uparrow$'. It does, however, tell us what conditions have to hold for it to be *possible* to construct any such definition. BICOND has many logical consequences in which '$\uparrow$' is the only non-logical predicate: only if all these consequences are true will it be *possible* to introduce the predicate 'Δ' in such a way as to make BICOND true. Let us call the totality of such claims the *theory of like-relatedness*.

It is interesting to investigate how we might axiomatize the theory of like-relatedness using the predicate '$\uparrow$' alone. The crucial notion we need is that of a *paradigm-pair* for a relation. Let us say that $\langle a, b \rangle$ is a paradigm-pair for r iff

$$\forall xy(xy\Delta r \equiv xy\uparrow_r ab).$$

BICOND entails that every relation—in fact, everything whatsoever—has at least one paradigm-pair. For any r, there are three possibilities: (i) r is uninstantiated (i.e. there are no x and y such that $xy\Delta r$), in which case any $\langle a, b \rangle$ is a paradigm-pair for r; (ii) r is both symmetric and instantiated, in which case any $\langle a, b \rangle$ such that $ab\Delta r$ is a paradigm-pair for r; (iii) r is non-symmetric and instantiated, in which case any $\langle a, b \rangle$ such that $ab\Delta r$ and not $ba\Delta r$ is a paradigm-pair for r. Hence BICOND entails the following principle in which the predicate 'Δ' does not occur:

PARADIGMS $\qquad \forall r \exists ab \forall xyzw(xy \uparrow_r zw \equiv (xy \uparrow_r ab \wedge zw \uparrow_r ab)$
$\qquad\qquad\qquad\qquad\qquad \vee (yx \uparrow_r ab \wedge wz \uparrow_r ab))$.

PARADIGMS suffices to axiomatize the theory of like-relatedness: that is, BICOND and PARADIGMS have the same logical consequences in which the only predicate is '$\uparrow$'. To prove this, note that any model PARADIGMS can be extended into a model of BICOND by interpreting

'$xy\Delta r$' as '$xy \uparrow_r f(r)g(r)$', where f and g are functions that map each r to an a and b as described in PARADIGMS. Hence, any sentence involving only the predicate '$\uparrow$' that is consistent with PARADIGMS is also consistent with BICOND.

PARADIGMS shows us how we might go about making the arbitrary choices that are required in order to assign a determinate extension to the predicate 'bears': provided that PARADIGMS is true, it will always be possible to find functions f and g such that 'x bears r to y' can appropriately be defined as '$xy \uparrow_r f(r)g(r)$'. In practice, of course, we haven't bothered to define any general notion of this sort. Rather than using names for relations and the single predicate 'bears', we use many different predicates, often associating more than one with a given relation. Thus, if there is a single non-symmetric binary relation t which underlies facts about temporal order, we have not decided whether to say that x bears it to y when x is earlier than y, or when y is earlier than x. But we evidently have somehow managed to make a distinction between 'x is earlier than y' and 'x is later than y'. One way we might have done this is to stipulate, concerning a paradigm pair $\langle a, b \rangle$ of times or events related by t, that 'x is earlier than y' shall be true just in case $xy \uparrow_t ab$, and 'x is later than y' shall be true just in case $xy \uparrow_t ba$.[17] Of course the actual process whereby our predicates come to mean what they do would have to be much more complicated than this in all sorts of ways. But this simple story at least gives us a sense of what we might expect to be involved in the analysis of especially basic non-symmetric predicates, if like-relatedness is primitive.[18]

---

[17] If we had wanted to, we could have introduced two predicates, '$bears_{ab}$' and '$bears_{ba}$', stipulating that 'x $bears_{ab}$ t to y' shall be true iff $xy \uparrow_t ab$, and that 'x $bears_{ba}$ t to y' shall be true iff $xy \uparrow_t ba$. We could, furthermore, have introduced two more names for t, 'beforeness' and 'afterness', together with the following convention of disambiguation: when we refer to t as 'beforeness' we are to interpret 'bears' as '$bears_{ab}$'; when we refer to it as 'afterness' we are to interpret 'bears' as '$bears_{ba}$'. We could even allow different disambiguations within the same sentence. If we did, 'x bears beforeness to y but does not bear afterness to y' could be true despite the truth of 'beforeness = afterness'. This would be a way to make non-contradictory sense of the puzzling doctrine, defended by Armstrong (1978, p. 42) and Williamson (1985), that non-symmetric relations have converses, but are identical to their converses.

[18] Like all analyses that make use of paradigms, the suggested analyses of 'before' and 'after' are subject to an important modal objection: if 'x is before y' is analysed as '$xy \uparrow_t ab$', it follows that, if a or b did not exist, nothing could be before anything. This difficulty can be circumvented to some extent by switching to a disjunctive analysis, and by allowing qualitatively similar "counterparts" of the paradigms to count as surrogates for the paradigms themselves; but intuitively, it seems that some things could have been before

The strategy of taking like-relatedness as primitive can be generalized to relations of higher degree. Just as we might introduce an $(n + 1)$-place predicate $x_1 \ldots x_n \Delta r$ to play the same role for n-ary relations that 'bears' plays for binary relations, so we might introduce a $(2n + 1)$-place predicate $x_1 \ldots x_n \underset{r}{\uparrow} y_1 \ldots y_n$ to play the same role for n-ary relations that '↑' plays for binary relations. The intended connection between these notions can be expressed using a generalized version of BICOND:

BICOND$_n$ $\quad x_1 \ldots x_n \underset{r}{\uparrow} y_1 \ldots y_n \equiv \bigvee_{k_1 \ldots k_n} \left(x_{k_1} \ldots x_{k_n} \Delta r \wedge y_{k_1} \ldots y_{k_n} \Delta r \right)$

(Here the right-hand side is a disjunction with $n!$ disjuncts, one for each way of assigning $k_1 \ldots k_n$ to some permutation of the first n positive integers.)

Can the set of logical consequences of BICOND$_n$ in which '↑' is the only non-logical predicate, be axiomatized using only the predicate '↑'? The most straightforward generalization of PARADIGMS would be the following claim:

$\forall r \exists a_1 \ldots a_n \forall x_1 \ldots x_n y_1 \ldots y_n$

$\left(x_1 \ldots x_n \underset{r}{\uparrow} y_1 \ldots y_n \equiv \bigvee_{k_1 \ldots k_n} \left(x_{k_1} \ldots x_{k_n} \underset{r}{\uparrow} a_1 \ldots a_n \wedge y_{k_1} \ldots y_{k_n} \underset{r}{\uparrow} a_1 \ldots a_n \right) \right)$

But this claim is not a consequence of BICOND$_n$. It fails, for example, in a model of BICOND$_n$ in which these are the only true atomic sentences involving the predicate 'Δ':

$abc\Delta r \quad def\Delta r$
$bca\Delta r \quad dfe\Delta r$
$cab\Delta r$

$\langle a, b, c \rangle$, for example, won't do as a paradigm sequence in this model: for we have $abc \underset{r}{\uparrow} def$, and $abc \underset{r}{\uparrow} efd$, but not $def \underset{r}{\uparrow} efd$. $\langle d, e, f \rangle$ is also

other things even if *no* actual particulars, or anything like them, had existed. One way to approach this problem would be to look to the direction-of-time literature for a satisfying theoretical characterization of the difference between past and future. Another would be to allow it to be an indeterminate matter which direction is which at such distant worlds, just as it is often thought to be an indeterminate matter whether a hand-shaped object in a world sufficiently unlike the actual world is left or right.

ruled out: for we have $def \uparrow_r abc$, and $def \uparrow_r acb$, but not $abc \uparrow_r acb$. However, it can easily be verified that in this model,

$$\forall xyz(xyz\Delta r \equiv (xyz \uparrow_r abc \wedge xyz \uparrow_r def)),$$

so the set $\{\langle a, b, c\rangle, \langle d, e, f\rangle\}$ can do the work that neither sequence can do on its own. BICOND$_n$ entails that it will always be possible to associate each relation with an appropriate set of paradigm n-tuples; moreover, at most $n! - 1$ paradigm n-tuples are needed for each n-ary relation.[19] So a counterpart of PARADIGMS for n-ary relations can be stated as follows:

PARADIGMS$_n$ $\quad \forall r \, \exists a_1^1 \ldots a_n^1 a_1^2 \ldots a_n^2 \ldots \ldots a_1^{n!-1} \ldots a_n^{n!-1} \, \forall x_1 \ldots x_n y_1 \ldots y_n$

$$\left(x_1 \ldots x_n \uparrow_r y_1 \ldots y_n \equiv \bigvee_{k_1 \ldots k_n} \bigwedge_{0 < i < n!} (x_{k_1} \ldots x_{k_n} \uparrow_r a_1^i \ldots a_n^i \wedge y_{k_1} \ldots y_{k_n} \uparrow_r a_1^i \ldots a_n^i) \right)$$

(Again, '$k_1 \ldots k_n$' ranges over all permutations of the first n positive integers.) This is a certainly a mouthful, but it is the simplest first-order axiomatization I have been able to find.[20]

---

[19] Sketch of proof: let the *extension* of r be the set $\{\langle x_1, \ldots, x_n\rangle | x_1 \ldots x_n \Delta r\}$. Let the *image* of any sequence $\langle a_1, \ldots, a_n\rangle$ be the set $\{\langle x_1, \ldots, x_n\rangle | x_1 \ldots x_n \uparrow_r a_1 \ldots a_n\}$. Let the *expanded extension* of r be the intersection of all the images that contain the extension of r. It is straightforward to show, using BICOND$_n$, that the expanded extension of r is equivalent to the extension of r for the purposes of defining like-relatedness: that is, $x_1 \ldots x_n \uparrow_r y_1 \ldots y_n$ is true iff $\langle x_{k_1}, \ldots x_{k_n}\rangle$ and $\langle y_{k_1}, \ldots, y_{k_n}\rangle$ are both members of the expanded extension of r, for some permutation $k_1 \ldots k_n$. Moreover, BICOND$_n$ entails that every image is a union of some of the permutations of the extension of r, i.e. the sets $\{\langle x_1, \ldots, x_n\rangle | x_{k_1} \ldots x_{k_n} \Delta r\}$. There are at most $n!$ such sets. Hence it is always possible to find some set containing at most $n! - 1$ images whose intersection is the expanded extension of r.

[20] There is another disanalogy between the case of binary relations and the general case which is worth noting. In the case of binary relations, the distinctions between possibilities described using the predicate 'bears', which we get to dismiss as spurious when we take '$xy \uparrow_r zw$' as primitive, are exactly those I argued against in Sect. 4. But in general, if we take '$x_1 \ldots x_n \uparrow_r y_1 \ldots y_n$' as primitive, we will have to classify as spurious certain distinctions between possibilities that could be perfectly genuine as far as the arguments of Sect. 4 are concerned. Consider, for example, two worlds, each of which contains just three particulars, a, b, and c, and a ternary relation r:

w_1 $\quad$ w_2
$abc\Delta r$ $\quad$ $abc\Delta r$
$bca\Delta r$ $\quad$ $bca\Delta r$
$cab\Delta r$

6. AGAINST PRIMITIVE LIKE-RELATEDNESS

It is time to take stock. We were led to consider taking the notion of like-relatedness as primitive by the following argument: if 'bears' is primitive, CONVERSES is a brute necessity; but there are no brute necessities; therefore 'bears' is not primitive. Could this be a good reason to adopt like-relatedness as a primitive instead? Surely not. For even if BICOND is not an analysis of '↑' in terms of 'bears', it certainly seems both necessary and a priori. If it is, then so are its logical consequences, including those whose only non-logical vocabulary is the predicate '↑'—what I have been calling the theory of like-relatedness. Hence, if '↑' is primitive, all of these consequences of BICOND are brute necessities, except for those that are logical truths. But the theory of like-relatedness includes many sentences—for example PARADIGMS—that are not logical truths. Hence, since there are no brute necessities, '↑' is not primitive.

Someone might respond to this argument by denying that the theory of like-relatedness is metaphysically necessary and/or a priori. The problem with this response is analogous to the problem I raised in Section 4 for someone who holds that 'bears' is primitive and denies that CONVERSES is necessary or a priori. If we take seriously the (metaphysical or epistemic) possibility that the theory of like-relatedness is false, we are forced to see distinctions between possibilities which even the most stalwart anti-verificationist should baulk at accepting as genuine matters of (metaphysically or epistemically) contingent fact.

Here is an example of such a distinction. Take some world w at which the theory of like-relatedness is true, where there are several binary relations $r_1 \ldots r_n$, at most one of which holds between any two objects. Let w' be a world derived from w by replacing all these relations with a single binary relation r, in such a way that $ab \uparrow_r cd$ is true at w' iff $ab \uparrow_{r_i} cd$ is true at w for any r_i. The theory of like-relatedness will be false at w'. Suppose that, at w, a and b are related by r_1 ($ab \uparrow_{r_1} ab$), and c and d are related by r_2: then, at w', a and b are related by r, and c and d are related by r, but these two pairs are *incomparable* as regards the direction in which r holds: '$ab \uparrow_r cd$' and '$ab \uparrow_r dc$' are both false. Here, then, is one example of the sort of question that strikes me as "metaphysical"

BICOND$_n$ entails that exactly the same sentences of the form $x_1x_2x_3 \uparrow y_1y_2y_3$ hold at w_1 and w_2. So if 'Δ' is analysed in terms of '↑', we will have to say that w_1 and w_2 are not really two different possibilities, but one possibility described in two different ways.

in the pejorative sense: do we live at a world with several binary relations, like w, or should we instead say that there is just one relation, holding in many different, incomparable ways, as at w'?

Some of the distinctions between possibilities in which the theory of like-relatedness fails have the same symmetric character as the distinctions I discussed in Section 4, which makes them especially difficult to take seriously. Suppose Metaphysician A and Metaphysician B agree about everything except for one relation r, regarding which they have the following disagreement: whenever Metaphysician A says that $ab \uparrow_r cd$, Metaphysician B says that $ab \uparrow_r dc$, and vice-versa. Given that they disagree in this way, they cannot both accept the theory of like-relatedness.[21] There is something especially repugnant, I think, about the conclusion that this is a determinate, objective dispute which cannot be resolved by a priori means. For, given the entirely symmetric character of the dispute, it seems clear that, unless at least one of the hypotheses can be conclusively ruled out a priori, there is no basis at all for assigning one of them higher credence than the other.[22]

These examples fall short of establishing that the whole of the theory of like-relatedness, as opposed to some substantial fragment of it, is necessary and a priori. From the point of view of the argument, this doesn't matter: a weaker brute necessity is just as unacceptable as a strong one. But in fact, I doubt there is any stopping point short of the whole theory: for *any* description of a situation in which the theory fails, there will be some description of a situation in which it holds, such that the distinction between the two descriptions has the spurious character to which I have been objecting.

---

[21] Suppose they did. Then whenever A says that $ab \uparrow_r cd$, by PARADIGMS, A must say that $ab \uparrow_r ab$ and $cd \uparrow_r cd$; hence B will say that $ab \uparrow_r ba$ and $cd \uparrow_r dc$; so by PARADIGMS, B too must say that $ab \uparrow_r cd$.

[22] PARADIGMS logically entails that the predicate '$\uparrow$' is subject to certain symmetries:

$$ab \uparrow_r cd \equiv cd \uparrow_r ab$$

$$ab \uparrow_r cd \equiv ba \uparrow_r dc$$

Even if '$\uparrow$' were primitive, I think we could still accept these biconditionals as necessary and a priori truths. In fact, they should be classified as *logical* truths, even though they are not theorems of standard logic. They merely express the fact that no semantic significance attaches to certain facts about the order in which the arguments of $\uparrow$ are written down, just as no semantic significance attaches to the choice of a typeface or the speed with which they are pronounced. It is just an artefact of our linear language that it forces us to choose a unique order for the four arguments of '$\uparrow$'. However, this way of explaining how a sentence involving only primitive predicates could be a logical truth only makes sense for biconditionals with atomic formulae on either side, and their logical consequences.

7. ANALYSING LIKE-RELATEDNESS

So far, I have argued that neither bearing nor like-relatedness is primitive. In this section I will survey several more systems of primitive predicates. In each of these systems, '↑' can be analysed in a natural and general way, whereas 'bears' can be analysed only relative to some arbitrary choices.

My arguments against these systems will be similar to those I gave against the primitiveness of 'bears' and '↑'. First, none of the new systems of primitive predicates allows us to give a natural analysis of '↑' on which the theory of like-relatedness turns out to be analytic. (By contrast, if we take 'bears' as primitive, the natural analysis of '↑'—i.e. BICOND—does render the theory of like-relatedness analytic.) If I am right that the theory of like-relatedness is necessary and a priori, this means that each of the new systems requires us to posit brute necessities.

Even if I am wrong that the entire theory of like-relatedness, as opposed to some fragment of it, is necessary and a priori, it doesn't matter much: the new systems of primitive predicates are also objectionable for a quite different reason. Whereas, if we take '↑' as our only primitive, there is simply no way to make sense of the question 'Do r_1 and r_2 hold between x and y in the same direction or in opposite directions?', in each of the new systems there *is* at least one natural translation of this question, on which both answers are logically consistent. In Section 4 I argued that such cross-relational comparisons are illegitimate, in the sense that there are no pairs of (epistemic or metaphysical) possibilities that differ only in the answers to questions of this sort. Thus, each of the new systems succumbs to the same objection as the view that 'bears' is primitive.

For the sake of brevity, I will present each of the new systems in a condensed format. In each case, I will begin by stating the natural analyses of like-relatedness and bearing in terms of the primitive predicates of the system. Next, I will list some plausible-looking axioms from which the theory of like-relatedness can be derived, given the analysis of like-relatedness. (These axioms will often be somewhat stronger, but also somewhat simpler, than the weakest possible set of axioms needed to derive the theory of like-relatedness.) Finally, I will present a second list of axioms, which are the counterparts of CONVERSES for the given system: only if they were necessary and a priori could spurious cross-relational comparisons be ruled out; but they cannot be necessary and a priori, since if they were they would be brute necessities. The point of stating all these axioms is to help make it clear just what sorts of bizarre possibilities one would have to countenance if one accepted any of these systems of predicates as primitive. Readers who are satisfied with the point should feel free to skip over them.

The first system is what we would end up with if we took the apparent quantification over "ways" in the expression 'a is related by r to b in the same way that c is related by r to d' at face value, as committing us to a new ontological category of *ways* alongside particulars and universals.

System A: Ways of being related

Primitive predicate

  'w is a way in which a is related by r to b' ('$ab\underset{w}{\Delta}r$')

Definition of like-relatedness

(A1) $\qquad ab\underset{r}{\uparrow}cd =_{df} \exists w(ab\underset{w}{\Delta}r \wedge cd\underset{w}{\Delta}r)$

Definition of bearing

(A2) $\qquad ab\Delta r =_{df} ab\underset{f(r)}{\Delta}r$

where f is a function that associates each relation with one of its ways.

Axiom needed to derive theory of like-relatedness

(A3) $\qquad (ab\underset{w_1}{\Delta}r \wedge cd\underset{w_2}{\Delta}r \wedge w_1 \neq w_2) \supset \forall xy(xy\underset{w_1}{\Delta}r \equiv yx\underset{w_2}{\Delta}r)$

Axioms needed to rule out cross-relational comparisons

(A4) $\qquad (ab\underset{w}{\Delta}r_1 \wedge cd\underset{w}{\Delta}r_2) \supset r_1 = r_2$

(A5) $\qquad ab\underset{w_1}{\Delta}r \supset \exists w_2(ba\underset{w_2}{\Delta}r)$

I doubt many philosophers would be seriously tempted to recognize these "ways" as a new fundamental ontological category: they are just too similar to relations.[23] A more appealing new fundamental ontological category is the category of *argument places*, considered not as numbers but as *sui generis* entities which can be associated with numbers only by some arbitrary convention.

---

[23] In fact, ways as conceived in this system are *exactly* like non-symmetric relations, as conceived by the proponent of CONVERSES. The only difference is that we now add a new fundamental category of entities corresponding to pairs of converse relations, and reserve the title 'relation' for these new entities.

System B: Argument places

Primitive predicate

'r holds between a and b with respect to the argument places α and β, respectively' ('$ab\underset{\alpha\beta}{\Delta}r$').

Definition of like-relatedness

(B1) $\qquad ab\underset{r}{\uparrow}cd =_{df} \exists\alpha\beta\left(ab\underset{\alpha\beta}{\Delta}r \wedge cd\underset{\alpha\beta}{\Delta}r\right)$

Definition of bearing

(B2) $\qquad ab\Delta r =_{df} ab\underset{f(r)g(r)}{\Delta}r$

where f and g are functions thought of as specifying a relation's "first" and "second" argument place, respectively.

Axioms needed to derive theory of like-relatedness

(B3) $\qquad ab\underset{\alpha\beta}{\Delta}r \equiv ba\underset{\beta\alpha}{\Delta}r$

(B4) $\qquad \left(ab\underset{\alpha\beta}{\Delta}r \wedge cd\underset{\gamma\delta}{\Delta}r\right) \supset ((\alpha = \gamma \wedge \beta = \delta) \vee (\alpha = \delta \wedge \beta = \gamma))$

Axiom needed to rule out cross-relational comparisons

(B5) $\qquad \left(ab\underset{\alpha\beta}{\Delta}r_1 \wedge cd\underset{\alpha\gamma}{\Delta}r_2\right) \supset r_1 = r_2$ [24]

A third ontological category that might be invoked in an analysis of '↑' is the category of *states of affairs*, entities that many philosophers believe in for reasons having nothing to do with the problems of non-symmetric relations. The most straightforward way to invoke states of affairs in the analysis of like-relatedness is to take the notion of *entering into states of affairs in the same way* as primitive. Kit Fine (2000) defends something very close to this view.

System C: States of affairs

Primitive predicates

  'a stands to b in state of affairs s_1 in the same way that c stands to d in state of affairs s_2' ('$abs_1 \Uparrow cds_2$')
  'x is a universal component of s' ('$x\mathbf{U}s$')

---

[24] This is the principle 'distinct relations have distinct argument places', which I offered in Sect. 4 as a metaphorical explanation of the incomparability of distinct relations. It works better as a metaphor: taken at face value (as a claim about fundamental entites) it has to be regarded as a brute necessity if it is necessary and a priori at all.

Definition of like-relatedness

(C1) $\quad ab \underset{r}{\uparrow} cd =_{df} \exists s_1 s_2 (r\mathbf{U}s_1 \wedge r\mathbf{U}s_2 \wedge abs_1 \Uparrow cds_2)$

Definition of bearing

(C2) $\quad xy\Delta r =_{df} \exists s(r\mathbf{U}s \wedge xys \Uparrow f(r)g(r)h(r))$

where h assigns each relation to a "paradigm state of affairs", and f and g label the components of that state of affairs as the "first" and "second", respectively.

Axioms needed to derive theory of like-relatedness

(C3) $\quad abs_1 \Uparrow cds_2 \equiv cds_2 \Uparrow abs_1$

(C4) $\quad abs_1 \Uparrow cds_2 \equiv bas_1 \Uparrow dcs_2$ [25]

(C5) $\quad (abs_1 \Uparrow cds_2 \wedge cds_2 \Uparrow efs_3) \supset abs_1 \Uparrow efs_3$

(C6) $\quad (r\mathbf{U}s_1 \wedge r\mathbf{U}s_2 \wedge abs_1 \Uparrow abs_1 \wedge cds_1 \Uparrow cds_2) \supset (abs_1 \Uparrow cds_2 \vee abs_1 \Uparrow dcs_2)$

Axioms needed to rule out cross-relational comparisons

(C7) $\quad (r\mathbf{U}s_1 \wedge abs_1 \Uparrow cds_2) \supset r\mathbf{U}s_2$

(C8) $\quad (r_1 \mathbf{U}s \wedge r_2 \mathbf{U}s) \supset r_1 = r_2$

If we accept more than one of the three new ontological categories we have considered, still further systems of primitive predicates suggest themselves. If we were willing to accept ways of being related alongside states of affairs, we might take 'w is a way in which a stands to b in s' as primitive; if we were willing to accept argument places alongside states of affairs, we might take 'a and b occupy the argument places α and β of s, respectively' as primitive. These two systems add nothing of interest to systems A and B. But we get a more interesting theory of argument places and states of affairs if we don't take 'a and b occupy the argument places α and β of s, respectively' as primitive, but instead analyse it as 'a occupies argument place α of s, and b occupies argument place β of s'.

System D: States of affairs and argument places

Primitive predicates

'a occupies argument place α of state of affairs s' ('$x\underset{\alpha}{\mathbf{C}}s$')
'x is a universal component of s' ('$x\mathbf{U}s$')

---

[25] (C3) and (C4) belong to the special category of *symmetries*, which, as I argued in n. 22, can properly be classified as logical truths, and so can be necessary and a priori even if '⇑' is primitive.

Definition of like-relatedness

(D1) $ab\underset{\alpha\beta}{\Delta}r =_{df} \exists s \left(rUs \wedge a\underset{\alpha}{C}s \wedge b\underset{\beta}{C}s \wedge \forall x(\exists y(x\underset{y}{C}s) \supset (x=a \vee x=b)) \right)$

(B1) $ab\underset{r}{\uparrow}cd =_{df} \exists \alpha\beta \left(ab\underset{\alpha\beta}{\Delta}r \wedge cd\underset{\alpha\beta}{\Delta}r \right)$

Definition of bearing

As in system B.

Axioms needed to derive theory of like-relatedness

(D2) $(rUs_1 \wedge rUs_2 \wedge x\underset{\alpha}{C}s_1) \supset \exists y \left(y\underset{\alpha}{C}s_2 \right)$

(D3) $\left(x\underset{\alpha}{C}s \wedge y\underset{\alpha}{C}s \right) \supset x = y$ [26]

Axioms needed to rule out cross-relational comparisons

(D4) $\left(rUs_1 \wedge a\underset{\alpha}{C}s_1 \wedge b\underset{\alpha}{C}s_2 \right) \supset rUs_2$

(C8) $(r_1Us \wedge r_2Us) \supset r_1 = r_2$

If we were prepared to embrace the thesis (defended in Armstrong 1978, pp. 91–3) that all relations are necessarily *irreflexive*—i.e. that things never bear relations to themselves—we could avoid the ontological commitment to argument places incurred by system D by regarding argument places as "abstractions" from states of affairs and their particular components. The idea is to take the formula 'the argument place that a occupies in s_2 = the argument place that b occupies in s_2' not, at face value, as involving genuine quantification over argument places, but as primitive.

System E: States of affairs without argument places

Primitive predicates

'a is a component of s_1 in the same way that b is a component of s_2' ('$as_1 A bs_2$')

'x is a universal component of s' ('xUs')

---

[26] (D3) entails that even the holding of a *symmetric* relation between a and b must involve two states of affairs, differing in the argument places occupied by a and b. It would perhaps be more intuitive to posit just one state of affairs in this situation, which has both a and b in the same argument place (see Fine 2000, p. 31). In fact, (D3) is a stronger axiom than we really need. Its work could be done instead by the weaker (but non-first-order) principle that an argument place is always occupied by the same number of entities in every state of affairs in which it is occupied at all.

Definition of like-relatedness

(E1) $abs_1 \Uparrow cds_2 =_{df} as_1\mathbf{A}cs_2 \wedge bs_1\mathbf{A}ds_2 \wedge \forall x(xs_1\mathbf{A}xs_1 \supset x = a \vee x = b)$
$\wedge \forall x(xs_2\mathbf{A}xs_2 \supset x = c \vee x = d)$

(C1) $ab\underset{r}{\uparrow}cd =_{df} \exists s_1 s_2 (r\mathbf{U}s_1 \wedge r\mathbf{U}s_2 \wedge abs_1 \Uparrow cds_2)$

Definition of bearing

  As in System C.

Axioms needed to derive theory of like-relatedness

(E2) $as_1\mathbf{A}bs_2 \equiv bs_2\mathbf{A}as_1$ [27]

(E3) $(as_1\mathbf{A}bs_2 \wedge bs_2\mathbf{A}cs_3) \supset as_1\mathbf{A}cs_3$

(E4) $(r\mathbf{U}s_1 \wedge r\mathbf{U}s_2 \wedge as_1\mathbf{A}as_1) \supset \exists x(as_1\mathbf{A}xs_2)$

(E5) $as\mathbf{A}bs \supset a = b$ [28]

Axioms needed to rule out cross-relational comparisons

(E6) $(r\mathbf{U}s_1 \wedge as_1\mathbf{A}bs_2) \supset r\mathbf{U}s_2$

(C8) $(r_1\mathbf{U}s \wedge r_2\mathbf{U}s) \supset r_1 = r_2$

Before we leave this survey of systems, it is worth noting an interesting feature which distinguishes systems D and E from all of the other systems of primitive predicates that we have considered. The other candidate primitive predicates are all specifically adapted for talking about *binary* relations. To accommodate relations of arbitrary degree within any of these systems, we would have to add infinitely many new primitive predicates, taking ever larger numbers of arguments, and governed by ever more complex systems of brute necessities. By contrast, systems D and E are both already equipped to deal with relations of arbitrary degree. Their analyses of '$ab\underset{r}{\uparrow}cd$', can both be generalized straightforwardly to yield analyses of '$a_1 \ldots a_n \underset{r}{\uparrow} b_1 \ldots b_n$', for any n. Moreover, given these generalized analyses, the axioms already listed suffice to entail the generalized theory of like-relatedness (i.e. to entail PARADIGMS$_n$ for every n), and to rule out spurious cross-relational comparisons. Thus, these two systems are more *economical* in their primitive predicates, and in their need to posit brute necessities, than the

---

[27] For the special status of this axiom, see n. 25.
[28] As in system D, if we wanted to allow that the holding of a symmetric relation between two things can involve just one state of affairs, we could replace (E5) with the weaker principle that, whenever $as_1\mathbf{A}bs_2$, the xs such that $xs_1\mathbf{A}bs_2$ are equinumerous with the ys such that $as_1\mathbf{A}ys_2$.

other theories of non-symmetric relations that we have considered. But if the reasons for ruling out brute necessities that I gave in Section 3 are good, they show that there are *no* brute necessities—not just that we should accept as few of them as possible.[29]

8. DOING WITHOUT NON-SYMMETRIC RELATIONS

We have been searching for a system of predicates with three features:

1. They do not allow for any credible analyses of the sentences 'r_1 and r_2 hold between a and b in the same direction' and 'r_1 and r_2 hold between a and b in opposite directions', on which both of these claims are consistent.
2. They allow for a credible analysis of the notion of like-relatedness, on which the theory of like-relatedness is analytic.
3. They allow for a credible analysis of 'All relations are symmetric'—or, equivalently, '$\forall xyr(xy \uparrow_r xy \supset xy \uparrow_r yx)$'—on which this claim is not analytic.

'Bears' lacks feature 1, as does any system of primitive predicates in which 'bears' has a plausible and non-arbitrary analysis. '↑' lacks feature 2. The systems considered in Section 7 lack both of these features. On the basis of this survey of candidates, I conclude that no system of predicates has all three features. I don't know how to *prove* this—as currently stated, indeed, it is too vague to admit of proof. The best I can do is to challenge those who doubt the conclusion to produce a counter-example.

But, as I argued in Sections 4 and 6, the true system of primitive predicates, whatever it is, must have features 1 and 2. Hence the true system of primitive predicates lacks feature 3. Either 'bears' is semantically defective, or it has an analysis on which 'x bears r to y' is equivalent to 'y bears r to x'; in either case, 'all relations are symmetric' is metaphysically analytic.

I am in fact inclined to favour the Nominalist view that 'bears' is semantically defective. Nevertheless, even for me it is worth seeing how the less radical view that there are relations all of which are necessarily symmetric could be a defensible one. For I suspect that considerations

---

[29] In Sect. 10, I will take up the question what we should believe about non-symmetric relations if we replace the outright rejection of brute necessities with this weaker methodological principle.

very similar to those I have discussed should lead a Nominalist to embrace a Nominalistic "paraphrase" of the claim that all relations are symmetric. Even if there are, *strictly speaking*, no relations at all, even *loosely speaking*—speaking "according to the fiction of universals"—all relations are symmetric.

To help ourselves get used to the conclusion that all relations must be symmetric, we should consider various ways for a theory containing non-symmetric polyadic predicates to be true despite the non-existence of non-symmetric relations. For of course the fact that a non-symmetric predicate can't be meaningful by "standing for" a certain relation doesn't entail that non-symmetric predicates can't be meaningful at all, and doesn't entail that they can't be used to state true theories.

It is not hard to show that every theory using non-symmetric predicates can be modelled in a world of symmetric relations. Imagine a world where there is a property of "ghostliness", and a symmetric binary relation of "shadowing" which places the non-ghostly things in one-to-one correspondence with the ghostly things. At such a world, any consistent theory with only two-place predicates could be true; on an interpretation on which all quantifiers are restricted to non-ghostly entities, every one-place predicate is associated with a property of non-ghostly entities, and every two-place predicate F is associated with a symmetric relation r_F that holds between non-ghostly and ghostly entities, with 'Fab' being analysed as 'r_F holds between a and b's shadow'. By postulating more than one ghostly realm, we can extend this method to interpret theories with non-symmetric predicates taking more than two arguments.

Of course—and fortunately for common sense—this is not the only sort of interpretation on which a theory containing non-symmetric polyadic predicates can be true. Many such theories can be interpreted without imposing any restriction on the quantifiers. For example, the predicate 'is part of', which occurs in the theory known as 'mereology' or 'the calculus of individuals', can be analysed in terms of a symmetric "overlap" relation: x is part of y iff whatever overlaps x overlaps y (see Goodman 1951, pp. 42–51). In other cases we do need to posit some new entities, but they are much more familiar and easier to believe in than the realm of "ghostly" entities. For example, the three-place non-symmetric predicate 'between' which might feature in a formalization of Euclidean geometry construed as a theory about points of space, might be analysed in terms of a binary symmetric "overlap" relation whose relata include line segments as well as points: 'x is between y and z' is taken to mean 'every line segment that overlaps both y and z overlaps x.'

Mathematical platonists will be glad to learn that set theory is one of the theories that can be interpreted in a world of symmetric relations without commitment to any new entities. According to orthodox (well-founded) set theory, there are some special sets called *ranks*, such that, whenever x is a member of y, there is some rank that contains x and not y, but no rank that contains y and not x. Allen Hazen (1999) has shown how this fact can be used to analyse membership in terms of two symmetric two-place predicates. Say that two things *overlap set-theoretically* iff one of them is a member of the other. Say that two things *are of the same rank* iff they are members of exactly the same ranks. It follows from orthodox set theory that a is a member of b iff a overlaps b and there is something of the same rank as b that overlaps everything of the same rank as a.[30] To account for the truth of set theory in a world of symmetric relations, we can adopt this biconditional as an analysis of 'is a member of' in terms of 'overlaps' and 'is of the same rank as', and posit a symmetric binary relation corresponding to each of these two predicates.[31]

Do we *ever* need to introduce new entities in order to interpret a theory containing non-symmetric predicates? It might be suggested that the answer to this question is 'no'. For couldn't we interpret any such theory by associating each non-symmetric two-place predicate F with a *ternary* symmetric relation r_F, analysing 'Fxy' as '$xyy\Delta r_F$'? Likewise, we could analyse '$Gxyz$' as '$xyyzzz\Delta r_G$'; and so on.

To me, this looks like cheating: it is consistent with the letter of the thesis that all relations must be symmetric, but not with its spirit. What

---

[30] If $a \in b$, then a overlaps b, and the *rank* which is of the same rank as b has everything of lower rank, and hence everything of the same rank as a, as a member. If $a \notin b$, then either a doesn't overlap b, or $b \in a$. But if $b \in a$, there is nothing of the same rank as b which is a member of everything of the same rank as a, and so there is nothing of the same rank as b which overlaps everything of the same rank as a. (Actually, this last claim is true only if there is at least one urelement; otherwise the case where b is the null set and a is its unit set is an exception. Hazen (1999) states a more complicated definition which can accommodate this case.)

[31] Since there are any number of different ways to define the notion of a *sequence* in set-theoretic terms, this interpretation of set theory gives us another perfectly general strategy for interpreting theories involving non-symmetric predicates: we simply associate each non-symmetric predicate F with a property p_F, analysing '$Fx_1 \ldots x_n$' as '$\langle x_1, \ldots, x_n \rangle$ instantiates p_F'.

difference does it make whether we think of an assignment of numbers to the relata of a relation as measuring the order of the relata, or as measuring how many times over each of them occurs as a relatum? The idea that there could be non-arbitrary sense to be made of the question which assignment of numbers is the correct one seems to face more or less the same problems either way. Just like the disputes I considered in Section 4, the dispute between two metaphysicians who agree about everything except that, whenever metaphysician A says '$xyy\Delta r$', metaphysician B says '$xxy\Delta r$', strikes me as a spurious one. If this analogy holds, then, just as we have concluded that '$xy\Delta r$' and '$yx\Delta r$' are metaphysically analytically equivalent, we should also conclude that '$xyy\Delta r$' and '$xxy\Delta r$' are metaphysically analytically equivalent.[32] Thus, the suggested strategy for interpreting arbitrary theories containing non-symmetric predicates is a failure. If we want to find ontologically conservative interpretations of such theories, we must seek them case by case.

9. THE INTUITION THAT NON-SYMMETRIC RELATIONS ARE POSSIBLE

I have not been shy of appeals to modal intuition in this paper: in fact, my method of argument relies essentially upon them. Thus, I should say something about the widely shared intuition that non-symmetric relations *are* possible. Unsurprisingly, I think that the force of this intuition is defeated by the argument I have presented. But this is not just a clash of equally matched intuitions: there are good reasons, independent of this argument, why we should be extremely tentative in our intuition that non-symmetric relations are possible.

---

[32] This would be true, for example, if the simple theory of states of affairs that I described in Sect. 2 were correct. For if '$xyz\Delta r$' is analysed as 'there is a state of affairs with x, y, and z as its only particular components and r as its universal component', '$xyy\Delta r$' and '$xxy\Delta r$' are indeed equivalent.

In fact, '$xyy\Delta r$' is equivalent on this analysis to '$xy\Delta r$'. Likewise, 'x bears r to x' is equivalent to 'x instantiates r'. A relation that things sometimes bear to themselves is really a *multigrade* universal: an entity that is sometimes instantiated like a property, and sometimes borne like an irreflexive relation. If we really wanted to block this conclusion, we could do so by tinkering with the analyses of 'instantiates' and 'bears'; for example, 'x instantiates y' could be analysed as 'x is the unique particular component of some state of affairs with y as its unique universal component, and no state of affairs with y as its universal component has more than one particular component'. But I'm not sure that the conclusion is odd enough to be worth blocking in this way.

First, let us consider a more general principle from which the possibility of non-symmetric relations might be derived. Say that a theory is *fundamental* iff it is true under an interpretation on which each of its predicates is interpreted as standing in the most direct possible way for some universal. Someone might hold that it is possible for *any* consistent theory to be fundamental. If this is correct, then, in particular, it must be possible for consistent theories that include non-symmetric predicates to be fundamental, and so it must be possible for there to be non-symmetric relations.

In fact, however, any believer in universals must accept that there are some limits on the forms that fundamental theories can take. Although logicians have generally been content to study languages whose atomic formulae consist of predicates together with ordered sequences of terms, one can imagine languages that attach semantic significance to quite different sorts of facts about the arrangement of the words that make up an atomic formula. For example, we can imagine a predicate that takes not a straightforward list of arguments, but a list of arguments embellished with an equal number of left and right parentheses: if F is such a predicate, 'Fa', '$Fa(bc)$', '$F(ab)c$', '$F(a)(b(c))$', '$Fa(bc)(d(ef))$' are all well-formed and logically independent formulae.

Surely it makes no sense to suppose that a predicate of this exotic sort could "stand in the most direct possible way" for a universal u_F. What simple fact involving just a, b, c, and u_F could make the difference between a situation in which '$Fa(bc)$' was true and one in which '$F(ab)c$' was true?[33] The true story about the interpretation of 'F', whatever it is, must be fairly complicated: we cannot simply say that F stands for a certain relation and leave it at that. For example, the analysis of F might involve set theory: we could associate F with a property p_F of sets, contextually analysing each formula '$F\varphi$' as 'φ^* instantiates p_F', where φ^* is a singular term derived from the parenthesis-embellished list φ by replacing all left and right parentheses with left and right curly braces, and putting another pair of curly braces around the whole expression.

---

[33] If we spoke a language with lots of these "parenthesis-embellished" predicates, we might find it natural to introduce a parenthesis-embellished version of the non-symmetric predicate 'Δ'; so we could answer the question posed in the text by saying that in the first case $a(bc)\Delta u_F$, while in the second case $(ab)c\Delta u_F$. My point is that we surely do not want to accept this new parenthesis-embellished predicate as primitive, or as definable in any very natural and simple way in terms of primitives.

Sentences of our language consist of words spread out along one dimension of time or space. So non-symmetric predicates seem to us to be the most natural thing in the world, whereas the parenthesis-embellished predicate F seems strange and unusual. But this fact is much too parochial to warrant our continuing to insist that it must be possible for non-symmetric predicates, unlike parenthesis-embellished predicates, to occur in fundamental theories. There could be a race of beings whose sentences took an entirely different form. For example, they could build up their sentences by collecting words in bags of different colours, collecting these bags inside other bags, and so on.[34] To the "speakers" of such a language, non-symmetric predicates might seem just as exotic as parenthesis-embellished predicates seem to us, while the equivalents of parenthesis-embellished predicates might strike them as utterly natural. If they were given to theorizing about universals, they might find it just as intuitive that there could be universals corresponding directly to parenthesis-embellished predicates as we find it intuitive that there could be non-symmetric relations.

Can any other basis be found for a principled distinction between non-symmetric predicates and parenthesis-embellished predicates? It might be suggested that the crucial difference is something about the predicates' role in *scientific explanation*: non-symmetric predicates can be explanatorily essential in a way that parenthesis-embellished predicates cannot. But this is false: we can imagine situations in which parenthesis-embellished predicates are just as useful in scientific explanation as non-symmetric predicates could ever be. Let's begin by recursively defining the predicate 'forms a nested circle around point p' as follows: Every material object forms a nested circle around its centre of gravity. A set forms a nested circle around p iff (i) each of its members forms a nested circle around some point, and (ii) all of these points are at the same distance from p (see figure 1). Now, suppose we discover some special new particles. As we move them around, we notice that certain arrangements lead to the emission of a distinctive kind of radiation from nearby points. Eventually we find a pattern, which we describe as follows: there are some special sets, built up from these particles, such that the distinctive radiation is emitted from a point iff one of those sets forms a nested circle around it. Moreover, we find

---

[34] Cf. Williamson (1985, p. 259).

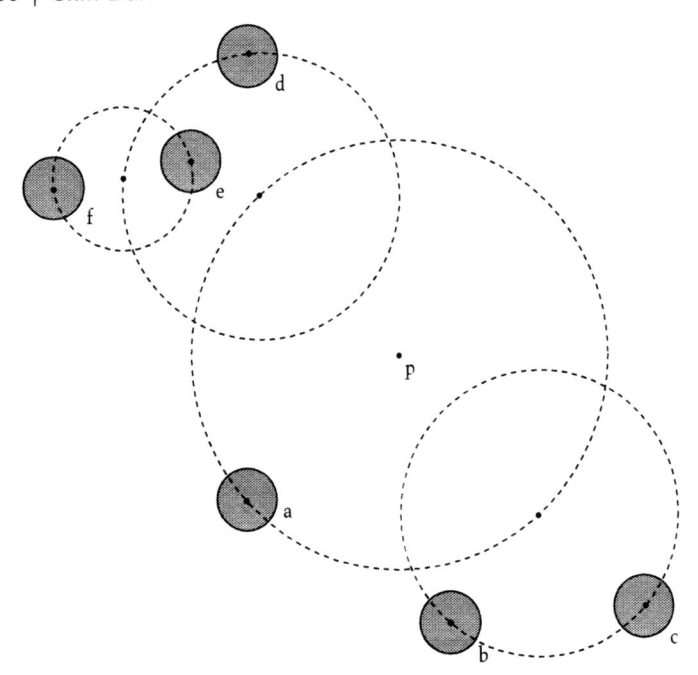

Figure 1: {a, {b, c}, {d, {e, f}}} forms a nested circle around p

absolutely no way to predict whether a given set has this feature given any other facts about its members and their relations. So we end up introducing a new basic physical law, involving a new monadic predicate F of sets: whenever an F set forms a nested circle around a point p, radiation is emitted at p.

It comes naturally to us to put the new law in terms of sets. But this isn't inevitable: we might instead introduce a new parenthesis-embellished predicate, writing 'Fa(bc)(d (ef))' instead of 'F{a, {b, c}, {d, {e, f}}}'. If we did this, the new parenthesis-embellished predicate would play just as essential an explanatory role in our theory as non-symmetric predicates could possibly play in any theory. The parenthesis-embellished predicate is not absolutely indispensable, since it can be replaced with an ordinary predicate of sets. But of course non-symmetric predicates can also be dispensed with in favour of symmetric predicates applicable to sets; and, as I've already shown (p. 182 above), set theory itself can be developed without reliance on non-symmetric predicates. Thus, there is no principled distinction between the roles that non-symmetric predicates and parenthesis-embellished predicates can play in scientific explanation: if the former are in fact more useful in science, this is just a contingent fact about the laws of the actual world.

Our intuition that non-symmetric relations are possible turns out to be a product of the linear structure of human language. If our languages had a different sort of structure, we would have had entirely different intuitions; and there is no clear sense in which our actual languages are objectively superior to those other possible languages. It seems to me that this consideration should greatly reduce our confidence in the intuition. Universals, if they exist, are *fundamental* entities, not mere projections onto the world of idiosyncratic facts about human language. We should, therefore, be very tentative in our intuitions about the possibility of universals corresponding to familiar sorts of predicates; we should always be sensitive to the possibility that these intuitions will be defeated by the 'rigorous programme for identifying and eliminating the illicit influence of linguistic structures on our theory of universals' which Williamson (1985, p. 262) rightly advocates, and which I have been attempting to carry out in this paper.

10. ECONOMY

My argument so far has depended entirely on the premise that there are no brute necessities. In this final section I will consider the question what those who deny this premise should think about the issue of non-symmetric relations.

If we cannot choose between different systems of primitive predicates by eliminating those that entail that there are brute necessities, how else are we make this choice? Do we suspend all judgement on the matter, or simply believe whatever we find most appealing? If we are to have any useful debate on the question, we need some objective basis for comparing systems. A natural suggestion is that *economy* should play this role. *Ceteris paribus*, we should believe the *simplest* system, where the simplicity of a system is determined by such factors as the number of primitive predicates it has, the number of arguments taken by those predicates, and the simplicity of its system of brute necessities (i.e. of the simplest set of axioms sufficient to entail all necessary and a priori truths involving only the primitive predicates of the system).

It seems to me that, if this sort of economy matters at all, it counts strongly against all but three of the systems of primitive predicates which I have considered in this paper: systems D and E from Section 7, and the simple theory of states of affairs which I described in Section 2 as an example of a system that rules out non-symmetric relations. (Recall that this system has just two primitive predicates: 'is a particular component of' and 'is a universal component of'.) All the other systems I have considered have primitive predicates specially adapted for talking about *binary* relations. But surely it would be unacceptably arbitrary to rule out the possibility of relations of higher degree than two, just as it would be unacceptably arbitrary to rule out the possibility of relations of higher degree than seventeen. That there are no such arbitrary limitations on the space of possibilities is one of our firmest modal intuitions.[35] So our theory of binary relations must carry over, *mutatis mutandis*, to relations of higher degree. This means that, if we adopt as primitive any predicates that are specifically adapted for talking about binary relations, we will end up having to recognize infinitely many primitive predicates, with ever-increasing numbers of argument places. And since each of these predicates will be governed by some brute necessities, the set of brute necessities will not be even finitely axiomatizable.[36]

Of the three systems that remain when the ones with infinitely many primitive predicates have been ruled out, the simple theory of states of affairs is clearly the most economical. Its primitive predicates take fewer arguments: it makes do with a two-place predicate ('x is a particular component of s') where they have, respectively, a three-place predicate ('x occupies argument place α of s') and a four-place predicate ('a is a

---

[35] See Bricker (1991).

[36] Moreover, the more arguments a primitive predicate takes, the more complex the system of brute necessities involving that primitive predicate will be. We have already met one example of this: as n increases, the length of PARADIGMS$_n$ increases factorially. Similarly, if we take 'bears' as primitive and accept CONVERSES as a brute necessity, we will also have to accept as independent, axiomatic brute necessities all sentences of the form

$$\forall r \exists r^*(x_1 \ldots x_n \Delta r^* \equiv x_{k_1} \ldots x_{k_n} \Delta r)$$

for each of the $(n! - 1)$ nontrivial permutations $k_1 \ldots k_n$ of the first n positive integers.

component of s_1 in the same way that b is a component of s_2'). More importantly, it requires much less in the way of brute necessities. I don't think it lets us do without brute necessities altogether: for example, we will probably have to accept the claim that *no state of affairs has more than one universal component* (C8) as a brute necessity. But for any sentence which the simple theory of states of affairs forces us to accept as a brute necessity, there will be a corresponding brute necessity in each of the other two systems. By contrast, if we adopt the simple theory of states of affairs, we have no need for any brute necessities corresponding to the other axioms listed in section 7 ((D2)–(D4) and (E2)–(E6)).

Each of these systems of primitive predicates admits of some further simplifications. For example, we could make the simple theory of states of affairs even simpler by making do with just one two-place primitive predicate, 'is a component of', analysing 'x is a universal component of y' as 'x is a component of y and x is a universal', and 'x is a particular component of y' as 'x is a component of y and x is not a universal'.[37] The predicate 'is a universal' which occurs in these analyses could be taken as primitive, or analysed somehow in terms of 'is a component of'. For example, following a suggestion of Russell's, we might analyse 'x is a universal' as 'all the states of affairs of which x is a component have the same number of components' (cf. Whitehead and Russell 1925, vol. I, pp. xix–xx).[38] Simplifications of a similar sort can be made in systems

---

[37] These analyses rule out the possibility of *higher-order* universals, i.e. universals that are sometimes instantiated by other universals. If we were unhappy with this consequence, we might try analysing 'x is a universal component of y' as 'x is a component of y that is of higher order than any other component of y', taking 'x is of higher order than y' as a new primitive predicate.

[38] MacBride (1999) objects that this analysis incorrectly entails the impossibility of *multigrade* relations. But this is hardly a fatal objection. Rather more counterintuitively, the analysis entails that every particular necessarily bears some relation to some other particular.

A different approach, not subject to these objections, is to analyse 'x is a universal' as 'x is a component of itself', or alternatively as 'x is not a component of itself'. But these proposals have an air of trickery that make them hard to take seriously. In part, this is because it seems to be much harder to accept 'everything that has components has exactly one component that is a component of itself' as a brute necessity than it is to accept 'everything that has components has exactly one universal component' as a brute necessity. The latter claim, at least, intuitively strikes us as necessary, while the former certainly doesn't.

In fact, no completion of the schema 'everything that has components has exactly one component that...' involving just the predicate 'is a component of' seems like a very good candidate to be a brute necessity. Thus, if we take 'is a component of' to be the only

D and E.³⁹ But these simplifications do not affect the basic terms of the comparison: it is still true that if we want to allow for non-symmetric relations we must do so at the cost of making our system of primitive predicates considerably less economical.

None of these systems is very economical with *ontological categories*, since they all require us to believe in states of affairs as well as particulars and universals. But there is another highly economical system—to my mind, perhaps the most appealing of all those I have considered—which lets us avoid commitment to states of affairs. In this system there is just one primitive predicate: '... holds among ...', taking one singular and one plural term as arguments.⁴⁰ This system clearly rules out non-symmetric relations: 'x bears r to y' can plausibly be analysed only as 'r holds among x and y', which is of course logically equivalent to 'r holds among y and x'.⁴¹ It's hard to say how this system should be compared with the others as regards the simplicity of its primitive predicates. Does a primitive predicate that takes one singular and one plural argument contribute more to the complexity of a system than a primitive predicate that takes two singular arguments, and if so, how much more?⁴² But by

primitive predicate, we may well end up agreeing with Ramsey (1925) that we cannot know a priori that the components of states of affairs can be divided into two classes different enough from one another to be appropriately labelled as 'particulars' and 'universals', even if we are in principle prepared to posit brute necessities.

³⁹ *Some examples*: (i) We could simplify system E by analysing 'x is a universal' as 'whenever x enters into a state of affairs, it does so in the same way' ($\forall s_1 s_2 (x s_1 \, \mathbf{A} x s_1 \wedge x s_2 \mathbf{A} x s_2 \supset x s_1 \mathbf{A} x s_2)$). (ii) We could simplify system D by analysing 'x is a universal component of s' as '$x \mathsf{C}_{\check{x}} s$' or as '$x \mathsf{C}_{\check{s}} s$'. (iii) We could analyse the three-place primitive predicate of system D in terms of the two-place primitive predicates of the simple theory of states of affairs; for example, we could take argument places to be *properties* of the things that "occupy" them, analysing '$x \mathsf{C}_\alpha s$' as 'there is an s' with x as its sole particular component and α as its sole universal component, and s' is a particular component of s'.

⁴⁰ Many philosophers and linguists have endorsed some general strategy for "analysing away" plural expressions: if they are right, predicates taking plural arguments cannot be primitive. To accept such a predicate as primitive, one would have to adopt the view—defended by Boolos (1984), and more recently by Oliver and Smiley (2001)—that plural terms are perfectly clear as they are, and stand in no more need of reduction or explanation than singular terms.

⁴¹ Armstrong (1997, p. 91) suggests this way of understanding what it is for something to bear a symmetric relation to something else; he attributes the idea to Lewis.

⁴² On the numerical measure of complexity described by Goodman (1951, ch. 3), any system one of whose primitive predicates takes a plural argument would be *extremely* complex—more complex than any system whose predicates take only singular arguments. But this judgement strikes me as quite wrong. At least, it certainly seems much *easier to believe* that a predicate that takes one singular and one plural argument is primitive than that, say, a seventeen-place predicate is primitive.

doing away with the ontological category of states of affairs, this system clearly does better than any of the others as regards the simplicity of its system of brute necessities. To take just one example, we now need no counterpart of the principle that every state of affairs has just one universal component.[43]

Thus, even if I am wrong that there are no brute necessities, considerations of economy count strongly in favour of the thesis that all relations must be symmetric. And there may be other things to be said in favour of the thesis as well.[44] Of course, these advantages must be weighed against the disadvantage of conflicting with our intuition that non-symmetric relations are possible. I won't presume to say which way the balance should tilt. But I hope that my discussion has made it plausible that the disadvantage is not as weighty as it may initially have seemed.

University of Pittsburgh

---

[43] This system can be simplified still further in the same way as the simple theory of states of affairs. Instead of taking '*r* holds among the *x*s' as primitive, we might analyse it as '*r* is a universal, and *r* and the *x*s are bound together', taking the predicate 'are bound together', which takes just one plural term as its argument, as our new primitive. '*x* is a universal' might be taken as primitive, or analysed in terms of 'are bound together'—perhaps, in the style of Russell, as 'whenever the *y*s are bound together, and the *z*s are bound together, and *x* is among both the *y*s and the *z*s, the *y*s and the *z*s are equinumerous'.

[44] David Lewis (1986; 1992, p. 200) objects to the theory of states of affairs on the grounds that it violates the principle of *uniqueness of composition*, according to which it is impossible for two things to have exactly the same components. Certainly a believer in states of affairs who also believes in the possibility of relations that are neither symmetric nor antisymmetric is under considerable pressure to deny this principle. If *a* bears a non-symmetric relation *r* to *b* and *b* bears *r* to *a*, there must be two states of affairs whose only components are *a*, *b*, and *r*. But if we give up on non-symmetric relations, and adopt the simple theory of states of affairs or one of its simplifications, there is no motivation at all for positing such failures of uniqueness.

Lewis also objects that the believer in states of affairs must accept a "non-mereological mode of composition", i.e. a notion of "componenthood" distinct from the notion of "parthood" which Lewis takes to be governed by the axioms of mereology. But this is not inevitable: if we wanted to, we could analyse '*x* is a component of *s*' as '*x* is simple, and *s* is a state of affairs, and *x* is part of *s*', taking 'is a state of affairs' as a new primitive predicate. Thus, even though (according to mereology) any object and any universal have a fusion, for the object to count as *instantiating* the universal, the fusion of the two must be a *state of affairs*, and both must be simple. (The restriction to simple things is needed to avoid having to count fusions of components of a state of affairs as further components of the state of affairs. The consequence that only simple things can instantiate or be instantiated is indeed surprising, but far from being entirely incredible.)

REFERENCES

Armstrong, David M. (1978) *A Theory of Universals*, vol. 2 of *Universals and Scientific Realism*, Cambridge University Press.
—— (1997) *A World of States of Affairs*, Cambridge University Press.
Boolos, George (1984) 'To Be is to be the Value of a Variable (or to be Some Values of Some Variables)', *Journal of Philosophy*, 81: 430–49.
Bradley, F. H. (1897) *Appearance and Reality*, 2nd edn, Oxford University Press; reprinted in *Writings on Logic and Metaphysics*, ed. James W. Allard and Guy Stock, Oxford University Press, 1994.
Bricker, Phillip (1991) 'Plenitude of Possible Structures', *Journal of Philosophy*, 88: 607–19.
Dorr, Cian (2002) *The Simplicity of Everything*, Ph.D. thesis, Princeton University.
—— (2003). 'Primitive Predicates', unpublished paper.
Fine, Kit (2000) 'Neutral Relations', *Philosophical Review*, 109: 1–33.
Goodman, Nelson (1951) *The Structure of Appearance*, Harvard University Press.
Hazen, A. P. (1999). 'A Simplification to Lewis's Set-theoretic Structuralism', unpublished paper.
Jackson, Frank (1998) *From Metaphysics to Ethics: A Defence of Conceptual Analysis*, Oxford University Press.
Kripke, Saul (1980) *Naming and Necessity*, Harvard University Press; first published 1972.
Lewis, David (1986). 'A Comment on Armstrong and Forrest', *Australasian Journal of Philosophy*, 64: 92–3; reprinted in Lewis (1999: 108–10).
—— (1992) 'Critical Notice of Armstrong's *A Combinatorial Theory of Possibility*', *Australasian Journal of Philosophy*, 70: 211–24; reprinted in Lewis (1999: 196–214).
—— (1999) *Papers in Metaphysics and Epistemology*, Cambridge University Press.
MacBride, Fraser (1999) 'On How We Know What There Is', *Analysis*, 59: 27–37.
Mellor, D. H. (1991) 'Properties and Predicates', in *Matters of Metaphysics*, Cambridge University Press, pp. 170–82.
Oliver, Alex and Timothy Smiley (2001) 'Strategies for a Logic of Plurals', *Philosophical Quarterly*, 51: 289–306.
Ramsey, F. P. (1925) 'Universals', *Mind*, 34: 401–17; reprinted in *Philosophical Papers*, ed. D. H. Mellor, Cambridge University Press, 1990.
Russell, Bertrand (1903) *The Principles of Mathematics*, Routledge.
Whitehead, Alfred North and Bertrand Russell (1925) *Principia Mathematica*, 2nd edn, Cambridge University Press; first published 1910.
Williamson, Timothy (1985) 'Converse Relations', *Philosophical Review*, 94: 249–62.

Part III

FREEDOM, CAUSAL POWERS, AND CAUSATION

8. The Mental Problems of the Many

Peter Unger

Many years ago, I blush to recall, I published some arguments against the existence of all sorts of commonly supposed entities—against rocks and desks, plants and planets, stars and salt shakers, human brains and bodies, and, perish the thought, against us human thinking experiencers, including even the one who's me.[1] By contrast, now I'm trying to develop, in a book I've been long writing, a humanly realistic philosophy, wherein my existence, and yours, has the status of a quite undeniable philosophic datum.[2]

As it seems to me now, certain *trying ideas* then deployed in such nihilistic reasoning may bear importantly on the question of what sort of a humanly realistic view we should adopt. These are ideas to the effect that, where I'm apt first to think that there's just this one human body,

[1] In chronological order, the most directly nihilistic of these papers are: "There Are No Ordinary Things", *Synthese*, 41 (1979): 117–54; "I Do Not Exist", pp. 235–51 in *Perception and Identity*, ed. G. F. MacDonald, London: Macmillan, 1979; and "Why There Are No People", *Midwest Studies in Philosophy*, 4 (1979): 177–222. The main thrust of these papers is the articulation of a nihilistic approach to various *sorites* arguments. Typically, these arguments trade on the (for all I really know perfectly correct) idea that an extremely minute difference between two ordinary entities—minute as regards propensities as well as all sorts of other things—will never mean the difference between one of them being a rock, for example, and the other not being a rock, or the difference between one being a thinking being and the other not being a thinking being. Less directly nihilistic are a few other papers, including "The Problem of the Many", *Midwest Studies in Philosophy*, 5 (1980): 411–67. In this paper none of the key ideas has anything much to do with any sorites arguments, or with "discriminative vagueness", though a casual glance at these key ideas may often give such an erroneous impression. Right now, I'll warn you against conflating these two very different sorts of nihilistic reasoning. And, in the bargain, I'll warn against mistaking, for any sorites argument, or any reasoning at all concerning discriminative vagueness, the trying thoughts I'm about to supply in this present essay. Finally, I signal that, while several of this essay's key ideas do arise from issues central to "The Problem of the Many", some of these presently central ideas go, in various important respects, far beyond anything considered in that old paper. (While there are great differences between the thoughts of this new essay and the ideas of the older one, an attempt to detail the differences looks to be more distracting than instructive.)

[2] Still in progress, the book is entitled *All the Power in the World*, to be published by Oxford University Press.

"my body", seated in just this one chair, "my desk chair", there are, more accurately, many billions of human bodies, each seated in many billions of chairs. And, where I'm first given to believe that there's just one healthy active brain, "my brain", promoting someone's mentality, there may be many billions of brains, each of them largely overlapping so many of the others, and each serving, quite equally, to promote a thinking, experiencing and choosing human being, or human self. Maybe each brain promotes the very same mind, or self, as do each of the others, in which case there's just one self promoted (rather redundantly?) by them all; or maybe each promotes a numerically distinct conscious individual, in which case many billions of experiencers may be, in my situation, simultaneously promoted. Right now, these remarks should seem no better than cryptic comments; but, in the course of this essay their import should become clearer.

These *trying ideas* might provide, I'll be suggesting, much force against the Scientiphical View that each of us is a highly complex wholly physical thing, with each of our powers just some sort of (physically derivative) physical power; or, on a less popular version of Scientiphicalism, each of us is epiphenomenal on, or supervenient on, a highly complex wholly physical thing.[3] And they might also provide much force against a related Emergentist View, on which each of us is a physical-and-mental complex.[4] Without further ado, let's encounter these trying ideas.

RECALLING THE PROBLEM OF THE MANY

In a paper called "The Problem of the Many", I introduced a problem for our everyday thinking, distinct from all sorites problems and, indeed, quite different from problems of "discriminative vagueness".

---

[3] Spelling it differently, as "Scientificalism", I first sketched this View, which is our dominant metaphysic, in "The Mystery of the Physical and the Matter of Qualities", *Midwest Studies in Philosophy*, 23 (1999): 75–99. Using philosophically more suggestive spelling, I discussed it further in "Free Will and Scientiphicalism", *Philosophy and Phenomenological Research*, 65 (2002): 1–25. One of the main aims of *All the Power in the World* is to explore, very critically, this Scientiphical Metaphysics that, for several decades at least, has been the dominant worldview among prominent mainstream philosophers, as well as many others.

[4] There's a discussion of this Emergentism in my "Free Will and Scientiphicalism". The excellent suggestion that I treat this view very seriously I owe to Dean Zimmerman.

Much as I found it useful to do then, let us start by considering certain cases of *ordinary clouds*, clouds like those we sometimes seem to see in the sky.

As often viewed by us from here on the ground, sometimes puffy "picture-postcard" clouds give the appearance of having a nice enough boundary, each white entity sharply surrounded by blue sky. (In marked contrast, there are other times when it's a wonder that we don't simply speak singularly of "the cloud in the sky", where each visible cloudy region runs so messily together with many other cloudy "parts of the sky".) But upon closer scrutiny, as may happen sometimes when you're in an airplane, even the puffiest, cleanest clouds don't seem to be so nicely bounded. And this closer look seems a more revealing one. For, as science seems clearly to say, our clouds are almost wholly composed of tiny water droplets, and the dispersion of these droplets, in the sky or the atmosphere, is always, in fact, a gradual matter. With pretty much any route out of even a comparatively clean cloud's center, there is no stark stopping place to be encountered. Rather, anywhere near anything presumed a boundary, there's only a gradual decrease in the density of droplets fit, more or less, to be constituents of a cloud that's there.

With that being so, we might see that there are enormously many complexes of droplets, each as fit as any other for being a constituted cloud. Each of the many will be a cloud, we must suppose, if there are even as many as just one constituted cloud where, at first, it surely seemed there was exactly one. For example, consider the two candidates I'll now describe. Except for two "widely opposing" droplets, one on one side of two overlapping cloudy complexes, way over on the left, say, and another way over on the right, two candidate clouds may wholly overlap each other, so far as droplets goes. The cited droplet that's on the left is a constituent of just one of the two candidates, not a component of the other; and the one on the right is a component of the other candidate, not the one first mentioned. So each of these two candidate clouds has exactly the same number of constituent droplets. And each might have exactly the same mass, and volume, as the other.

Now, all around the outer portion(s) of a supposedly single cloud, what obtains is a gradual change of droplet density, along ever so many paths, from the considered cloud's central portion(s) to what is merely its droplet-infested environment. In actuality, there's not just one "problematic pair of opposing droplets". Rather, there are very many such *distinct* pairs, that is, many pairs of peripheral droplets each of which has no droplet in common with any of the other pairs. So there's certainly nothing special about the opposing pair that, above, fueled some peculiar thinking. Indeed, any droplet from any one of the many opposing pairs might be coupled equally well, instead, with at least one of the two droplets from (almost) any other one of these very many pairs. This being so, the mathematics of combinations will have it that, in the situation where one first supposes a single concrete cloud, there are *very many millions* of clouds present. Each of these many millions of cloud candidates has precisely as many droplets as does each of the others. And, in every way plausibly deemed relevant for cloudhood here, each is the exact equal of all the others. By contrast with considerations central to sorites arguments, here there is *no* difference at all between any one of these complexes' current cloud credentials and the credentials of any of the millions of others.

Though it's not needed to generate our problem, it's sometimes fun to combine what's just been offered above with some considerations concerning vagueness. So, in the case we've been considering, the extremely good cloud candidates are not limited, of course, to the exactly equally good ones that differ only as regards two such opposing peripheral constituent droplets. In addition, there's a candidate that's plenty good enough for current cloudhood that *lacks not just one but both of* the peripheral "opposing" droplets first considered. If there are any real clouds here at all, this will be a cloud that's just one "droplet's worth" less massive than either of our first two candidates, and just slightly smaller in volume, too. And, there's another perfectly good candidate that *has not just one but both of* those peripheral droplets as constituents. As regards both mass and volume, it will be just two droplets' worth larger than the candidate considered a moment ago, and just one droplet larger than each of the two complexes we first considered above. With even just this much thrown into our cloudily explosive mix of considerations, our situation's recognized cloud population rises enormously.

While there should be limits to how far such "numerically differential shuttling" can be taken, lest sorites arguments here lead to nihilistic ideas, we won't be anywhere close to approaching those limits with differences of just two peripheral droplets in the cloudy complexes we're considering. Indeed, even with differentials of *five* such peripheral droplets, even five on *either* side of our initially chosen "tied clearest current cloud case", we won't be anywhere close to threatening any such limits. Now, these matters concerning vagueness have been, as I predicted, some fun to consider. But, they themselves are peripheral to what are here the main issues, to which we now return.

Even as concerns the main issues, there's not an absolutely perfect parallel between a common cloud and its constituting droplets on one hand, and a water droplet and (at least some of) its constituting molecules, or atoms, or elementary particles on the other. But there's no important difference between the two. We may grant, if needs be, that there are routes from a drop's center into its mere environs with breaks that are quite clean. Even so, there'll be many others that are very much messier, quite messy enough to allow for "opposing" pairs of plausible enough constituents. With these opposing pairs of "particles", we may reason, in a relevantly parallel fashion, that there are many millions of water droplets where at first there would seem to be just one. And, as it is with water droplets, so it is also with rocks and desks, planets and plants, and human brains and bodies.

Where at first there seems to be just a single human body, here, which is just "my body", there may really be vastly many human bodies. And where I take your single brain to be ensconced in your one head, there may be very many human brains (each equally "yours"), all similarly ensconced in vastly many human heads (each "yours").

All this sounds very strange. But, maybe there isn't anything in it that should be very disturbing. So long as we're clear as to what are the relations among which brains, and which bodies, maybe there needn't be any serious problem. For instance, we can be clear enough about what we may correctly express when saying that none of your brains is in, nor are any of your brains a part of, any of my many bodies. And, we may be similarly clear about saying that each of my brains is in, and is a part of, all of my bodies. And, even as many of your brains each overlap with many other brains that are yours, none of your brains overlap with any of mine, of course. At the same time, it's also clear that none of my many bodies ever nest in, nor do any ever greatly overlap with, any one of your many bodies.

Now, even on the face of things, the problems of the many just canvassed, or rehearsed, concern nothing of much greater moment, or depth, than what's commonly found with many merely semantic issues. There seems nothing of much metaphysical moment in these problems with common thoughts about quite grossly complex physical entities. (Nor does there seem any perplexing problems of moral moment, or any deep difficulty concerning rational concern.) Should every "problem of the many" be no worse than these noted problems—about many overlapping clouds, and brains, and human bodies—there may be no very serious philosophical problem to be found along these lines. Is there, perhaps, such a relatively untroubling situation happily in the cards for us here?

THE EXPERIENTIAL PROBLEM OF THE MANY

Maybe so; but maybe not. Indeed, matters may start to get much worse, I'll suggest, should we be unable to quash the thought that, in what I take to be just my own situation, there are really very many experiencing thinkers, each promoted by a different one of the very many brains that, above, I bid us recognize as "my brains".

But, can anything much like *that* be right? In addition to me myself, whose conscious metaphysical struggles are, apparently, producing these awkward sentences, are there many other thinkers, too, each similarly responsible, and maybe each of us then just barely responsible, for producing these strangely disquieting philosophical utterances? Right here and now, "in my situation", are there vastly many experiencing thinkers, each with a protracted illusion of being, in this very present situation, quite singular and unique? While anything's possible, as we say, the idea that there are, along with me, so many distinct likeminded experiencing thinkers is incredible.

Am I being, perhaps, overly self-centered here? I don't think so. In fact, when I consider a similar "experientially explosive" suggestion about you, and about the many bodies and brains "in your situation", I find the thought of billions of like-minded experiencers just as incredible as in my own case. Whether it's for my own case or for yours, with our Experiential Problem of the Many there's a very serious issue of credibility.

Just a few sentences make clear how very much such an experientially explosive supposition flies in the face of our commonsense thinking about ourselves. Possibly excepting what happens when certain rarified metaphysics is done, each one of these many supposed billions thinks that, at least among all the people on earth right now, he alone is experiencing—immediately, complexly, and totally—in the precise way or fashion that, at the moment, he manifests, or exemplifies. As I take it, you're not experiencing in a way that's precisely like the way I'm experiencing right now, even though we may be near each other in the same room. For one thing, I have a tingling condition "in my left foot" that, I believe, is quite different from any felt condition you now suffer. For another, my perspective is different from yours, which almost certainly means a notable difference in our visual experiencing. Obviously we could go on and on; but, just as obviously, that's enough.

Matters quickly go from bad to worse; incredible thoughts compound incredibly. Am I to think that, with vastly many experiencers promoted by vastly many brains "in my situation", each may be communicating his innermost thoughts to all of the enormously many other experiencing thinkers, across the vastly many tables between us, promoted by the vastly many brains "in your situation"? Such an idea is, I think, patently absurd.

Something has gone badly wrong here. And, as we are now dealing with human thinking experiencers, with the likes of you and me, what's gone wrong concerns what's central for any humanly realistic philosophy.

Indeed, whatever philosophical projects one may find interesting, this present matter presents an issue that one should recognize as philosophically puzzling and disturbing. Part of what makes the matter so puzzling may be that it concerns what has been called, in recent years, the "subjectivity of experience". This so-called subjectivity is closely related to—and it may even be the same thing as—what was called, in earlier years, the "privacy of experience". Very sketchily put, that is indeed my partial diagnosis. In a way that may resonate intuitively, I'll try to amplify on this diagnostic idea.

The thought that there are, "in my situation", vastly many individuals each similarly experiencing the sweet taste of chocolate is, to my mind, a very disturbing suggestion. It is far more disturbing than the thought that, in this situation, there are vastly many complex entities each of whom is chewing a sweet piece of chocolate, or digesting a sweet piece of chocolate. A digesting of the sweet chocolate that's very much like my (body's) digesting it may as well be ascribed—quite indifferently, tolerably, and readily—to each of however many human beings (or human bodies) may very largely overlap me (or mine). This contrasting thought concerning digesting is far less deeply puzzling, and far less disturbing, than the thought concerned with experiencing.

With the digesting of the chocolate, the situation seems far more relaxed than with the experiential tasting of anything. With so much more relaxed a matter, it seems little more than a matter of choosing what forms of words to use. Following common sense, even if perhaps speaking loosely, we may say that there's just one process of digesting now going on "in my situation". Or, paying less attention to common thought, and maybe more to certain principles of differential constitution, we may instead say that, with many similar overlapping entities each engaged in a very similar digestive process, there are many similar overlapping digestive happenings. As it seems, this latter description is only somewhat less intuitively palatable.

Not so, it seems, with my experiencing as I do. Rather, it seems, my power to experience will be radically different from my power to digest (or, perhaps better, from my very many bodies' powers to digest.) The latter is just a highly derivative physical propensity; it's a metaphysically superficial power ascribed, perhaps properly enough, to many such ontologically superficial complexes as are typical human bodies, or entirely physical human organisms. By contrast, a power to experience may be a radically emergent mental propensity, in no wise any mere physical power, neither derivative nor non-derivative. For some, this contrast will be both evident and even profound. But, for others, further discussion may be useful.

For the sake of the argument, or the diagnostic exposition, just suppose, for the moment, that a Substantial Dualism holds. And, further, suppose that I causally interact, quite equally, with each of very many overlapping complex physical bodies, each of which thus may be called, properly enough, one of *my bodies*. Must there be very many other Cartesian thinkers, in addition to myself, who also causally interact, quite equally, with (so many of) these same physical complexes—so that (many of) my bodies are also *their bodies*? Certainly not. Indeed, it may be a great advantage of this Dualism that its most plausible versions won't have things turn out this way. As a matter of metaphysical fact, all the bodies "in my situation" serve to promote only myself, and not any other sentient self. On such a Substantial Dualistic View, there may be much reason to take each of these many bodies to be one of my bodies, but not to take any of them to be anyone else's.

Even as I may have so many human bodies, none of which are anyone else's bodies, so I may then also have very many *digestive systems*, many of them greatly overlapping many of the others, while each such system has a slightly different group of basic physical constituents from all the rest—perhaps an "extra" electron here, or one less hydrogen atom there. To be sure, this sounds like it's squarely against commonsense thinking, and ordinary biological thinking. And, very possibly, it is. Still, there's nothing that is all that disturbing in any of it. Indeed, there's nothing very disturbing, either, in going on to think many further thoughts, elaborations on these materially explosive ideas. For instance, without very much disturbance, we may think that each of my many digestive systems may undergo, or be engaged in, a process of digestion—a digesting—that's ever so similar to the digestive processes undergone, simultaneously, by ever so many overlapping digestive systems. Readily enough, I trust, we may accept the idea that all these systems are mine, and mine alone, and all these digestings are mine, and mine alone. Though it's somewhat unnatural for us to say such profligate things, there's no grave philosophical error, I'll suggest, in being so liberal about these metaphysically material matters.

For the same reasons that I might be said to have billions of digestive systems, I may also be said to have vastly many *nervous systems*, each largely overlapping very many others, and each having slightly different physical constituents from all the rest. Indeed, it seems established that *my* causal interaction with all these systems is much more direct than *my* interaction with any of my digestive systems. Anyhow, much as we might readily tolerate the thought that my many overlapping digestive systems may be engaged in many overlapping digestive processes, so we might also easily tolerate the thought that my many overlapping nervous systems may be engaged in many overlapping neural processes.

But, may we similarly tolerate the idea that each of these many nervous systems may undergo, or may be engaged in, a process of *experiencing* that's quite simultaneous with, and ever so similar to, the experiencings undergone by ever so many other largely overlapping nervous systems? I certainly don't think so. More cautiously, may we fairly happily think that, even as each of very many particular experiencings may occur during exactly the same time as ever so many others, each may occur in very much the same place as so many others? May we think this nearly as happily, at least, as we may think parallel thoughts about my digestings? Again, it certainly doesn't seem so to me. By contrast, this following seems a much more intuitively congenial expression of what's apparently happening experientially. More *directly* than any other comparable part of my body, or parts of my bodies, each of the many nervous systems now in "my situation" physically *promotes just a single (total) process of (total) experiencing*, which is just *my experiencing*, even as I myself am the single experiencer that's physically promoted by (any of) the nervous systems now in this particular situation. Briefly put, here's a reasonably plausible way for how all that may be so, even if it is also a rather nicely amazing way. In whatever serves to constitute my nervous systems, there's a propensity to the effect that there will be a limit placed—(almost always) a limit of just one—on how many experiencing particulars may be promoted by the optimally arranged basic physical constituents—optimally arranged, that is, for the promoting of any experiencing individuals. In the same way, we may hypothesize that each of my simple physical constituents—every single one of them—has a marvelous propensity with regards to how it may interact with very many others, so that, in optimal arrangements for promoting consciousness, there's an effective *singular resolution* as to what experiencer they promote. And so also is there a singular resolution of what experience, or what experiencing, is then promoted by them.

In the last several paragraphs, we've been supposing that the correct metaphysical view is a Substantial Dualism, not terribly different from the classical view of Descartes. Now, let's drop that supposition and, to the contrary, suppose that a more materialistic view of mentality is correct—maybe some form of materialism itself, maybe some more relaxed version of our Scientiphical Metaphysic, as with a suitable Scientiphical Epiphenomenalism. Or maybe what's correct is something as moderately different from Dualism as the Emergentism that, in this is paper's preamble, I mentioned so briefly. Now, on this Emergentist View, there are radically emergent mental powers, all right, but they all inhere in physical complexes, in the very same complex objects that also have so many physically derivative physical powers.[5] *Insofar as* we may maintain one of these more materialistic views, quite comfortably and intuitively, we may not find it disturbing, at all, to think that, in my situation right now, there are billions of experiencing thinkers. But,

---

[5] As noted earlier, I discuss this Emergentism in my "Free Will and Scientiphicalism".

then, *how far is it* that, all the while doing it quite comfortably and intuitively, I actually can sustain the thought that, in my situation right now, there are billions of experiencing individuals, each enjoying his very own experiencing, numerically distinct from the similar experience of all the others? Not very far at all, that's for sure. And, as I suspect, pretty much the same is true of you.

For most of us, all this should be fairly intuitive, maybe even highly intuitive. For that reason, all this should be, for most of us, a point in favor of Substantial Dualism—as against the Scientifical Metaphysic and, as well, as against the Emergentism lately noted.

THE EXPERIENCING OF SPLIT-BRAIN PATIENTS UNDERSCORES THIS DISTURBING PROBLEM

The previous section offered a fairly succinct presentation of the Experiential Problem of the Many. Now, I aim to amplify on that. With the further considerations I'll discuss in this amplification, we may see that this problem provides a more clearly forceful point in favor of Dualism, even if, perhaps, not yet any point that's enormously forceful.

At all events, it's extremely interesting to think about human "split-brain" patients—epileptics whose main neural connection between their two cerebral hemispheres, their corpus callosum, was severed so that they might gain relief from frequent severe seizures. When these patients are placed in certain specially designed experimental setups, as some of them actually were, in many cases their behavior almost cries out for exotic psychological interpretation.

Here's a simple case, contrived for illustrative purposes, that's relevantly similar to striking actual cases. Our psychological subject, a cooperative split-brain patient, is asked to handle some regularly shaped solid figures, each object being either a cylinder, or a cube, or a pyramid, or a sphere. And, right after handling a solid object, our subject is to write down the sort of object she just handled, inscribing just one of these four common words for shapes, the one that seems suitable to her: "cylinder", "cube", "pyramid", and "sphere". Now, none of these objects is ever seen by the subject; the solids are all behind an opaque screen that obscures even the surface of the table on which they rest. Usefully, the screen has two holes in it, while each hole has an easily movable but always visually obscuring flap. At all events, our subject places her left arm through the hole on her left, and her right arm through the one on her right. So her left hand can handle objects on the table's left side, from her perspective; but, it can't handle any on the table's right side. Why not? Well, protruding upward from center of the table's surface, there's a large solid barrier, which precludes any left–right, or right–left, crossover. In this way the right hand is conversely limited; with her right hand she can handle only the objects to the right of the barrier.

That's our experimental setup. Now, we suppose that, within about a minute of putting her arms through the appropriate holes, her right hand grasps a cube, and no other regular solid object, while the sole object her left hand grasps is a sphere. For a few seconds, she holds the two objects like that. Then, she withdraws her hands from the holes, as instructed. And, then, on the near side of the screen, she places her hands on two pieces of paper and is given two pencils, one placed in her left hand and one in her right. Then our ambidextrous subject, who can readily employ both hands at once, is asked to write, on each of the pads, just one of the four words: "cylinder", "cube", "pyramid", "sphere". Something quite amazing now happens. With her right hand, she writes "cube", while with her left hand, she writes "sphere". In this strangely diverse writing activity, our subject evinces no hesitation, conflict, or ambiguity. Rather, as far as her behavior seems to indicate, (it's as though) "a part of her" experienced a cube tactiley, and not any sphere, while at the very same time "another part of her" experienced tactiley only a sphere, and no cube at all.

Many actual cases are, as I said, very like this contrived example.[6] They strongly suggest that, in many actual experimental setups with split-brain patients, the subjects become involved, at once, in two quite separate experiencings, or "streams of experience". Of course, these split-brain episodes are very unlike what we imagined above for our very many "largely overlapping experiencers". With those very many overlappers, each of *very many millions* of experiential streams was supposed to be *qualitatively extremely like* each of the others; with our

---

[6] For a nice presentation of some of these actual cases, along with an interesting discussion of what might be much of their philosophic import, see Thomas Nagel, "Brain Bisection and the Unity of Consciousness", *Synthese*, 22 (1971). This essay is widely reprinted, notably in Nagel's *Mortal Questions* (Cambridge University Press, 1979), pp. 147–64.

split-brain subjects, by contrast, each of *just two* presumed experiential streams is qualitatively very *unlike* the only other.

What's going on here, with a split-brain patient in a dually productive setup? To provide a sensible answer to this question, we first put to one side all our problems of the many. That done, what's going on seems to be this: along with a good deal of the subject's nervous system that's not cerebral—her brain-stem, for example—one of her hemispheres serves (most directly) to promote one sort of experiencing that the subject's written answer indicated she enjoyed—say, her tactile experiencing as of a cube. And, in a relevantly complementary way, the other hemisphere serves (most directly) to promote another sort of experiencing, a tactile experiencing as of a sphere, and not as of a cube. Now, except as regards cerebral hemispheres, a big exception here, what's promoting the one experiencing, is the same entity—presumably the same physical complex—as is promoting the other; or, at the very least, the one precisely coincides with the other. In exactly the same way, the physical complex (most directly) promoting one of these experiences has a promotionally important part that is the same as, or that coincides with, the physical complex that's (most directly) promoting the other experience. And at the same time, of course, each complex lacks a promotionally important part, a whole hemisphere, that is a crucial part of the other.

Far be it from me to think that in these cases everything is readily amenable to our customary ways of thinking about human experiencers and our experiencings. On the contrary, the apparent simultaneous "contrary" experience is very puzzling. Here's just some of what's so puzzling. With each numerically different total momentary experiencing, there is a numerically different experiencer—or so we're strongly inclined to believe. So, in the case that's in focus, we have a certain inclination to think that there is one experiencer who writes only "cube" when reporting her experiencing, and another who doesn't write "cube", but writes only "sphere", when reporting her tactiley very different simultaneous experiencing. So, intuitively, there's a certain difficulty here for our thinking that in this experimental situation there's just one single experiencer.

But, that inclination isn't our only proclivity here. Can there really be two human people in this situation? Can there really be, in this experimental setup, an experiencing writer who is not a human person? As it certainly seems, there's *also* a difficulty for our thinking that in this setup there's *not* always just one experiencer. Indeed, there might be an even greater difficulty here.

For the moment, though, suppose there's not just one, but two experiencers here, each tactilely experiencing quite differently from the other. Well, what happens when these two experiencers are removed from the artificial setup, when each hemisphere again gets very much the same stimulation as the other? Do we have only one experiencer once again, the same single person who went into the experiment (say, about a year after she had her split-brain operation)? That suggestion seems strangely implausible. Where was she in the intervening period, this one experiencer, when (as we're supposing) there were the two simultaneous different experiencers? Was she just a certain one of these two? That seems quite absurd. Did she go out of existence altogether, just when the experimental setup was introduced, and then come to exist again, just when the differentially stimulating setup was removed? This suggestion also seems unsatisfactory.

As a still further alternative, there's the conjecture that, not just during the experimental setup, but ever since her operation first affected how she experienced, our split-brain patient was engaged in not one, but two experiencings. Quite dramatically, during the differentially stimulating setup of the experimental situation, her experiencings were qualitatively very different, and not just numerically distinct. Less dramatically, before the post-operative patient was introduced to this setup, her two (streams of) experiencings were qualitatively very alike. (But, for all their qualitative similarity, these experiencings were numerically different from each other.)

What are we to make of these conjectures? And what are we to make of various further proposals, which may also be, at once, both somewhat attractive and somewhat problematic? I do not know. It is all very puzzling; and, it seems, quite *deeply* puzzling. But even in our deeply puzzled ignorance we might make, I think, some useful comments.

Let us meanwhile continue to suppose that, during the puzzling middle period of the experimental setup, a certain apparently exclusionary diversity of experiencing is all at once promoted. And let's suppose, just a little explosively perhaps, that then there is not just one sentient being, but *two experiencers*. Though that thought is somewhat uncomfortable, it's not nearly as disturbing as the thought that there are *many billions of human thinkers experiencing* as of a cube; nor is it nearly as unsettling as the thought that billions are each tactiley *experiencing only spherically*. (Far more disturbing yet is the thought that there are billions experiencing tactiley only in the first way, and billions only in the second way.)

However, unless we believe in a naturally resolving limit on the experiencers promoted, how are we rationally to reject the thought that, with so very many exceptionally similar complexes of matter, there are, right then and there and all at once, so very many experiencers as *that*?

Recall the speculation that, before and after the experimental setup with our patient—or with our two "neighboring" patients—there may be two quite parallel experiencings promoted. Supposing that's really so, a somewhat plausible explanation will run rather like this. One of these parallel experiencings is promoted by a neuronal system featuring only the left hemisphere as its distinctively highest region or part, and the other by a nervous system that, lacking the left, similarly features just the right hemisphere. Whatever one thinks of this speculation—I myself don't think it's all that plausible—there's nobody, I trust, who thinks there are many billions of experiencings physically promoted largely by the left hemisphere, and billions more promoted largely by the right. But, to avoid such a numerically explosive idea, in a properly principled fashion, we must accept, again, that there is a resolving limit on what, by way of experiencers and their experiencings, is physically promoted by various mentally productive arrangements of physical constituents.

Almost everything we've been discussing in this section strikes me as not only puzzling, but *deeply* puzzling. Far from being concerned only with semantics, or with the application conditions of some concepts, these puzzles seem to concern, beyond all that, metaphysically deep considerations. And, if that's right, they may point to some matters of much metaphysical import. Below, I'll try to make these points more clearly vivid.

Recall our remarks as to how we might take it upon ourselves to say that, "in my situation", there are many different digestive systems, each involved with a different simultaneous digesting. While that's a rather unnatural thing to say, and while the motivation supplied for saying it may be somewhat puzzling, there is nothing in it that's *deeply* puzzling. Nor is there any deep puzzle concerning whether we should continue always to think that, "in my situation", there's always just one digester, presumably a certain human organism, or whether there are very many digesters, most of them largely overlapping many others. So, here again, we find an intuitively striking difference between our experiencing and, on the other side, such evidently physical processes as our digesting. This difference may indicate something deep metaphysically.

MIGHT THE SINGULARITY OF COMMON EXPERIENCING FAVOR SUBSTANTIAL DUALISM?

To deal effectively with our deep puzzles about our experiencing, perhaps we might accept, if only very tentatively and somewhat skeptically, a certain Substantial Dualism. Central to this Cartesian doctrine is the thought that each of us is a non-physical experiencer, though an experiencer who (causally) *interacts with* certain physical things.

With such a suitable Dualistic doctrine, there may be a singular resolution for our Experiential Problem—featuring just a single experiencer "in my situation" that isn't so horribly arbitrary as to be terribly incredible. Well in line with this Dualism, we can conjecture that "in my situation" very many overlapping physical complexes—physical brains, perhaps—may altogether serve to promote, causally or quasi-causally, a single non-physical experiencer, or a singular mind, or exactly one individual soul, even while each of the complexes may do its promoting in what is really a quite derivative sense or way. In the case of each mentally promoting physical complex, the derivation will proceed, of course, from the basic (enough) physical components of the very complex in question, and from the physical relations obtaining among its particular components, to the complex's being a (derivative) promoter of just a single sentient self. And so, in each of very many worldly derivations, it may be the very same sentient self, or experiencing mind, that the complexes in question each serve (derivatively) to promote. In a happy enough sense, then, the (physically derivative) promoting of this single mind, *by any one of* these physical complexes, will be a *causally redundant* promoting. Of course, there won't be any complex that's doing any of this (derivative) promoting without there being, all at once, a great many each doing it rather redundantly.

In any very direct sense or way, it will be this promoted single non-physical mind itself—just me myself—that has a power to experience. So, it will be only in a very attenuated sense or way that an experiential power will be possessed by any of the concrete physical complexes that serve to promote the experientially powerful non-physical being.

Nowadays, it's very hard for respectable philosophers to believe in mentally powerful non-physical beings. But, even for us now, this may be *less* incredible than the thought that *just a single one* of our considered physical complexes itself has this power—with all those other slightly overlapping complexes being quite powerless experientially, even all of those others that, in mass, in volume, and in number of basic constituents, are each precisely the same as the supposedly sole experiencing physical complex. And it's *also* less incredible than the thought that just a single one of the basic (enough) physical entities here—say, a certain particular quark—has the power to experience richly—with all the other quarks "in my situation" being quite powerless in such a mentally rich regard. And it's certainly less incredible than the thought that some mere abstraction from what's physical, and nothing concrete at all, should be the sole entity, "in my situation", with the power to experience, a power that's manifested, this very minute, in *my presently experiencing* precisely as I now do.

As easy as it is for us to think, quite rightly, that each of us is a concrete being, not a mere abstraction, or abstractum, it's equally hard for us, in this present day and age, to believe that we are not spatially extended beings. Indeed, it's enormously hard to believe anything about ourselves that's very different from how our Scientiphicalism has us be. What's more, it's hardly ever that I manage to get further from the Scientiphical Metaphysic than the nearby Emergentism that I've been trying to take very seriously. Yet, as this essay has been suggesting, this Emergentism is deeply embroiled with the Experiential Problem of the Many, as deeply as Scientiphicalism itself.

Among the metaphysical options not so embroiled with this apparently deep problem, Substantial Dualism is, so far as I can tell, the available view that departs least radically from our dominant Scientiphical Metaphysic. It's a much less radical departure, certainly, than is any fundamentally mentalistic metaphysic, whether such an exhaustively mental view be called "idealism", or "phenomenalism", or, as seems more fashionable nowadays, "panpsychism". Wishing not to be radical metaphysically, I'll suggest that, in the face of the Experiential Problem of the Many, we take Substantial Dualism, in its most coherent and tenable forms, rather seriously; or, if that is not yet psychologically possible for us, at least we should take it rather more seriously than almost all prominent professional philosophers have done in recent decades.

Professionally socialized as I am, even this much is very hard for me now to do. Apparently, I need a good deal more help, psychologically, than what's afforded by the Experiential Problem, to give any very substantial departure from our dominant Scientiphicalism, even so much as just a very moderately serious run for the money. So in the following section I'll try to provide some potentially liberating thoughts, perhaps novel enough to help us get beyond the circumscribed bounds dictated by our unquestioning allegiance to Scientiphical thinking.

THE PROBLEM OF TOO MANY REAL CHOOSERS

For the Scientiphical view of ourselves, and for our noted Emergentism, too, there's a mental problem of the many that's yet more disturbing, and far more baffling, than the disturbingly baffling Experiential Problem of the Many. It's the Problem of Too Many Real Choosers.

In order that our metaphysical meditations could begin most manageably, we haven't yet addressed issues concerning the choosing of our thinking experiencers. But now it's high time to explore them. When exploring these issues persistently, we may find it absolutely incredible that there should be, "in my situation", very many experiencing choosers, rather than just me choosing all alone.

As with everyone else, there are some sorts of things I'm far more prone to imagine than things of some other sorts. For example, I'm far more prone to imagine a pretty woman than an ugly plant. But, with regards to many (other) things, there's no great difference in my imaginative proclivities. For example, this may happen with my imagining a horse, or else a cat, or else a dog, where each of the options is to exclude each of the others. Equally, it may occur with my imagining something wholly red, or else something wholly blue. With many groups of real alternatives for imagining, then, I have no enormous disposition toward just one of the mutually exclusive options for me.

What's more, even with something I'm strongly prone *not* to imagine, (not always but) often I can choose to imagine it experientially nonetheless. I have just done some demonstrative imagining. Counter to my proclivities, I chose to imagine an ugly plant. And because I chose that option for my imagining, I actually imagined a pathetic weed, very dry and brown. What's the moral of this little exercise? Dramatically put, the point is this: the domain of my power to choose encompasses a very great deal of the domain of my power to imagine experientially. Often enough, I can choose to imagine experientially even counter to my quite strong imaginative proclivities.

Having taken note of my power to choose even contrary to my strong proclivities, we turn to an easier case. Here, I'm to choose among roughly equal options for my imaginative activity, where my proclivities for each option are about equally strong. And so, just for the sake of it, I'll choose to imagine experientially either a horse, or else a cat, or else a dog. And, just for the sake of some potentially instructive reasoning, let's now suppose that the experiential imagining I'm about to perform will be a *purely mental* act of mine, entirely isolated from the world's physical realm. Not only will this imagining not be anything physical, but we suppose it to lack any real physical cause. And, both concurrently and in the future, it will have no physical effect or manifestation. (Later we'll drop this pretense of mental purity; but not just yet.)

All right, I'm now imagining just one of the three mentioned sorts of very common domesticated animal. Make a guess, please, as to which of the three I'm imagining. You might guess, I suppose, that I'm imagining a cat. Or you might guess that it's a dog I'm imagining. Or you might guess it's a horse. Whatever you may have guessed, I'm now done with that bit of imagining. Now, as you'll recall, I said that my chosen imagining won't have any physical manifestation, not even in its future. Sticking with that supposition, I won't ever communicate to you, in (physical) writing, what sort of animal it was that I actually did just imagine.

For the sake of instructive reasoning, let's make the *supposition* that it was a cat I just imagined. And let's proceed to reason from that supposition.

When I put the question of this three-way choice as a little exercise for myself just now, did billions of very similar people, all of them "in my situation", each similarly put the question to himself? And, when I made a choice among my three specified options for imagining, each an alternative excluding the others, did each of them also effectively choose? How many of them effectively chose to imagine a cat experientially, the alternative we're supposing that I effectively chose?

If there really are vastly many people in my situation, then the only plausible thing to suppose about them is that, like myself, each of them has his own power to choose. And, since this is a real power to choose fully, and freely, *each* of these thinker's powers to choose is relevantly *independent of the power of each of the others*, including, of course, my own power to choose. So it's only plausible to suppose, further, that, when I made my effective choice to imagine a cat experientially, each of them made an equally effective choice to imagine that was independent of my choice, and also independent, of course, of the choice of each of the others.

That being so, it would be an astounding coincidence, and not a credible occurrence, if all these billions of people should also imagine a cat, each freely choosing to imagine the very sort of animal that, of the three exclusive options, I freely chose to imagine. (After all, we've been properly supposing that, just as with me, none of these billions of "overlappers", each so similar mentally to me, *is not much more* prone to imagine a cat than he is to imagine a dog, or a horse.) Indeed, it would be extremely unlikely that there should be, among the billions of choosers "in my situation", fewer than ten million real choosers who imagined a dog, when I myself was imagining a cat. And, equally, it would be extraordinarily unlikely that should there be, among the billions with independent powers, fewer than ten million who would choose, quite effectively, to imagine a horse experientially. With *any less* diversity of chosen animal images than *that*, among my overlapping physical-and-mental cohort of independent full choosers, there would be *far* too little qualitative experiential diversity, among "the population in my situation" for an outcome that's even the least bit credible.

The point here is, in its essentials, quite the same as a point about choice concerning me and you, and billions of other relevantly independent choosers, thinkers who *aren't* largely overlappers, thinkers who *aren't* "in numerically the same situation". For this case of "spatially separated choosers", or choosers with spatially separate bodies, and brains, we may playfully consider the most suitable two billion subjects, for a very widespread but temporally tiny psychological experiment, selected from among the world's current population, which numbers a bit over six billion. Now, as we may similarly suppose here, very few of these two billion have a tremendous proclivity toward imagining cats, as against horses or dogs. The great majority have a roughly equal propensity in each of the three specified directions. So, if fewer than ten million of us choose, freely and effectively, to imagine a dog, while almost all of us choose to imagine a cat, that is an unbelievably great coincidence. I myself would not believe in such an outcome. Rather than accepting that overly coincidental nonsense, I'd go back and question various propositions that we were supposing to hold true. Was there, perhaps, mass mesmerization going on globally, so that almost all of us were made to imagine a cat, with few really able to exercise his power to choose?

Whether overlapping or not, it's just incredible that billions of real choosers should all choose to imagine a cat experientially, with hardly any opting for a dog or a horse, when those two are, quite as forcefully, presented as appropriate alternatives. But at the same time it's not really credible, either, that there really was, in my situation, truly substantial diversity in experiential imagining, when I was (supposedly) just imagining a cat. So it's just incredible that, overlapping with me right now, there are many other complex entities, many physical-and-mental beings, who really do choose.

In one of its endless variations, that is the Problem of Too Many Real Choosers. Maybe I'm being overly quick about the matter, or even simply quite dense. But, in any case, I suspect that this problem may be an insuperable difficulty for the dominant Scientiphical Metaphysic. And, as I also suspect, it may undermine the Emergentist View.

THIS PROBLEM AND THE EMERGENTIST IDEA OF PHYSICAL-AND-MENTAL COMPLEXES

On the Emergentist view we've been exploring, each of us is a physical-and-mental complex. By contrast with our severe Scientiphical View, which has all our power as physical propensities, whatever the details of their physical derivations, on this Emergentism each of us will have, in *addition* to ever so many physical proclivities, various non-physical radically emergent mental powers. Yet, on the Emergentist View, any being that has such radical mental powers must be, at the same time, a complex physical entity. Indeed, it is precisely this aspect of our Emergentism that has it as a *more conservative* departure from Scientiphicalism, or *less of* a departure, than a Cartesian View, or any Substantial Dualism concerning mind and body.

In my "Free Will and Scientiphicalism", I argued that Scientiphicalism is, in several ways, incompatible with our thought that we really choose from among real alternatives for our thoughtful activity. And after offering those arguments, I observed that, so far as any of us could then tell, this fairly conservative Emergentist View might be as free of such Scientiphical Incompatibilisms as is Substantial Dualism. Our Emergentism *might be* tenable, but only insofar as a complex physical being's real physical features are no obstacle to her having, as well, many non-physical mental powers, saliently including a radically emergent purely mental power to choose. And, as it was then suggested, that might be quite far indeed; for, as it then appeared, there wasn't any such obstacle; there wasn't any real philosophic difficulty. Well, that was then; and, this is now.

In the light of our current discussion, there does appear to be a very real philosophic difficulty. In the first place, it appears that, "in your situation right now", there are very many different physical-and-mental complexes (each greatly overlapping with many others)—supposing, of course, that "in your situation right now" there's at least one complex physical entity with radically emergent non-physical mental powers. Though it may be logically possible that there is a great plurality of spatially extended real choosers, each of whom may share much of your space with you now, this is a proposition that defies belief. Indeed, this conflict becomes quite unbearable when we reflect, as we have, that the almost perfectly certain consequence of this is that, from time to time, there'll be great qualitative diversity in the chosen mental lives of the largely overlapping physical-and-mental beings.

Nor is there, on our Emergentist View, a credible way out of this philosophic difficulty. In a "messily gradual" world like this actual one, with very many very similar physical complexes to be found "in the situation of" any alleged physical-and-mental complex being, there's no credible resolution as to *which one,* among all the very many overlapping complexes, alone has the power to choose. Nor is it credible that, while each of the many complexes has a power to choose, there's somehow just one physical-and-mental complex, among the billions overlapping, that, at any given moment of time, gets to exercise his power. Nor is there any other credible way to offer a suitably singular resolution of the matter. But the only alternative, we have just observed, is an incredible diversity of choosers diversely choosing experientially. So, at least in any world much like our messily gradual actual world, the Emergentist View is not a credible alternative to our besieged Scientiphicalism.

A SINGULAR PHYSICAL MANIFESTATION OF THE POWER TO CHOOSE UNDERSCORES THIS PROBLEM

To make the presentation of the problem both vivid and manageable, the initial offering of the Problem of Too Many Choosers featured just such choosing as might be considered quite purely mental activity, and even quite isolated from all physical happenings. It may now profit us further, I imagine, to explore cases of choosing an imaginative option where the agent, just before she starts to imagine as she chooses to do, communicates to others what she's imagining, presumably via an appropriate physical sign or signal.

As before, again I'll now imagine either a horse, or a cat, or a dog. And, while I'm imagining it, I'm going to produce a physical signal of what it is that, because I just chose to imagine it, I'm now imagining experientially. (Pretend that I'm communicating by writing on a pad in plain view, or by an electronic instant messaging system.) Anyway, with this very physical sentence that I've just produced and that you're now reading, I tell you that it's a dog I'm now imagining, not a horse or a cat.

In producing that writing, I made a certain change in physical reality. And this change was a real result, of course, of the choice I just effected.

Putting aside our previous worries, maybe we can somehow make it palatable to ourselves that, this time "in my situation", there are millions of people choosing to imagine a horse, quite effectively, and millions of others choosing to imagine a cat, as well as the millions who, like me, were imagining a dog. Each of the people, though overlapping ever so many others, chose quite independently and very effectively, with each managing to alter his own imaginative experiencing just as he independently chose freely to do. Well, maybe that's too far-fetched really to be palatable. Even so, let's *suppose* that there are all these overlapping choosers, independently and effectively choosing images of striking qualitative diversity. If, quite fantastically, that should be true, will it help our Emergentism?

No, it won't. Even if we allow ourselves this supposition, there will arise, or will remain, this parallel problem: with each of our three animal options chosen by many millions, each of them an independent chooser though overlapping so many other free choosers, *how is it that just those who chose to imagine a dog* managed to produce an intended (revealing) signal change—but not those millions who imagined a horse, or imagined a cat? Here's one specific suggestion. Maybe it's a matter of the numbers, as with a voting procedure; and maybe more chose to imagine a dog than chose a cat, or a horse. But, though that idea may occur more obviously than most of its equally specific alternatives, it's no less absurd than so many other terribly incredible thoughts.

All this just brings home to us how incredible is the idea that, in my situation, or in yours, there are very many real choosers. Indeed, it's absurd for us to believe anything in the neighborhood. It's absurd to think that there are many overlapping people here—but only one of them has the power really to choose. It's also absurd to think that there are many with this power—but at any one time only one gets to exercise the power; and, so on, and so forth.

DOES THIS PROBLEM OF REAL CHOOSERS FAVOR SUBSTANTIAL DUALISM?

Recall our remarks about how *each of many* overlapping nervous systems, "in my situation", might be one of *my* nervous systems. In what serves to constitute my overlapping nervous systems, there are propensities to the effect that there's a limit to be placed—a limit of just one—on how many experiencing particulars may be promoted by these overlapping systems. How so? Here's a way. Each of a system's simple physical constituents, as with each of its constituting quarks, has marvelous propensities regarding how it may interact with very many other simple physical things, so that, in their optimal arrangements for promoting experience, there's an effective *singular resolution* as to what experiencer they may promote. And, because there's that singular resolution, there's also a nice singular resolution as to what experiencing may be promoted by them all.

It was hard to believe, we said before, that the single experiencer thus promoted should be a complex physical thing, whether or not the complex should have radically emergent purely mental powers. For, as it surely appears, no good candidate for being the single experiencing complex, "in the situation", is any better a candidate than each of very many extremely similar and massively overlapping others. It's hard to believe that, somehow or other, *just a single* one of these should have the power to experience richly, while all the others should be perfectly powerless in this salient regard. (Yet it's *also* hard to believe that, running very much in parallel with me, there are *vastly many* highly similar distinct experiencers promoted, rather than just me experiencing here alone.) Indeed, if a certain one of these physical complexes should somehow be the sole experiencer here, what happens when it loses one of its peripheral constituents, as will surely happen quite soon? Does this sole experiencer go out of existence? That's incredible. Does it, rather, come to coincide with a just slightly smaller complex, previously "nested" in it, while having only one fewer simple component than just before the slight loss? Will there be, then, an experiencing complex that's materially coincident with an insensate complex? That too is incredible. Will there then be, alternatively, two experiencing complexes, one previously experiencing and one just now newly experiencing? That's also incredible. Is a further alternative markedly more credible than these patently fantastic claims? I can't see any further alternative to be much more credible. In line with our Scientiphical Metaphysic, or even in line with our noted Emergentism, there's no credible resolution, I submit, to our Experiential Problem of the Many.

So, for folks so accepting of Scientiphicalism, myself included, there's a disturbing problem with the Experiential Problem of the Many. But, as I've lately been arguing, we may find the Problem of Too Many Choosers to be still more disturbing. With that Problem, there's the following dilemma: on the one hand, it's blatantly absurd to think that there are *very many* real experiencing choosers "in my situation", sometimes many choosing in a certain experiential way and many others choosing in a very different experiential way. This is yet more disturbing, I think, than our thinking there to be, "in my situation", very many experiencers, where it may always be that each of them experiences, immediately and totally, in much the same way as all the others. But on the other hand, and just as with the Experiential Problem, it's also absurd to think that there's a single *complex physical* being that's the only real chooser here; rather, any promising candidate for being such a choosing complex appears no better at all, not even the least bit more qualified or promising, than each of very many extremely similar, and massively overlapping, complexes.

Well, then, are there other alternatives for the Scientiphically inclined to favor here, evidently less absurd for us to accept? While there are other logical possibilities, I suppose, I can't see any that are notably more credible options. Certainly not that *I'm a simple physical* thing. So far as I can tell, there are ever so many quarks, or maybe superstrings, each of which might be a simple physical thing. But, then, it's not at all credible that *I'm* a quark, or whatever. (The matter can't be improved by suggesting I might be a simple physical-and-mental thing. For, any such entity must be a simple physical thing, of course, whatever else also might be true of it.) And, not that I'm a complex spatially extended entity that's not physical, with substantial simple spatial parts that aren't physical parts. Nor is it at all credible that I'm any other, still different, sort of spatial or physical thing.

Now, remember, I'm an independent real chooser, a conscious being who, at least from time to time, chooses fully and freely his own conscious activity. So, I'm not any mere epiphenomenal being, nor anything that merely supervenes on a base that's fully physical. In all of our Scientiphicalism, there's nothing that does much justice to my being a real chooser.

While still believing in a vast heterogeneous physical reality, what are we now to think ourselves to be? Among the traditionally available options, the least implausible view may be a Substantial Dualism, rather like the Cartesian View noted earlier. As I'm suggesting, then, maybe we should think that our mental problems of the many, especially the Problem of Too Many Choosers, mean a point in favor of such a Dualistic Metaphysic. (This may be so, of course, even if these problems also favor views that depart still further than does Dualism from the Scientiphical Metaphysic now so widely accepted, as with many Idealistic worldviews.)

I myself cannot yet believe in a metaphysic that departs even as much as a Substantial Dualism departs from our standard metaphysical conception. For one thing, I can't believe that I really haven't any spatial extension; at least, not yet I can't. And, as I suspect, you're in the same commonsensical boat. So, what are we to do?

Three main courses strike me as available.

First, we may go back over what our investigation has so far offered, and look for serious errors. Then, we may come to think, perhaps quite rightly, that there's no mental problem of the many, nor any other difficulty, that's truly a serious problem for our widely accepted Scientiphicalism. I hope that you will try this very seriously. And, whether successful or not, I hope you may be so good as to tell me what you find. As for myself, however, at this point in time this option has been exhausted and, in the wake of my laborious struggles, is not widely available. So, for me, right now, that leaves two courses.

Second, we may ask ourselves what are the most disturbing aspects of a Cartesian View. And, after trying our best to articulate them well, we might then endeavor to show how they might really give far less cause for intellectual disturbance than at first they appear to do. Yet, this has been often tried before, by many others. So, while I think I should try to do something here, I have doubts as to how much I might accomplish in this way.

Third, and finally, there's a more novel and speculative approach, though it's not wholly divorced from the Dualistic course just noted. Perhaps, in addition to many physical and spatial parts, many of them overlapping many others, I might have a single non-physical non-spatial part. And perhaps it may be that it's only in this non-physical part of me, in my "soul", that I'm mentally propensitied and empowered. It's through my exercise of certain powers inhering in this soul, my soul, that I may perhaps choose various aspects of my mental life, and sometimes even choose how it is that my body moves.

Though it's pretty speculative, so far that's not novel, but just old hat. In bare and sketchy terms, here's something that, far from being so old hat, is even more strangely speculative: though this non-physical part of me—my mind, or my soul—may *not* have any *spatial extension*, at least not in any strict or narrow sense of the terms, perhaps it may *have* some *non-spatial spacelike extension*. In what's only a very schematic way indeed, I'll try to say something about the general tenor of this strange speculation.

Now, as it *seems* to me, *space* is the *only clearly non-temporal dimension of concrete reality* in which I exist. But that appearance may be an illusory appearance. As it might really be, space is but one of the clearly non-temporal dimensions in which I exist; as I'm speculating, there's at least one other such dimension in which, quite equally, I also participate—in which I also exist. Even as my many substantial physical parts exist in space, I may have another enduring substantial part (or maybe more than one) that *does not* exist in space itself. This non-spatial part of me, this soul of mine, if you will, may exist in some other clearly non-temporal dimension (or in more than one) that is *extended*, all right, *but not spatially* extended.

No easy matter; it remains for us to suggest for these speculative ideas some helpfully more concrete terms, not so abstract as those I've just employed or offered. Since they require our engagement with the most profoundly radical sort of imaginative thinking, we may need to connect the offered abstract speculations with some of our (more nearly) experiential thinking, or at least with some thinking of ours that's more experientially informed. With no great confidence that I'll have much success in any such positive effort, I postpone this for another occasion. Anyway, and as with almost everything else in first philosophy, here too it may be that only the problems rightly last long with us, while our attempted resolutions are all fleeting, fashionable, and, maybe, flat-out futile as well.

New York University

9. Properties and Powers
John Heil

> I suggest that anything has real being that is so constituted as to possess any sort of power either to affect anything else or to be affected, in however small a degree, by the most insignificant agent, though it be only once. I am proposing as a mark to distinguish real things that they are nothing but power.
>
> Plato, *Sophist*, 247d–e

1. INTRODUCTION

In what follows, I take up the question of how properties and powers might be related. In the foreground is an idea expressed by Plato's Eleatic Stranger: all there really is to an entity is its power to affect and be affected by other entities. Assuming that an entity's powers depend on its properties, this suggests that there is no more to a property than the powers or dispositionalities it confers on its possessors; properties are "pure powers".

A view of this kind fits comfortably with the idea that science is the measure of all things. The business of science is to tease out fundamental properties of objects. Properties are what figure in laws of nature, and laws govern the behavior of objects. Properties, then, are features of the world that make a difference in how objects behave or would behave.

Such a conception of properties faces two difficulties. First, for most English-speaking philosophers, it is an article of faith that powers are contingent. Gelignite is explosive because it possesses a certain chemical

---

Versions of this paper were presented at the New Zealand Philosophy Conference (Wellington, December 2000), LaTrobe University, the University of Sydney, and at the Australasian Association of Philosophy Conference (Hobart, July 2001). I am grateful for the many criticisms and suggestions offered on those occasions. I owe a special debt to David Armstrong, John Bigelow, Brian Ellis, Toby Handfield, David Robb, and Dean Zimmerman for extensive criticism and discussion, and to the Department of Philosophy, Monash University, for its hospitality and support. C. B. Martin is responsible for the core ideas on dispositionality that lie at the heart of this paper (see Martin 1997).

constitution, but it could have been otherwise. Had the laws of nature been different, gelignite might have been as benign as pizza dough. If properties *are* powers, however, there could be no question of its being contingent that a given property confers a given power; if all there is to the property is the power it confers, there is no prospect of properties and powers varying independently: what makes gelignite gelignite is its disposition to explode under the right conditions.

Second, it is hard to find room in a world of pure powers for familiar qualities. These include, in addition to much-discussed qualities of conscious experience (the *qualia*), qualities of ordinary objects. On the face of it, a qualitatively empty world is indistinguishable from the void. The worry here is not just that a world barren of qualities would be dull and listless. A weighty tradition, going back at least to Berkeley, has it that the notion of a world without qualities is incoherent: a wholly nonqualitative world is literally unthinkable.

After discussing these and related issues, I undertake to defend the suggestion that properties (intrinsic properties of concrete objects) might be both qualitative and dispositional. Such a conception takes seriously considerations driving the "pure power" account of properties, while acknowledging the force of traditional worries concerning a world bereft of qualities. My aim is to convince you that a particular conception of properties—properties as simultaneously qualitative and dispositional—deserves serious consideration. The conception has been advanced recently by C. B. Martin, but I believe it is rooted in Locke's *Essay*. I shall have succeeded if considerations raised here lead you to doubt that the ways we have become accustomed to think about qualities, dispositions, and properties generally are the only ways.

2. PROPERTIES AS POWERS

Philosophers of many persuasions have been attracted to the thesis that properties are powers or dispositions.[1] More precisely, the thesis is that

[1] I shall use "power" and "disposition" interchangeably. My focus here is on properties of concrete spatio-temporal objects. I leave aside *abstracta*, *possibilia*, and their cousins. Philosophers who have regarded properties as powers include Plato's Eleatic Stranger; Boscovich (1763); Priestley (1777); Harré (1970); Harré and Madden (1975); Mellor (1974; 2000); Shoemaker (1980); and Swoyer (1982), although Shoemaker has apparently changed his mind; see Shoemaker (1998).

intrinsic properties of concrete objects make distinctive contributions to the powers or dispositionalities of their possessors. A view of this kind could strike you as inevitable if you began with the thought that impotent properties would be undetectable (assuming that detection requires causal interaction of some kind between detected and detector), hence unknowable; the presence or absence of a flatly undetectable property is not something anyone could lose sleep over. This sounds verificationist. Certainly, it is not obvious how we could have access to causally inert properties. But doubts about non-dispositional properties outstrip epistemological worries. A property that made no difference to the causal powers of its possessors would, it seems, be a property the presence of which made no difference at all.

This suggests a principle of property identity:

(PI) Necessarily, if A and B are properties, $A = B$ just in case A and B make the same contribution to the causal powers of their (actual or possible) possessors.

Sydney Shoemaker, a prominent exponent of the properties-as-powers thesis, provides considerations favoring such a principle:

Suppose that the identity of properties consisted of something logically independent of their causal potentialities. Then it ought to be possible for there to be properties that have no potential whatever for contributing to causal powers, i.e., are such that under no conceivable circumstances will their possession by a thing make any difference to the way the presence of that thing affects other things or to the way other things affect it. Further, it ought to be possible for there to be two or more different properties that make, under all possible circumstances, exactly the same contribution to the causal powers of things that have them. Further, it ought to be possible that the potential of a property for contributing to the production of causal powers might change over time, so that, for example, the potential possessed by property A at one time is the same as that possessed by property B at a later time, and that possessed by property B at the earlier time is the same as that possessed by property A at the later time. Thus a thing might undergo radical change in its causal powers without undergoing any change in the properties that underlie these powers. (Shoemaker 1980; 1984, pp. 214–15)

If you find such possibilities hard to swallow, you will be moved to accept something like principle (PI).

Related to this thought is what Graham Oddie (1982) calls "the Eleatic Principle" and Jaegwon Kim (1993a, p. 202) dubs "Alexander's

Dictum": to be real is to possess causal powers. Something akin to the Eleatic Principle appears to underlie the suggestion that predicates like "is three miles south of a red barn" fail to express genuine properties. Consider Jerry Fodor's H-particles: a particle has the property *being an H-particle* just in case it is a particle and a coin tossed by Fodor lands heads (Fodor 1988, p. 33). Such "properties" are "mere Cambridge properties". Their being possessed (or being gained or lost) by objects "makes no difference" to those objects.

This sounds question begging. Surely causally idle properties would "make a difference" to their possessors, just not a *causal* difference: such properties would have no effect on what their possessors do or would do. Perhaps it is equally question begging to lump all quiescent properties with "mere Cambridge properties". The latter are relational: their possession by an object depends on distal objects (barns on the far side of the county; Fodor and his coin). But this gives us no reason to doubt the possibility of purely qualitative *intrinsic* properties.[2] Indeed, a long philosophical tradition distinguishes categorical properties from dispositional properties precisely on the grounds that categorical properties are intrinsic and dispositional properties are not. An object's being square is intrinsic to the object and (thereby) categorical. A square peg's having the power to pass smoothly through a square hole is, in contrast, a relational property, one the possession of which depends on the peg's standing in an appropriate relation to square holes. Or so it is thought.

3. TERMINOLOGICAL PRELIMINARY

The terms "categorical" and "dispositional" are difficult to pin down. Are these meant to pick out kinds of *predicate*? Or are *properties* dispositional and categorical? Confusion is abetted by an informal convention whereby "categorical" has come to mean "non-dispositional", suggesting that the terms designate mutually exclusive, exhaustive classes of entity (see Mumford 1998).

[2] Intrinsicality is notoriously difficult to characterize informatively; see Humberstone (1996); Lewis and Langton (1998). Elsewhere (Heil 1992, p. 24) I have characterized intrinsic properties this way: "An intrinsic property... is *nonrelational* in the sense that its possession by an object does not (logically or conceptually) require the existence of any separate object or the existence of that same object, or a part of that same object, at some other time. An object, o_1, is separate from an object, o_2, just in case o_1 is not identical with o_2 or with any part of o_2."

In an effort to diminish terminological confusion, I shall use "qualitative" to designate intrinsic qualitative properties of objects, properties often described as "categorical". I shall use "dispositional" to designate properties that bestow powers on their possessors in the following sense: it is solely by virtue of possessing a given dispositional property that an object possesses a given power. Dispositional properties, if there are any, have their powers "built in". The idea is to distinguish properties that themselves amount to causal powers from those that bestow powers on their possessors, if at all, only indirectly: via contingent laws of nature, for instance.

If, like D. M. Armstrong, you think that objects' possession of causal powers depends on laws of nature that could vary independently of objects' intrinsic properties, then, in my terminology, you are thinking of objects' intrinsic properties as qualitative, but not dispositional. Such properties could bestow a power on their possessors, but only given laws of nature. (Armstrong, himself, conceives of laws as higher-order relations among qualitative properties. The possession of a qualitative property by an object confers a power on the object because the qualitative property bears appropriate relations to other properties.)

4. ARE DISPOSITIONS RELATIONS?

You might be attracted to the idea that dispositions are relations for reasons that have nothing to do with Armstrong. Consider Locke's secondary qualities.[3] These, according to Locke, are powers possessed by objects to produce certain effects in conscious observers.[4] Colors and tastes are secondary qualities. An object's being red, for instance, is a matter of that object's possessing a power to produce in observers experiences of a particular kind. This might be thought to turn powers into relations.

---

[3] Locke (1690; II, viii). A caveat. Although I associate certain views with Locke, my interest is in ontology, not Locke scholarship. If you read Locke differently, so be it. Sophisticated discussions of Locke can be found in Smith (1990); Lowe (1995, ch. 3). For a pointedly different construal of Locke, see Langton (1998, chs. 7–8).

[4] Locke also mentions tertiary qualities, powers possessed by objects (in virtue of those objects' possession of certain primary qualities) to produce changes in the qualities of other objects. The power of the sun to melt wax is a tertiary quality. Because the difference is irrelevant to this discussion, I shall henceforth follow custom and lump together secondary and tertiary qualities.

One of Locke's motives for distinguishing primary and secondary properties can be appreciated by reflecting on how we might explain objects' appearances. Being square is, for Locke, a primary quality. When an object looks or feels square to an observer, this is because it *is* square. Compare an object's looking red. An object looks red because (let us say) its surface incorporates a particular micro-arrangement of primary qualities. These structures reflected light in a particular way. Light thus structured affects our eyes so as to bring about an experience of red.[5] Here, a secondary quality, being red, is characterized relationally: by reference to its actual or possible manifestations. Primary qualities, in contrast, can be denominated non-relationally.[6] An object's being square is an intrinsic quality of the object, a way the object is quite independently of its actual or possible effects on any other object.

It is tempting to assimilate Locke's primary–secondary distinction to a distinction between qualitative and dispositional properties—a distinction between qualities and powers. The temptation should be resisted. Primary qualities, no less than secondary qualities, are power-bestowing. In virtue of being square, an object would produce in us an experience of its being square; in virtue of being square, an object would leave a square-shaped impression were it pressed against your skin. As I read Locke, primary qualities are *both* intrinsic qualities *and* powers.

What of the secondary qualities? Locke sometimes describes these as "pure powers". This suggests that *all there is* to being a secondary quality is its being a power. What Locke has in mind might be something quite different, however. A secondary quality is a power possessed by an object in virtue of its possession of certain primary qualities. Philosophers fond of the dispositional–categorical distinction find it natural to think of this in-virtue-of relation in terms of supervenience: secondary qualities supervene on primary qualities. Supervenience is a

---

[5] I do not offer this as an account of color, only as an example of what Locke has in mind.

[6] Locke includes among the primary qualities "solidity, extension, figure, motion, or rest, and number" (1690/1978; II, viii, 9). Elsewhere (II, viii, 10) he supplements this list by adding bulk and texture. Primary qualities are intrinsic, at least in the sense that they can be possessed by a single particle alone in the void. Locke's inclusion of number among the primary qualities is at first puzzling. Perhaps he had in mind a "naturalistic" conception of number similar to that advanced in Bigelow (1988). More likely, Locke regards this as a consequence of the view that divisions we find in the world are objective and natural. The question "How many?" always has a mind-independent answer. What of motion? Locke regards motion as intrinsic to moving objects rather than as a relation between a moving object and something else (a stationary object, for instance, or space).

modal notion, however. If As supervene on Bs, there can be no A-difference without a B-difference. But then the question is *why*? What grounds the supervenience claim, what is its truth maker?[7]

One popular idea is that secondary qualities (the dispositions) are *realized by* the primary qualities (the categorical "grounds" or "bases" of these dispositions). The realizing relation here is the relation that philosophers of mind appeal to in holding that states of mind are realized in sentient creatures by biological states of various sorts (or, more generally, that mental properties are realized by physical properties).

I shall return to this conception of dispositionality in Section 6. For the moment, note merely that the idea that dispositional properties are realized in, or grounded by, qualitative properties does not itself imply that secondary qualities (dispositions) are relations. Rather, it makes secondary qualities out to be "higher-level" properties, properties possessed by objects by virtue of those objects' possession of certain "lower-level" properties—their realizers. This thesis is independent of the idea that dispositions are relations. The inspiration for a relational conception of dispositions arises from another source: our practice of identifying dispositions conditionally, identifying them by reference to their possible manifestations.[8] A vase is fragile: it would shatter *if* struck by a solid object or dropped; a pill is poisonous: it would bring about illness or death *if* ingested; a ball is red: it would look red to normally-sighted perceivers *if* observed in sunlight.

Such characterizations relate dispositions to their manifestations conditionally: D is a disposition to yield manifestation M if C occurs. Might such conditional characterizations capture all there is to a disposition? Alternatively, what are the prospects of analyzing talk of dispositions conditionally?[9] Rather than addressing this vexed question here, let us grant that the practice of characterizing dispositions conditionally is warranted, even unavoidable. The question is whether this should lead us to regard dispositions as relations.

---

[7] This point was originally impressed on me by Brian McLaughlin. It is discussed in Blackburn (1984, p. 186); Kim (1990); Horgan (1993, esp. §8); and Heil (1998a). The point is just that a variety of different kinds of condition can ground a supervenience claim—assuming supervenience to be characterized in the usual way. As will supervene on Bs, for instance if As *are* Bs, or if As are composed of Bs, if As are caused by Bs, if A and B have a common cause, ...

[8] C. B. Martin calls these "typifying manifestations": see Martin (1997) and his contribution to Armstrong *et al.* (1996).

[9] See Mellor (2000). For reasons to doubt the possibility (and utility) of such analyses, see Martin (1994).

Consider a red object—a red billiard ball, for instance. Suppose Locke is right: the ball's being red is a matter of the ball's having a particular sort of power or disposition: a power to cause experiences of certain distinctive kinds in observers. Is the billiard ball's possessing this power a matter of the ball's (or some property of the ball's) standing in an appropriate relation to observers' experiences? Imagine a world consisting of the billiard ball and nothing else. Is the billiard ball red in such a world? Locke's considered view is, I believe, that the ball *is* red. An object's powers do not fluctuate owing simply to the removal of objects requisite for the manifestation of those powers.

Here is an alternate route to the same conclusion. It would be mad to require every actual disposition to be manifested. There might be red objects located in remote regions of the universe that, owing solely to their remoteness, could never look red to anyone. If you agree that an object might possess a disposition that it never manifests—and, perhaps because it is outside the light cone of whatever would be required for its manifestation, a disposition it *could* never manifest—then you should not balk at the thought that this same disposition might be possessed by an object located in a world altogether lacking in whatever might be required for its manifestation.

We deploy conditionals to characterize dispositions, but this does not oblige us to regard dispositions as relations. We might characterize water as a liquid that would look, feel, and taste a certain way were it seen, felt, or tasted by a human being. This does not make water (or, if you prefer, the property of being water) relational. The stuff we pick out in this conditional way could exist in a world altogether lacking in conscious agents.

To regard dispositions as relations between the disposition itself (or some property grounding the disposition) and its actual or possible manifestations is to confuse a feature of our way of characterizing dispositions—conditionally by reference to their possible manifestations—for the dispositions themselves. This is perhaps most clear in cases in which a single disposition is capable of different kinds of manifestation. Suppose an object's being red is a matter of the object's possessing a particular disposition, R. R will manifest itself differently with different kinds of reciprocal disposition partner.[10] R will, for

---

[10] The expression "reciprocal disposition partner" is C. B. Martin's; see Martin (1997); Martin and Heil (1999); and Martin's contribution to Armstrong, *et al.* (1996).

instance, differently affect distinct kinds of ambient light radiation—with the result that objects possessing R will sometimes look red and sometimes look brown or gray. (Your visual experience is itself a mutual manifestation of dispositions belonging to light radiation and dispositions of your visual system.) If R is a relation, which of these is it a relation to? Or is R relationally multifaceted? Rather than puzzling out an answer to such questions, we should do better to abandon the thesis that R is a relation.

There is, I believe, no compelling reason to regard dispositions (or, for that matter, Locke's secondary qualities) as relational. Dispositions can be conditionally characterized in a way that invokes their actual or possible manifestations. But this does not turn dispositions into relations. The existence of a disposition does not in any way depend on the disposition's standing in a relation to its actual or possible manifestations or to whatever would elicit those manifestations.

You might agree with all this, yet regard dispositions as relational for an altogether different reason. Suppose you were attracted to Armstrong's idea that an object possesses a disposition in virtue of the object's possessing a certain qualitative property together with that property's standing in an appropriate relation to a contingent law of nature. A vase's being fragile, for instance, might be its possession of a particular kind of micro-structure *together with* laws of nature that insure that anything with this structure would shatter if struck. If you thought this, you might regard dispositions as relations between categorical properties and laws of nature (laws regarded as entities of certain sorts, and not merely as sentences or statements).

5. ARMSTRONG ON DISPOSITIONALITY

According to Armstrong, a qualitative property bestows a power on its possessors owing to contingent laws of nature. (Armstrong takes laws of nature to be higher-order relations: relations that take properties as relata.) An object is fragile in virtue of its possession of a qualitative property, F, in concert with some law of nature, L. Because L is contingent, it is contingent what powers F bestows on its possessors.

To sharpen the focus, consider a variant of the Armstrong view. A qualitative property, Q, might endow its bearers with the property of being fragile because Q itself possesses a certain property, ϕ.

Q possesses φ only contingently, however: you could imagine a world in which Q lacks φ. In the imagined world, objects qualitatively indiscernible from fragile objects in the actual world would not be fragile. Here, a disposition is taken to be a higher-*order* property, a property possessed by a lower-order qualitative property.

It would be easy to confuse a conception of this kind with Armstrong's. For Armstrong, however, powers do not reside in higher-order properties; powers reside in ordinary qualitative properties. It is just contingent which powers reside in which qualities. The idea that powers or dispositions amount to higher-order properties differs from Armstrong's. It differs as well from an influential account of dispositionality developed by Elizabeth Prior, Robert Pargetter, and Frank Jackson.

6. PRIOR, PARGETTER, AND JACKSON

Prior, Pargetter, and Jackson's (henceforth Prior *et al.*) (1982) account of dispositions has come to occupy what could be regarded as the *default* position on dispositionality. According to Prior *et al.*, powers or dispositions are higher-level properties that objects possess by virtue of those objects' possession of lower-level qualitative (categorical) properties.[11] Dispositional properties resemble (or perhaps *are*) functional properties. The dispositional property, being fragile, is a property possessed by a given object by virtue of that object's possession of some qualitative— probably structural—property.

Dispositionality might be thought to be a higher-level phenomenon because dispositions appear to be "multiply realizable". Many different kinds of object are fragile: a sheet of glass, a kneecap, an antique watch. In every case, a fragile object is fragile by virtue of possessing some property, but the lower-level "realizing" properties can vary widely across kinds of object. The property of being fragile cannot be reduced to or identified with any of these lower-level properties. Being fragile, then, must be a higher-level property: a property possessed by objects by virtue of their possession of some distinct lower-level property.

---

[11] Although the terms are frequently interchanged, I distinguish higher-and lower-*level* properties from higher- and lower-*order* properties. A higher-*order* property is a property of some (lower-order) property. A higher-*level* property is a property possessed by an object in virtue of that object's possession of some distinct, lower-level "realizing" property.

A closer look at the idea that dispositional properties are higher-level properties with categorical "realizers" reveals a number of apparent anomalies. First, and most obviously, it is unclear how higher-level properties could themselves figure in causal relations. This is the so-called problem of causal relevance, a problem that has plagued functionalist accounts of mind. If mental properties are higher-level properties possessed by agents in virtue of their possession of lower-level "realizing" properties, it looks as though the realizing properties figure in causal relations in a way that pre-empts or "screens off" higher-level realized properties (see e.g. Kim 1993a; Jackson 1997; Heil 1999).

You might regard this not as a difficulty, but merely as a surprising consequence of the view. Consider, however, the peculiar ontological credentials of dispositions regarded as higher-level properties. These properties are introduced in the course of a discussion of powers possessed by objects to behave in various ways under various circumstances. Yet the properties introduced themselves apparently have no part in producing the effects they have been introduced to explain! It is hard to credit an account of powers that centers on the postulation of epiphenomenal properties. This is the theoretical tail wagging the ontological dog.[12]

Frank Jackson, himself a proponent of the two-level view, regards the idea that dispositional properties might be causally operative as amounting to "a curious and ontologically extravagant kind of overdetermination" (1997, p. 202). But surely it is the postulation of causally inert higher-level properties that is curious and extravagant. What are these properties supposed to explain? On the view favored by Jackson, every causally operative qualitative property is accompanied by an epiphenomenal dispositional property. A vase is fragile; it is disposed to shatter if struck by a sufficiently massive solid object or dropped. Its being fragile is a matter of its possession of some higher-level dispositional property grounded in a distinct lower-level categorical property. If the vase should shatter, however, this is not, strictly speaking, because it is fragile, but because it possesses a certain lower-level qualitative

---

[12] Dean Zimmerman points out that some philosophers will object to my describing higher-level properties so conceived as epiphenomenal. After all, references to such properties might figure in causal explanations and in causally grounded counterfactuals. I regard explanation as an epistemological concept. When a term figures in a true causal explanation, the question remains: what is it about the world that makes the explanation true? The same point holds for counterfactual truths.

property. Why not dispense with the higher-level dispositional property altogether? This would leave us with a qualitative property the possession of which would *itself* amount to the possession of a power. Now, however, we are back to a conception of properties as powers.

Locating the disposition in the qualitative "realizing" property requires rejecting the idea that fragility is a single (higher-level) property. Instead, we should suppose that the predicate "is fragile" is satisfied indifferently by objects possessing any of a family of properties (all those properties, namely, that Prior, *et al.* would regard as fragility's realizers). A conception of this kind is analogous to the Armstrong–Lewis conception of functional properties, what Ned Block calls the "functional specifier" conception, as distinguished from the "functional state identity" conception of such properties (see Armstrong 1968a; Lewis 1966, 1994; Block 1980; see also Heil 1999).

7. HUMEAN CONTINGENCY

Nowadays most philosophers follow Armstrong in regarding laws of nature as contingent. If dispositionalities were built into properties—if, for instance, properties were characterized as they are in (PI) or as Shoemaker suggests in the passage quoted in Section 2—contingency goes by the board. God does not create the objects and properties and then decree the laws. Instead, laws of nature "logically supervene" on the properties: when God fixes the properties, He thereby fixes the laws (see Swoyer 1982; Elder 1994). If a sugar cube is water-soluble by virtue of possessing a certain property S, then it is flatly impossible that an object could possess S, yet fail to be water soluble. This seems too strong, however. We can imagine sugar cubes failing to dissolve; we can imagine that the laws of nature might have been different so that gold, but not sugar, was water-soluble; that bars of steel, but not Micen vases, were fragile.

Not so fast. An object's dispositionalities depend on its overall makeup. If you encase a sugar cube in Lucite, you will make the cube-encased-in-Lucite impervious to water. In regarding properties as powers, you would be imagining that every property contributes in a distinctive way to the powers of its possessors. What powers an object possesses would depend on its entire compliment of properties. Sphericity can provide an object with the power to roll, but only in concert with various other properties. A spherical cloud lacks the power to roll. A sugar cube could be thought to possess the power to dissolve in water contingently in the sense that the cube might have been encased in Lucite, with the result that the cube-encased-in-Lucite would not be water soluble.

Similarly, if you vary an object's circumstances, you may affect the way an object's powers are manifested. A match will ignite when struck against an abrasive surface. It would not ignite, however, if oxygen were not present. The presence or absence of oxygen does not affect the match's dispositional makeup, but it does have an effect on how those dispositions are manifested.

Might such considerations account for the impression we have that objects' dispositionalities are contingent? Balls *could* fail to roll, sugar *could* fail to dissolve, matches *could* fail to light, not because powers are contingent, but because the manifestation of a power can be effected, often dramatically, by the presence or absence of other powers.

This would scarcely satisfy a dedicated Humean, of course. If the laws of nature are contingent, then the very same sugar cube that dissolves in water might have failed to dissolve in the very same liquid under the very same conditions. On this view, it is a purely contingent fact that the properties of sugar cubes and water in virtue of which sugar cubes are water-soluble could have been such that they contributed in utterly different ways to powers of their possessors. Given the laws of nature, sugar cubes must behave as they do, but the laws of nature could have been different.

Perhaps the impression of contingency is partly an epistemological matter. For all we know, the laws could be very different from what we at any time believe they are. This, however, does not imply that the laws could have been different from what they are. In imagining worlds indiscernible from ours with respect to the properties, but discernible with respect to the laws, we are perhaps imagining worlds with different (though similar-seeming) properties. Laws of nature would be contingent insofar as it is contingent that the actual world includes the properties it includes.

All this is just to say that the apparent contingency of natural processes might be due not to those processes (or laws governing them) being contingent, but to our ignorance concerning the processes or laws. Note that, even on a view that grounds laws of nature in the properties, it will be contingent what the laws are if it is contingent what the properties are.

One worry here is that the dispute between Armstrong and someone like Shoemaker, who regards powers as built into the properties, is at bottom a dispute over labels. Suppose a property, P, makes a distinctive contribution to the dispositionalities of its possessors. Now consider a merely possible property, P', qualitatively similar to P, but making a different contribution to the powers of its possessors. Armstrong could describe this as a case in which the same property affords its possessors different powers owing to differences in laws of nature ($P = P'$); Shoemaker, in contrast, could describe the case as one in which a different property is on the scene ($P \neq P'$).

Is this all there is to the dispute? I doubt it. The dispute concerns the nature of properties: whether a property's dispositionality is built into the property or is a contingent add-on. On one side are those who regard properties as nothing more than conferrers of powers. If you thought that, you would not think that properties and powers could vary independently. On the other side are those who regard properties as qualities possessed by objects that, *in addition*, affect the dispositionalities of their possessors. I shall attempt a reconciliation of these conceptions of properties presently. First, however, let us look more carefully at the idea that properties are "pure powers".

8. PURE DISPOSITIONALITY

The exciting idea that to be real is to possess causal powers can lead directly to the thought that properties are purely dispositional: *all there is* to a property is its contribution to the dispositionalities of its possessors.[13] (Qualitative properties, if there are any, stand outside the causal order: qualities exist only in the minds of conscious observers.) Joseph Priestley, for instance, echoing Roger Boscovich, held that the world comprises

> certain *centres of attractions and repulsions*, extending indefinitely in all directions, the whole effect of them to be upon each other;... a compage of these centres, placed within the sphere of each other's attraction, will constitute a body that we term *compact*. (Priestley 1777/1972, p. 239).[14]

---

[13] A reminder: what I have to say is intended to apply to properties of concrete objects, not to *abstracta*.

[14] Cited in Harré and Madden (1975, p. 172).

What we regard as solid bodies are, in reality, bundles of powers: *"power centres"*. The material world is wholly made up of what, two hundred years later, Harré and Madden were to describe as "an interacting system of powerful particulars" (1975, p. 7).

A conception of this kind might be read as incorporating a two-fold reduction: (1) objects are reduced to bundles of properties; (2) properties are reduced to powers. The result is a conception of objects as power loci. The world is viewed as a network of powers rather than as a system of self-contained interacting substances.

Although a conception of properties as pure powers does not force the abandonment of a substance–property ontology, the daring thought that all there is to the material world are "centres of attractions and repulsions" pushes in the direction of a "bundle theory" of objects, a theory that promises to banish all but powers from the material world. If an object's qualities are reduced to or replaced by pure powers, anything resembling substantial nature fades away. Substances wholly bereft of qualities are difficult to envision (see Section 9). Far from considering this a problem to be overcome, a proponent of the thesis that properties are pure powers could regard the demise of the traditional substance–property ontology as liberating. A dynamic conception of reality replaces the static Aristotelian conception of inert substances propelled by external forces.

Despite its appeal in some quarters, many philosophers have been struck by the thought that a properties-as-powers view leads to an embarrassing regress.[15] Suppose *A*s are nothing more than powers to produce *B*s, *B*s are nothing more than powers to produce *C*s, *C*s are nothing more than powers to produce *D*s, and so on for every concrete spatio-temporal thing. How is this supposed to work? Imagine a row of dominos arranged so that when the first domino topples it topples the second, which topples the third, and so on. Now imagine that, *all there is* to the first domino is a power to topple the second domino, and *all there is* to the second domino is a power to be toppled and a power to topple the third domino, and so on. If all there is to a domino is a power to topple or be toppled by an adjacent domino, nothing happens: no domino topples because there is nothing—no thing—to topple.

---

[15] See, e.g. Blackburn (1990); Campbell (1976, pp. 93–4); Foster (1982, pp. 67–72); Martin (1997, 213–17); Swinburne (1980). A related argument is advanced in Armstrong (1961, ch. 15, and 1999).

Or so it appears. Some philosophers disagree. Richard Holton, for instance, thinks that a conception of the world as comprising pure powers is a viable, even attractive, option (Holton 1999; see also Dipert 1997). Holton, assuming a relational model of dispositionality, argues that, if we could coherently describe a world consisting wholly of objects "entirely characterized" by relations they bear to other objects, this would be tantamount to describing a world consisting of objects whose nature is exhausted by pure powers. Holton invites us to imagine a world consisting of four points: A, B, C, D. A is to the left of B and above C; B is to the right of A and above D; C is below A and to the left of D; and D is below B and to the right of C. Such a world can be depicted via a diagram:

A • B •
C • D •

Each of the points in the illustration is meant to be "entirely characterized" by its relations to the remaining points. In one regard the diagram is misleading. The world we are being invited to imagine is not a world of corpuscles or material particulars arranged in the way depicted. The world in question is made up of entities whose nature consists of nothing more than relations they bear to other entities. A description of such a world need not issue in a regress. Entities are constituted by relations they bear to every other entity. The relations in question, then, are web-like, mutually supporting, not linear.

The diagram depicts four points appropriately located relative to one another. According to Holton (1999), "there really is nothing more to A, B, C, and D than that given by the descriptions [of their relations]. So do not think that, in describing them I have helped myself to the non-dispositional notion of a point" (p. 10). To get the idea, you would need to subtract the points and keep the relations. This is none too easy. Engaging in Locke's abstraction or "partial consideration", you could, perhaps, *consider* the relations without considering the points. Subtracting the points, however, and keeping the relations is no less challenging than subtracting the cat and keeping the smile. Relations are, or certainly seem to be, dependent on their relata. The idea of relata wholly constituted by relations is hard to credit.

Perhaps I am being unfair to Holton.[16] Imagine that A, B, C, and D are spatial points—as distinct from material "atoms". In that case, A, B,

---

[16] Toby Handfield pressed this point.

C, and D might indeed seem to be wholly constituted by relations each bears to the others. If this is right, and if there might be purely spatial worlds, then the possibility of exclusively relational worlds might be vindicated.[17]

I am not so sure. It is hard to see how turning A, B, C, and D into spatial points helps with the matter at hand. First, as Armstrong makes clear in an argument I shall discuss in the following section, it is hard to see how purely relational worlds would differ from worlds consisting of nothing but empty space. Second, space is not *made up* of spatial points in the way a lump of coal is made up of bits of coal. The idea is not that spatial points, being infinitely small, could never add up to a spatial expanse. Spatial points are not infinitesimal particles of space. If space were made up of spatial points in the way a lump of coal is made up of bits of coal, it would be false that spatial points are wholly constituted by relations to other points.

I am not denying that space might turn out to be granular, made up perhaps of particle-like entities—as imagined by Plato in the *Timaeus*, for instance. In that case, space itself would be substance-like. Still, we should want to distinguish empty space from a space occupied by material bodies. If we regard bodies as nothing more than relations or as nothing more than powers to affect other bodies, it is not clear that we have left ourselves with sufficient conceptual resources to make this distinction (see Section 9).

Even if, as I believe, powers are not relations, worries about entirely relational worlds extend to worlds comprising objects wholly constituted by powers. These worries are made vivid by Keith Campbell in a discussion of Boscovich's Holton-like ontology (Boscovich 1763). Boscovich depicts the world as consisting of material points, the intrinsic nature of which is exhausted by their power to accelerate other points. "What," asks Campbell, "is at a material point?"

What distinguishes a location in space where there is a point from one where there is no such thing? All we can say is: at a material point there is something which accelerates other somethings which in turn accelerate somethings (including the first) which in turn.... But what an odd object this is. Its *only* feature is to have an effect on things which have an effect on things which have an effect on things which.... We seem to be caught in a regress or circle,

---

[17] Could there be purely spatial worlds? Not if space requires occupants; see Lowe (1998, pp. 163–4).

240 | John Heil

forever unable to say what these things *are* which have an effect on each other.[18] (Campbell 1976, p. 93)

Boscovich's world is a world of pure powers located at points. It is not merely that we can know material points only by knowing their effects on other material points, but that this is all there is to being a material point.

When one point moves another, all that has been shifted is a power to shift powers to shift.... But powers to shift *what*? To be coherent, I consider that Boscovich's points must be *somethings* which have the power to shift one another. They must have some intrinsic features which make them things in their own right, and they must in addition have the power to shift one another. Then, and only then, will there be something to move about. There must be some answer to the question What is at a point? independent of accelerative capacity. (Campbell 1976, p. 93)

Campbell concludes with the observation that "we do not understand Boscovich's theory until we know just how a universe with exactly one material point in it would differ from a universe containing none at all".[19]

9. AN ARGUMENT FROM ARMSTRONG[20]

Before delving deeper into the nature of properties, let me mention an argument offered by Armstrong against the possibility that all properties might be Locke's primary qualities: shape, size, position, duration, movability, divisibility, and solidity.[21] Think of these as properties of the atoms from which everything else is made. Armstrong asks, "Do these qualities suffice to give us a physical object?" His answer: they do

---

[18] The same point has been made by many others; see note 7.

[19] (Campbell (1976, p. 94). Campbell goes on to consider possible emendations of the theory involving attempts to specify "that intrinsic quality, whatever it is, which material points have and other points lack", but these appear both ad hoc and at odds with the idea that material points are pure powers. Dipert (1997) envisages a graph-theoretic world that incorporates conscious episodes at graphical vertices.

[20] The argument discussed here can be found in Armstrong (1961, ch. 15). Armstrong himself no longer endorses the argument, but, as Dean Zimmerman pointed out to me, a related argument, developed independently, can be found in Robinson (1982, ch. 7), and in Unger (1999; forthcoming).

[21] As Armstrong notes, versions of the argument were advanced by Berkeley (*Principles of Human Knowledge*, §10) and by Hume (*A Treatise of Human Nature*, I, iv, § 4). See also J. J. C. Smart (1963, pp. 73–5). I omit number because, Armstrong contends, it does not obviously belong; see n. 6 above.

not. "These qualities just by themselves do not suffice to differentiate a physical object from empty space."[22]

Armstrong is thinking of the primary qualities, in the way a physicist might, as wholly non-qualitative. (In this regard, a world made up of objects possessing only the primary qualities resembles a purely relational world or a world of pure powers.) Some of these qualities make up extensive magnitudes; others, perhaps, constitute relational magnitudes. Imagine an exhaustive quantitative description of the world and its contents, a description that mentioned only relations among objects and those objects' non-qualitative, primary qualities. How, asks Armstrong, would such a world differ from a world consisting entirely of empty space? Shape, size, duration, and position are primary qualities, but a region of space could have a *shape, size,* or *duration*. If space is absolute, every spatial point or region will have an absolute *position*. If space is a relation among material bodies, then appeals to position, because they presuppose material bodies, cannot be used to distinguish material bodies from regions of empty space. Divisibility is a primary quality, but regions of space are *divisible* into sub-regions. *Motion,* another primary quality, belongs to bodies moving through space (or moving relative to other bodies). Armstrong takes this to mean that a body is in motion if it occupies adjoining spatial regions over successive intervals. But if this were all there were to motion, motion would be analyzable in terms of shape, size, position, and duration. If these other concepts are insufficient to distinguish bodies from empty space, the addition of motion to the list cannot help.

What of *solidity*? Solidity, according to Locke, is what "hinders the approach of two bodies when they are moving one towards another" (1690, II, iv, §1). This comes close to equating solidity with impenetrability. If this were all there were to solidity, adding it to the mix would not help. Regions of space are themselves mutually impenetrable in the sense that no region could be "occupied" by another region. Locke, perhaps recognizing this point, regards solidity as including impenetrability plus "something positive". The presence of this additional ingredient might provide a way of distinguishing impenetrable bodies from empty regions of space. Armstrong is doubtful: a distinction between pure impenetrability and impenetrability plus "something positive" "is a distinction without a difference" (p. 187).

---

[22] Armstrong (1961, p. 185); parenthetical references below are to this work.

242 | John Heil

We are left, according to this line of thought, without a coherent conception of material bodies. This suggests that "objects must have at least one further quality over and above the [primary qualities]" (p. 187). Any such quality must satisfy two conditions. First, the quality "must not be analyzable solely in terms of the [primary qualities]" (p. 187). Second, given that relations among material bodies presuppose material bodies, "the new quality or qualities must not be relations that physical objects have to other physical objects".[23] Armstrong suggests that the only qualities satisfying both conditions are the traditional secondary qualities: colors, sounds, tastes, smells, and the like, or as yet unknown counterparts of these.

These reflections exhibit affinities with Berkeley's contention that the primary qualities are metaphysically dependent on the secondary qualities. Berkeley parlays this observation into an argument for anti-realism about the material world: if the secondary qualities are mind-dependent, then so are the primary qualities, and indeed so are material bodies generally.[24] Armstrong declines the anti-realist option by refusing to accede to the mind-dependence of the secondary qualities. Primary and secondary qualities subsist side by side, neither being reducible to the other.

Although there is much to be said for it, I believe that this kind of solution is, in the end, unstable. I shall explain why this is so in the course of sketching an alternative conception of properties.

10. THE IDENTITY THEORY

Rather than attempting detailed refutations of opposing views, I propose to sketch a conception of properties that avoids pitfalls associated with its competitors while accommodating what might seem right about them. The conception I have in mind has been propounded by C. B. Martin.[25] Martin speaks of it as "the surprising identity"; I shall call it the identity theory:

---

[23] Armstrong (1961, pp. 187–8). For reasons of the sort discussed already, the missing qualities could not be relations of any sort.
[24] For more recent thoughts along these lines, see Foster (1982); Robinson (1982); Blackburn (1990); Langton (1998).
[25] See Martin (1997); Martin and Heil (1999); and Heil (1998b, ch. 6).

(IT) If P is an intrinsic property of a concrete object, P is simultaneously dispositional and qualitative; P's dispositionality and qualitativity are not aspects or properties of P; P's dispositionality, P_d, is P's qualitativity, P_q, and each of these *is* P: $P_d = P_q = P$.

This means, in effect, that every property of a concrete spatio-temporal object is both qualitative and dispositional. A property's "qualitativity" is strictly identical with its dispositionality, and these are strictly identical with the property itself.

You might regard a conception of this kind as unintelligible. It will strike you as unintelligible, certainly, if you assume from the outset that dispositionality and qualitativity are mutually exclusive, if you assume that every property is either dispositional or qualitative, and no property could be both. Recall, however, Locke's primary qualities. Unlike Armstrong, I take these to be paradigmatically properties of the sort I am envisaging.[26] Being spherical is a manifest quality of a baseball. But it is in virtue of being spherical that a baseball can, for instance, roll: sphericity is, it would seem, a power possessed by the ball. Recognizing this, you might be inclined to reason (as many philosophers are wont to reason): if sphericity is a power, then it cannot be a quality. On the contrary; the ball's sphericity *is* a quality possessed by the ball and *is* a power. Locke is right to think of primary qualities as *qualities*.[27]

As in the case of the thesis that properties are pure powers, it is convenient, although potentially misleading, to describe properties as powers, or as qualities, or as both powers and qualities. Rather, properties could be thought of as contributing in distinctive ways to the dispositionalities and qualities of their bearers. The dispositionalities and qualities possessed by a given object depend on all its properties. A key of a certain size and shape will open a lock, but only if it is sufficiently rigid.

The identity theory does not regard the dispositional and the qualitative as "aspects," or "sides," or higher-order properties of properties. A property's dispositionality and its qualitativity are, as Locke might

---

[26] For a very different view, see Langton (1998, ch. 7). Langton suggests that Kant's "phenomenal world" is a world of pure relations (see e.g. p. 162).

[27] This enables us to make sense of Locke's otherwise puzzling insistence that solidity is not pure impenetrability. *Contra* Armstrong, solidity endows its possessors with qualities and with powers, and so for any property.

have put it, the self-same property differently considered. The identity theory diverges as well from the popular thesis that dispositionality is somehow grounded in the non-dispositional. Sometimes this is put by saying that dispositional properties supervene on categorical properties (or on categorical properties together with laws of nature). An identity theorist need have no objection to the supervenience claim—nor for that matter to the claim that every property is a power. These follow as trivial consequences of the identity thesis.

We have seen already that it is easy to turn examples of qualities into examples of powers. Think of a quality—being white, for instance, or being sweet. It is surely in virtue of its being white that a cupcake looks white and in virtue of its being sweet that the cupcake tastes sweet. Being white and being sweet are powers of the cupcake to affect us in particular ways. The mistake—not, I like to think, a mistake made by Locke—would be to conclude from this that whiteness and sweetness are *mere* powers. True, Locke does from time to time describe the secondary qualities as mere powers. But what are the secondary qualities? These are powers possessed by an object (owing to its possession of particular primary qualities) to produce certain kinds of experience in us. Secondary qualities are primary qualities distinguished by reference to certain of their manifestations: their effects on conscious observers.

The resulting conception is straightforward. Objects have various (primary) qualities. Arrangements of these yield experiences in conscious observers. In some cases, experiences can be reliable guides to their causes. This is so for shape, size, and (if Locke is right) the remaining primary qualities. In other cases experiences are less reliable indicators of their causes. A red triangle looks triangular because it has a triangular shape. It looks red because its surface exhibits (Locke speculates) a certain kind of micro-texture. Describing secondary qualities as powers is Locke's way of bringing this point home. If we identify an object's color with the micro-texture of its surface, we cannot say that this texture is a pure power. On the contrary, the surface has complex qualities and powers, among these the power to produce in us experiences of distinctive sorts.

The sciences are sometimes said to be in the business of identifying powers. The mass of an electron, its spin and charge, could be regarded as powers possessed by the electron. Physics is silent on an electron's qualities. (Perhaps, insofar as an electron can be thought of as occupying a fuzzy region of space, an electron could be thought of as having something rather like a shape.) It would be a mistake to interpret silence as outright denial, however. Just as your failure to perceive something need not be a matter of your perceiving its absence (see Armstrong 1968b), physics' silence on qualities does not amount to an affirmation that there are no qualities. Physics aims at a description of the world centered around quantifiable relations among objects. In this regard, physics nicely reflects our capacity for partial consideration.

I can think of two reasons to suppose that properties of the elementary constituents are (as I have claimed every property is) simultaneously qualitative and dispositional. First, the denial of this view apparently leads to a conception of properties of the fundamental things as pure powers; I have argued that such a conception is prima facie implausible. Second, although you may find it difficult to imagine how charge or charm could be qualities, you probably find it natural to ascribe qualities to ordinary middle-sized objects: tables, stones, trees. It would be comforting to think that qualities of these middle-sized items are what you get when you combine elementary things in the right ways. The mechanism here is largely combinatorial: the qualities of wholes are built up from qualities of the parts (and the arrangement of these).[28] This suggests that there must be some route from qualities of parts to qualities of wholes. Such a route need not be analytical or available to us a priori. This is something we acknowledge in everyday life. Cooks explain qualities of dishes they have prepared by citing qualities of their ingredients; painters explain the qualities of different colors and textures of paint by reference to qualities of constituent pigments; audiophiles trace the qualities of amplified sounds emitted by loudspeakers to qualities of the components.

Is it flatly outrageous to think that the mass or charge of an electron are qualities? Evidently not. Many philosophers are attracted to the idea that powers are grounded in categorical properties. If an electron's mass and charge are powers, then on this view mass and charge are grounded in unspecified qualities of the electron. If mass and charge are taken to be purely categorical bases of powers, they are no less qualities. In either case, the mass and charge of an electron are associated with qualities of the electron. The identity theory interprets this association as strict

---

[28] Might qualities "emerge"? I have nothing against emergence, but I do not think that the properties of wholes emerge in any sense that involves an addition of being to the properties of parts of a whole (suitably organized).

identity: the quality associated with the mass of an electron is strictly identical with the power associated with that mass. Neither is reducible to nor grounds the other.

The identity theory implies that you could not vary an object's qualities without varying its dispositionalities, and you could not vary an object's dispositionalities without changing it qualitatively. In altering a ball's shape, a quality, you alter its disposition to roll; in changing its color, another quality, you change its disposition to reflect light in a particular way. Altering the ball's disposition to roll or to reflect light in a particular way requires changing the ball's qualitative makeup.

The widespread influence of functionalism on our conception of properties has made it especially difficult to appreciate the force of such examples. A central tenet of functionalism is that objects can be dispositionally indiscernible but differ qualitatively as much as you please. Functionalists make this idea plausible by describing functional processes at an elevated level of abstraction. Egg-beaters share causal powers *vis à vis* eggs, but could be utterly different with respect to their qualities. This is so, however, only so long as you characterize egg-beaters—and their inputs and outputs—in a relatively "abstract", non-specific way.

The point applies to the Prior *et al.* (1982) "default" conception of dispositionality, according to which a disposition is a higher-level property possessed by an object by virtue of its possession of some distinct lower-level qualitative property. One consideration thought to favor this conception is that dispositional properties appear to be "multiply realizable". Consider being fragile. Objects can be fragile in virtue of having very different compositions and very different structures. So: same disposition, different qualitative (or structural) basis.

All this will seem plausible only so long as you are content to characterize fragility in a relatively non-specific way. If being fragile is described as shattering when struck by a massive solid object, for instance, this is something shared by a light bulb, an ice cube, and a kneecap: same higher-level dispositional property, different lower-level realizing properties. Light bulbs, ice cubes, and kneecaps shatter in very different ways, however. These "ways" reflect these objects' possession of distinct, though similar, dispositions. We need not posit a higher-level property here. We have, rather, a range of similar properties all satisfying a single, moderately imprecise predicate, "is fragile". Functionalists mistake a non-specific predicate satisfied by a range of imperfectly similar states or properties for a specific predicate satisfied by a unique higher-level "multiply realized" state or property (Heil 1999). Putative lower-level realizers of fragility are really just different ways of being fragile.

If this is right, then it is less obvious that dispositions and qualities *could* vary independently. If you change a fragile object qualitatively, you change it dispositionally as well. It might remain fragile but become fragile *in a different way*. Of course, you could change a fragile object qualitatively in a way that has no bearing on its fragility. If you dye an ice cube pink, you do not affect its disposition to shatter. But, if I am right, dyeing the ice cube must change it dispositionally in *some* way. And, indeed, it does: a pink ice cube reflects light differently than does a colorless ice cube.

To be sure, Armstrong could agree with all this: qualitativity and dispositionality go hand in hand—but only contingently, only given contingent laws of nature.[29] What advantage might the identity theory offer over the contingency thesis?

The identity theory provides a straightforward account—indeed, the simplest account imaginable—of the connection between an object's powers and its qualities. For Armstrong, the connection requires distinct laws of nature. Why, we might ask, do such laws connect qualities and dispositionalities as they do? The answer, insofar as the question concerns the fundamental qualities and powers, is that they just do. An identity theorist agrees that there is no further explanation for the fact that certain qualities endow their possessors with certain powers (that is, for the fact that actual properties are what they are), but, if powers and qualities are identified, this is not something that could require explanation. The brute fact is that these properties *are* instantiated.[30] If you are keeping score, an identity theorist is committed to a single brute fact: that these properties are instantiated. Armstrong is committed to a pair of brute facts: that these properties are instantiated and that these laws of nature obtain.[31]

A proponent of an Armstrong-style view would no doubt insist that this is a price well worth paying in order to preserve the contingency of

---

[29] Dean Zimmerman made this point. I am grateful to Dave Robb for discussion of it.
[30] By "instantiated" I mean only that the properties are properties of actual objects. I mean to leave open the possibility that properties are tropes.
[31] A worry about the Armstrong view that I shall mention but not discuss concerns the puzzling nature of the necessitation relation introduced by Armstrong's higher-order universals.

the relation between qualities and powers. To this, an identity theorist might reply that the contingency is only apparent, or perhaps better; the source of the appearance resides not in the power–quality connection, but in which properties are in fact instantiated.

11. DISPOSITIONAL AND QUALITATIVE PLURALISM

Many readers will remain unmoved. You might agree that it is a mistake to regard dispositional properties as higher-level properties extruded somehow by categorical properties, and you might even be willing to concede that it is a bad idea to regard every property as a pure power or disposition. But you might draw the line at the thought that properties are simultaneously dispositional and qualitative. Why not embrace a pluralistic approach, allowing that there are two mutually exclusive kinds of property: dispositional and qualitative? The actual world (and maybe any possible world of concrete objects) includes both.

The idea that dispositions and qualities are kinds of property could seem altogether natural. Cases I have offered to illustrate the identity theory—a ball's sphericity or color, for instance—might be reconstrued as cases in which property pairs are present: one qualitative and one dispositional. Perhaps properties making up these pairs co-occur as a matter of natural necessity: a contingent law of nature insures that, whenever the one is on hand, the other is as well. There is no question of every property's being purely dispositional; but so long as some objects possess properties that are not purely dispositional—properties that would, presumably, be purely qualitative—this should be enough to block the kinds of regress associated with purely dispositional properties (and discussed in Section 8).

Here I can only fall back on previous observations. A pure quality, a property altogether lacking in dispositionality, would be undetectable and would, in one obvious sense, make no difference to its possessor. Even if you conceive of such properties as nomologically connected to dispositions (even if, as a matter of natural law, purely qualitative properties co-occurred with dispositional sidekicks), they would remain idle.[32] The whole notion of purely qualitative properties appears ill-conceived and unnecessary.

---

[32] And of course the question remains: what *is* it to conceive of such properties?

Where, then, does this leave the idea that some properties are purely qualitative and some purely dispositional? We should have to suppose that a world containing such a mixture of properties would be a world of pure powers mixed with undetectable, wholly idle qualities. I am not prepared to argue that such a world is flatly impossible. It does strike me, however, as combining two ill-considered conceptions of properties (properties as pure powers or dispositions and properties as pure qualities) into a single ill-considered whole. Philosophers who have grown accustomed to thinking of properties on the categorical–dispositional model may find this a remarkable claim. My contention, however, is that the categorical–dispositional model, despite its comfortable familiarity, is deeply flawed.

Before moving on, let me belabor a point touched on earlier. The identity theory is sometimes described (not by its proponents) as a "dual aspect" conception of properties: every property has a dispositional aspect and a qualitative aspect. I am not sure what aspects are, but one possibility is that aspects are properties.[33] If this were so, then we might imagine that qualities and dispositionalities were bestowed on objects by properties in virtue of those properties' themselves possessing higher-order properties.

Such a position strikes me as objectionable for at least two reasons. First, and most simply, it is hard to see how this is an advance over the idea that there are two kinds of property, qualitative and dispositional. Why should the promotion (or is it demotion?) of dispositional and qualitative properties to the status of higher-order properties render this bifurcation more plausible?

Second, it is not clear what a property's possessing the envisaged higher-order properties could amount to. We are trying to imagine a *property*—sphericity, say—having the property of being (as it were) qualitative sphericity and the property of being dispositional sphericity. Call the base property P, and P's higher-order properties, Q and R. Bearing in mind that P is a property, not an object, what is there to P beyond Q and R? (The truth maker for ascriptions of properties to P is P itself.) But if P just *is* Q and R, then either P is composite (in which case the idea that Q and R are higher-order properties of P drops out and we are back with the categorical–dispositional property model) or the

---

[33] This seems to be what proponents of Spinozistic double-aspect accounts of the mind–body relation had in mind. See e.g. Hirst (1959, chap.7).

double aspect view collapses into the identity theory: *P is Q* and *P is R*, so *Q is R* (alternatively: *Q* and *R* are not different components or aspects of *P*, but *P* itself, differently considered).

You might object that a capacity for partial consideration presupposes distinctions in the world, and distinctions are a matter of differences in properties. If a property, *P*, could be considered either as a disposition or as a quality, then, unless we are suffering an illusion, *P* must incorporate distinct features answering to these two modes of consideration. Talk of distinguishable features, however, is just an oblique way of indicating distinct properties.

Thoughts along these lines maintain an air of plausibility so long as the model for *P* is an object. Objects have multiple properties. Considering the same object in different ways (now as something round, now as something red) is often a matter of considering distinct properties possessed by the object. In the case before us, however, the focus is on properties, not objects. The model, if you want one, is an ambiguous figure—a Necker cube, for instance—that can be seen now one way, now another. This need not be a matter of attending to different properties of the figure. Rather, we consider the figure as a whole in different ways.

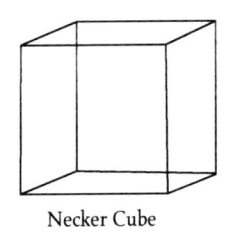

Necker Cube

To my mind, the identity theory is independently attractive, but even if it were not, it appears to win by default. Purely qualitative properties are uninviting, as are pure powers. Mixing these does not help, nor does turning dispositionality and qualitativity into aspects or kinds of higher-order property.

12. CONCLUDING REMARK

Perhaps I have said enough to persuade previously uncommitted readers to take the identity theory seriously and regard it as at least within the realm of possibility that every property—every intrinsic property of a concrete object—is qualitative and dispositional. There are no purely qualitative properties; there are no pure powers. The human mind, as Locke noted, has a capacity for partial consideration. We can consider an object's properties as dispositions or powers or we can consider them as qualities. In so doing we consider not two kinds of property, but the self-same properties in different ways.

Why should any of this matter? I believe that misconceptions about properties have spawned confusion and despair in the philosophy of mind. Nowadays consciousness is frequently cited as the deepest mystery confronting philosophers and scientists. Against this background, it is widely acknowledged that current theories are inadequate. What appears to be called for is not more of the same—more neuroscience, more epicycles in going theories—but an utterly different kind of approach.[34]

Let me mention a single example: the status of mental qualities, the *qualia*. Philosophers' suspicions of *qualia* stem, in some measure, from more general suspicions of qualities per se. But if, as I have urged, everything has qualities, if every property is qualitative, then it would be a bad idea to treat putative mental properties as dubious solely because they are qualitative. More immediately, if the identity theory is correct, it would be a mistake to imagine that mental qualities could vary independently of the dispositions of conscious agents. You could put this by saying that, if the identity theory is correct, "zombies" are impossible.[35]

The moral: we need to re-examine certain of our fundamental assumptions. These constrain the space of possibilities open to us. Residual dogmas over the nature of properties infect theories that presuppose them. Only by recognizing alternatives and seeing where these lead do we have any hope of moving ahead. If nothing else, perhaps these remarks can serve to direct attention to foundational issues that have been too long ignored in the philosophy of mind.

Monash University

---

[34] David Chalmers (1996) offers *both* more of the same *and* something utterly different. Incidentally, I do not mean to denigrate neuroscience. My point is that a satisfactory way of conceptualizing minds and their place in nature is not something to be deduced *ex post facto* from a successful neuroscience.

[35] A zombie is a fanciful creature, identical to a conscious agent in every physical respect, but differing mentally. Zombies are dispositionally indiscernible from conscious agents, but qualitatively different: zombies lack conscious qualities. See Chalmers (1996).

REFERENCES

Armstrong, D. M. (1961) *Perception and the Physical World*, London: Routledge & Kegan Paul.
Armstrong, D. M. (1968a) *A Materialist Theory of Mind*, London: Routledge & Kegan Paul.
Armstrong, D. M. (1966) "The Headless Woman Illusion and the Defense of Materialism", *Analysis*, 29: 48–9.
Armstrong, D. M. (1989) *Universals: An Opinionated Introduction*, Boulder, CD: Westview Press.
Armstrong, D. M. (1999) "The Causal Theory of Properties: Properties According to Ellis, Shoemaker, and Others", *Philosophical Topics*, 26: 25–37.
Armstrong, D. M., C. B. Martin, and U. T. Place, (1996) *Dispositions: A Debate*, ed. Tim Crane, London: Routledge.
Bigelow, John (1988) *The Reality of Numbers: A Physicalist's Philosophy of Mathematics*, Oxford: Clarendon Press.
Blackburn, S. (1984) *Spreading the Word: Groundings in the Philosophy of Language*, Oxford: Clarendon Press.
Blackburn, S. (1990) "Filling in Space", *Analysis*, 50: 62–5.
Block, Ned (1980) "What is Functionalism?" in Ned Block (ed.), *Readings in Philosophy of Psychology*, vol. 1, Harvard University Press, pp. 171–84.
Boscovich, R. J. (1763/1966) *A Theory of Natural Philosophy*, trans. J. M. Child, Boston: MIT Press.
Campbell, Keith (1976) *Metaphysics: An Introduction*, Encino, CA: Dickenson.
Chalmers, David (1996) *The Conscious Mind: In Search of a Fundamental Theory*, New York: Oxford University Press.
Cohen, L. J. and M. Hesse, eds. (1980) *Applications of Inductive Logic*, Oxford: Clarendon Press.
Dipert, Randall R. (1997) "The Mathematical Structure of the World: The World as Graph", *Journal of Philosophy*, 94: 329–58.
Elder, C. (1994) "Laws, Natures, and Contingent Necessities", *Philosophy and Phenomenological Research*, 54: 649–67.
Fodor, Jerry (1988) *Psychosemantics: The Problem of Meaning in the Philosophy of Mind*, Cambridge, MA: MIT Press.
Foster, John (1982) *The Case for Idealism*. London: Routledge & Kegan Paul.
Harré, R. (1970) "Powers", *British Journal for the Philosophy of Science*, 21: 81–101.
Harré, R. and E. H. Madden (1975) *Causal Powers: A Theory of Natural Necessity*, Oxford: Basil Blackwell.
Heil, John (1992) *The Nature of True Minds*, Cambridge University Press.

Heil, John (1998a) "Supervenience Deconstructed", *European Journal of Philosophy*, 6: 146–55.

Heil, John (1998b) *Philosophy of Mind: A Contemporary Introduction*, London: Routledge.

Heil, John (1999) "Multiple Realizability", *American Philosophical Quarterly*, 36: 189–208.

Heil, John, and A. Mele (eds.) (1993) *Mental Causation*, Oxford: Clarendon Press.

Hirst, R. J. (1959) *The Problems of Perception*, London: George Allen & Unwin.

Hoffman, Joshua and Gary Rosenkrantz (1994) *Substance and Other Categories*, Cambridge University Press.

Holton, Richard (1999) "Dispositions All the Way Round", *Analysis*, 59: 9–14.

Horgan, Terence (1993) "From Supervenience to Superdupervenience: Meeting the Demands of a Material World", *Mind*, 102: 555–86.

Humberstone, Lloyd (1996) "Intrinsic/Extrinsic", *Synthese*, 108: 205–67.

Jackson, Frank (1997) "The Primary Quality View of Color", *Philosophical Perspectives*, 10: 199–219.

Kim, J. (1990) "Supervenience as a Philosophical Concept", *Metaphilosophy*, 12: 1–27.

Kim, J. (1993a) "The Non-Reductivist's Troubles with Mental Causation", in Heil and Mele (1993: 189–210); reprinted in Kim (1993b: 336–57).

Kim, J. (1993b) *Supervenience and Mind: Selected Philosophical Essays*, Cambridge University Press.

Langton, Rae (1998) *Kantian Humility: Our Ignorance of Things in Themselves*, Oxford: Clarendon Press.

Lewis, David (1966) "An Argument for the Identity Theory", *Journal of Philosophy*, 63: 17–25.

Lewis, David (1994) "Reduction of Mind", in Samuel Guttenplan (ed.), *A Companion to the Philosophy of Mind*, Oxford: Basil Blackwell, pp. 412–31.

Lewis, David and Rae Langton (1998) "Defining 'Intrinsic' ", *Philosophy and Phenomenological Research*, 58: 333–45.

Locke, John (1690/1978) *An Essay Concerning Human Understanding*, ed. P. H. Nidditch, Oxford: Clarendon Press.

Lowe, E. J. (1995) *Locke on Human Understanding*, London: Routledge.

Lowe, E. J. (1998) *The Possibility of Metaphysics: Substance, Identity, and Time*, Oxford: Clarendon Press.

Lowe, E. J. (2000) "Locke, Martin, and Substance", *Philosophical Quarterly*, 50: 499–514.

Martin, C. B. (1980) "Substance Substantiated", *Australasian Journal of Philosophy*, 58: 3–10.

Martin, C. B. (1994) "Dispositions and Conditionals", *Philosophical Quarterly*, 44: 1–8.
Martin, C. B. (1997) "On the Need for Properties: The Road to Pythagoreanism and Back", *Synthese*, 112: 193–231.
Martin, C. B. and John Heil (1999) "The Ontological Turn", *Midwest Studies in Philosophy*, 23: 34–60.
Mellor, D. H. (1974) "In Defense of Dispositions", *Philosophical Review*, 83: 157–81; reprinted in Mellor (1991: 104–22).
Mellor, D. H. (1991) *Matters of Metaphysics*, Cambridge University Press.
Mellor, D. H. (2000) "The Semantics and Ontology of Dispositions", *Mind*, 109: 757–80.
Mumford, Stephen (1998) *Dispositions*, Oxford: Clarendon Press.
Oddie, Graham (1992) "Armstrong on the Eleatic Principle and Abstract Entities", *Philosophical Studies*, 41: 285–95.
Priestley, Joseph (1777/1972) "Disquisitions of Matter and Spirit", in *The Theological and Miscellaneous Works of Joseph Priestley*, vol. 3, New York: Kraus Reprint Co.
Prior, Elizabeth W., Robert Pargetter, and Frank Jackson (1982) "Three Theses about Dispositions". *American Philosophical Quarterly*, 19: 251–7.
Robinson, Howard (1982) *Matter and Sense: A Critique of Contemporary Materialism*, Cambridge University Press.
Shoemaker, Sydney (1980) "Causality and Properties", in Peter van Inwagen (ed.), *Time and Cause*, Dordrecht: Reidel, pp. 109–35; reprinted in Shoemaker (1984: 206–33).
Shoemaker, Sydney (1984) *Identity, Cause, and Mind: Philosophical Essays*, Cambridge University Press.
Shoemaker, Sydney (1998) "Causal and Metaphysical Necessity", *Pacific Philosophical Quarterly*, 79: 59–77.
Smith, A. D. (1990) "Of Primary and Secondary Qualities", *Philosophical Review*, 99: 221–54.
Smart, J. J. C. (1963) *Philosophy and Scientific Realism*, London: Routledge & Kegan Paul.
Swinburne, R. G. (1980) "A Reply to Shoemaker", in Cohen and Hesse (1980: 316–17).
Swoyer, Chris (1982) "The Nature of Natural Laws", *Australasian Journal of Philosophy*, 60: 203–23.
Unger, Peter (1999) "The Mystery of the Physical and the Matter of Qualities: A Paper for Professor Shaffer", *Midwest Studies in Philosophy*, 23: 75–99.
Unger, Peter (forthcoming) *All the Power in the World: Body, Mind, and Freedom*, New York: Oxford University Press.

10. The Intrinsic Character of Causation
Ned Hall

1. INTRODUCTION

There is surely something to the idea that the causal structure of a process is *intrinsic* to it—determined, that is, by the intrinsic natures of the events that make up the process, together with the ways in which they are juxtaposed with one another, together with the laws that govern that process. Consider a simple case.

> *Suzy Alone*: Suzy, an expert rock-thrower with a taste for minor acts of destruction, throws a rock at a bottle. The rock hits the bottle, shattering it. Her throw is a cause of the shattering. Isn't it also clear that, in addition to the laws, whatever *makes* it a cause of the shattering is to be found wholly within the sequence consisting of the throw, the shattering, and the events in between?[1] Whatever is happening off-stage, as it were, would seem to have no bearing on the causal status of her throw.

As further evidence that some such thesis of Intrinsicness (as I will call it) guides our thinking about causation, consider a variant.

> *Suzy First*: This time Suzy's friend Billy throws a rock at the bottle, too. He's just as expert as she is, but a bit slower. Consequently, her rock gets there first; but if she hadn't thrown it, the bottle would have shattered all the same, thanks to his throw.

Billy's throw in Suzy First disrupts the neat nomological relationships that held between Suzy's throw and the shattering in Suzy Alone. For example, the shattering no longer counterfactually depends on her throw; nor does her throw belong to a unique set of non-redundant

---

[1] Maybe we didn't need to say "in addition to the laws"—maybe, that is, the fact that the process is governed by such-and-such laws is itself intrinsic to that process. We will come back to this issue later.

sufficient conditions for the shattering.[2] No wonder that cases like Suzy First make such trouble for philosophical analyses of causation. But they don't trouble our intuitions in the slightest; far from being a borderline case of causation, Suzy's throw in Suzy First is just as clearly a cause of the shattering as in Suzy Alone (and, equally clearly, Billy's is *not*). Plausibly, what is guiding our judgments about the more complex case is that the extra complexity Billy's throw brings with it is *extrinsic to*— and therefore irrelevant to the evaluation of—the sequence connecting Suzy's throw to the shattering. Think of the matter this way. We begin with the pared-down situation, where Suzy alone is present, and throws. We now *add* elements to the situation—we add Billy, his throw, the flight of his rock toward the bottle—but in such a way as to leave unchanged the intrinsic characteristics of the process that begins with Suzy's throw and ends in the shattering.[3] And so, of course, Suzy's throw remains a cause of the shattering.

The Intrinsicness thesis that I will articulate and explore in this paper aims at codifying the powerful intuitive conviction that such extrinsic additions can make no causal difference. This thesis is valuable for a number of reasons, but the one that I will place front and center is this: it allows us to solve what would otherwise be an intractable problem posed by depressingly simple examples of causal overdetermination. (Suzy First is a typical instance.) Other benefits, which I will have space only to sketch, are these: it provides the ingredients for an elegant account of *symmetric* causal overdetermination, and it helps illuminate the notion of *causal efficacy* for event properties. It also has some striking consequences; for if it is correct, then the core idea behind counterfactual analyses of causation is false, and, furthermore, there is no such thing as causation by omission. Of course, those consequences will look rather *too* striking to some: they will seem more accurately labeled "costs". Later we will see how to restate them in ways that will make them

---

[2] Some would object, either on the grounds that the shattering *does* still depend on Suzy's throw—for without her throw the window would have shattered moments later, and that would have made for a numerically different event—or on the grounds that the nomological relations I have attended to are too simple, and that more intricate ones can be found to distinguish Suzy's from Billy's throw. The first objection is pretty clearly misguided; the second, while obviously too open-ended for decisive refutation, becomes implausible on close inspection. I'll explain all this in Sect. 5 below.

[3] Well, *almost* unchanged, and at any rate unchanged in any *relevant* respect. We will examine the need for the qualifications—and how to state them in a way that is not objectionably weaselly—in Sect. 8 below.

appear less drastic: namely, by taking Intrinsicness to characterize one central *kind* of causation.[4]

The plan is as follows. After some preliminaries, I will give the formulation of the Intrinsicness thesis I prefer, and then raise several questions about it. Answering these questions will take us through a number of topics. The first concerns the motivation for the Intrinsicness thesis; here I will lay out the philosophical problem posed by causal overdetermination. The second focuses on the reasons why the Intrinsicness thesis needs to have the somewhat complicated form that I will give it. The third concerns the applications of the Intrinsicness thesis just alluded to. It is here that I will argue against counterfactual analyses, and the claim that there is such a thing as causation by omission; I will also offer my solution to the problem of overdetermination, and indicate in passing how to leverage the thesis into an adequate account of symmetrical overdetermination. The fourth topic concerns the need for a certain key refinement of the Intrinsicness thesis; I will sketch what I think is the best way to undertake that refinement—and, again, indicate in passing how this refinement helps explain what causal efficacy consists in. Finally, I will close with a brief discussion of an important objection, some of the reply to which will help to draw out what I take to be a deeper motivation behind the Intrinsicness thesis. To foreshadow: I think that, if we wish to have the means for elucidating, in a manageable form, the nomological structure of our world, then we need a causal concept governed by Intrinsicness.

Now to the preliminaries, the first of which aims to forestall confusion about the nature of the Intrinsicness thesis.

2. TWO ROADS NOT TAKEN

Some authors would find the statement of the Intrinsicness thesis to be simplicity itself, holding that, whenever an event c causes an event e, this causal relation simply *is* intrinsic to the pair (c, e). To be sure, the relation is *external*, in that (like spatio-temporal relations) whether it obtains is not solely determined by the respective intrinsic properties of c and e. But it is nevertheless intrinsic to the pair—and that is the end of the story.[5]

---

[4] This view is developed more fully in Hall (2003).
[5] For a representative statement, see Menzies (1999).

This position is most naturally developed as part of a certain kind of *non-reductionist* position about causation, according to which facts about what causes what are metaphysically primitive (Tooley 1990). To see why, start with what must seem an obvious and decisive objection to this statement of <u>Intrinsicness</u>. Let c be the lighting of a fuse, and let e be an explosion some time later. Supposing c to be a cause of e, how could this fact possibly be *intrinsic* to the pair (c, e)? Surely the facts that make it the case that c causes e would need to include one that is *extrinsic* to the pair—namely, the fact that *this* fuse is connected to *that* bomb. So the claim that causation is a relation intrinsic to the events that exhibit it seems a non-starter.

But a non-reductionist can respond that the objection presupposes an ontology at odds with—because more spartan than—the ontology that he is committed to. As I understand it, the latter ontology simply *includes* causation as one of the fundamental properties and relations that characterize the world; the more spartan alternative does not. This contrast closely parallels another major difference of opinion that characterizes the literature on causation: namely, whether causal facts *reduce to* facts about what happens, together with facts about the fundamental laws of nature that govern what happens. One who says "yes" will, by way of clarifying her reductionist position, likely endorse something like the following picture. *All* facts about the world somehow reduce to or are constituted by or obtain in virtue of facts about which fundamental physical objects instantiate which fundamental physical properties and relations, together with facts about the fundamental physical laws.[6] And she will add that the list of fundamental relations is in all likelihood extremely *short*—perhaps comprising just spatio-temporal relations, perhaps a few more, e.g. if certain versions of quantum mechanics are right. At any rate, it does *not*, on her view,

---

[6] Of course, there is room for further dispute among reductionists. Some will say that to include facts about the laws is redundant, since these themselves reduce to facts about the instantiation of properties and relations by things. Some will insist that "physical objects" had better include space–time itself. Some will demur about the restriction to the physical, wishing to allow, for example, that minds might be among the fundamental objects. (Note that such dualism does nothing at all to threaten the *reductionist* element in the physicalist position sketched in the text.) And there will be further disagreement about whether the reductionist claim is necessary or contingent—and, if contingent, contingent on *what*. None of these disagreements matter for present purposes; what is important is the philosophical sentiment that unites all the various forms of reductionism about causation.

include causation itself. By contrast, her principal opponent thinks there is no hope of reducing causation to such a limited set of facts—and not for fancy reasons, but simply because he thinks (typically on the basis of various thought-experiments: see Tooley 1990) that causal facts don't even *supervene* on these other facts. He—at least, in some of his incarnations—therefore sees fit to introduce causation itself as a further fundamental relation. And it is therefore open to him to stipulate further that this relation is an intrinsic one.

I will side with the reductionist, although without making any attempt to resolve her dispute with the anti-reductionist. It is important to realize, however, that the appeal of <u>Intrinsicness</u> does not at all depend on endorsing, tacitly or otherwise, the kind of anti-reductionist view about causation just sketched. Think again about Suzy and Billy. When we judge that the extrinsic addition of Billy and his throw is irrelevant to the causal status of Suzy's throw, this judgment does *not* turn on conceiving of her throw as somehow directly connected to the shattering by the instantiation of a fundamental, metaphysically primitive causal relation. It turns, rather, on noticing at once that the addition does not affect in any relevant way the intrinsic character—the *ordinary*, garden-variety intrinsic character—of the process connecting Suzy's throw to the shattering.

So much for the first of the roads not taken. To map out the second road requires another brief digression. Distinguish two very different varieties of reductionism about causation. The first variety seeks to define some kind of *nomological entailment* relation that holds between cause–effect pairs. Examples will suffice to give the idea. We might hold that c is a cause of e iff, from the proposition that c occurs, together with the proposition that encapsulates the fundamental laws, it follows (with metaphysical necessity, say) that e occurs. Or we might try something more sophisticated: c is a cause of e iff, from the proposition that c occurs, together with the proposition that encapsulates the fundamental laws, together with some suitably chosen proposition about conditions that obtain at the time of c's occurrence, it follows that e occurs, where it is essential to the entailment that we include the premise that c occurs (Mackie 1965, more or less). Or we might hold that c is a cause of e iff, had c not occurred, e would not have occurred—where this entailment relation between the proposition that c does not occur and that e does not occur counts as nomological because of the central role played by the fundamental laws in fixing the truth-conditions of the counterfactual.

Or we might hold that causation is the ancestral of this relation of counterfactual dependence (Lewis 1986b). Examples of this kind of approach abound in the literature, becoming more and more intricate the closer one gets to the present. As will become clear (Section 6), I endorse this approach (though not in its currently popular counterfactual form), and in fact will argue that one of the virtues of Intrinsicness is that it provides the key to making a nomological entailment account work, even in the face of stubborn cases like Suzy First.

Contrast a very different kind of reductionist account, which seeks to define causation in terms of some kind of *physical connection*—often involving the "transfer" of some physical quantity—between the cause and its effect. Again, I'll lean on examples. We might say, with Fair (1979), that causation consists in the transfer of *energy*; or, with Ehring (1997), in the transfer of a *trope*; or, with Dowe (1992) and Salmon (1994), in the transfer of some *conserved quantity*—where appeal is made to fundamental physics for an inventory of such quantities. This last example shows that fundamental laws have, or at least can have, a place in such accounts; all the same, their role is evidently much less direct than it is in nomological entailment accounts.

Physical connection accounts may vindicate some version of an Intrinsicness thesis—at least, insofar as the physical connections appealed to are intrinsic to processes that exhibit them.[7] In addition, some such account may well prove successful in capturing what causation is in worlds with laws like ours—*provided* we restrict our attention to causation between microphysical events. The qualifications appear unavoidable, as there seems little hope of employing the simple and austere connections of these accounts to map out causal relations in the messy macroscopic realm, or in possible worlds whose fundamental physics doesn't involve the transfer of anything. With respect to the former problem, consider that I drank coffee this afternoon, and a short while later became jittery as a result. It's not terribly plausible to think that we could arrive at some illuminating analysis of this causal process by focusing on the transfer of energy, momentum, charge, or any other fundamental physical quantity, or by searching for tropes that pass from the coffee to my body. After all, I drank *milk* with my coffee, and doing *that* presumably had nothing to do with my jitters—even though it effected the transfer of fundamental physical quantities to my body no

---

[7] Fair's position may be a counter-example, since *kinetic* energy, at least, has its value only relative to an inertial frame of reference.

less than did the coffee-drinking.[8] So I see no interest in trying to understand Intrinsicness by means of such theories, since their scope is far too limited.

I turn now to what I hope will prove a more fruitful way of developing the Intrinsicness thesis, taking a necessary detour through some further preliminaries.

3. ASSUMPTIONS

Let me now lay out some basic assumptions that will serve as my starting points. As noted—and like many philosophers who work on causation—I am going to assume that the *fundamental* causal structure of the world is given by the purely contingent facts about what happens, together with the facts about what the fundamental laws are that govern what happens. I think of these fundamental laws on the model of physics: namely, as something like rules that specify how complete physical states of the world generate successive physical states.[9] If you like, then, the fundamental causal facts take the following form: complete-physical-state-P_1 causes complete-physical-state-P_2. There is, of course, ample room, and even a pressing need, within such a conception for much more circumscribed causal facts involving correspondingly circumscribed and localized events, for example the fact that my pressing this letter on the keyboard caused that letter to appear on the screen. But again, like many philosophers, I take the further step of holding that these causal facts somehow *reduce to* facts about what happens, together with the laws that govern what happens—and do so in a way that careful philosophical analysis can elucidate. By "reduce to" I mean something

---

[8] Granted, a detailed *scientific* understanding of the causal process leading from coffee-drinking to jitters would require examining its relevant micro consituents, and the relevant relations among them. But notice that use of the word "relevant" is inescapable here: e.g., the coffee transfers *heat* to my body, but that fact presumably does not matter to why the coffee makes me jittery. A proper philosophical account of causation ought to illuminate *what it is* about drinking the coffee that was causally responsible for my jitters, and it is a mark against transference theories that they lack the resources to do so. See Hall and Paul (2002) for more details.

[9] See Maudlin (1996) for an excellent exposition of this conception of law. Even though this is the way I think of the laws, all that is really necessary for me to assume is that there is a firm distinction between worlds that are, and worlds that are not, *nomologically possible*. So it is compatible with everything I have to say that the world be infinitely complex, in the sense that it has no "fundamental" level (see Schaffer 2003).

stronger than merely "supervene on"; for the former relation is patently asymmetric, whereas the latter is not. (And in the present case, it would not be that surprising if it turned out that both the facts about what happens and the facts about the fundamental laws supervene on the totality of causal facts expressible in the form "event c causes event e".) I will say a bit more later about the form that I think such a reductionist analysis should take.

I have implicitly suggested, and hereby explicitly endorse, the view that the basic causal relata are events. I won't try to say what "basic" means here, save to point out that some such qualification is necessary, since, after all, people, rocks, and other ordinary particulars can in some sense cause things, as perhaps can items from still other ontological categories (*facts*, as it might be). I also won't try to say what events are, although I will assume this much about them: like other particulars, they have detailed intrinsic natures. Such natures correspond to easily recognizable facts about events. Suppose, for example, that I throw a rock. Then there are facts about exactly how long the throw lasts, exactly what shape region it occupies at each moment of its occurrence, the exact mass the rock has at each of these moments, etc. I take these to be facts about the *intrinsic properties* of my throw. More generally, I assume that, for any event e, the totality of such facts serve to specify exactly— but do no more than serve to specify exactly—how e occurs, down to the most minute detail. I will therefore further assume that it makes sense to compare any two events with respect to their intrinsic *similarity*. I will likewise assume that structures built up out of events[10] have intrinsic natures—exhausted, I will suppose, by the intrinsic natures of their constituent events, together with the facts about how those events are spatio-temporally juxtaposed with one another. (I count the time order of its constituent events as an intrinsic feature of an event structure, so that two such structures that are temporally inverted with respect to each other qualify, for that reason, as being intrinsically *dis*similar.) All of this will be important in what follows, for we will see that stating the Intrinsicness thesis carefully requires us to make use of the notion of intrinsic similarity between entire event structures.

I am going to make the simplifying assumption that the fundamental laws are deterministic, and that they permit neither backwards caus-

---

[10] "Built up" how? By mereological fusion, I suppose—although those uncomfortable with extending mereology into the domain of events could probably substitute some set-theoretical surrogate.

ation nor action at a temporal distance. At various points in what follows I will briefly indicate where complications arise when we give up these assumptions, but I won't pursue those complications in any detail.

Let us turn now to the Intrinsicness thesis. The crude statement of the thesis was that the causal structure of a process is intrinsic to it. We can arrive at a better statement if we focus on simple examples. I will choose the ones we started with—Suzy's throw, with and without Billy's backup throw—but will represent their structure abstractly, by means of the "neuron diagrams" popularized by Lewis. Thus, in Figure 1, neuron **a** fires, sending a stimulatory signal to **e**, causing it to fire; we represent the firings of **a** and **e** by shading their respective circles, and represent the passage of the stimulatory signal by the arrow connecting these circles. Note that the order of events is left to right.

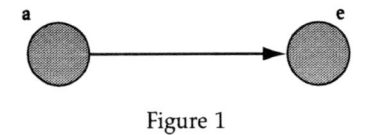

Figure 1

In Figure 2 exactly the same events happen, plus some additional ones: neuron **b** fires a few moments after **a**, sending a stimulatory signal to **e** that has almost reached **e** by the time **e** fires. (We represent this fact by drawing an arrow from **b** that doesn't quite reach **e**.)

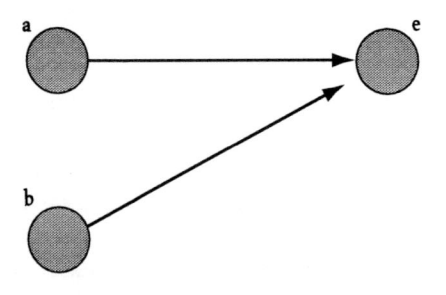

Figure 2

The addition of **b** and its signal does nothing at all to alter the status of *a* as a cause of *e*. (Throughout, I will use italicized letters to represent the events consisting in the firings of the associated neurons.) Here, then, is the thought: fix on an event *e*, and take the structure consisting of that event together with all of its causes back to some earlier time t. Then altering the *environment* of that structure while holding the structure itself fixed cannot alter the fact that the events in the structure (distinct from e) are *causes* of e. In that sense, causal relations are *stable* under perturbations of the environment of the process exhibiting them.

That statement of the thesis has the distinct advantage of being both intuitive and plausible. But it is important to restate the thesis in a way that makes clear what we mean when we talk about holding a structure of events "fixed" while changing the environment. Hence this final version of the thesis:

> <u>Intrinsicness</u>: Let S be a structure of events consisting of event e, together with all of its causes back to some earlier time t. Let S′ be a structure of events that intrinsically matches S in relevant respects, and that exists in a world with the same laws. Let e′ be the event in S′ that corresponds to e in S. Let c be some event in S distinct from e, and let c′ be the event in S′ that corresponds to c. Then c′ is a cause of e′.

So stated, the thesis raises a number of questions. Five stand out.

4. QUESTIONS AND BRIEF ANSWERS

First question: What is the motivation for the thesis?

Answer: First, there is the intuitive motivation brought out by contrasting cases like Suzy Alone and Suzy First. Second, the thesis offers an elegant solution—and perhaps the *only* solution—to what I am calling the "overdetermination problem" (Sections 5 and 7). Third, reflection on the *function* of our causal concepts suggests that at least one such function, and a central one, is to provide us with tools for the piecemeal representation of the nomological structure of our world; the <u>Intrinsicness</u> thesis, if correct, goes a long way towards explaining how our causal concepts can play such a role (Section 9).

Second question: Why is the thesis so complicated? In particular, why must S be so comprehensive as to include *all* the causes of e (back to some earlier time t)?

Answer: Causes produce their effects *by way of* causal intermediates, and *with the help of* other causes with which they combine; state the thesis in a way that ignores these truisms, and you expose it to trivial counter-examples. (Section 6).

Third question: Why the qualification "in relevant respects"?

Answer: Because non-causes can make small and irrelevant differences to the manner in which causes occur. Add Billy's throw so as to convert Suzy Alone into Suzy First, and you inevitably introduce ever-so-subtle changes in the flight path of her rock (due, for example, to gravitational attraction from Billy's rock) (Section 8).

Fourth question: What does this qualification mean?

Answer: Roughly this: S' must be intrinsically similar to S in those respects in which S and other "blueprints" like it are similar to each other. Begin with Suzy Alone, and introduce slight variations in her throw (or in the window) that make no difference to the causal structure of the processes that lead up to the shattering: the multitude of ways of doing so provides us with a set of "blueprints". These blueprints, in turn, allow us to set up standards of comparison by means of which we can distinguish relevant from irrelevant respects of similarity (Section 8).

Fifth question: What are the consequences of the thesis?

Answer: It provides a solution to the overdetermination problem. It provides a novel argument that counterfactual dependence is not sufficient for causation, and likewise that there is no causation by omission. It provides the materials for a clean account of symmetric overdetermination, and of at least one notion of "causal efficacy" (Sections 7 and 8).

On to more detailed answers.

5. THE OVERDETERMINATION PROBLEM

Let's start with reasons for believing the Intrinsicness thesis. I have already talked about the intuitive motivation for the thesis by comparing and contrasting the events depicted in Figures 1 and 2. I now want to put those examples to use for a different purpose, in order to bring out the serious problem that the Intrinsicness thesis may offer the only good hope of solving.

Recall one of our starting points: I assumed that philosophical analysis should be able to show how causal facts reduce to facts about what happens, together with facts about what the laws are that govern what happens. As noted in Section 2, a thriving tradition has it that a successful analysis of causation should reveal that relation to be a kind of *nomological entailment* relation. Once again, some illustrative examples (of which the literature offers countless variations):

> *Crude sufficient condition account*: c causes e iff c and e both occur, and from the fact that c occurs, together with the laws, it follows that e occurs. More precisely: c causes e in world w iff c and e both occur in w, and in any world w′ in which c occurs, and which has the same laws as w, e occurs.
>
> *Crude necessary condition account*: c causes e iff c and e both occur, and from the fact that e occurs, together with the laws, it follows that c occurs. More precisely: c causes e in world w iff c and e both occur in w, and in any world w′ in which e occurs, and which has the same laws as w, c occurs.
>
> *Mackie-style regularity account*: c causes e iff c and e both occur, and from the fact that c occurs, together with some suitable auxiliary premises describing contingent facts about the circumstances in which c occurs, together with the laws, it follows that e occurs; but this fact does *not* follow from the auxiliary premises and the laws alone. (This is roughly Mackie's view: causes are necessary parts of sufficient conditions for their effects.)
>
> *Simple counterfactual account*: c causes e iff c and e both occur, and had c not occurred, e would not have occurred.
>
> *Lewis-style counterfactual account (circa 1976)*: c causes e iff c and e both occur, and there is a (possibly empty) set of events $\{d_1, d_2, \ldots, d_n\}$ such that if c had not occurred d_1 would not have occurred; and if d_1 had not occurred d_2 would not have occurred; ... and if d_n had not occurred, e would not have occurred. (This is the analysis offered in the classic Lewis 1986b.)
>
> *Updated Lewis account (circa 2000)*: c causes e iff c and e both occur, and there is a (possibly empty) set of events $\{d_1, d_2, \ldots, d_n\}$ such that c influences d_1, d_1 influences d_2, ..., d_n influences e; one event *influences* another just in case, roughly, any of a large number of slight counterfactual variations in the first would be followed by corresponding variations in the second (see Lewis 2003).

In each case, the analysis attempts to show causation to be a kind of *entailment* relation (using that term in a permissive sense, so that it covers, e.g., counterfactual accounts as well as regularity accounts) between the fact that the cause occurs and the fact that the effect occurs (sometimes going from cause to effect, sometimes from effect to cause), where that relation is, crucially, mediated by the fundamental laws. While the search for such an entailment relation can easily go astray— e.g. none of the foregoing analyses succeeds—the motivation behind it is, to my mind, fundamentally sound. At the very least, the project of pursuing this kind of reductionist analysis of causation is fruitful enough, even where it fails, to deserve serious and sustained attention.

Reflecting on Figure 2, however, it can seem utterly hopeless. For what is so striking and dispiriting about this example is that the events a and b bear, apparently, *exactly the same* nomological entailment relations to e. Each is a necessary part of some sufficient condition for e; e counterfactually depends on neither—but would so depend had the other not occurred; both a and b influence e (indeed, to pretty much the same degree); etc. Moreover, the usual tricks for handling cases of overdetermination—for example interpolating some intermediate event such that the cause bears the appropriate entailment relation to it and it bears that relation to the effect (see Lewis 1986b)—seem to be of no avail.[11] Notice, in this regard, that the close parallel in nomological entailment relations to the effect persists as we move from a and b to successive pairs of events more and more causally proximate to the effect.

At this point we might want to try more desperate measures. For example, perhaps it matters crucially that if **a** had not fired, e would have fired at a slightly different time, whereas the same would not be true if **b** had not fired. More generally, we might want to distinguish causes by saying that they are the events upon which the detailed manner of occurrence of the effect depends. But not only will this maneuver let in far too many events as causes (namely, by erasing the distinction between events that *cause* a given effect and events that merely make a difference to the *way* in which that effect occurs), it is also embarrassingly easy to tinker with our example so as to render it

---

[11] Terminological point: I am calling cases like Fig. 2 cases of "overdetermination", where some (e.g. Lewis 1986b) would use the term "redundant causation"—reserving "overdetermination" for *symmetric* cases (as when two neurons simultaneously stimulate a third).

ineffective. Suppose, for example, that the signal from a exerts a retarding force on the signal from b, slowing it down slightly. Suppose that the exact strength of this force is such that, had a not fired, the signal from b would have arrived at e at exactly the same time that the signal from a in fact arrives. Then not only does the firing of e not depend on the firing of a, but nothing *about* the firing of e—not its timing, or any other feature of its manner of occurrence—depends on the firing of a. (We can further suppose that the retarding force is of just the right strength that, for exactly the same reason, e exhibits a total lack of dependence on each of the events that consist in the passage of the stimulatory signal from a to e.)

More desperate measures still? Perhaps we could insist that causes be connected to their effects via spatio-temporally continuous causal chains. But of course there *are* spatio-temporally continuous chains connecting b to e. For example, the stimulatory signal from b emits radiation as it moves along, and some of this radiation strikes e at the exact moment that it begins to fire. And anyway, it seems drastic to be forced to accommodate such a simple example by ruling out action at a distance a priori. (Note that we would be ruling out not merely action at a *temporal* distance—a restriction which we need not find so troubling—but also action at a spatial distance. And that is the one kind of action at a distance for which the history of physics provides some precedent.)

There are, of course, other and still more elaborate constructions that one might try. Vast tracts of the literature on causation are littered with their remnants. But there is no further profit to be had in sifting through them.[12] Enough has been said to underscore how serious is the problem posed by such simple cases of overdetermination as that depicted in Figure 2. I will just add that their very simplicity argues for a correspondingly simple solution. It would be disappointing if we could handle such mundane examples only by means of an intricate technical apparatus. We will see, happily, that the Intrinsicness thesis offers an attractively elegant solution. The key idea is to find a nomological entailment relation that succeeds in capturing the causal structure of a process when circumstances are *nice* (as they are, for example, in Figure 1), and to use the Intrinsicness thesis to "transfer" that causal structure into circumstances that are not so nice (e.g. Figure 2). But

---

[12] For excruciatingly detailed discussion, see Hall and Paul (2002).

before developing this idea, let us first consider why that thesis needs to have the form I have given it.

6. MOTIVATING THE CONSTRAINTS

What the Intrinsicness thesis allows us to do is to fix on one structure of events, and then to "transfer" its causal characteristics over to another, intrinsically matching, structure. But the two structures must exist in worlds with the same laws, and the structure we begin with must be comprehensive enough to consist of an event together with all of its causes back to some earlier time. It may be unclear why these constraints should be in place. That is what I will explain in this section. What I will do is to show by example that the most obvious ways of relaxing them do not give us a workable version of the Intrinsicness thesis.

6.1 Laws

Begin with the constraint on laws. Recall Figure 1: **a** fires, emitting a stimulatory signal which travels to **e**, at which point **e** fires. The relevant underlying laws hold that **e** will fire iff (and when) a stimulatory signal reaches it. But suppose the laws to be radically different. Suppose they dictate that **e** fires spontaneously every two seconds. (By "spontaneously", I do not mean *without any causes*, but just without any *external* causes.) Suppose further that the laws specify no role for the signals that neurons sometimes emit when they fire. Such laws permit an exact duplicate of the events depicted in Figure 1: **e** has been firing spontaneously, every two seconds, since the dawn of time; **a** fires, emitting its signal in the direction of **e**; that signal reaches **e**—purely by coincidence—at exactly the moment at which **e** is beginning one of its firings. To be sure, in realistic examples we could probably discern subtle intrinsic differences in the two event structures, differences that bore witness to the drastic difference in underlying laws. But I would have you imagine that in our highly abstracted neuron worlds the *only* difference is in the underlying laws. The *a–e* event structures, in each case, are intrinsically *exactly* alike.

The *causal* structures are completely different, of course. The appropriate conclusion is one that might seem a truism: the fundamental laws play an essential role in fixing causal structure. The best way to implement this lesson in the development of the Intrinsicness thesis is to require that intrinsic similarity make for similarity in causal structure, *provided* that these laws are held fixed.[13]

On to the less obvious constraint that requires us to pick an event structure that consists of an event *e*, together with *all* of its causes back to some earlier time t. I will explain in stages why this constraint should be in place.

6.2 Causal mediation

Suppose we tried to defend this simpler statement of the Intrinsicness thesis: when a pair of events (*c*, *e*) intrinsically matches another pair of events (*c'*, *e'*), and both pairs exist in worlds with the same laws, then the same causal relations obtain in each case—i.e., *c* is a cause of *e* (likewise *e* of *c*) iff *c'* is a cause of *e'* (respectively, *e'* of *c'*). That is hopeless, even when we make it clear that, in order for such pairs intrinsically to match each other, they must duplicate the spatio-temporal relations exhibited by their members. For whether we have causation in each case obviously depends on what sorts of connections, if any, there *are* between the events in question. And the existence or lack thereof of such connections is not going to be a fact intrinsic to the pairs.

Consider Figure 3. Here, **a** fires, sending a signal to **b**, causing it to fire. A little later, **c** fires (as a result of causes that are not depicted—but *not* as a result of *b*), sending a signal to **e**, causing it to fire. The (*a*, *e*) pair depicted in Figure 3 is, we can suppose, intrinsically *exactly* like the (*a*, *e*) pair depicted in Figure 1. But the causal relation that obtains in this latter case does not transfer to the former.

There are two distinct lessons to learn from this case. For the first, suppose that we have some event structure, picked out in some manner, that consists in part of event *a* and later event *e*. Suppose further that *a* is *not* a cause of *e*. This structure might, for example, be the one consisting of all the events depicted in Figure 3. Then it will almost always be possible to embed an intrinsic duplicate of this structure in an

---

[13] One might think this proviso unnecessary, on the grounds that the fact that a process is governed by such-and-such laws is itself an *intrinsic feature* of that process. As was implicit in my discussion of the spontaneously firing neuron, I disagree. But nothing hangs on this question; if I am wrong, the worst that happens is that my statement of the Intrinsicness thesis is somewhat redundant.

The Intrinsic Character of Causation | 271

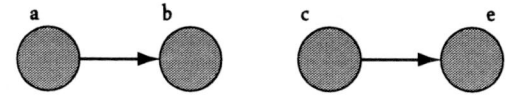

Figure 3

environment that provides sufficient "connecting material" to make the event corresponding to *a* a cause of the event corresponding to *e*—as for example in Figure 4, where we insert a stimulatory connection between b and c. Granted, it might in rare cases *not* be possible, namely if the structure with which we begin is so "fat" that it leaves no room for such connecting material. But there is no interest in trying to come up with a condition that will guarantee such "fatness". So the first lesson is this: in constructing our Intrinsicness thesis, we should expect to come up with a principle that enables us to transfer only *positive* causal characteristics from one event structure to another. Once we have identified our "blueprint" structure S, and have picked out some event structure S′ that intrinsically matches S, we should expect only that, where *c* in S causes *e* in S, the intrinsic similarity between S and S′ guarantees that *c*′ in S′ causes *e*′ in S′ (where, as usual, *c*′ is the event in S′ corresponding to *c* in S, etc.). We should *not* expect, in addition, that, where *c* in S does *not* cause *e* in S, the intrinsic similarity between S and S′ guarantees that *c*′ in S′ does not cause *e*′ in S′.

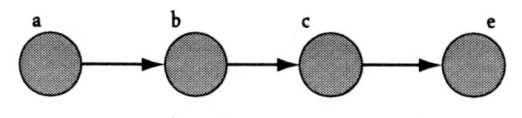

Figure 4

The second lesson concerns the way in which the event structure we begin with must be specified. For suppose this structure contains events *c* and *e*, where *c* is a cause of *e*; but suppose it *fails* to contain every event that is causally intermediate between *c* and *e*—that is, every event that is both an effect of *c* and a cause of *e*. Then, as Figures 1 and 3 show, it will almost always be possible to embed an intrinsic duplicate of this structure in an environment that "deletes" the relevant intermediate causes, and that guarantees that *e* is brought about by other, *independent* means. In any such environment, c (or its duplicate) will no longer be a cause of (the duplicate of) e. The simplest way to avoid this problem is to require that the event structure with which we begin include, for every pair of events c and e where c is a cause of e, all the causal intermediates between c and e.

6.3 Causal combination

So far, we have come up with constraints motivated by the need to attend to the essential role that laws play in fixing causal structure, and to the fact that causes typically yield their effects only *by way of* causal intermediates. But causes also typically yield their effects only with the *help* of other causes with which they combine, and this fact introduces the need for one more constraint, as a pair of examples will show.

Suppose that neurons can fire with different "polarities"—say, positive and negative—emitting stimulatory signals with those same polarities. Suppose that neuron e in Figure 5 requires two stimulatory signals in order to fire (we represent this fact by drawing it with a thick border), and further requires that these signals be of the same polarity. Suppose finally that the way in which e fires is not at all sensitive to whether it receives two positively polarized or two negatively polarized stimulatory signals. Here, **a** and **b** both fire with positive polarity (represented by hatching their circles), sending positively polarized signals to e, which fires as a result.

Now consider Figure 6. Again, **a** fires with positive polarity, sending a positively polarized signal to e. But e receives only one such signal; the reason it fires is that it also receives two negatively polarized signals (represented by diagonal lines), one from **b** and one from **c**. It is sheer coincidence that these signals reach it, and thus cause it to fire, at exactly the same moment that the signal from **a** reaches it.

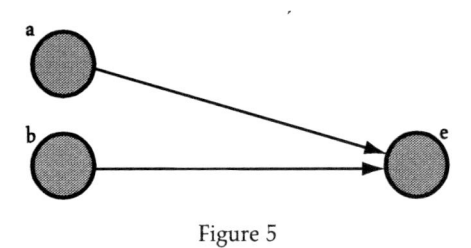

Figure 5

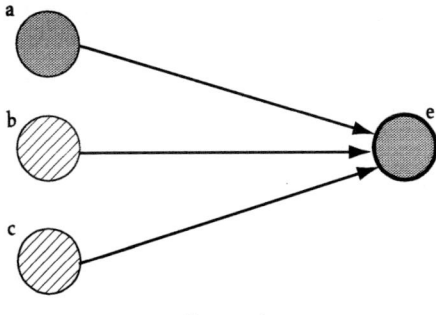

Figure 6

In Figure 5 *a* is a cause of *e*, but in Figure 6 *a* is not a cause of *e*. Nevertheless, if we pick out, from the events depicted in Figure 5, a structure consisting of *a*, *e*, and all the events causally intermediate between *a* and *e*, we see this structure duplicated *exactly* in the events depicted in Figure 6. We are obviously not entitled to use this similarity as grounds for transferring the causal characteristics of the *a–e* sequence in Figure 5 over to the *a–e* sequence in Figure 6.

The problem is that we have not properly incorporated the fact that in Figure 5 *a* does not cause *e* all by itself: it requires the assistance, as a kind of combining cause, of *b*. We should therefore require that, when the event structure S contains *c* and *e*, with *c* a cause of *e*, then it must also contain the other causes with which *c* combines to bring about *e*. (Typically, these will be those causes of *e* that are contemporaneous with *c*.)

Let us now put all this together. We set out to provide a recipe for specifying an event structure in such a way as to guarantee that any other structure that intrinsically matches it will also share its causal characteristics. We have seen that the two structures need to exist in worlds with the same laws. We have seen that we can only expect sharing of "positive" causal characteristics. We have seen that the event structure we begin with must meet a certain closure condition: it must be comprehensive enough that, when it includes an event *e* and one of its causes *c*, it likewise includes all events causally intermediate between *c* and *e*, as well as the events with which *c* combines to bring about *e*. The next step is to replace these two explicitly causal notions—"causal intermediate" and "combining cause"—with non-causal surrogates. What allows us to do so is the assumption that there is neither action at a temporal distance nor backwards causation. Without the first restriction, we would have to contend with the possibility that a cause *c* combines with other causes not contemporaneous with it. (*Example*: two magicians cast spells, at different times, that jointly act at a temporal distance to bring about some effect.) Without the second, we would have to contend with the possibility that, even where *c* precedes its effect *e*, some of the events causally intermediate between *c* and *e* lie outside the time interval between them. Such possibilities make trouble for a clean statement of the Intrinsicness thesis, as well as for the project of using the Intrinsicness thesis to extend the scope of a reductive analysis of causation (see the next section); it would be distracting and profitless, at this point, to explore how to handle this trouble. Instead, we will take advantage of our assumptions to arrive at a particularly simple specification of the kind of event structure that meets our closure condition: it should consist of an event *e*, together with all of its causes back to some earlier time t. It is therefore such structures—structures that we will henceforth call "*e*-blueprints"—that our statement of the Intrinsicness thesis concerns.

7. CONSEQUENCES OF THE THESIS

Let us turn to three applications of the Intrinsicness thesis. The first is a solution to the problem of overdetermination (which yields, as a kind of byproduct, an account of *symmetric* overdetermination as well). The second is an argument that counterfactual dependence does not suffice for causation. The third is an argument that there is no causation by omission. I will take these in order.

7.1 Solving the problem of overdetermination

Recall the contrast between the two cases Suzy Alone and Suzy First. Here is a natural way to think about that contrast. We can get to Suzy First by starting with Suzy Alone, and simply adding things to the environment—Billy, his throw, the flight of his rock through the air, etc. The crucial point is that, while making these additions, we can *hold fixed* the event structure consisting of Suzy's throw, the flight of her rock to the window, the shattering of the window, and, for completeness, the prior presence of the window itself. That is, we can hold fixed a structure consisting of the shattering of the window together with all of its causes back to the time of Suzy's throw. And what I mean by "hold fixed" is that making these additions to the environment does not alter—or at least, does not alter in any relevant respect—the intrinsic character of that structure. Since Suzy's throw in Suzy Alone is, obviously, a cause of the shattering, it therefore follows from the Intrinsicness thesis that in Suzy First her throw is a cause of the shattering. For short, Suzy First contains within it an event structure that (i) includes Suzy's throw as part; and (ii) intrinsically matches some shattering-blueprint (namely, the one provided by Suzy Alone). It is in virtue of (i) and (ii) that Suzy's throw counts as a cause of the shattering.

Now try to do the same with Billy's throw. We might start by imagining a situation—call it "Billy Alone"—in which Billy throws a rock at the window, breaking it, and Suzy is absent. We might then try to imagine ringing changes on this situation so as to add Suzy and her throw, arriving by these changes at Suzy First. But notice that if we begin, in Billy Alone, with a structure consisting of the shattering together with all of its causes back to the time of Billy's throw, then we cannot possibly hold this structure fixed in intrinsic respects while morphing the situation into Suzy First. In particular, the spatio-temporal relations that the shattering bears to the events constituting the flight of Billy's rock through the air will change in crucial respects: a spatio-temporal gap will open up where formerly there was none.

That is the intuitive idea behind the way in which the Intrinsicness thesis allows us to distinguish the causal status of Suzy's throw from the status of Billy's throw, in Suzy First. It is important that its intuitive force not be obscured by the following unavoidable caveat: namely, that what matters is not merely that in morphing Billy Alone into Suzy First we are forced to make *changes* to the intrinsic character of the given event structure (for the same is true, when we change Suzy Alone into Suzy First), but that these changes must inevitably be changes in *relevant respects*. I sketch, in the next section, an account of what distinguishes relevant from irrelevant respects. For now, I want to show how the Intrinsicness thesis can be welded to a reductive analysis of causation in such a way as to enable that analysis to overcome the problem of overdetermination.

Suppose we have an analysis of causation that is *partial*, in that it issues verdicts about some situations, but simply falls silent about others. Suppose further that when it issues a verdict it never makes a mistake, and that in at least some situations it does more than merely identify the causes of a given event: in addition, it successfully identifies them as being *all* the causes. In particular, suppose that the analysis, as applied to Suzy Alone, correctly identifies all the causes of the shattering (back to the time of Suzy's throw), and correctly identifies them *as being* all the causes. But, finally, suppose the analysis falls silent about the more complicated Suzy First.

It will help to have an example, so let me quickly sketch an analysis with these features. I do not mean to argue for this analysis here (though something like it is developed and defended in Hall (2003, 2004), but only to use it for purposes of illustration).

Consider an event e, and some time t earlier than the time at which e occurs. Let the set S consist of events occurring at t. Say that S is *sufficient* for e if and only if e would still have occurred, had only the events in S occurred at t. Say that S is *minimally sufficient* for e if and only if it is sufficient for e; but no proper subset of it is. Then the analysis says that, *if* (note: not "if and only if") S is the unique set of t-events minimally sufficient for e, then the events in S are all the *causes* of e occurring at t. Observe that this analysis falls squarely within the tradition of nomological entailment accounts.

In Suzy Alone we can be sure that, at each time before the shattering, there is a unique set of events minimally sufficient for the shattering. The analysis will therefore say that the events in such sets are all causes of the shattering, and indeed that they are the *only* causes (occurring at the given time). The problem with Suzy First, of course, is that at each time before the shattering there is more than one set of events minimally sufficient for the shattering: on the one hand, there is a set containing (depending on the time) either Suzy's throw or one of the events in the flight of her rock to the window; on the other hand, there is a set containing either *Billy's* throw or one of the events in the flight of *his* rock to the window. Since the analysis only aims at providing a sufficient condition for causation—a condition that *requires* a unique minimally sufficient set—it falls silent about Suzy First. Thus, while the analysis succeeds in identifying the complete causal history of the shattering in Suzy Alone, it says nothing about Suzy First.

But *any* analysis that succeeds in this former task can automatically be extended to cover Suzy First by the addition of the Intrinsicness thesis.[14]

---

[14] Provided, that is, that the analysis is *consistent* with the Intrinsicness thesis. We'll see shortly how important this qualification is.

For it is a consequence of the analysis that, in Suzy Alone, the structure of events consisting of the shattering, together with Suzy's throw and the flight of her rock, together with the prior presence of the window itself, just *is* a shattering-blueprint: a structure consisting of the shattering together with all of its causes back to the time of Suzy's throw. Since Suzy First contains an intrinsic duplicate of this structure, it follows from the Intrinsicness thesis that in Suzy First, Suzy's throw is a cause of the shattering.

The picture is this. We started by observing that simple cases of asymmetric overdetermination threatened to block the progress of any analysis of causation that attempts to reduce causation to some kind of nomological entailment relation. We therefore retreat, attempting to come up with an analysis that *doesn't get those cases wrong*—avoiding such refutation simply by falling silent about them. We then see that as long as our analysis can get the "blueprint" cases—cases like Suzy Alone—right, then, augmented by the Intrinsicness thesis, it will automatically cover the troublesome cases of asymmetric overdetermination as well. It is in this way that the Intrinsicness thesis dissolves the threat to the project of analyzing causation posed by asymmetric overdetermination.

At least, this will be so *provided that* we can arrive at any case of asymmetric overdetermination by starting with some blueprint case, and adding details to it extrinsic to the causal process featured in it (in the way that we could arrive at Suzy First by starting with Suzy Alone). It is plausible that we will always be able to do so. After all, what marks a case of asymmetric overdetermination *as* such? Presumably, that it contains, in addition to the genuine causal processes that yield the given effect, backup processes that would have done so, had the genuine causes been absent. Working backwards, then, we can construct a blueprint for such a case simply by stripping away these idle backup processes. The only worry would be that in doing so, we might inevitably—i.e. with nomological necessity—substantially alter the intrinsic character of the structure consisting of the effect together with the genuine causal processes. But if the absence of the "idle" backup processes would *have* to make such a difference, then it is no longer clear that they are really idle: Some of them, at least, should have been counted among the genuine causes in the first place.

Before proceeding to the more destructive consequences of the Intrinsicness thesis, let us pause to consider how it lends itself to an account of *symmetric* causal overdetermination. Full discussion of this topic would take us too far afield, so I will limit myself to a single illustrative example.

Same Time: Billy and Suzy both throw rocks at a window, each with sufficient force to shatter it. The rocks strike the window at exactly the same time. The window breaks.

This kind of case puzzles us. Should Billy's throw count as a cause of the shattering? If so, then so should Suzy's; but isn't that redundant? If not, then neither should Suzy's; but doesn't that leave the shattering uncaused? Never mind. It is not our concern here to resolve these puzzles, but rather to answer a prior question: What distinguishes cases like this *as* cases of symmetric causal overdetermination—the kinds of cases that give rise to these puzzles?

The literature provides various answers, none particularly successful.[15] It has not provided the one that I think is most attractive, and that I will now sketch. Consider two ways that we could arrive at Same Time. First, we could begin with Suzy Alone and then add stuff to the environment: Billy, his throw, the flight of his rock to the window. Second, we could begin with Billy Alone and add stuff to the environment: Suzy, her throw, the flight of her rock to the window. In each case, the extrinsic additions do not alter in any relevant respect the intrinsic characteristics of the event structures we start with.[16] So it follows from the Intrinsicness thesis that in Same Time *both* Billy's and Suzy's throws are causes of the shattering. More to the point, it follows that Same Time contains within it two distinct event structures, each of which intrinsically matches some blueprint: one of these event structures matches the blueprint provided by Suzy Alone, the other the blueprint provided by Billy Alone. In this sense, then, Same Time contains within it two distinct *complete causal histories* of the shattering—where what marks an event structure as a complete causal history of some event e (back to some time t) is that, when augmented by e itself, the resulting structure intrinsically matches some e-blueprint. I suggest that in general, symmetrically overdetermined events are exactly those with multiple complete causal histories.

---

[15] For an extended argument that this is the case, see Hall (2004).

[16] Or if they do—say, by dramatically altering the manner in which the window shatters—then we should reverse our original verdict, and count Same Time a case of *joint* causation rather than a case of symmetric overdetermination.

7.2 Intrinsicness and the Counterfactual Analysis

It might seem that this *blueprint strategy* for handling asymmetric overdetermination could be pursued in any of a number of ways, by grafting the Intrinsicness thesis onto any of a number of partial analyses of causation. In particular, it might seem that it could be grafted onto a partial *counterfactual* analysis of causation. Suppose for example that one started with the simplest counterfactual analysis, but took it to provide only a sufficient condition for causation: *c* is a cause of *e* if *e* would not have occurred if *c* had not occurred. And suppose further that one could somehow add a "completeness" condition allowing one to tell, at least for sufficiently "nice" situations, that the sufficient condition has identified *all* the causes of some given event. Add the Intrinsicness thesis, and it now appears that the counterfactual analyst has a solution to the problem of overdetermination.

Not quite. We can use the Intrinsicness thesis to extend a partial analysis of causation only if that thesis is *consistent* with the analysis with which we begin. The problem for the counterfactual analyst is that Intrinsicness contradicts the claim that counterfactual dependence suffices for causation. More carefully, the combination of these two claims yields consequences so dramatically at odds with our basic intuitions about causation as to make it implausible that an analysis founded jointly upon them will have any utility.

To see why, consider a situation in which *e* depends on *c* only because *c* cancels some threat to *e*. In Figure 7 neuron **c** fires at time 0, sending an inhibitory signal to **d** that switches it off at time 1. (Lines with blobs at the end represent these inhibitory signals.) At time 2, **b** fires,

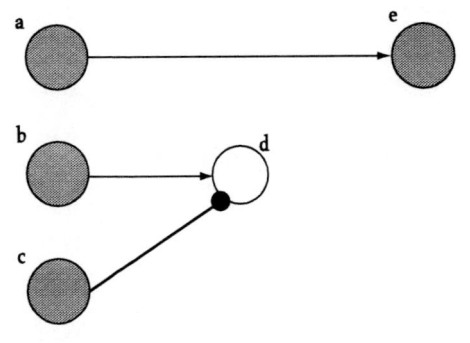

Figure 7

emitting a stimulatory signal that reaches **d** at time 3 (and that has no effect). Also at time 3, **a** fires, sending a stimulatory signal to **e** which causes it to fire at time 5. Figure 8 depicts what would have happened had **c** not fired. Here, the stimulatory signal from **b** causes **d** to fire; **d** in turn sends an inhibitory signal to **e** that reaches it at time 4, turning it off before the signal from **a** arrives. Consequently, **e** never fires.

These diagrams display as clean a case of counterfactual dependence as could be desired. In Figure 7 **c** fires; then **e** fires; but if **c** had not fired, **e** would not have fired. Suppose we conclude that *e* has among its causes *c*, along with the events making up the passage of the inhibitory signal from **c** to **d**, and the protracted event consisting in **d**'s being in a turned off state from time 1 to time 3. That is, we collect together as causes of *e* not merely *a*, together with the events making up the passage of the stimulatory signal from **a** to **e**, but also all other events upon which *e* depends. If the core thesis behind the counterfactual analysis—that counterfactual dependence suffices for causation—is correct, then the structure consisting of *e*, together with all of these events, *just is* a structure consisting of *e*, together with all of its causes back to time 0.

The problem is that this structure will be duplicated—duplicated *exactly*, down to the most microscopic detail—in a situation in which *c* is clearly not a cause of *e*, simply because there was no threat to be canceled. For suppose that **b** never fires. More dramatically, suppose that **b** simply does not exist, and that there is nothing taking its place that threatens to stimulate **d**. Then we would have the situation depicted in Figure 9: **c** fires, sending an inhibitory signal to **d**, switching it off. Meanwhile, **a** fires, sending a signal to **e**, causing it to fire.

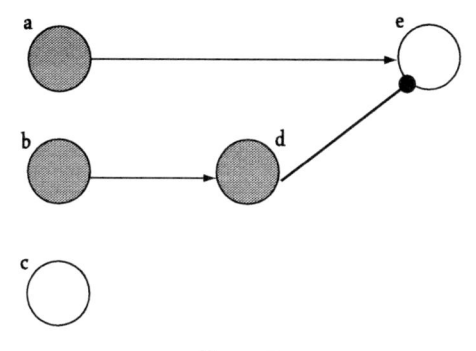

Figure 8

Here, *e* clearly does not depend on *c*. More to the point, *c* can in no sense be considered causally responsible for *e*. In Figure 7, its causal responsibility was exhausted by the fact that it canceled a threat to *e*; Figure 9, containing no threat to be canceled, does not allow *c* even that limited role.

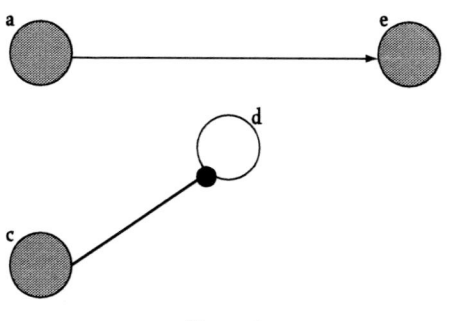

Figure 9

There is, to be sure, a sense in which *c* can be said to "safeguard" *e*; for *c* guarantees that certain threats, *were* they to materialize, *would* be canceled. Far from helping the counterfactual analyst, this point helps bring her mistake into sharper focus, for there seems little future in an approach to causation that cannot distinguish between safeguarding and causing. The crucial point is that when something threatens to prevent *e*, the threat's status *as* a threat will typically result partly from factors *extrinsic* to the causal history of *e*. Once you see the trick, it is child's play to multiply examples indefinitely. Partly just for fun, but partly also to return from the neuron world to the real world, I will provide one more.

> *Disappointed*: Suzy and Billy want to have lunch together. Suzy leaves a note pinned to her front door, telling Billy where to meet her. On his way to her house, Billy trips over a tree root. He tries, but fails, to catch himself in time. He falls over. He bumps his head, and is knocked cold. He never reaches Suzy's house, and so never sees the note. Later, Suzy, waiting at the restaurant, becomes disappointed.

Let *e* be the onset of Suzy's disappointment. Let *c* be Billy's trip. We have the right pattern of dependence: if Billy had not tripped, Suzy would not have become disappointed (because Billy would have made it to her house, seen the note, met her at the restaurant on time, etc.). According to any of a large number of counterfactual analyses, c is therefore a cause of e. Now compare

> *No Note*: Suzy and Billy want to have lunch together. But Suzy forgets to leave a note pinned to her front door, telling Billy where to meet her. On his way to her house, Billy trips over a tree root. He tries, but fails, to catch himself in time. He falls over. He bumps his head, and is knocked cold. Again, he never reaches Suzy's house. Later, Suzy, waiting at the restaurant, becomes disappointed.

No Note exhibits both a failure of dependence and a failure of causation: for if Billy had not tripped, he would have arrived at Suzy's house, seen no note, and gone back home in confusion; hence Suzy would have been disappointed all the same. It would therefore be absurd to count the trip a cause of Suzy's disappointment. But then the same verdict must hold for Disappointed, if the Intrinsicness thesis is correct. For the only intrinsic difference between the two situations concerns the disposition of the note—and this is a difference that on *any* sane view is extrinsic to the causal history of e, in Disappointed. In that situation, e has a no doubt complex causal history involving various psychological and perceptual episodes, as well as a number of other events that our story has left unspecified; if the counterfactual analyst is right, it also has among its causes Billy's trip. But even she will agree that it does not have among its causes the presence of Suzy's note on her front door. And so all should agree that, whatever the causal history of e is, in Disappointed that causal history is duplicated *exactly* in No Note. The Intrinsicness thesis then yields the conclusion that, if c is a cause of e in Disappointed, so too is it a cause of e in No Note. The false consequent shows again how Intrinsicness conflicts with the thesis that counterfactual dependence suffices for causation.[17]

Why not blame Intrinsicness? After all, the idea that threat-cancelers such as Billy's trip are causes is not unattractive, at least to some. (See Schaffer 2000b for a spirited and skillful defense of this view.) Perhaps

---

[17] It is perhaps worth mentioning that the provisional analysis of causation sketched above can be developed in a way that makes it clear that it does *not* conflict with Intrinsicness. See Hall (2004) for discussion.

cases of threat-canceling simply reveal a curious way in which the causal structure of a process can fail to be intrinsic to it. (Lewis 2003 makes exactly this claim.) I think this position is defensible but unattractive—in part because of the clear intuitive appeal of Intrinsicness, but more importantly because rejecting this thesis seems likely to render the problem of overdetermination intractable. At the very least, those who want to defend the claim that counterfactual dependence suffices for causation should recognize that they thereby render the problem of overdetermination vastly more difficult.

7.3 *Intrinsicness* and causation by omission

We can obtain very similar results about causation by omission. Now, in order even to consider how to apply the Intrinsicness thesis to cases of causation by omission, we must take up an awkward question, which is whether to treat omissions as a kind of event, or instead to take reference to them as a mere manner of speaking, capable, perhaps, of being paraphrased away. In order to streamline discussion, I will simply take the first option (although it turns out not to matter: see Hall 2004 for discussion).

So we will assume that omissions are genuine events, just like kisses, collisions, and conversations. Well, not *just* like these other events, of course, for it is presumably of the essence of omissions that they "happen" just in case no *ordinary* event of some appropriately specified type happens.[18] Suppose, for example, that in Figure 10 b never fires. Then we might wish to credit its non-firing—the omission of its firing—as a cause of *e*, since, if it *had* fired (within an appropriate time interval), e would not have fired (Figure 11).

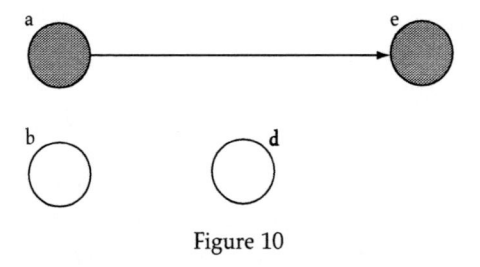

Figure 10

---

[18] Very occasionally, ordinary language obscures this point, as when I say, "Oops—I failed to leave the lights on", meaning of course not that some ordinary kind of event failed to happen, but rather that an ordinary event of the switch-flipping kind *did* happen.

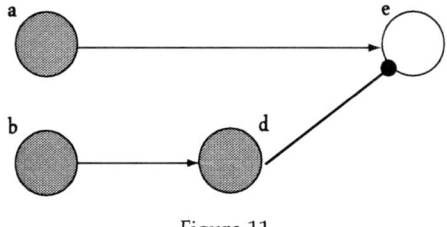

Figure 11

A problem now emerges that stands in the way of straightforwardly applying the Intrinsicness thesis to the events depicted in Figure 10. Suppose we wish to collect together, into one event structure S, *e* together with all of its causes back to the time of **a**'s firing. Suppose further that we wish to include among these causes **b**'s failure to fire (along with other omissions, presumably). Our problem is to figure out exactly what contribution this omission makes to the intrinsic character of S. For an ordinary event this problem is easy to solve. We first locate the event, then figure out which particulars it involves, then figure out which properties they exemplify during the event's occurrence, singling out for attention those properties whose combined exemplification constitutes the given event. But how are we to execute this procedure, in the case of **b**'s failure to fire? Where, to begin with, should we locate this "event"? We might say that the omission is located where **b** is, during the relevant time interval. But the arbitrary nature of this answer becomes clear once we notice that **b**'s failure to fire can "occur" even if **b** does not exist. Suppose, for example, that shortly before time 0 something destroys **b**. We would still want to say that **b**'s failure to fire between time 0 and time 1 was a cause of *e*. (That is, if we should ever countenance a case of causation by omission, we should countenance this one.) But without **b** to serve as a peg on which to hang this omission, where are we to locate it?

Never mind. Suppose that we somehow solve this location problem. We still have not answered our original question: what does **b**'s failure to fire add to the intrinsic character of the event structure S? One defensible answer would be: nothing. For, even if we agree to treat omissions as a species of genuine event, an excellent reason for sharply distinguishing them from kisses, collisions, and conversations is that, unlike these ordinary events, they lack intrinsic natures. If so, then the intrinsic character of S is exhausted by the intrinsic character of the ordinary events that make it up, together with the spatio-temporal relations among them.

Still, one could fairly defend a different answer. One could insist, for example, that, once we have located b's failure to fire as occurring throughout the spatio-temporal region R, we can specify the contribution that this omission makes to the intrinsic character of S as consisting in those intrinsic properties of R in virtue of which it contains no firing of b (together with the spatio-temporal relations region R bears to the other parts of S). This maneuver would guarantee that including b's failure to fire as part of S makes a genuine difference to the intrinsic character of S, and so makes a difference to whether some alternative situation contains an event structure intrinsically matching S. Let us henceforth assume that this is how omissions contribute to the intrinsic character of event structures containing them.

Consider Figure 10 again. It provides a canonical example of causation by omission. And now consider the situation depicted in Figure 12, where neuron d is absent, and so not available to be stimulated by b, and so not available to send an inhibitory signal to e. Here b's failure to fire is causally irrelevant to e. But on the proposal under consideration, the event structure S drawn from Figure 10, and taken to *include* b's failure to fire, will have in Figure 12 a perfect intrinsic duplicate. So, if we try to extend the Intrinsicness thesis to cover the kind of causation by omission exhibited in Figure 10, we get the incorrect result that in Figure 12 b's failure to fire is (still) a cause of e. More generally, we get the result that, when the occurrence of an event of some type merely *could*—if circumstances had permitted—have been a threat to some outcome e, then the failure of an event of that type to occur causes e.

Notice the parallel with the discussion of threat-canceling: just as those who say that threat-cancelers are causes are forced, if they endorse the Intrinsicness thesis, to the absurd conclusion that events that

Figure 12

"cancel" *non*-threats are nevertheless sometimes causes in virtue of doing so, so too are those who say that omitted threats are causes forced to say that omitted *non*-threats are sometimes causes as well. The fundamental reason is exactly the same in each case: the status of a threat *as such* often depends crucially on facts extrinsic to the causal history of the event being threatened.

I have stated these conclusions in an overly hard-nosed manner. If the Intrinsicness thesis is correct, then counterfactual dependence does not suffice for causation, and there is no causation by omission (i.e., situations that should provide examples of causation by omission, if *any* do, in fact fail to do so). I do not in fact believe these conclusions, so stated. That is because I think we should take seriously a third option, according to which there are different kinds of causal relation, one of which I call "production" and which is characterized (in part) by Intrinsicness, and another of which can be identified with counterfactual dependence.[19] Cases of overdetermination exhibit production without dependence; cases of threat-canceling and causation by omission, dependence without production. I think a reductionist about causation should find this sort of causal pluralism entirely unremarkable. At any rate, if such a position is correct, then the key conclusion of this section needs a slight modification: counterfactual dependence may suffice for one kind of causation (which kind includes, I suppose, causation by omission), but if Intrinsicness is correct then it cannot suffice for all. In particular, it cannot suffice for the kind of causation exhibited by Suzy's throw in Suzy First. It is perhaps worth noting in passing that if this last claim is correct, then there is little interest in developing a counterfactual analysis of causation: for if dependence is the target then this is too easy, whereas if causation in all of its varieties is the target then it is impossible.

8. RELEVANT SIMILARITY

Let me turn to the need for a refinement in the statement of the Intrinsicness thesis—a refinement hidden up to now in the claim that intrinsic match *in relevant respects* is what makes for similarity in causal characteristics.

[19] More or less. There are complications, explored in detail in Hall (2004).

8.1 Need for the qualification

Why must Intrinsicness include this qualification? Because of the way we have used it to solve the problem of overdetermination. Recall the contrasting cases Suzy Alone, Billy Alone, and Suzy First. Suzy Alone and Billy Alone each contain a shattering-blueprint. We would like to say that Suzy's throw, in Suzy First, is a cause of the shattering because it belongs to an event structure that intrinsically matches the shattering-blueprint in Suzy Alone. But "matches" cannot mean "perfectly duplicates", since Billy's rock causes gravitational effects that perturb the trajectory of Suzy's rock ever so slightly—and "ever so slightly" is quite enough to destroy perfect duplication. On the other hand, we cannot make due with mere intrinsic similarity, since *Billy's* throw, in Suzy First, belongs to an event structure that is intrinsically similar to the shattering-blueprint in Billy Alone, but cannot thereby qualify as a cause of the shattering. So we need it to turn out that this latter event structure is not intrinsically similar *in relevant respects* to the shattering-blueprint in Billy Alone, whereas the event structure containing Suzy's throw *is* intrinsically similar in relevant respects to the shattering-blueprint in Suzy Alone.

It would be disappointing if we could say nothing about what makes for similarity in relevant respects; for many, leaving this notion unexplained would give the Intrinsicness thesis a "whatever it takes" cast that would smack of triviality. That is not our situation, as I will shortly explain. But before doing so, observe that even if we were not able to—even if the explanation I offer fails disastrously—the charge of triviality would be inappropriate. For a weaker version of Intrinsicness—one that requires perfect intrinsic duplication rather than intrinsic similarity in relevant respects—is manifestly strong enough to secure the conclusions reached in the last section concerning threat-canceling and causation by omission. That's enough to show that Intrinsicness is non-trivial. (Of course, it's another question whether the weaker version would be worth defending without the stronger: one reason to think not is that the weaker version is *too* weak to support a solution to the preemption problem.[20])

I will now present what I think is a promising and intuitive strategy for elucidating the notion of "relevant respects".

---

[20] Thanks, here, to Jonathan Schaffer.

8.2 Relevant similarity defined

Here is the key idea: Suppose we have some e-blueprint S, and some other event structure S′ that is intrinsically similar to S. Such intrinsic similarity provides prima facie grounds for the claim that S′ has the same causal structure as S; more exactly, for the claim that, whenever c in S is a cause of e, then c' in S′ is likewise a cause of e'. But these prima facie grounds can be overridden: in particular if the intrinsic similarity between S and S′ does not extend to those intrinsic characteristics of S *that matter to its having the causal structure it does*. It is exactly those characteristics that pick out the *relevant* respects of similarity. What remains is to provide some means for drawing them out. I will use our familiar cases to show how.

Begin by focusing on Suzy Alone. Suzy, unattended by Billy or anyone else, throws a rock at the window, breaking it. Imagine ringing very slight changes on this situation—not by adding anything to or subtracting anything from the environment, but by changing, in tiny ways, the intrinsic characteristics of the event structure S that consists of the shattering together with all of its causes back to the time of Suzy's throw. For example, we might change the exact angle of Suzy's throw, or the exact force that she imparts to the rock, or the mass of the rock, or the angular velocity it has during its flight, or its shape, or some of the details of its chemical composition, etc. Again, we might change the exact size of the window, or its thickness, or its internal chemical structure, or its color, etc. Or we might change several of these details at once. And now let us add two constraints: that in making these changes we stay within the realm of nomological possibility, and that we leave causal structure invariant. That is, we require first that no change lead us to a situation that violates the fundamental laws at work in Suzy Alone; and we require second that the result S′ of making slight intrinsic modifications to S have exactly the same causal structure as S.

The second requirement carries presuppositions that deserve to be brought out explicitly. I will take it that, in order for S and S′ to count as having the same causal structure, there must be some non-arbitrary way of imposing a one–one map from the parts of one to the parts of the other, such that c and e in S stand in some causal relation iff the corresponding events c' and e' in S′ stand in that causal relation as well. What will make such a mapping non-arbitrary is for corresponding events to be reasonably intrinsically similar, and for them to occupy similar positions within their respective event structures. When such a non-arbitrary map exists, it need not be *unique*. Suppose for example that we modify our event structure S—the one drawn from Suzy Alone—by having Suzy throw slightly more forcefully, thereby shortening the duration of her rock's flight. Then there will evidently be more than one way to non-arbitrarily match up the events constituting the slightly quicker flight of her rock in S' with the events constituting the slightly slower flight of her rock in S. No matter. What we need to require is simply that on any such way of non-arbitrarily imposing a one–one map from the events in S to the events in S', the two event structures will come out isomorphic with respect to their causal characteristics.

What we have done is to focus attention on all the nomologically possible ways of ringing slight changes on the intrinsic characteristics of S *that make no difference to its causal structure*. Quite obviously, there will be an indescribably large number of ways of doing so. Collect together their results into a set of nomologically possible alternatives to S; call this set the "blueprint-class" for S. There will be certain respects of similarity that all of the members of this blueprint-class share. In fact, these members will be intrinsically similar to one another, *except* in those respects that do not matter to their (shared) causal structure. So: they will be intrinsically similar to one another only in respects that *do* matter to their causal structure. So: for some event structure S' to be similar to S "in relevant respects" is just for it to be intrinsically similar to S in those respect in which S and other members of its blueprint-class are similar to one another.[21]

Let us apply this formula to our familiar cases. Start by letting S be the shattering-blueprint in Suzy Alone, and S' the event structure in Suzy First consisting of Suzy's throw, the flight of her rock, the shattering, and the prior presence of the window—i.e. the event structure

---

[21] Certain constraints on the notion of a "respect of similarity" need to be in place, else this account of relevant similarity is a non-starter. Suppose the blueprint-class for S contains the event structures S_1, S_2,.... Then consider the highly disjunctive intrinsic property picked out by the predicate "perfectly duplicates S_1 or perfectly duplicates S_2 or..." If sharing of this intrinsic property counts as a genuine respect of similarity, then, obviously, the only event structures that will be similar to S in all those respects in which S and other members of its blueprint-class are similar to one another will be members of this blueprint-class. That won't do. So we evidently need to require that genuine respects of similarity correspond to not-too-disjunctive intrinsic properties. Happily, our ordinary notion of "respect of similarity" quite clearly meets this requirement.

most intrinsically similar to S. Again, S' will not perfectly duplicate S, thanks to the perturbing presence of Billy's rock. But the slight intrinsic differences between S' and S will not be differences in any respect in which S and other members of its blueprint-class are similar to one another. Hence S' will, by Intrinsicness, have the same causal structure as S; hence Suzy's throw in Suzy First counts as a cause of the shattering.

Now let S be the shattering-blueprint in Billy Alone, and S' the event structure in Suzy First consisting of Billy's throw, the flight of his rock, the shattering, and the prior presence of the window—i.e. the event structure most intrinsically similar to S. As before, S' will not perfectly duplicate S. But this time, at least one of the intrinsic differences between S' and S *will* be a difference in a respect in which S and all other members of its blueprint-class are similar to one another. For it is true of every event structure in this blueprint-class that the rock strikes the window, whereas this is not true of S'. So S' does not count as intrinsically similar to S in relevant respects, and so Intrinsicness does not yield the conclusion that Billy's throw is a cause of the shattering.

8.3 Causal efficacy

Let us pause for a brief digression. The ideas that led to an account of "relevant similarity" also give content to at least one notion of "causal efficacy". Let me point to the notion I have in mind by focusing on Suzy's throw in Suzy Alone. Intuitively, certain aspects of this throw matter to its status as a cause of the shattering, and certain other aspects do not. For example, it is important that the velocity her throw imparts to the rock is above some critical threshold, else the rock will not reach the window; likewise, it is important that the mass of the rock be above some threshold, else it will bounce harmlessly off the window. By contrast, the exact position of Suzy's pinky finger is not important, nor is the color of the rock. How shall we draw this distinction between *efficacious* and *inefficacious* aspects of Suzy's throw?

Here is an attractive way to do so. As before, let S be the shattering-blueprint in Suzy Alone, and construct its blueprint-class. Consider just those members of the blueprint-class that differ with respect to Suzy's throw, but *not* with respect to the intrinsic characteristics of the causes of the shattering that are contemporaneous with Suzy's throw. Equivalently, begin with S, and ring slight changes *only* on Suzy's throw (making necessary adjustments down the line to ensure nomological possibility); leave other factors such as the constitution of the window fixed. (Why hold these other factors fixed? Because if, for example, we weaken the window, then the momentum the rock needs to have in order to break it decreases, leading us to underestimate the causally relevant threshold value for this momentum.) The resulting subset of the blueprint-class for S picks out those intrinsic features of the throw that are efficacious: a feature is efficacious iff it is shared by the throws in each member of this subset.[22] For example, ringing changes on the *color* of Suzy's rock will result in a nomologically possible shattering-blueprint that is causally isomorphic to S; ringing (sufficient) changes on its *mass* will not.

It was important that we considered the pared-down situation provided by Suzy Alone, in carrying out this test for efficacy. For if we add stuff to the environment—even stuff that is, in fact, causally idle—the test fails. Consider:

> *Testy Demon*: This case is just like Suzy Alone, save that a Demon is standing by, set on blocking Suzy's throw if (but only if) her rock is *red*. In fact, her rock is blue, and the Demon does nothing.

In Testy Demon, is the color of Suzy's rock—more exactly, its property of not being red—efficacious with respect to the shattering? Perhaps yes, in *some* sense; but there also seems a clear sense (the one I am trying to elucidate here) in which it is not: as before, it seems that all that matters about the throw are the mass of the rock, the angle and velocity imparted to it, etc. But the foregoing test does not yield this result. Change the color of the rock to red, while holding other contemporaneous factors fixed, and one does not arrive at a nomologically possible shattering-blueprint.

My tentative suggestion is that we treat causal efficacy in general as parasitic on causal efficacy, as exhibited in pared-down situations like Suzy Alone. Suppose we have some event c, and one of its effects e. To determine which aspects of c are efficacious with respect to its status as a cause of e, we should proceed by (i) identifying some e-blueprint S that contains c as one of its initial constituents (i.e., c is part of S, and no event earlier than c is part of S); (ii) identifying some (possibly distinct)

---

[22] As before, we should restrict attention to not-too-disjunctive intrinsic features; see n. 21.

event structure S′ that intrinsically matches S in relevant respects, and that exists in "pared down" circumstances containing no back-up processes whose initiation is sensitive to the manner of occurrence of c'; (iii) identifying the efficacious aspects of c' according to the foregoing test. We can then take the efficacious aspects of c to be exactly the same as the efficacious aspects of c'.[23]

9. A POTENTIAL COUNTER-EXAMPLE, AND SOME LESSONS

Trouble for the Intrinsicness thesis comes in the form of a kind of example that appears to draw forth firm intuitions clearly at odds with that thesis.[24] This section presents the example (due to Steve Yablo), along with a diagnosis that goes some way toward preserving Intrinsicness in the face of it. The diagnosis will suggest some deeper lessons about the way in which Intrinsicness functions to structure at least one of our central causal concepts.

9.1 The example

Here is the case, which we imagine to take place in a Magic world, in which wizards regularly cast spells. (We'll see shortly that it's a mere convenience to rely on "magic".)

---

[23] It may have been noticed that my account of the intrinsic character of causation makes no provision for perfectly coincident events that (i) are numerically distinct, because they differ in which of their categorical properties are *essential* to them; and (ii) have different causes and effects (see e.g. Lewis 1986c and Yablo 1992). For example, when I shut a door by slamming it, some would have us distinguish two closings of the door: one that is *essentially* a slamming, and one that is only *accidentally* a slamming. Those who draw such distinctions will typically want to go on to distinguish the causes and effects of such perfectly coincident events. As stated, Intrinsicness rules out such causal distinctions, since any event structure containing one of a pair of perfectly coincident events will have a perfect duplicate that contains the other. One could, perhaps, modify Intrinsicness to allow for causal distinctions between perfectly coincident events, but I think a much better course is to argue that any philosophical work to be done by such distinctions can be better carried out by a careful analysis of causal efficacy, perhaps along the lines sketched in this subsection. I explore this issue in much more detail in Hall (2004).

[24] I bypass here discussion of other alleged counterexamples, e.g. the "trumping" cases considered by Schaffer (2000a), and the "switching" cases examined in Hall (2000). By contrast with the kind of case considered in the text, none of these cases strike me as particularly rich in probative value. But for full discussion of these and other examples, see Hall and Paul (2002), and Hall (2004).

Meddling Wizards: Suzy throws a rock at a bottle. Two wizards, Merlin and Morgan, are standing by. Morgan casts a spell to make her rock disappear in mid-flight. Merlin casts a spell to make a rock appear, flying towards the bottle. It so happens that the two spells dovetail so perfectly in their effects that the instant Suzy's rock disappears, its place is taken by Merlin's rock. What's more, Merlin's rock is intrinsically just like Suzy's, and flies towards the bottle in just the way Suzy's would have, had it not disappeared. The bottle shatters.

It seems perfectly clear that, in Meddling Wizards, Suzy's throw is *not* a cause of the shattering. But now consider a variant, in which the two wizards are absent, Suzy throws in exactly the same way, and the bottle shatters. That variant contains a shattering-blueprint S that is, we are supposing, duplicated *exactly*, down to the most minute detail, in Meddling Wizards (for that is how perfectly the two spells dovetail). By <u>Intrinsicness</u>, then, Suzy's throw in Meddling Wizards should be a cause of the shattering.[25]

If we are careful about how to describe the laws in this world, we will see that we need to consider a quite different causal gloss that could be put on the example—one that is in fact consistent with the verdict that Suzy's throw causes the shattering. For it is possible that the causally loaded locutions with which we described Morgan's and Merlin's spells illegitimately prompted the troublesome intuitions about the case. So suppose that, as is appropriate, we describe the spells in non-causal terms, by simply specifying what events must (given the laws) take place, consequent upon their casting. Presumably, the right such "non-loaded" description is as follows. (i) In a situation in which neither spell is cast, the rock follows a certain trajectory T. (ii) In a situation where Morgan's but not Merlin's spell is cast, the rock vanishes at a certain point in its trajectory. (iii) In a situation where Merlin's spell is cast, the rock follows trajectory T (regardless of whether Morgan's spell is cast). We could put (iii) more cagily, thus: in a situation where Merlin's spell is cast, a certain trajectory-shaped region of space–time is rock-filled. It

---

[25] One might worry that the shattering-blueprint is *not* duplicated exactly, since Merlin's rock is not (numerically) the same as Suzy's. That is a red herring: just rewrite the example so that it doesn't involve a persisting object like the rock, but rather some other sort of process. For example, let Suzy light a fuse, Morgan cast a spell to snuff out the traveling spark, and Merlin cast a spell to reignite it.

is now not so perfectly clear what the causal structure of Meddling Wizards is. In particular, it is not clear why we should reject the following gloss: the effect of Merlin's spell is merely to *neutralize* Morgan's spell. And that is a gloss which preserves Suzy's throw as a cause of the shattering.

In the end, I do not think this gloss is appropriate; I think rather that the original verdict stands. But it is exceedingly useful to ask *why* it is inappropriate. Do not say: because it is sheer coincidence that Morgan's and Merlin's spells dovetail in the way that they do. For that is a feature of the case that is easily erased: let God have ordained, since the dawn of time, that the two wizards cast their spells just so. Do not say: because the shattering counterfactually depends on Merlin's spell, and not on Suzy's throw. For again, that is a feature easily erased, by addition of suitable extrinsic details (e.g. in the form of an even more powerful wizard who will act so as to guarantee that the shattering occurs in just the manner it does, should Suzy, Morgan, and Merlin collectively fail to do so). And do not say: because if Suzy had thrown, say, a watermelon, then it would still have been a rock that shattered the window (so that there is no counterfactual covariation of the manner of the shattering with the manner of her throw). For it's easy to *introduce* such covariation in a way that does not alter our intuitions about the case (e.g. let the more powerful wizard stand ready to intercede, if Merlin fails to produce an object perfectly matching whatever Suzy threw). But do not, finally, dismiss the case as having nothing to teach us. On the contrary: there is a natural explanation for the strength—even in the face of the alternative gloss—of the intuitive judgment that Suzy's throw is not a cause of the shattering.

To see what this natural explanation is, it will help to represent Meddling Wizards abstractly, using our handy neuron diagrams. In Figure 13 neurons **a** (Morgan), **b** (Suzy), and **c** (Merlin) fire simultaneously, at time 0; their signals reach **e** at time 1; an instant later, **e** fires. Let the laws dictate that (i) **e** will always fire upon receiving a signal from **c**; (ii) if **c** does not fire, then **e** will fire upon receiving a signal from **b**, provided it does not also receive, simultaneously, a signal from **a**; (iii) **e** will not fire unless it receives a signal from at least one of **b** and **c**.

It appears that we could describe the events depicted in Figure 13 in either of two ways. On the one hand, we could say that *c* alone causes *e*, while *b* is not also a (symmetrically overdetermining) cause because of the inhibiting signal from **a**. On the other hand, we could say that

The Intrinsic Character of Causation | 295

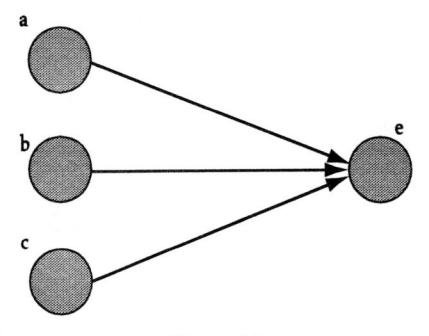

Figure 13

the signal from **c** helps bring about *e* only by neutralizing the inhibitory signal from **a**, thus allowing the signal from **b** to do its work. What considerations can we adduce that would favor one description over the other?

9.2 The intrinsic character of prevention

The crucial consideration is brought out by Figure 14. As before, **a** and **b** fire at time 0, sending signals that reach **e** at time 1; but because no signal from **c** reaches **e**, **e** fails to fire an instant later. So the signal from **a** prevents **e** from firing. But there is a second, distinct kind of preventative relationship that these events manifest as well: the signal from **a** prevents the signal from **b** from causing **e** to fire. I claim that this second relationship is intrinsic to the event structure that manifests it. That is, consider the event structure S consisting of (i) the firing of **a**, together

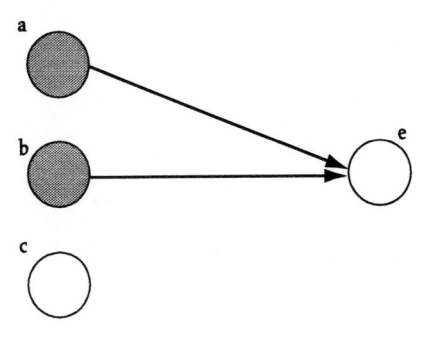

Figure 14

with the passage of its signal to **e**; (ii) the firing of **b**, together with the passage of *its* signal to **e**; (iii) the presence of neuron **e** from time 0 to time 1. It is *not* a fact intrinsic to S that **e** fails to fire an instant after time 1; hence it is not a fact intrinsic to S that the signal from **a** prevents **e** from firing (since **a** prevents **e** from firing only if **e** does not fire). But the claim that the signal from **a** prevents the signal from **b** from causing **e** to fire does not entail the claim that **e** fails to fire an instant after time 1. So it is tenable to suppose that the fact that the signal from **a** prevents the signal from **b** from causing **e** to fire *is* intrinsic to S. I propose—with a slight qualification shortly to come—that it is not merely tenable, but true.

A full defense and elaboration of this proposal belongs elsewhere. Suppose this work done, so that we have available to us an upgraded version of Intrinsicness that applies not just to causation but to prevention (in the way indicated in the last paragraph). Let us see how to apply it to the analysis of Figure 13. Observe that Figure 13 depicts, among other things, a perfect intrinsic duplicate of S. In addition, it contains a perfect duplicate of the *e*-blueprint exhibited in Figure 15. Making use of the Intrinsicness thesis, we should therefore conclude that, in Figure 13, (i) the signal from **a** prevents the signal from **b** from causing **e** to fire (thanks to the match between Figures 13 and 14); and (ii) the signal from **c** causes **e** to fire (thanks to the match between Figures 13 and 15). But, given (i), it cannot *also* be that the signal from **b** is a cause of *e*. So *c* is the *sole* cause of *e*.

A problem remains. What we have done is to take note of certain causal structures in Figures 14 and 15, and to make use of Intrinsicness to project these causal structures into Figure 13. But why is it not just as

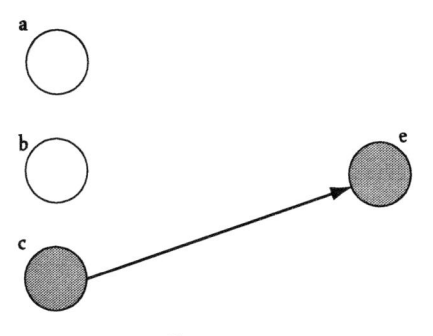

Figure 15

a
○

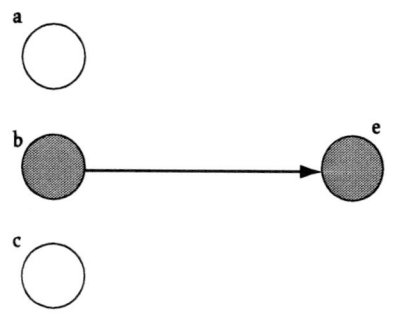

b ● ⟶ ● e

c ○

Figure 16

legitimate to take note of the causal structure in Figure 16, and use Intrinsicness to project *it* into Figure 13? We know that we cannot project both, on pain of inconsistency. But what favors projecting the instance of prevention, as opposed to the instance of causation?

A proper answer needs to weigh the costs of each alternative. On the one hand, if we project the causal structures in Figures 14 and 15, then we must say, *contra* Intrinsicness, that, even though Figure 13 contains a perfect duplicate of the e-blueprint found in Figure 16, b is not a cause of e. On the other hand, if we insist that b *is* a cause of e, then we must say—also *contra* Intrinsicness (as modified to accommodate prevention)—that, even though Figure 13 contains a perfect duplicate of the prevention-blueprint in Figure 14, a does not prevent b from causing e. So far the score is even. But there is an *extra* cost to this latter alternative. For taking it *also* requires us to assign to c, in Figure 13, a novel causal role: namely, that of "neutralizing" the inhibitory signal from **a**. That doing so is inappropriately *ad hoc* emerges when we observe that there are no *other* circumstances, qualitatively distinct from those exhibited in Figure 13, that would attest to such a role. Thus the balance tips in favor of the first alternative.

9.3 Intrinsicness and the function of our causal concepts

The picture we arrive at is this: causation—or, at least, one important kind of causal relation—is governed by the Intrinsicness thesis. But it is governed loosely, in that conflicts can arise *from that thesis itself*: very occasionally, Intrinsicness will offer contradictory advice about what causal structure to assign to some sequence of events. Resolving such conflicts requires appealing to higher principles, principles that will pick out the particular bit of advice that should be heeded. The argument of the last paragraph tacitly appealed to such principles—without, to be sure, articulating them at all explicitly. What, then, are these principles, and what grounds them?

I must leave these as open questions. But not without suggesting what seems to me an attractive line of investigation. Consider that reductionists like me—philosophers, that is, who hold that the *fundamental* causal structure of the world is given by what happens (what the complete physical state is, at each moment of time), together with the fundamental laws that govern what happens—face an excellent question: why, by our lights, should there be any *need* for a concept of a causal relation that applies to anything less grand than a complete physical state? A promising answer is that, given our relatively impoverished epistemic circumstances, such a concept can play the crucial role of allowing us to capture—in a manner that is both approximate and piecemeal but, above all, *manageable*—facts about the fundamental causal structure of the world.

Think of the matter this way. As we amass more and more facts of the form "*c* caused *e*", "*a* prevented *e*", "*a* prevented *c* from causing *e*", etc., we build up, bit by bit, a better and better picture not just of what happens in our world, but of what the fundamental laws are that govern what happens. I suggest that, in order for our causal concept to best play this role, it should be governed by something like the Intrinsicness thesis; for then we will be able to use it to delimit the causal features of novel situations, by discerning in them already-familiar patterns in the form of event structures intrinsically similar, in relevant respects, to ones whose causal characteristics we have antecedently settled. Put another way, we want a concept of causation that will allow us to describe the nomological shape of the world as efficiently and clearly as possible in terms of *repeatable causal structures*. Given that aim, it makes exceedingly good sense to employ a concept governed by Intrinsicness. For without it it seems that, whenever we encountered some slightly novel situation, differing in some small respect from those with which we are familiar, we would not be entitled to use our experience of similar situations to make even a provisional guess as to its causal structure. Rather, we should have to start afresh. Imagine, in this regard, being familiar with innumerable cases like Suzy Alone, and then encountering Suzy First: is it really plausible that we would start afresh *here*, simply *ignoring* the deep intrinsic similarities between this new case and the old ones? If so, then surely—given its *counterfactual* structure—our first guess as to the *causal* structure of Suzy First should be that it is a case of symmetric overdetermination. Nobody, but *nobody*, makes *that* mistake.

When, finally, we face one of those rare occasions where this thesis endorses contradictory descriptions, we should settle on the one that best fits our overarching aims. In the case of Figure 13, we violate these aims if we assimilate its causal structure to that of Figure 16. For in doing so we are forced to introduce a causal structure (the "neutralization" of the a-signal by c) that is not only novel, but *unrepeatable*, outside of circumstances exactly like those of Figure 13. Assimilating the structure of Figure 13 to that of Figures 14 and 15, by contrast, carries no such cost.

Massachusetts Institute of Technology

REFERENCES

Collins, John, N. Hall, and L. A. Paul (eds.) (2003) *Causation and Counterfactuals*, Cambridge: MIT Press, forthcoming.

Dowe, Phil (1992) "Wesley Salmon's Process Theory of Causality and the Conserved Quantity Theory", *Philosophy of Science*, 59: 195–216.

Ehring, Douglas (1997) *Causation and Persistence*, Oxford University Press.

Fair, David (1979) "Causation and the Flow of Energy", *Erkenntnis*, 14: 219–50.

Hall, Ned (2000) "Causation and the Price of Transitivity", *Journal of Philosophy*, 97: 198–222.

Hall, Ned (2003) "Two Concepts of Causation", in Collins *et al.* (2003), forthcoming.

Hall, Ned (2004) *Causation*, Oxford University Press, forthcoming.

Hall, Ned and L. A. Paul (2002) "Causation and the Counterexamples: A Traveler's Guide", Unpublished MS.

Lewis, David (1986a) *Philosophical Papers*, vol. II, Oxford University Press.

Lewis, David (1986b) "Causation", with "Postscripts", in Lewis (1986a): 159–213; originally published in *Journal of Philosophy*, 70 (1973): 556–67.

Lewis, David (1986c) "Events", in Lewis (1986a), pp. 241–69.

Lewis, David (2003) "Causation as Influence", in Collins *et al.* (2003), forthcoming.

Mackie, J. L. (1965) "Causes and Conditions", *American Philosophical Quarterly*, 2: 245–64.

Maudlin, Tim (1996) "A Modest Proposal Concerning Laws, Counterfactuals, and Explanation", Unpublished MS.

Menzies, Peter (1999) "Intrinsic versus Extrinsic Conceptions of Causation", in Sankey. (1999).

Salmon, Wesley (1994) "Causality without Counterfactuals", *Philosophy of Science*, 61: 297–312.

Sankey, Howard (ed.) (1999) *Causation and Laws of Nature*, Boston, MA: Kluwer.

Schaffer, Jonathan (2000*a*) "Trumping Preemption", *Journal of Philosophy*, 97: 165–81.

Schaffer, Jonathan (2000*b*) "Causation By Disconnection", *Philosophy of Science*, 67: 285–300.

Schaffer, Jonathan (2003) "Is There a Fundamental Level?" *NOUS*, forthcoming.

Tooley, Michael (1990) "Causation: Reductionism versus Realism", *Philosophy and Phenomenological Research*, 50 (Supplement): 215–36.

Yablo, S. (1992) "Cause and Essence", *Synthese*, 93: 403–49.

11. Recombination, Causal Constraints and Humean Supervenience: An Argument for Temporal Parts?

Ryan Wasserman, John Hawthorne, and Mark Scala

According to the doctrine of four-dimensionalism, our world and everything in it consists of *stages* or *temporal parts*; moreover, where an object exists at various times, it does so, according to the four-dimensionalist, in virtue of having distinct temporal parts at those times. While four-dimensionalism is often motivated by its purported solutions to puzzles about material objects and their persistence through time, it has also been defended by more direct arguments. Three such arguments stand out: (1) the argument from temporary intrinsics, (2) the argument from vagueness, and (3) the argument from recombination, Humean supervenience, and causal constraints. Not surprisingly, each of these arguments originates in the work of four-dimensionalism's most prominent modern defender, David Lewis.[1] The third of these arguments has received, by far, the least attention, critical or otherwise; it is now time to begin to address this imbalance.[2]

Thanks to Tamar Szabo Gendler, Ted Sider, and Dean Zimmerman for helpful discussion and for comments on earlier drafts of this paper.

[1] For Lewis's formulation of the argument from temporary intrinsics, see Lewis (1986a, pp. 202–5). Theodore Sider develops the argument from vagueness (1997, pp. 197–231). Sider's argument is an extension of the argument for unrestricted composition that is presented in Lewis (1986a, pp. 212–13). Finally, for the argument from recombination, causal constraints, and Humean supervenience, see Lewis (1983, pp. 73–7).

[2] Harold Noonan's recent commentary offers a striking endorsement of this argument. As he sees it, the three-dimensionalist will have to resist by rejecting the supervenience thesis underpinning the move from four to five. But Noonan claims, "Apart from the incompatibility with three-dimensionalism that Lewis's argument exposes, [it] seems philosophically uncontentious" (Noonan 2001, p. 128). As will become clear, this evaluation is somewhat misguided.

The argument in question makes its first appearance in Lewis's *"Postscripts to* 'Survival and Identity' ". Here is the bulk of the argument, as presented by Lewis:

First: it is possible that a person-stage might exist. Suppose it to appear out of thin air, then vanish again. Never mind whether it is a stage *of* any person (though in fact I think it is). My point is that it is the right sort of thing.

Second: it is possible that two person-stages might exist in succession, one right after the other but without overlap. Further, the qualities and location of the second at its appearance might exactly match those of the first at its disappearance. Here I rely on a *patchwork principle* for possibility: if it is possible that X happen intrinsically in a spatio-temporal region, and if it is likewise possible that Y happen in a region, then also it is possible that both X and Y happen in two distinct but adjacent regions. There are no necessary incompatibilities between distinct existences. Anything can follow anything.

Third: extending the previous point, it is possible that there might be a world of stages that is exactly like our own world in its point-by-point distribution of intrinsic local qualities over space and time.

Fourth: further, such a world of stages might also be exactly like our own in its causal relations between local matters of particular fact. For nothing but the distribution of intrinsic local qualities constrains the patter of causal relations. (It would be simpler to say that the causal relations supervene on the distribution of local qualities, but I am not as confident of that as I am of the weaker premise.)

Fifth: then such a world of stages would be exactly like our own simpliciter. There are no features of our world except those that supervene on the distribution of local qualities and their casual relations.

Sixth: then our world is a world of stages. (Lewis 1983, pp. 76–7)

The first premise in this argument is an unobjectionable modal claim— here Lewis merely asserts the possibility of a short-lived object whose intrinsic history duplicates part of the intrinsic history of a possible person. The third premise is merely an extension of the first two premises. The conclusion certainly follows from the previous five premises.[3] That leaves us with the second, fourth, and fifth premises as likely

---

[3] Standard four-dimensionalism claims that this world is a world filled with fusions of *instantaneous* beings. This is not strictly entailed by the conclusion. Further, standard four-dimensionalism assumes, with standard mereology, that any set of such instantaneous beings has a unique fusion. That is not strictly entailed by the conclusion either. But the conclusion does secure a good part of what the standard four-dimensionalist wants: in any given person's life, there is a series of short-lived objects, existing in succession, each of whose intrinsic character exactly matches the intrinsic character of the person for the short period that it exists.

targets. These premises rely, respectively, on a combinatorial principle, a principle about what constrains causal facts, and a weakened version of Humean supervenience. In the following three sections we will evaluate each of these premises, along with their motivating principles. As we hope to show, each step of the argument faces significant—and instructive—problems, and so the defender of three-dimensionalism needn't worry about Lewis's argument.[4]

RECOMBINATION

The second premise of Lewis's argument may be read as a conditional: if two person-stages are possible, then two person-stages of that sort are *com*possible, and moreover they might exist one right after the other and without overlap. According to Lewis, this premise is motivated by a combinatorial principle:

> I rely on a *patchwork principle* for possibility: if it is possible that X happen intrinsically in a spatio-temporal region, and if it is likewise possible that Y happen in a region, then also it is possible that both X and Y happen in two distinct but adjacent regions. (Lewis 1983, p. 77)

Combinatorial principles come in different persuasions, depending on what sort of entity one wants to combine. One might, for example, defend a combinatorial principle for local intrinsic properties, or defend a principle for concrete material objects. Lewis, however, invokes a combinatorial principle for *events*—this, at least, is suggested by the word "happen". Let us take the notion of two events being *duplicates* as primitive.[5] We may then say that two regions are *event-wise duplicates* just in case the events that occur at those two regions are duplicates. We also help ourselves to the notion of adjacency: two regions are *adjacent* if and only if they do not overlap, and the union of those regions is a continuous region. Then:

---

[4] We note that Lewis himself writes: "I do not suppose the doubters will accept my premises, but it will be instructive to find out which they choose to deny" (Lewis 1983, p.76). On this point we can all agree.

[5] The notion of duplication is intimately tied to the idea of an *intrinsic property*, and there are several different accounts of this relation—and several different definitions of 'intrinsic'—in the literature. See e.g. Lewis and Langton (1994). We do not think that the ideas in this paper are much affected by which definition (if any) we employ.

A Combinatorial Principle for Events (CPE): Let R_1 and R_2 be any pair of possible spatio-temporal regions. Then, for any way W of making R_1 and R_2 adjacent,[6] it is possible for there to be two non-overlapping spatio-temporal regions R_1^* and R_2^* such that (i) R_1^* and R_1 are event-wise duplicates, (ii) R_2^* and R_2 are event-wise duplicates, and (iii) R_1^* and R_2^* are adjacent in way W.[7]

Invoking something like CPE at this stage of the argument is a bit puzzling, since all we are working with here are *person-stages*, and it is at best tendentious to treat person-stages as events. Moreover, the nature of events—in particular, Lewis's theory of events—is extremely controversial.[8] A more neutral combinatorial principle is desirable.

Perhaps a combinatorial principle for local intrinsic properties, or *qualities* for short, would do the trick. Roughly stated, the idea is that any distribution of qualities across the space–time manifold is possible. More carefully, let p be any space–time point. Then Q is a *quality profile for p* just in case Q is the set of all the qualities instantiated at p.[9] A point-by-point quality profile for an extended spatio-temporal region will then be a function of the quality profiles for all of the points

---

[6] The notion of 'a way of making a pair of regions adjacent' should be intuitive enough: given two rectangles, 1 in. × 2 in., one way of making the pair adjacent is to form a 4 in × 1 in. rectangle; another way of making that pair adjacent is to form a 2 in. × 2 in. square. The idea can be rigorized as follows. The *adjacency set* for a pair of regions R_1 and R_2 is a non-empty set of continuous regions; and a continuous region r is a member of that set if and only if r is the union of two adjacent regions $R_1{}^*$ and $R_2{}^*$ which intrinsically match R_1 and R_2 with regard to topology and metric. Let a mode of adjacency be any maximal subset of the adjacency set whose members are alike with regard to topology and metric. So, for example, the set of possible spherical regions that are 3 in. in diameter is a mode of adjacency as between a pair of regions, the first of which is a solid spherical region of 3 in diameter (except for a fish-shaped hole), the second of which is a fish-shaped region that is exactly the size of that hole.

[7] For ease of exposition, we presuppose Lewis's commitment to Modal Realism so that we may meaningfully quantify over possible non-actual entities, like regions of space. Accordingly, we will also presuppose Lewis's counterpart theoretical analysis of *de re* modal claims (though nothing of import turns on this last assumption).

[8] See Lewis (1986b, pp. 241–69) for his theory of events.

[9] We have borrowed Lewis's term 'instantiated at'—we trust that it is well enough understood. Note that, in the relevant sense, a quality need not be instantiated *by* a point in order for it to be instantiated *at* that point. (For example, it may be that the quality is instantiated by a particle that is located at that point.) In what follows we follow Lewis in ignoring complications about haecceitistic properties. We also ignore complications connected with the fact that some three-dimensionalists take fundamental property instantiations to be temporally relativized. We believe that such complications at best point to issues of fine-tuning, not to fundamental difficulties with the argument.

of that region. Finally, let us also say that two regions R_1 and R_2 are *qualitative duplicates* just in case there is a one-to-one function f between the points of R_1 and R_2 that (i) preserves topological and metrical features[10] and (ii) is such that, if Q is the quality profile of some point x in R_1, Q will also be the quality profile of $f(x)$ in R_2.[11] We can now state our new combinatorial principle.

> *Combinatorial Principle for Qualities* (CPQ): Let R_1 and R_2 be any pair of possible spatio-temporal regions. Then, for any way W of making R_1 and R_2 adjacent, it is possible for there to be two non-overlapping spatio-temporal regions R_1^* and R_2^* such that (i) R_1^* and R_1 are qualitative duplicates, (ii) R_2^* and R_2 are qualitative duplicates, and (iii) R_1^* and R_2^* are adjacent in way W.

CPQ is superior to CPE with regard to neutrality about the metaphysics of events. But CPQ does no better than CPE as a ground for the second premise of Lewis's argument. Person-stages, whatever they are, are no more quality profiles than they are events. It is worthwhile to clarify exactly what the problem is. From the first step of Lewis's argument, we know that it is possible for there to be a spatio-temporal region, R_1, that is exactly occupied by a person-stage, and that it is also possible for there to be a spatio-temporal region, R_2, that is likewise exactly occupied by a person-stage. CPQ, then, licenses the following inference: it is possible for there to be two (non-overlapping) spatio-temporal regions, R_1^* and R_2^*, that are qualitative duplicates of R_1 and R_2 and whose union is a continuous spatio-temporal region. But that is not the inference made in the second premise of Lewis's argument. What Lewis wants is the possibility of there being *two person-stages* that exactly occupy regions R_1^* and R_2^*. That conclusion says something about *what objects* are located at these regions. But CPQ cannot deliver *that* conclusion—it can only tell us about the *quality distributions* at those regions. Taking note of this fact, the three-dimensionalist might say something like the following:

---

[10] For example, if some metric relation holds between two points x and y in R_1, then it also holds between $f(x)$ and $f(y)$. The holding of this relation between x and y is intrinsic to R_1; highly extrinsic relations like 'being a third of the size of space–time' won't count.
[11] We assume that literally one and the same quality can be instantiated at multiple points. One who denied this—the trope-lover, for example—may wish to complicate matters further by invoking a duplication relation as between qualities.

I grant the possibility of a person-stage exactly occupying some region, R_1, and I grant the possibility of some person-stage exactly occupying some other region, R_2. Moreover, I am perfectly willing to accept CPQ. So I think that there is a world—call it w—where there are two regions, R_1^* and R_2^*, which are qualitative duplicates of R_1 and R_2, respectively, and whose union is a continuous region. But I (consistently) deny that there are two person-stages at w, occupying R_1^* and R_2^*, respectively. Rather, there is one *enduring* object at w, exactly occupying the fusion of R_1^* and R_2^*.

The upshot, then, is that Lewis requires a stronger combinatorial principle—a combinatorial principle for *concrete material objects*. Let us say that two regions R_1 and R_2 are *object-wise duplicates* just in case (i) R_1 and R_2 are qualitative duplicates; (ii) there is a one–one function, f, from the objects and points in R_1 to the objects and points in R_2 such that, if some object x instantiates some quality F at some point y in R_1, then $f(x)$ instantiates F at $f(y)$; and (iii) an object x exactly occupies[12] a set of points S_1 in R_1 if and only if $f(x)$ exactly occupies the corresponding set of points S_2 in R_2 (where a set of points in R_2 corresponds to a set of points in R_1 just in case f provides a one–one mapping from the former to the latter). We can now state our combinatorial principle for objects.

A Combinatorial Principle for Objects (CPO): Let R_1 and R_2 be any pair of possible spatio-temporal regions. Then, for any way W of making R_1 and R_2 adjacent, it is possible for there to be two non-overlapping spatio-temporal regions R_1^* and R_2^* such that (i) R_1^* and R_1 are object-wise duplicates; (ii) R_2^* and R_2 are object-wise duplicates; and (iii) R_1^* and R_2^* are adjacent in way W.

Here, finally, we seem to have a combinatorial principle that can do the work Lewis intends. Given the possibility of two person-stages, CPO allows us to infer the possibility of two distinct objects, each a duplicate of one of our person-stages, occupying adjacent spatio-temporal regions.

Now we have to ask: should the three-dimensionalist accept CPO? As an entering wedge, let us introduce a principle about parthood and spatial extension that is denied by several prominent three-dimensionalists.

---

[12] An object exactly occupies a set of points comprising a region if and only if it occupies all and only the points that belong to that set.

The Doctrine of Arbitrary Undetached Parts (DAUP): Necessarily, for every material object M, if R is the region of space exactly occupied by M at time T, and if sub-R is any occupiable subregion of R whatever, there exists a material object that exactly occupies the region sub-R at T and that is a part of M at T.[13]

Rejecting DAUP does not, on the face of it, commit one to too much. All that is required for the falsity of DAUP is the *possibility* of a material object that doesn't have a material object as a part at *some* subregion of the region occupied by the object in question. However, some philosophers who deny DAUP would do so even if it were restricted to objects in the actual world. In fact, some would deny DAUP even if it were restricted to particular material objects like you. To take one concrete example, some philosophers who deny DAUP will go so far as to deny that there is a material object exactly occupying the region that we would normally say is occupied by your left arm. Perhaps such philosophers would even go so far as to say that it is, strictly speaking, *impossible* for there to be a region, R, that qualitatively duplicates the region you occupy and that has a subregion exactly occupied by an arm-shaped material object. Let us say that some region, R_1, *part-prohibits* some subregion, R_2 of R_1 if and only if it is impossible that there be two regions R_1^* and R_2^* such that (i) R_2^* is a subregion of R_1^*, (ii) R_1^* qualitatively duplicates R_1, (iii) R_2^* qualitatively duplicates R_2, and (iv) there is an object exactly occupying R_2^*. The philosophers we are imagining hold that the region that you occupy part-prohibits the subregion in which common sense claims that there is a left arm. Such philosophers subscribe (among other things) to the following claim.

Part-Prohibition: It is possible that there exists an object, O, and regions R_1 and R_2 such that (i) O exactly occupies region R_1, (ii) R_2 is a subregion of R_1, and (iii) R_1 part-prohibits R_2.[14]

Of course, such philosophers could consistently allow that an arm-shaped object exists, even one with an intrinsic profile that matches the arm-shaped subregion in which it is said that your arm exists. Indeed, such philosophers could, consistently, subscribe to the following general claim.

[13] Cf. van Inwagen (1987, p. 123).
[14] And also to *Actual Part Prohibition*: there exists an object O and regions R_1 and R_2 such that (i) O exactly occupies region R_1, (ii) R_2 is a subregion of R_1, and (iii) R_1 part-prohibits R_2.

Occupation: For any possible object, O, if R is a continuous subregion of the region exactly occupied by O, it is possible for there to be a region R^* such that (i) R^* qualitatively duplicates R and (ii) there exists an object that exactly occupies R^*.

One who subscribes to Part-Prohibition and Occupation ought not to subscribe to CPO. Here's why. Take as a sample case someone who thinks that the region you occupy part-prohibits the arm-shaped region we would normally suppose that your left arm occupies. Suppose that philosopher were to subscribe to Occupation: then it remains possible that there is an object exactly occupying a region that qualitatively duplicates the region occupied by all of you except (loosely speaking) your left arm. It is likewise possible for there to be an object exactly occupying a region that qualitatively duplicates the region we would normally say is occupied by your left arm. (We can imagine the first object to simply be a disfigured doppelganger of you, the second object to be an arm that is not attached to a living being.) According to CPO, then, it is possible for there to be two non-overlapping regions (of space, let us say) such that (i) one region is exactly occupied by a duplicate of your disfigured duplicate, (ii) one region is exactly occupied by a duplicate of the lonely arm, and (iii) the regions are adjacent to one another in just the way that the left-arm-shaped region in your vicinity is adjacent to the rest-of-you-shaped region. In short, CPO gives us a region that qualitatively duplicates *you*, but counts among its subregions one occupied by a left-arm-shaped object. And *that* is inconsistent with the thesis that the region that you occupy part-prohibits the region occupied by your left arm.

The above discussion focused on *spatial* parts. But we also have corresponding principles for *temporal* parts. To begin,

The Doctrine of Arbitrary Undetached Temporal Parts (DAUTP): Necessarily, for every material object O, if I is the interval of time exactly occupied by O, and if sub-I is any occupiable sub-interval of I whatever, there exists a material object that exactly occupies the interval sub-I and is a part of O at sub-I.[15]

While certain three-dimensionalists reject DAUP, it seems clear that *every* three-dimensionalist should reject DAUTP. For DAUTP is simply

---

[15] Cf. van Inwagen (1987, p. 137).

the claim that four-dimensionalism is a necessary truth.[16] Moreover, it would not be surprising if a three-dimensionalist were to believe that certain space–time regions part-prohibit some temporally smaller subregions. For example, such a three-dimensionalist may insist that, while it is possible that there be a short-lived object that duplicates the first three years of Descartes' life, it is not possible that there be a space–time region that duplicates Descartes' entire life that contains such a short-lived object in its first three-year temporal segment. On this view, the space–time region occupied by Descartes' life part-prohibits the subregion corresponding to the first three years of his life. Such a version of three-dimensionalism is not at all unnatural. And, for reasons analogous to those just considered, the proponent of such a theory will reject CPO and, with it, the second premise of Lewis's argument.[17]

What about those three-dimensionalists who do not subscribe to the combination of Occupation and Part-Prohibition? Well, it is certainly consistent, at least, for such philosophers to deny CPO.[18] The key point here is that such philosophers may still cling to weaker combinatorial principles such as CPE or CPQ in order to capture what is right about combinatorialism. However, we suspect that some three-dimensionalists may still find CPO appealing. Such philosophers, it seems, must accept the second premise of Lewis' argument. Must they also accept the doctrine of temporal parts? To answer that question, we must investigate the remaining premises of Lewis's argument.

CAUSAL CONSTRAINTS

We said at the outset that Lewis's argument relies crucially on three different principles. We have already discussed the principle of

---

[16] Cf. Sider (1997), where something like DAUTP is defended as the proper articulation of the central thesis of four-dimensionalism. Some readers will no doubt believe that four-dimensionalism involves more than DAUTP. We shall not be engaging with such readers here. Cf. fn. 4.

[17] Some of the ideas explored in this section are echoed in van Inwagen (2000).

[18] Notice that, even if Occupation does not hold with full generality, Part-Prohibition may still make trouble for CPO, so long as certain particular sorts of objects are possible. If the region occupied by Descartes life part-prohibits the subregion occupied by the first three years of his life, then, so long as it is possible that there is an object that intrinsically matches the first three years of his life and an object that intrinsically matches the rest of his life, CPO will have to be rejected.

recombination. Humean supervenience will be the topic of the following section. Here we discuss the fourth premise of Lewis's argument and the topic of causal constraints.

The premise in question says something like the following. If it is possible for a stage-world to be exactly like our world with respect to its distribution of qualities, then it is possible for a stage-world to be exactly like our world with respect to its distribution of qualities *and* its causal facts. As Lewis puts it, "nothing but the distribution of local qualities constrains the pattern of causal relations" (1983, p. 77). It is not exactly clear what the scope of this generalization is. For example, is Lewis requiring his opponents to accept that the laws of nature cannot put additional constraints on the pattern of causal relations beyond the distribution of local qualities? We need not pause to consider such issues here, since a restricted version of the principle will serve Lewis's purposes just as well. Put informally, this version of the principle states that boundary facts—facts about where the boundaries of objects lie—do not place additional constraints on the pattern of causal relations beyond those imposed by the distribution of local qualities. We develop this idea in what follows.

Let us say that the boundary profile, B, for a world is the set of regions that are exactly occupied by an object in that world. Let us say that causal profile, C, for a world is a set of pairs of space–time points, such that a pair $<p_1, p_2>$ belongs to C if and only if there is a line of causal influence running from p_1 to p_2. (A line of causal influence connects p_1 and p_2 just in case the instantiation of some quality at p_1 is causally related to the instantiation of some quality at p_2.)[19] Recall that a point-by-point quality profile is a function from space–time points to sets of qualities. Q is the quality profile for world w just in case the following is true: given any space–time point p as an input, Q delivers as output all and only the qualities instantiated at p in w. We also need the notion of a

---

[19] Some readers may wonder why a causal profile is not constructed in terms of events. On some metaphysics of events, this will clearly not serve Lewis's purposes. Suppose an event is individuated in part by which object undergoes it. Then, clearly, boundary profiles will be constitutively relevant to what events occur in a world, which, given an event-theoretic conception of causal profiles, will automatically render boundary profiles constitutively relevant to causal profiles. Once again, we steer clear in the text of tendentious issues concerning the metaphysics of events. We do freely acknowledge the possibility of a critique of Lewis's fourth premise based on the idea that the concept of causal influence cannot be ultimately understood in a way that is neutral as to which objects exist and where: if that is right, then our best efforts at reconstructing Lewis's premise will not be ultimately coherent.

Q-type quality profile, a B-type boundary profile, and a C-type causal profile. First, say that two quality profiles are duplicates just in case there is a one–one function from values of the one to duplicate values of the other (one that preserves topological and metrical features). Duplicates of a quality profile Q form a class of *Q-type quality profiles*. Similarly, duplicates of a boundary profile B form a class of *B-type boundary profiles* and duplicates of a causal profile C form a class of *C-type causal profiles*. The principle that Lewis needs can now be stated as follows:

> *A Principle Concerning Causal Constraints* (PCC): For any quality profile Q, causal profile C, and boundary profile B: if there is a possible world with a Q-type quality profile and C-type causal profile, and if there is a possible world with Q-type quality profile and a B-type boundary profile, then there is a possible world with a Q-type quality profile, a C-type causal profile, and a B-type boundary profile.

Here is how PCC licenses the inference made in the fourth premise of Lewis's argument. Let Q_A be the quality profile of the actual world and let C_A be the causal profile of the actual world. It is clear, then, that there is a possible world with a Q_A-type quality profile and a C_A-type causal profile, since the actual world is such a world. The third premise of Lewis's argument tells us that there is a possible world with the boundary profile of a stage-world and the quality profile of the actual world. Let us say that the boundary profile of such a world is a B_S-type boundary profile. The third premise then tells us that there is a possible world with a Q_A-type quality profile and a B_S-type boundary profile. Applying PCC, we can infer that there is a possible world with a Q_A-type quality profile, a B_S-type boundary profile, and a C_A-type causal profile. In other words, there is a stage-world exactly like our world with respect to the distribution of qualities and the causal relation. This is exactly what Lewis wants.

The question now before us is whether or not the three-dimensionalist ought to accept PCC. We mention two possible sources of resistance. (There may be others.)

Some three-dimensionalists, if they are to be taken at their word, claim that there are no informative criteria of identity over time.[20] But

---

[20] See e.g. Merricks (1998).

most three-dimensionalists, we take it, are not in this camp. Most three-dimensionalists will say that there is informative analysis available of what it takes for something at one time to be identical to something at another time. Others will believe that there are at least informative necessary conditions upon endurance. Whether providing an analysis or merely necessary conditions upon identity, three-dimensionalists typically have recourse to *causal* notions. In particular, as most three-dimensionalists see it, there will be certain causal requirements upon an object's enduring through time.

Presumably Lewis did not intend his argument to speak merely to those who believe that causal facts supervene on quality distribution. A good thing too: many three-dimensionalists would contest such an assumption. Let us suppose then that (i) there are causal requirements upon identity, but that (ii) causal facts—and, in particular, the kinds of causal facts relevant to diachronic identity—do not supervene on the distribution of qualities. Given these two assumptions, PCC is in trouble. According to the three-dimensionalist, our world is a world of enduring objects—persisting objects like you and I are "wholly present" at each moment of our existence. Let us suppose, then, that we have an enduring material object, m, at region R_1 and an enduring material object, n, at region R_2. Let us also assume that m is identical to n. Assuming that there are causal requirements upon endurance, only certain possible causal profiles will be compatible with the fact that an enduring object occupies R_1 and R_2: others will be incompatible. Call the quality profile of the actual world Q_A. If we allow that the causal facts pertinent to diachronic identity do not supervene on the quality distribution of a world, then it will come as no surprise that there is some causal profile C compatible with Q_A but incompatible with the existence of a single persisting object that occupies R_1 and R_2. We now have a counter-example to PCC: call the actual boundary profile B_A. Q_A is compatible with B_A. Q_A is compatible with C. But, contra PCC, Q_A is not compatible with B_A.

The point can be even more vividly illustrated with a simple thought experiment. The three-dimensionalist will likely be happy to embrace a world w containing a single enduring particle.[21] The boundary profile

---

[21] The general point obviously does not require that the three-dimensionalist believe that single particle worlds are possible. The toy example is chosen merely to illustrate the point at hand.

B_w of such a world is simple enough: there is a single boundary corresponding to the life of the particle. Suppose one believes that some line of causal influence that traces the trajectory of the particle is a necessary condition upon such a boundary profile, and that this line of causal influence does not supervene on the quality profile. Since the line of influence is not supervenient, there are worlds where the quality profile of w, Q_w, is combined with a causal profile that is incompatible with that line of influence. Consider one such profile C. C is compatible with B_w. Meanwhile, from the description of the case, Q_w is compatible with B_w. If PCC is true, then B_w, Q_w, and C are compatible also; but that is just what has been denied.

The previous line of thought relied on a conception of causation that is anti-Humean. A more Humean three-dimensionalist may face pressure from a different source. Let us assume that Lewis's view on the laws of nature is correct—laws are the simplest and most informative generalizations concerning the world. We now pose a simple question: might not boundary profiles bear on which generalizations are the most simple and informative? Two worlds w_1 and w_2 might be alike in their qualitative profile and yet, owing to different boundary profiles, enjoy differences such as the following. It is true in w_1, but not in w_2, that nothing persists once it is both F and G at the same time. It is true in w_1, but not in w_2, that nothing stops being H once it is H. It is true in w_1, but not in w_2, that, as soon as something that is I passes out of existence, everything that is J turn to K. By Lewis's own lights, differences like this might make for differences in the laws of nature. And this, in turn, will make a difference to the causal facts. Consider the last of our list of contrasts. Owing to the difference, it may be that, in w_1, some K-event is caused, *inter alia*, by an I thing passing out of existence; but the corresponding K-event in w_2 has no such cause. Allow that differences in laws of nature are in turn constitutively relevant to the causal facts, and we will be forced to deny that nothing beyond qualitative profile constrains the causal facts. Thus, PCC has to be rejected. Assuming Lewis's own conception of laws, PCC is a principle that (i) should be accepted only by four-dimensionalists and (ii) should be restricted to the "inner sphere" (assuming that the four-dimensionalist admits three-dimensionalist worlds in the "outer sphere").

We have not shown that PCC is incompatible with three-dimensionalism as such. The combination of three-dimensionalism with a Humean conception laws may preclude commitment to PCC.

Meanwhile, those who think that causal facts are irreducible but who also use those facts to describe certain purported necessary conditions upon diachronic identity will also reject PCC. But there may be certain three-dimensionalists who remain committed to both PCC and CPO. Such theorists must accept the second and fourth premises of Lewis's argument. So they should be very interested in the remainder of that argument.

WEAK HUMEAN SUPERVENIENCE

If we grant Lewis the first four premises of his argument, we grant the possibility of a stage-world that is exactly like our own world in its distribution of qualities and causal facts. What the fifth premise of Lewis's argument says is this: such a world is exactly like our world *simpliciter*. That is, a world of stages exactly like our world in its distribution of qualities and causal facts is exactly like our world in *all* respects. Lewis is not relying here on Humean supervenience, the doctrine that everything supervenes on the distribution of intrinsic, local properties; he merely requires that "there are no features of our world except those that supervene on the distribution of local qualities *and their causal relations*" [italics ours] (1983, p. 77). Let's refer to this claim as the doctrine of *weak* Humean supervenience. If we grant Lewis weak Humean supervenience, along with CPO and PCC, the conclusion of his argument appears to be established.

But here the dialectical shortcomings of the argument are especially apparent. We wish to pursue two themes in this connection.

Our first theme concerns the contingency of Humean supervenience. According to Lewis, weak Humean supervenience (like strong Humean supervenience) only holds at our world and at worlds like ours. But the first four premises of Lewis's argument only give us the mere *possibility* of a stage-world like ours in its quality distribution and causal profile—they do not locate that world at the inner or outer sphere of possibility. Now, if the stage-world in question is located in the outer sphere, the appeal to weak Humean supervenience is out of place. If a stage-world is located in the outer sphere, then it is straightforwardly *false* that such a world is like ours *simpliciter*. For, if such a world is located in the outer sphere, it is a world where weak Humean supervenience fails. So Lewis needs to claim that the stage-world under discussion is an inner sphere world—it is a world like ours. But this is a claim that the three-dimensionalist may well reject. She may insist that stage-worlds, while possible, are not "worlds like ours", and summarily reject Lewis's fifth premise. Noting that Lewis himself admits the possibility of an endurance-world can sharpen the point here:

[There] are worlds in which things persist through time not by consisting of distinct temporal parts, but rather by bilocation in space–time: persisting things are wholly present in their entirety at different times. (Lewis 1999, p. 227)

Lewis, of course, is about as generous with possibility as one can get. So, if he grants the possibility of endurance-worlds, we take it that he will also grant the possibility of an endurance-world exactly like our own in its distribution of qualities and causal facts. But, given *that* admission, the three-dimensionalist should be free to argue as follows:

It is possible for there to be an enduring world exactly like our own in its distribution of qualities and causal facts. But, by weak Humean supervenience, there are no features of our world except those that supervene on the distribution of local qualities and their causal relations. So an enduring world is exactly like our world *simpliciter*.[22]

Sauce for the goose is sauce for the gander. The only response available to Lewis, it seems, is to claim that endurance-worlds are outer sphere, so that the appeal to weak Humean supervenience is out of place. The three-dimensionalist may, of course, say the same thing about stage-worlds. So we seem to have reached an impasse.[23]

---

[22] Rea (1998, pp. 249–50) suggests a similar response to Lewis's argument.

[23] Lewis once believed that he had a way of making the distinction between inner and outer worlds that was independent of Humean supervenience: outer sphere worlds include alien properties, inner sphere worlds do not. Alien properties are properties that don't appear at the actual world. Now, if this is an adequate way of drawing the inner sphere/outer sphere distinction, the premise in question would be in much better shape. Here is why: the stage-world built up in the first four premises of the argument didn't include any alien properties—the stage-world, after all, is supposed to be a *qualitative duplicate* of the actual world. That, together with the claim that all outer sphere worlds have alien properties, puts the stage-world in the inner sphere. And, once we have located the stage-world in the inner sphere, the appeal to weak Humean supervenience is perfectly legitimate. The problem, of course, is that the attempt to make the inner sphere/outer sphere distinction by way of alien properties fails. Or so, at least, says Lewis (see Lewis 1999, p. 227). At the time that the argument we are discussing was proposed, Lewis had not properly reckoned with the possibility of endurance worlds, and in particular their bearing on the doctrine of Humean supervenience and the inner sphere/outer sphere distinction.

Perhaps the impasse can be broken. Lewis claims the doctrine of weak Humean supervenience is contingent. Some philosophers, however, are at least willing to consider the claim that weak Humean supervenience is a necessary truth.[24] What happens if we break with Lewis and endorse such a strong claim? Well, we no longer have to worry about locating our stage-world in the inner sphere, since, if we take weak Humean supervenience to be a necessary truth, the inner sphere/outer sphere distinction no longer exists. So, if it is possible for there to be a stage-world exactly like ours in its distribution of qualities and causal facts, and if it is a necessary truth that any world like ours in those respects is like ours *simpliciter*, we can infer that our world is indeed a world of stages. The catch, of course, is that the necessity of weak Humean supervenience is a highly questionable matter. Since Lewis himself does not even endorse such a claim, it seems unreasonable to expect as much of the three-dimensionalist.[25]

We briefly turn to a second theme. We noted earlier that only certain three-dimensionalists will be sympathetic to PCC; more specifically, that principle will appeal only to the kind of three-dimensionalist who believes that there are no causal conditions upon diachronic identity. But that kind of three-dimensionalist will likely have no sympathy at all for weak Humean supervenience. After all, a three-dimensionalist who thinks that there are no causal conditions on diachronic identity will almost certainly believe that worlds may differ from the actual one with regard to boundary facts while duplicating the qualitative and causal profile of the actual world. Consider, for instance, a particle in our world that endures from t_1 to t_2. There are other possible worlds in which that particle (or its counterpart) ceases to exist sometime between t_1 and t_2 and is immediately replaced by an exactly similar particle. A three-dimensionalist who believes that there are causal criteria of diachronic identity will insist that there is a causal difference between these two scenarios. But a three-dimensionalist who believes that diachronic identity is, so to speak, 'brute'—thus admitting of no causal criteria— will be prepared to concede that the pair of scenarios may be alike causally and qualitatively. She will, in that case, have no sympathy at

---

[24] See, e.g. Robinson (1989).

[25] Those readers who are compelled by the thesis that weak Humean supervenience is a necessary truth may wonder whether there is any plausible version of three-dimensionalism that can be rendered compatible with that thesis. We shall not pursue the matter further here.

all for weak Humean supervenience.[26] In sum, there simply are no clear-headed three-dimensionalists who will sympathize with the combination of PCC and weak Humean supervenience. There are thus no clear-headed three-dimensionalists whom Lewis's argument will embarrass.

CONCLUSION

In conclusion, let us review the responses to Lewis's argument that we advocate on behalf of the three-dimensionalist. If a three-dimensionalist upholds Part-Prohibition and Occupation, we say that she should reject the combinatorial principle required by Lewis's argument, CPO. In so doing, she may reject the second premise of his argument. Alternatively, if a three-dimensionalist does not count herself among those just mentioned, she may still feel free to reject CPO in favor of a more modest combinatorial principle like CPE or CPQ. Again, such a three-dimensionalist may reject the second premise of Lewis's argument. A three-dimensionalist may in any case have powerful reasons for rejecting PCC. That three-dimensionalist may reject the fourth premise of Lewis's argument. A three-dimensionalist who accepts the fourth premise of Lewis's argument may think that the world that it posits belongs to the 'outer sphere', in which case it fails to fall under the scope of weak Humean supervenience. That in turn can provide a basis for questioning the move from premise four to premise five. Moreover, three-dimensionalists who accept PCC ought in any case to have no sympathy for weak Humean supervenience (even as a contingent truth). This will also provide a basis for rejecting the move from premise four to premise five. What about the philosopher bent upon accepting CPO, PCC, and the necessity of weak Humean supervenience? Such a philosopher will, indeed, have to reject three-dimensionalism. However, we know of no contemporary three-dimensionalist who has anything to fear from Lewis's argument.

Rutgers University (Hawthorne and Wasserman)
and Syracuse University (Scala)

---

[26] Spinning-disk thought experiments are also suggestive here. Particularly relevant is Zimmerman (1998).

REFERENCES

Langton, R., and D. Lewis (1994) 'Defining Intrinsic', *Philosophy and Phenomenological Research*, 58: 333–45.

Lewis, D. (1983) 'Postscripts to "Survival and Identity"', in his *Philosophical Papers*, vol. I. Oxford University Press, pp. 73–7.

Lewis, D. (1986*a*) *On the Plurality of Worlds*, Oxford: Blackwell.

Lewis, D. (1986*b*) 'Events', in *Philosophical Papers*, vol. II, Oxford University Press, pp. 241–69.

Lewis, D. (1999) 'Humean Supervenience Debugged', in his *Papers in Metaphysics and Epistemology*, Cambridge University Press, pp. 224–47.

Merricks, T. (1998) 'There are no Criteria of Identity over Time', *Nous*, 32: 106–24.

Noonan, H. (2001) 'The Case for Perdurance', in G. Preyer and F. Siebeldt (eds.), *Reality and Humean Supervenience: Essays in the Philosophy of David Lewis*. Lanham, MD: Rowan & Littlefield.

Rea, M. (1998) 'Temporal Parts Unmotivated', *Philosophical Review* 107: 225–60.

Robinson, D. (1989) 'Matter, Motion and Humean Supervenience', *Australasian Journal of Philosophy*, 67: 394–409.

Sider, T. (1997) 'Four-Dimensionalism', *Philosophical Review*, 106: 197–231.

van Inwagen, P. (1987) 'The Doctrine of Arbitrary Undetached Parts', *Pacific Philosophical Quarterly*, 62: 123–37.

van Inwagen, P. (2000) 'Temporal Parts and Identity across Time', *The Monist*, 83: 437–59.

Zimmerman, D. (1998) 'Temporal Parts and Supervenient Causation: The Incompatibility of Two Humean Doctrines', *Australasian Journal of Philosophy*, 76: 265–88.

INDEX

Adams, F. 54
Adams, R. M. 47 n., 49 n.4, 49 n.5, 55, 56 n., 57 n.16, 85 n.6, 88 n.14, 96 n.27
Aristotle 88, 143, 237
Armstrong, D. M. 9, 10 n., 18 n.5, 85 n.8, 87 n.10, 159 n.7, 169 n.17, 178, 190 n.41, 227–247
Augustine. 47 n., 83–84

Baxter, D. L. M. 139–153
Berkeley, G. 9, 224, 240 n.21, 242
Bigelow, J. 15 n.2, 47 n., 50 n., 60 n., 84 n.2, 85 n.6, 85 n.7, 87 n.11, 94–96, 228 n.6
Blackburn, S. 229 n.7, 237 n., 242 n.24
Block, N. 234
Boolos, G. 190 n.40
Boscovich, R. J. 224 n., 236, 239–240
Bradley, F. H. 139, 156 n.4
Braun, D. 54
Bricker, P. 188 n.35,
Broad, C. D. 19 n.
Brogaard, B. 47 n.,
Burgess, J. 107
Burton, S. C. 30

Callender, C. 15 n.1
Campbell, K. 237 n., 239–240
Chalmers, D. 251 n.34, 251 n.35
Chisholm, R. M. 47 n., 52, 94, 95 n.24, 96 n.25, 118 n.
Christensen, F. M. 47 n.
Church, A. 123

Cohen, R. S. 123 n.8
Crisp, T. 21–36

Davidson, D. 31
Descartes, R. 111, 202, 204, 210, 215, 220–221,
Dipert, R. R. 152, 238, 240 n.19,
Dorr, C. 150, 152
Dowe, P. 260

Ehring, D. 260
Elder, C. 234
Emt, J. 62 n.

Fair, D. 260
Feyarabend, P. K. 123 n.
Fine, K. 47 n., 48 n.1, 61 n.24, 76 n.47, 167 n., 176, 178 n.23
Fitch, G. W. 47 n., 48 n.6, 67
Fodor, J. 226
Foster, J. 237 n., 242 n.24
Frege, G., 117–118

Geach, P. T. 84 n.2
Goodman, N. 9, 10 n. 113, 123 n.8, 151 n., 181, 190 n.42

Harre, R. 224 n., 236 n., 237
Hawthorne, J. 143 n., 145 n.7, 146 n.8, 147 n.10, n.11
Hazen, A. P. 5 n.4, 182, 182 n.30
Heil, J. 144
Hibbert, C. 88 n.13
Hinchliff, M. 15 n.1, 47 n., 51, 84 n.2, 89 n.15
Holton, R. 238, 239

Horgan, T. 229 n.7
Howell, R. 62 n.
Humberstone, L. 226
Hume, D. 234–235, 240 n.21, 301–317

Jackson, F. 84 n.4, 156 n.3, 232, 233

Kant, I. 243 n.26
Kaplan, D. 54
Keller, S. 47 n.
Kim, J. 225, 229 n.7, 233
Kripke, S. 22 n.2, 34 n., 58 n.19, 157 n.5, 162

Langton, R. 226 n., 227 n., 242 n.24, 243 n.26, 303 n.5
Laurence, S. 121 n.
Leibniz, G. W. 95 n.22, 96 n.26, 142
Levinson, J. 62 n.
Lewis, D. 23 n.2, 40, 76 n.48, 85 n.6, 85 n.7, 85 n.8, 86 n.9, 87 n.10, 95 n.23, 98, 109, 113, 125–131, 139, 141, 141 n., 144, 145, 145 n.6, 151, 190 n.41, 191 n.44, 226 n., 234, 260, 263, 266, 267, 267 n.11, 283, 292 n.23, 301, 301 n.2, 302, 303, 303 n.5, 304, 304 n.7, 304 n.9, 305, 306, 309, 310, 310 n.19, 311, 312, 313, 314, 315, 317
Lewis, S. 113
Locke, J. 9, 224, 227, 228, 230, 231, 238, 240, 241, 243, 244, 251
Lombard, L. 15 n.1
Long, A. A. 47 n., 50 n., 60 n.
Lowe, E. J. 227 n.3, 239
Lucretius 47 n., 50 n., 60 n.
Ludlow, P. 37–46
Lycan, W. 124 n.9

MacBride, F. 147 n.9, 189 n.38
Macdonald, C. 121 n.

MacDonald, G. F. 195 n.1
Mackie, J. L. 87 n.10, 260, 266
Madden, E. H. 224 n., 236 n., 237
Markosian, N. 15 n.2
Martin, C. B. 223 n., 224, 229 n.8, 229 n.9, 230 n., 237 n., 242
Maudlin, T. 261 n.9
Maxwell, N. 75 n.46
McCall, S. 47 n.
Meinong, 7, 89 n., 98, 126–130
Melia, J. 123 n.7
Mellor, D. H. 159 n.7, 224 n., 229 n.9
Menzies, P. 257 n.5,
Merricks, T. 15 n.1, n.2, 47 n., 311 n.
Monton, B. 47 n., 75 n.46
Mumford, S. 226

Nagel, T. 206 n.
Nelson, M. 47 n.
Newton-Smith, W. H. 77 n.51
Nolan, D., 8 n.7
Noonan, H. 301 n.2

Oddie, G. 225
Oliver, A. 190 n.40
Oppy, G. 54

Pargetter, R. 232
Parsons, J. 84 n.4
Parsons, T. 7, 8 n.8, 89 n.15, 128
Paul, L. A. 261 n.8, 268 n.12, 292 n.24
Plantinga, A., 9, 10
Plato, 8, 107–138, 140, 182, 223, 224 n., 239
Priestley, J. 224 n., 236
Prior, A. N. 4 n.3, 22, 40, 47 n., 48 n.1, 57 n.17, 60 n., 61, 70 n.38, 75 n.46, 76 n.47, 84 n.2, 88 n.14
Prior, E. 232, 234, 246
Putnam, H. 75 n.46, 121, 121 n.

Quine, W. V. O. 9, 50 n., 90 n.16, 111, 113–114, 117, 118 n., 121, 123, 124

Ramsey, F. P. 125, 146, 159 n.7, 190 n.38
Rea, M. 15 n.1, 315 n.22
Robb, D. 247 n.29
Robinson, D. 316 n.24
Robinson, H. 240 n.20, 242 n.24
Rosen, G. 87 n.10, 107
Routley, R. 128
Russell, B. 133, 140, 141, 148, 155 n., 189, 191 n.43

Salmon, N. 54, 62 n., 87 n.11
Salmon, W. 260
Sartre 112
Schaffer, J. 261 n.9, 282, 292 n.24
Sedley, D. N. 47 n., 50 n., 60 n.
Sextus Empiricus 48 n.1, 50 n., 60 n.
Shoemaker, S. 224 n., 225, 234, 236
Sider, T. 15 n.1, 25 n., 48 n.1, 60 n., 69, 301 n.1, 309 n.16
Simons, P. 144
Smart, J. J. C. 84 n.3, 240 n.21
Smiley, T. 190 n.40
Smith, A. D. 227 n.3
Smith, Q. 16 n. 3, 47 n., 48 n.1, 57 n.18
Smythies, J. R. 249 n.

Spinoza 249 n.
Stecker, R. 54
Swinburne, R. 237 n.
Swoyer, C. 224 n., 234
Sylvan, R. *see* R. Routley

Thomasson, A. 109
Tichy, P. 16 n. 3
Tooley, M. 19 n., 48 n.1, 50 n., 60 n., 84 n.3, 88 n.12, 258, 259

Unger, P. 240 n.20

Van Inwagen, P. 62 n., 87 n.11, 307 n.13, 308 n.15, 309 n.17

Wartofsky, M. W. 123 n.8
Whitehead, A. N. 189
Williams, D. C., 9, 10 n., 84 n.3, 90 n.17, 141 n.
Williamson, T. 166 n.13, 167 n., 169 n.17, 185 n., 187
Wittgenstein, L. 141
Wolterstorff, N. 48 n.1, 57 n.17, 109

Yablo, S. 292

Zalta, E. N. 61 n. 24, 76 n.47
Zimmerman, D. W. 15 n.1, 16 n.2, 48 n.1, 50 n., 60 n., 84 n.2, 233, 240 n.20, 247 n.29, 317 n.